DISCRETIONARY BEHAVIOR AND PERFORMANCE IN EDUCATIONAL ORGANIZATIONS: THE MISSING LINK IN EDUCATIONAL LEADERSHIP AND MANAGEMENT

ADVANCES IN EDUCATIONAL ADMINISTRATION

Series Editor: Anthony H. Normore

Recent Volumes:

ADVANCES IN EDUCATIONAL ADMINISTRATION
VOLUME 13

DISCRETIONARY BEHAVIOR AND PERFORMANCE IN EDUCATIONAL ORGANIZATIONS: THE MISSING LINK IN EDUCATIONAL LEADERSHIP AND MANAGEMENT

EDITED BY

IBRAHIM DUYAR

University of Arkansas at Little Rock, Arkansas, USA

ANTHONY H. NORMORE

*California State University, Dominguez Hills,
Carson, Los Angeles, California, USA*

Emerald

United Kingdom – North America – Japan
India – Malaysia – China

Emerald Group Publishing Limited
Howard House, Wagon Lane, Bingley BD16 1WA, UK

First edition 2012

Copyright © 2012 Emerald Group Publishing Limited

Reprints and permission service
Contact: booksandseries@emeraldinsight.com

British Library Cataloguing in Publication Data
A catalogue record for this book is available from the British Library

ISBN: 978-1-78052-642-3
ISSN: 1479-3660 (Series)

ISOQAR certified
Management Systems,
awarded to Emerald for
adherence to Quality
and Environmental
standards ISO 9001:2008
and 14001:2004,
respectively

Certificate Number 1985
ISO 9001
ISO 14001

INVESTOR IN PEOPLE

CONTENTS

**PART III: CONCLUSIONS AND IMPLICATIONS
FOR FUTURE RESEARCH**

To my mother, Dudu Duyar, and all mothers who unconditionally dedicate their life to future generations. Without expecting anything in return, mothers are the ultimate performers of discretionary behavior.

Ibrahim Duyar

LIST OF CONTRIBUTORS

Yahya Altınkurt	Dumlupınar University, Faculty of Education, Turkey
Betty Y. Ashbaker	Brigham Young University, USA
Inayet Aydin	Ankara University, Turkey
Elena Belogolovsky	Israel Institute of Technology, Israel
Michael F. DiPaola	College of William and Mary, Williamsburg, VA, USA
Ibrahim Duyar	University of Arkansas, Little Rock, AR, USA
Yeung Lee	University of Hong Kong, Hong Kong, SAR
Noriah Abdul Malek	Ministry of Higher Education, Malaysia
Jill Morgan	Swansea Metropolitan University, Wales, UK
Judy Nagy	University of South Australia, Australia
Anthony H. Normore	California State University, Dominguez Hills, Carson, Los Angeles, CA, USA
Izhar Oplatka	Tel Aviv University, Israel
Nancy L. Ras	St Mary's College of California/Walden University, USA
Tamara Savelyeva	University of Hong Kong, Hong Kong, SAR
Anit Somech	University of Haifa, Faculty of Education, Israel
Fatt Hee Tie	University of Malaya, Malaysia

xi

David L. Turnipseed   University of South Alabama, USA

Elizabeth VandeWaa   University of South Alabama, USA

Kursad Yılmaz   Dumlupınar University, Faculty of
                          Education, Turkey

FOREWORD

The contributors of this volume provide new insights and perspectives on discretionary behaviors in educational organizations. Such behaviors have long been recognized as essential to organizational effectiveness. Long ago Barnard (1938) characterized the willingness of individual employees to contribute cooperative efforts to an organization as indispensable. Katz and Kahn (1966) argued that extra-role behaviors are crucial in improving organizational effectiveness and that when individuals only perform prescribed duties, failure is inevitable.

During the past three decades researchers have attempted to define, measure, and assess the impact of employees' discretionary behaviors in both public and private sector organizations. Organ and his colleagues (Bateman & Organ, 1983; Smith, Organ, & Near, 1983) offered a definition of organizational citizenship behaviors (OCB) as employees' discretionary behaviors in organizations that promote effectiveness, but are neither required, nor formally rewarded.

In the decades that followed, Organ, as well as other scholars from various disciplines, continued to characterize, redefine, and operationalize discretionary behaviors in a variety of organizational and cultural contexts. Studies of private sector organizations, which tested the relationship between OCB and effectiveness, reported positive relationships between discretionary behaviors and measures of organizational effectiveness. Research on OCB also provided evidence that OCB are context specific.

Studies of discretionary behaviors in school organization were first reported in 2001 (DiPaola & Tschannen-Moran). The work on OCB in schools, grounded in Organ's conceptualization of discretionary behaviors, defined and operationalized OCB of teachers in PK-12 schools. Building theory and research on discretionary behaviors in educational organizations is critical because employees of educational organizations differ from those found in most private sector organizations.

The work of educational organizations is performed by professionals who have a high level of expertise and adhere to ethical standards of commitment and service to students, their clients. Their work is complex, requires professional judgments, and cannot simply be defined in job descriptions or contracts. Thus, the discretionary behaviors of educators, which enhance the success of their students and colleagues, are important aspects of the performance of educational organizations.

This volume's focus on the theoretical foundations and conceptual underpinnings of discretionary behavior in educational contexts is unique. It not only offers studies of organizational citizenship and other discretionary behaviors, but also studies of the proactive behaviors and initiatives that result from these discretionary behaviors in educational contexts.

Michael F. DiPaola

Chancellor Professor, The College of William and Mary

REFERENCES

Barnard, C. I. (1938). *The functions of the executive.* Cambridge, MA: Harvard University Press.

Bateman, T. S., & Organ, D. W. (1983). Job satisfaction and the good soldier: The relationship between affect and employee citizenship. *Academy of Management Journal, 26*(4), 587–595.

DiPaola, M. F., & Tschannen-Moran, M. (2001). Organizational citizenship behavior in schools and its relationship to school climate. *Journal of School Leadership, 11*(September), 424–447.

Katz, D., & Kahn, R. L. (1966). *The social psychology of organizations.* New York, NY: Wiley.

Smith, C. A., Organ, D. W., & Near, J. P. (1983). Organizational citizenship behavior: It's nature and antecedents. *Journal of Applied Psychology, 68*(4), 653–663.

INTRODUCTION

Organizational environment where the organizational behavior takes place and the task roles employees need to perform have become increasingly *complex* in today's organizations. To respond to this complexity, modern organizations need willing, flexible, and proactive employees who go beyond narrow task requirements and who approach work proactively by showing personal initiative (Crant, 2000; Ohly, Sonnentag, & Pluntke, 2006; Parker, 2000; Sonnentag, 2003). In an era where the responsibility and decision making have shifted downward through transformational leadership and shared decision-making, employees have started taking part in both decision making and implementation process without constant close supervision (Frese & Fay, 2001; Sonnentag, 2003). They are expected to demonstrate discretionary behaviors that may go beyond their formally identified job descriptions to carry out the current expectations and *comprehensive* and *complex tasks*. Discretionary behavior refers to the employee behavior that is not directly or explicitly recognized by the formal reward system, and in the aggregate promotes the efficient and effective functioning of the organization (Organ, Podsakoff, & MacKenzie, 2006; Van Dyne, Cummings, & McLean Parks, 1995). Employee discretionary behaviors contribute to maintenance and enhancement of the social and psychological organizational context which supports task performance and organizational effectiveness (McBain, 2004; Organ, 1997). As Den Hartog and Belschak (2007) stated, employee discretionary behaviors are crucial for organizations to be able to stay competitive in today's global economy.

Although growing number of authors has emphasized the need for research on discretionary work behaviors (e.g., Borman & Motowidlo, 1993; Den Hartog & Belschak, 2007), this line of research is still in its early stage in the organizational citizenship behavior domain and rudimentary in the proactive behavior area. The literature is not short of studies examining an array of constructs (e.g., taking charge, proactive behavior, prosocial behavior, personal initiative, organizational citizenship behavior) of discretionary behavior at the work place. Very often, however, these studies fail to relate their focus to the domain of discretionary behavior. They also fail to incorporate their focus with the similar constructs in the same domain. Therefore, many constructs with overlapping focus create disarray in the scholarly community. The *lack of parsimony* within the same domain requires an integrative and inclusive perspective toward the development of a sound theory of discretionary behavior at the workplace. Similarly, the existing literature suffers from a *lack of a coherent* view on the dimensions (e.g., directed toward organization vs. individual or positive vs. negative) of discretionary behavior (Bennett & Stamper, 2002; Borman, Penner, Allen, & Motowidlo, 2001). Furthermore, the existing literature *lacks an integrative* conceptual focus and fails to identify the variables in the overall picture and the relationships among these variables. In this regard, the studies dealing with the identification of the antecedents of discretionary behavior usually have presented limited focus by studying only one of the task, individual, or organizational domain variables. Studies linking leadership in organizations to the discretionary behavior are very few. Therefore, there is a need for inclusive and integrative studies for a *parsimonious and coherent theory* in discretionary behavior at workplace.

Education offers a perfect context for the application and testing of discretionary behavior theory. Teachers, school administrators, and other professional educators are now challenged with emerging needs and expectations which require them to carry out complex tasks and which require them to perform beyond their formal job roles and responsibilities. They are also expected to be self-starting, proactive, flexible, and persistent in overcoming difficulties that arise in addressing the new complex and comprehensive roles and functions. In other words, the educational work-force is expected to engage discretionary behaviors that may not necessarily be required explicitly or directly by the formal reward systems to promote the efficient and effective functioning of the organization. Toward this end, the collective efforts of authors in this volume would contribute to the development of a parsimonious and coherent theory and to the understanding of employee discretionary behaviors in educational organizations. The volume sets a stage for the discussion of significance and timeliness of discretionary behavior toward solving significant long lasting issues in educational organizations. Furthermore, it creates an environment where the future discourse and direction in relevant research, policy, and practice in the field of education. Few studies have investigated discretionary behavior and performance of teachers, assistant principals, principals, and other professional educational workforce in K-12 education. Similarly, the relevant literature in higher education organizations is also scarce. In addition to the apparent neglect by the scholarly community, common issues of educational workforce (low satisfaction, low commitment, and high attrition) further complicate the situation and call for immediate attention to discretionary behavior in educational organizations.

In this sense, there is a great need for future research examining the antecedents, outcomes, and processes of discretionary behavior in educational settings. This volume addresses to this neglected yet emerging field by highlighting advances in the discretionary behavior in education. To achieve this goal, editors of the book have invited some of the scholars who have been most active in the field to share their latest studies and thoughts on the topic. Written by educational and organizational scholars, this book is aimed primarily at scholars in educational studies, management (i.e., human resources management and organizational behavior), and industrial and organizational psychology. The book also is designed to help graduate students in these fields grasp the key issues, theories, concepts, and studies in discretionary behavior. It can be used an excellent source by graduate students in their relevant coursework and/or research.

The book includes conceptual and empirical (both qualitative and quantitative) studies exploring the dynamics of discretionary behavior in educational organizations. Both K-12 education and higher education organizations (i.e., community colleges and traditional universities) were included in the chapters. Organized into 12 chapters, this volume of *Advances in Educational Administration* is divided into three integral parts. Part I, titled *Theoretical Foundations of Discretionary Behavior* sets the stage for the rest of the book. The contributors mainly focus on the theoretical foundations and conceptual underpinnings of discretionary behavior in education. They delve into the antecedents of discretionary behavior, relationships between/among discretionary behavior, and other relevant constructs. In Chapter 1, David L. Turnipseed and Elizabeth Vandewaa examine the psychology of discretionary behavior by focusing on the employee emotions in business school and nursing school environments. They use a four-factor emotional intelligence framework to test influence of emotional intelligence dimensions on engaging in organizational citizenship behaviors. The findings of this study show that the management of emotions, one of the four dimensions, significantly linked to five of the eight organizational citizenship behaviors in two different professional higher education settings. This result presents important implications for policy and future research.

In Chapter 2, Elena Belogolovsky and Anit Somech examine the boundaries and multidimensionality of teacher discretionary behavior from the perspectives of direction, context, and time. They explore whether different role-holders in schools (i.e., principals, teachers, parents) perceive the boundary between in-role and extra-role behaviors differently. The results of this study attest to the dynamic and subjective nature of the boundary between teachers' task and discretionary behaviors. This study points out the absence of any clear-cut common understanding about the boundaries between discretionary behaviors and in-role behaviors across teachers at different career stages, as well as across different educational stakeholders. The authors argue that the definition of a given discretionary behavior as in-role or extra-role depends on the rating source and on the employee's assumed career stage. The complexity and the lack of clear definition of discretionary behaviors in educational settings pose methodological implications for future research.

Continuing the discussion of the theoretical foundations of discretionary behavior, in Chapter 3, Nancy L. Ras examines the relationships between teacher culture, teacher discretionary behaviors, and transformational leadership in schools. She argues that the characteristics of teacher culture predispose those who become teachers to perform discretionary behaviors. To this conceptual study, due to its participatory style, transformational leadership may result in either a motivating or de-motivating influence on teacher discretionary behaviors depending on the perceived values congruence between teacher culture and leadership goals and behavior. The possibility of overlooked de-motivating influences of transformational leadership on teacher discretionary behavior offers a new view on the conventional perspectives regarding effects of transformational leadership and it presents various implications for practice.

Continuing the discussion of antecedents and outcomes of teacher discretionary behavior, Ibrahim Duyar and Anthony H. Normore explore whether teacher self-efficacy, collective efficacy, perceived organizational support, and principal leadership styles predict teachers' work performance and career aspirations in Chapter 4. Applying an inclusive social-cognitive perspective, their study expanded on relevant research by combining the previously disparate elements in the person (employee), organization, and leadership domains to provide a more comprehensive and dynamic perspective on the relation between teachers' work performance (including both task and discretionary performance) and career aspirations. Results of this study indicate that teacher self-efficacy, collective efficacy, and perceived organizational support significantly predict certain aspects of teacher discretionary behavior, task behavior, and career aspirations of teachers. Consistent with the relevant research in other fields, this study identifies a strong significant relationship between teachers' task performance and discretionary performance. The results of the study present significant implications for human resource management and future research. These authors call for in-depth further research on the dimensions of significant factors.

In Chapter 5, Noriah Abdul Malek and Fatt Hee Tie focus on conceptual borders between discretionary and task performance and examine the influence of employee demographic attributes on their engagement in discretionary behaviors. The results of their study indicate that gender, recruitment status, job grade, promotion, and excellence award received are related to overall and some select dimensions of organizational citizenship behavior. An interesting finding is that more than half of the instructor organizational citizenship behaviors identified by community college supervisors fall into the "organizational compliance" dimension. This finding provides additional support for the subjectivity of discretionary behavior definitions and the fluid conceptual borders between discretionary and task behaviors.

Part II, titled *Applications of Discretionary Behavior in Educational Organizations* draws attention to the organizational citizenship behavior or voice or silence behaviors in regards to teachers; proactive behavior or personal initiative in regards to assistant principals, and such. Authors focus on several constructs including the *target of discretionary behavior, comprehensive conceptual perspectives*, and *emerging discretionary behavior constructs*. Effects of these *multidimensional* discretionary behaviors on creating organizational change, enhancing school improvement, and/or developing learning communities are introduced. In Chapter 6, Tamara Savelyeva and Yeung Lee apply an ecological model to explore the role of discretion and the mechanism of discretionary behavior alignment across school levels during the process of introducing a technology-based educational innovation in Hong Kong schools. These authors view discretion as a situational variable that moderates the degree of organizational processes and outcomes and argue that an alignment of discretionary behavior of both principals and teachers is the key to successful technology introduction in schools. This study reveals a discretionary behavior model including the following domains: shared vision, empowerment, institutional commitment, collaboration, and school culture. Their analysis also presents a major criterion, which they called a "focus on students' needs," which bonded the five domains and ensured instances of positive discretionary behavior by school leaders and their teachers. The successful utilization of ecological approach to examine discretionary behaviors in schools is one of the major contributions of this study. Ecological approach appears to meet the challenge for creating a synergetic understanding of the multiple factors, players, and phenomenon, thus, presenting advantages in the analysis of nonlinear discretionary behaviors across different levels of school organizations.

In Chapter 7, Judy Nagy examines the dynamics of discretionary behaviors in organizational settings where the roles are not clearly articulated. Her study discusses factors that impede discretionary academic leadership behaviors in Australian higher education and suggests strategies to develop leadership capabilities and competencies, and empowers academics to engage with discretionary teaching and learning responsibilities. Her study is a good example of increasing work condition what Van Dyne and Ellis (2004) call *job creep*. Nagy examines the discretionary behaviors of subject/program coordinators who function without clearly identified roles, which essentially is detriment to the careers of these individuals and which also is unsuited to the current hybrid, open, and distributed forms of learning in higher education. Her study offers various strategies (e.g., empowerment and targeted professional development, and capacity building) to enhance engagement with discretionary behaviors.

Continuing the discussion of the applications of discretionary behavior, Nancy L. Ras suggests a relationship between discretionary behaviors and teachers' perception of shared values and common goals in Israeli schools in Chapter 8. In this study, Ras examines the antecedents and outcomes of teacher discretionary behaviors through the lenses of social identity and social categorization theories. Discretionary behaviors have generally been considered at an individual level of analysis using social exchange models. Ras' study methodologically distinguishes itself with the utilization of group as the level of analysis. This longitudinal, mixed-method, case study of teachers during a curricular reform suggest that teacher discretionary behaviors may be the means to teacher socialization and the outcome of teacher social identification. Similar to several other chapters in the volume, this study suggests a connection between the individual, curricular, and organizational priorities of the context. Considering teacher discretionary behaviors as obligatory proof of group membership presents interesting avenues for future research, particularly for educational organizations with poor and problematic organizational cultures.

In Chapter 9, Kursad Yılmaz and Yahya Altınkurt examine the relationships between organizational justice, organizational trust, and discretionary behaviors in Turkish secondary schools. Consistent with studies in other fields, their study identifies organizational justice as a significant predictor of teacher organizational citizenship behaviors. This study also identifies trust as a significant predictor of teacher organizational citizenship behaviors. Even though trust in colleagues and trust in principals are both significant factors predicting teacher organizational citizenship behaviors, trust in colleagues appeared to be the strongest predictor. The effect of organizational justice on organizational citizenship behavior is mediated through organizational trust. The authors offer valuable insights on how national culture might have influenced the findings.

Concluding this part of the book, in Chapter 10, Jill Morgan and Betty Y. Ashbaker examine teachers' role paradox as supervisor of teaching assistants in Wales and England. They offer extensive review of literature to overview the discrepancies between format structures (i.e., law and policies) versus daily life in schools. The authors offer recommendations for building the teacher's supervisory role into the infrastructure of schools, rather than relying on its emergence as a discretionary behavior.

Part III, titled *Conclusions and Implications for Future Research* concludes the volume with focus on the outcomes of discretionary behavior, the impact of current research on discretionary behavior, and its implications on future research. In Chapter 11, Izhar Oplatka examines the organizational, individual, student outcomes of teacher discretionary behaviors within the context of drug and alcohol prevention education in Israeli high schools. Contrary to the expectations of positive outcomes, this study identifies both positive and negative consequences of discretionary behaviors. Oplatka argues that the positive outcomes were somehow absent while negative outcomes were more prevalent. Among the negative consequences are poor or adversary relations with colleagues, depletion of personal energy, and limited time with the family. Positive consequences included self-fulfillment, social acknowledgment, trust, and sense of professional effectiveness. The negative consequences of engaging discretionary behaviors present an interesting venue for the conceptual multi-dimensionality of discretionary behaviors. While studies in other fields identify the negative types or consequences of discretionary behaviors toward organizations, additionally, this study brings to the light the negative consequences of discretionary behaviors directed toward individuals.

In the final chapter of this volume, Chapter 12, Ibrahim Duyar and Inayet Aydin examine how discretionary performance and task performance of assistant principals take shape where no clear role specifications exist. The authors provide a comprehensive review of antecedent, processes, and outcomes of discretionary behaviors in educational and other organizations. The results of this study indicate that personal initiative and organizational support significantly predict assistant principals' work performance and career aspirations. Their cross-national study also examine whether the relationships among the study variables differ in two different countries,

United States and Turkey. In fact, the national origin appeared to be a significantly differentiating factor of the assistant principals' task performances, discretionary performances, and future career aspirations. This finding presents important implications about the conceptual validity of discretionary behaviors, as well as the relationships with other relevant constructs across different cultures and nations.

Preparing this book was a collective labor of love by all contributors. To begin, we must thank the authors who have contributed to this book. Their work has blazed an emerging yet significant field: discretionary behavior in educational organizations. We thank them greatly for allowing us to showcase their pioneering efforts. We pay special thanks to our reviewers, B. Dean Bowles, Michael F. DiPaola, and Carolyn L. Pearson. We would like to thank Thomas Dark, our editor at Emerald, for his invaluable help in bringing our project to fruition. We also wish to thank Chris Hart at Emerald for his faith in our project. His professional guidance not only made this book possible, but it did so in a most enjoyable fashion.

Ibrahim Duyar
Anthony H. Normore

REFERENCES

Bennett, R., & Stamper, C. L. (2002). Corporate citizenship and deviancy: A study of discretionary work behavior. In C. S. Galbraith (Ed.), *Strategies and organizations in transition* (Vol. 3, pp. 265–284). Kidlington, UK: Elsevier Science.

Borman, W. C., & Motowidlo, S. J. (1993). Expanding the criterion domain to include elements of contextual performance. In N. Schmitt & W. C. Borman (Eds.), *Personnel selection in organizations* (pp. 71–98). San Francisco, CA: Jossey-Bass.

Borman, W. C., Penner, L. A., Allen, T. D., & Motowidlo, S. J. (2001). Personality predictors of citizenship performance. *International Journal of Selection and Assessment, 9*, 52–69.

Crant, J. M. (2000). Proactive behavior in organizations. *Journal of Management, 26*, 435–462.

Den Hartog, D. N., & Belschak, F. D. (2007). Personal initiative, commitment and affect at work. *Journal of Occupational and Organizational Psychology, 80*, 601–622.

Frese, M., & Fay, D. (2001). Personal initiative: An active performance concept for work in the 21st century. *Research in Organizational Behavior, 23*, 133–187.

McBain, R. (2004). Developing organisational citizenship behaviour. *Henley Manager Update, 16*, 26–33.

Ohly, S., Sonnentag, S., & Pluntke, F. (2006). Routinization, work characteristics, and their relationships with creative and proactive behaviors. *Journal of Organizational Behavior, 27*, 257–279.

Organ, D. W. (1997). Organizational citizenship behavior: It's construct clean-up time. *Human Performance, 10*, 85–97.

Organ, D. W., Podsakoff, P. M., & MacKenzie, S. B. (2006). *Organizational citizenship behavior: Its nature, antecedents, and consequences.* Thousand Oaks, CA: Sage.

Parker, S. K. (2000). From passive to proactive motivation: The importance of flexible role orientations and role breadth self-efficacy. *Applied Psychology: An International Review, 49,* 447–469.

Sonnentag, S. (2003). Recovery, work engagement, and proactive behavior: A new look at the interface between non-work and work. *Journal of Applied Psychology, 88,* 518–528.

Van Dyne, L., Cummings, L. L., & McLean Parks, J. (1995). Extra-role behaviors: In pursuit of construct and definitional clarity (a bridge over muddied waters). *Research in Organizational Behavior, 17,* 215–285.

Van Dyne, L., & Ellis, J. B. (2004). Job creep: A reactance theory perspective on organizational citizenship behavior as over-fulfillment of obligations. In J. A-M. Coyle-Shapiro, L. M. Shore, M. S. Taylor & L. E. Tetrick (Eds.), *The employment relationship: Examining psychological and contextual perspectives* (pp. 181–205). Oxford, UK: Oxford University Press.

PART I
THEORETICAL FOUNDATIONS OF DISCRETIONARY BEHAVIOR

CHAPTER 1

THE RELATIONSHIP BETWEEN THE FOUR BRANCH MODEL OF EMOTIONAL INTELLIGENCE AND DISCRETIONARY BEHAVIOR OF UNIVERSITY EDUCATORS

David L. Turnipseed and Elizabeth VandeWaa

ABSTRACT

Typical organizations comprise members whose behaviors range from the minimum possible to maintain membership, to those discretionarily engaging in job-related behaviors above that expected or required. These discretionary behaviors are beyond the job description and often are not recognized by the formal reward system. Possibly, individuals with high emotional intelligence are more prone to engage in discretionary behaviors. The relationship between the dimensions of emotional intelligence and discretionary citizenship behaviors has not previously been explored. Using samples of nursing and business university professors, this study investigates the relationship between discretionary behaviors of educators and the four branch model of emotional intelligence. Discretionary behaviors comprised a set of traditional

Discretionary Behavior and Performance in Educational Organizations: The Missing
Link in Educational Leadership and Management
Advances in Educational Administration, Volume 13, 3–29
Copyright © 2012 by Emerald Group Publishing Limited
All rights of reproduction in any form reserved
ISSN: 1479-3660/doi:10.1108/S1479-3660(2012)0000013006

organizational citizenship dimensions, and those behaviors beyond the expected unique to higher education. Salovey and Mayer's four branch model was used to assess emotional intelligence. Data were analyzed with correlation analysis and multiple regressions. The regression results indicate that managing emotion (the ability to manage one's emotions and emotional relationships) had the greatest number of significant positive relationships with discretionary behaviors in both samples. Perceiving emotions and understanding emotions produced negative relationships with sportsmanship in the nursing sample. The nursing sample produced more relationships between emotional intelligence and discretionary behaviors than the business faculty sample. Overall results support the idea that emotional intelligence is linked to discretionary citizenship behavior. The study results provide evidence to support the organizational value of emotional intelligence. Also, the results provide ideas for fruitful further research which may hold promise for increasing organizational effectiveness and efficiency.

Governmental funding and other support for higher education have become rather meager over the past decade. In addition, athletics, tuition levels, faculty work loads, and even academic tenure have come under attack. The recession of the late 2000s put additional stress on higher education, and the governmental funding paradigm appears certain to change with public funds contributing less to the education budget. As a result of financial hardship, many universities have severely reduced hiring; salaries have been frozen in many states, and minimal increases in others. Because of the high unemployment rate, more people are going back to school: the result is that fewer university faculty are teaching more students with less resources. This scenario may be demoralizing and put downward pressure on individual productivity and efficiency.

University faculty have a uniquely wide range of desirable work attributes. The hours are flexible with the exception of classroom teaching times, and the intensity and effectiveness of job performance is difficult to measure. Consequently there are many opportunities to "slack off," and many opportunities to go beyond the minimum or the expected. Given the deteriorating situation of higher education, it is logical to expect faculty to respond by reducing their level of output. However, this does not appear to be the case most of the time.

Faculty work almost exclusively in a high degree of interaction with others: other faculty, students, staff, and persons in the community. Therefore, reducing effort and output would have the effect of reducing the quantity and quality of interpersonal relationships among some or all of these groups. Poor interpersonal relations would likely motivate their own remediation as individuals generally are averse to be in a climate characterized by poor social relationships. Some individuals would sense a deteriorating social climate and be able to interpret the social cues, understand the reason for the worsening climate, and formulate some type of response. This response may be management of their own feelings, or attempts to manage the feelings and actions of their peers. These individuals and others that they influence may respond by discretionarily engaging in positive behaviors intended to help their several constituencies (peers, students, the university per se, and the community).

The concept of discretionary job-directed organizational behavior going beyond that of a minimalist has its origin in Barnard's (1938) global idea of the "willingness to cooperate." This idea was expanded by Katz and Kahn (1966, 1978) to include a distinction between formal in-role, versus discretionary, extra-role behavior instrumental for the effective functioning of organizations. The popular term describing the wide range of discretionary, pro-organization behaviors that are beyond formal roles is organizational citizenship behavior or OCB (Bateman & Organ, 1983). Examples of traditional OCB include helping others with job-related problems, taking time to help new employees, trying to prevent problems with other workers, encouraging other employees when they are down, attending non-required functions to help the organization's image, not spending a lot of time complaining about trivial matters, and focusing on the positive side of situations rather than what is wrong (Podsakoff, Ahearne, & MacKenzie, 1997).

OCB was formally defined by Organ (1988) as "individual behavior that is discretionary, not directly or explicitly recognized by the formal reward system, and that in the aggregate promotes the effective functioning of the organization. By discretionary, we mean that the behavior is not an enforceable requirement of the role or the job description, that is, the clearly specifiable terms of the person's employment contract with the organization; the behavior is rather a matter of personal choice, such that its omission is not generally understood as punishable" (p 4). In 2006, Organ, Posakoff, and MacKenzie added efficiency as a consequence.

Discretionary behaviors benefiting the organization or those in the organization are valuable for three reasons: they serve to create a harmonious, pleasant work environment; they advance the organization; and there is no direct cost for these actions. Positive discretionary behaviors may indirectly increase organizational performance by improving the organizational climate, decreasing Herzburg – type (Herzberg, Mausner, & Snyderman, 1959) sterile factors or dissatisfiers in the workplace, and increasing motivators and thus job satisfaction. Smith, Organ, and Near (1983) established that job satisfaction is antecedent to OCB.

In any organization there are members who go the extra mile, act as good soldiers, and discretionarily engage in positive behaviors aimed at the organization or its members. Similarly, there are minimalists, who do the least possible to maintain organizational membership. An important question is why some individuals regularly go beyond the minimum and the expected, while others perform at a minimal level. Scholars and managers are interested in identifying the characteristics of individuals likely to engage in organizationally beneficial discretionary actions.

Prior study has shown that affective responses to the work environment, and work exchange relationships, which involve implicit assumptions about job-related tasks, are antecedents of OCB (c.f. Cardona, Lawrence, & Bentler, 2004; Ilies, Scott, & Judge, 2006; Schnake, 1991; Turnipseed & Rassuli, 2005; Witt, 1991). Cognitions associated with managerial and coworker behaviors, advancement opportunities, pay, and working conditions are also related to OCB (Williams & Anderson, 1991). The present university environment is one of increasing work, diminishing resources, stress, and uncertainty. There is little in the typical university milieu to trigger positive affect and cognitions, and consequently, positive discretionary behaviors. Yet these actions continue: university faculty continue to labor along, doing good jobs, and engaging in discretionary, good soldier behaviors for their universities, their students, and the communities.

The current difficult period in higher education is an opportune time to examine discretionary behavior. Obviously there is little to engender positive affect, and tangible rewards that could provide positive cognitions are scarce; however, professors continue to work and go beyond the minimum. What is it about these very intelligent, highly educated individuals that make them discretionarily go the extra mile? Possibly it is their social abilities, specifically the ability to recognize, interpret, understand, and act on the subtle currents of emotionality, or their emotional intelligence (EI). Perhaps individuals with high EI are likely to engage in discretionary behaviors. In this study we investigate the relationship between EI and positive job-oriented discretionary workplace behaviors.

EMOTIONAL INTELLIGENCE

A recent idea in the organizational behavior literature EI, which is suggested as another type of intelligence. EI is conceptualized as one's ability "to monitor one's own feelings, to discriminate among them, and to use this information to guide one's thinking and action" (Salovey & Mayer, 1990). This basic definition evolved to a four-branch model beginning with perception of emotion, which is the emotional area most directly related to emotions. The second branch is using emotion, the third, understanding emotion, and finally the fourth branch is managing emotion, which is the area most general to personality (Mayer & Salovey, 1997).

In normal adult populations, the effect of EI manifests in social situations and at work. EI is linked to good social relations, productive working relationships, effective interpersonal behaviors, and general social competency (Bracket, Rivers, Shiffman, Lerner, & Salovey, 2006). EI is also linked to understanding relationships in business environments; it predicts organization goal-supportive behavior (Côté & Miners, 2006), performance and leadership rankings (Carmeli & Josman, 2006; Kerr, Garvin, & Heaton, 2006), and development of good working relationships (Rosete & Ciarrochi, 2005). Individuals high in EI tend to be relatively higher achievers in their personal lives (Carmeli & Josman, 2006).

EI is linked to the traditional OCB dimensions of altruism and compliance (Carmeli & Josman, 2006). Highly EI individuals are skillful at identifying, interpreting, and responding to emotions. Therefore it is logical to expect that these emotionally intelligent individuals will have a relatively greater propensity to assist their peers. Individuals with high EI may perceive and interpret organizational stimuli differently than those with lower EI, and may engage in different patterns of behavior which include discretionary behavior. The focus of this study is to determine whether EI is linked to positive discretionary behavior and to identify any differences in the relationships of the four branches of EI, specifically, what is the incremental contribution of each of the branches.

Perception of Emotion

The first branch of EI is perception, which is the ability to detect and understand emotions in one's self and in others (Mayer & Salovey, 1997). Perceiving emotions is the basic part of EI that makes all other processing of EI possible (Salovey & Grewal, 2005). Emotional perception has been suggested to increase altruistic behaviors. Persons high in perceiving emotion will likely recognize and understand their peers' feelings (Carmeli & Josman, 2006). Individuals with greater ability to distinguish emotions may be more likely to have and use better social skills, and less likely to violate social norms. The ability to perceive emotions may make individuals more sensitive to the expressive behavior of others.

The connection between an empathetic perspective and EI has been established (Schutte et al., 2001). Empathy, an emotional reaction in one to the perceived affective state of another (Blair, 2005), has also been linked to EI (Mayer, Caruso, & Salovey, 1999), self-monitoring, and the social context. High self-monitors may have the ability to modify their self-presentation as a result of self-appraisal (Schutte, et al., 2001). Individuals high in EI and self-monitoring, and who are empathetic, are more likely to understand the needs and problems of coworkers, and to take discretionary actions to help, suggesting,

H_1. Perception of emotion is positively related to discretionary organizational behavior.

Using Emotion

Using emotion, the second branch of EI, is the ability to utilize emotions to assist with various cognitive activities such as thinking and solving problems. Individuals high in EI can use their emotions to help master a task or to match the immediate requirements of a task at hand (Salovey & Grewal, 2005). Highly emotional intelligent individuals who can use their emotions adaptively are likely to have and use better social skills and be more socially adept (Schutte et al., 2001). Social skills include the ability to choose and employ information from an interpersonal context to determine appropriate goal-directed behavior and to execute behaviors that maximize the probability of goal attainment and maintenance of good relationships with others (Beauchamp & Anderson, 2010). High EI individuals who have the ability to shift quickly and easily between positive and negative mood states are able to respond to peers' feelings more appropriately (Abraham, 1999).

Prioritization of thinking is included in using emotion. When a stimulus elicits an emotional response, maximum attention is usually directed toward the stimulating event: the use of emotions directs attention toward important things. Individuals with high EI can take advantage of changing moods to optimally match mood with a given task (Salovey & Grewal, 2005).

If an employee with high EI recognizes that a coworker is having problems, he or she may avoid any interactions when in a bad or sad mood, and wait until happy to help. The ability to use emotions may increase one's propensity to engage in discretionary behaviors that are individually and organizationally beneficial, thus,

H_2. Using emotion is positively related to discretionary organizational behavior.

Understanding Emotion

The third branch of EI is understanding or thinking with emotions and is defined as one's ability to comprehend emotions and appreciate complex relationships and nuances among various emotions. Understanding emotion includes solving emotional problems such as determining similarities and dissimilarities of emotions, and the relations they express (Mayer, Caruso, & Salovey, 2000). Highly emotional intelligent individuals are prone to be sensitive to, and understand, the many complex social relationships found in organizations. Understanding emotion includes sensitivity to even very small variations between emotions, such as the difference between sad and morose; and the ability to recognize a temporal progression of emotion, such as when shock turns to grief (Salovey & Grewal, 2005).

The ability to understand emotions may equip individuals to more genuinely express their emotions. Individuals high in EI are skillful at putting themselves in states of positive affect; and consequently, have the ability to experience states of negative affectivity without significant negative effects (Carmeli & Josman, 2006). Emotions convey information that may lead to behavior: for example, fear usually reflects one's wish to escape a situation, and anger typically indicates the desire to attack others. Anger is correlated with various behavioral responses such as attacking, seeking revenge, peacemaking, or situational withdrawal for a calming period. Understanding the meaning of emotions, and the ability to reason about the meanings are requisite to totally understanding emotions (Mayer & Salovey, 1997). An individual with high ability to understand the social relationships in an organization and to think with emotions may be likely to engage in discretionary organizational behavior, which suggests that,

H_3. Understanding emotion is positively related to discretionary organizational behavior.

Managing Emotion

Emotional management, the fourth branch of EI, is the ability to manage one's emotions and emotional relationships to achieve personal and interpersonal growth (Mayer, Caruso, Salovey, & Sitarenios, 2001). Management of emotions includes understanding the implications of social action on emotions, and the regulation of emotion in one's self and others (Mayer, et al., 2000). Thus understanding the result of one's actions on emotions, and the ability to regulate one's emotions may be positively linked to engaging in discretionary behaviors.

Emotions are managed in the context of the individual's goals, self-knowledge, and social awareness. Consider a small child being taught to "count to 10" before getting mad. When the child becomes adult, the means of managing emotions have expanded, and the individual has the ability to avoid feelings or to alter appraisals for self-control or self-assurance (Mayer, Salovey, & Caruso, 2004). Engaging in discretionary behaviors is more likely for individuals with emotional management abilities who can cognitively justify their actions and rationalize their failures.

Individuals with high EI have the ability to detect and understand emotions, utilize emotions to assist various cognitive activities such as thinking and solving problems, and to comprehend emotions and appreciate complex relationships and nuances among various emotions. Individuals high in EI are less likely to lose emotional control: they have the ability to control their emotions, as well as those of others (Salovey & Grewal, 2005). An emotionally intelligent individual is capable of harnessing emotions – both positive and negative – and managing them to achieve desired results (Salovey & Grewal, 2005). Turnipseed (2002) suggested that citizenship behavior may be an individual-specific general predisposition to view the workplace in a particular manner. Perhaps EI is that predisposition, which suggests the hypothesis,

H₄. Managing emotions is positively related to discretionary organizational behavior.

METHODS

Procedure

Volunteer participants were solicited from the faculty of a nursing school and business school in a southern university. Traditional OCBs, plus discretionary behaviors unique to a university were measured. Also, the four branches of EI – perceiving, thinking, understanding, and managing emotion – were measured. The samples were analyzed in the aggregate and separately. Descriptive statistics and Cronbachs's alpha coefficient of internal reliability were calculated. Person correlations were calculated to assess the relationships among the study variables. Multiple regression analyses were used to determine the incremental contribution of the four EI branches to the variance in of the discretionary behavior metrics.

Samples

Sample 1
Sample 1 comprised 43 full-time faculty at a doctoral granting College of Nursing in a Southeastern university. The average participant's age was 46.6 years (std dev 8.6), with an average time in higher education of 9.8 years (std dev – 6.9). Seventy three percent were female, and 93% were white.

Sample 2
The second sample was 30 faculty from a College of Business in a Southeastern University. The average age was 47.9 (std dev – 10.4), and the average time in higher education was 14.1 years (std dev – 11.1). Ninety-five percent were white, and 47% were male.

Measures

Traditional Organizational Citizenship Behavior
The 13-item scale of Podsakoff, Ahearne, and MacKenzie (1997) was used to measure traditional OCB. Respondents were presented with the scale statements and requested to indicate their agreement on a 1–7 Likert-type scale. Example statements are: "I encourage other employees when they are down"; "I act as a peacemaker when others in the organization have disagreement"; "I take steps to try to prevent problems with other workers"; and "I do not consume a lot of time complaining about trivial matters".

University-Specific Discretionary Behaviors
Traditional OCBs are relevant to almost all organizations. However, there are also discretionary behaviors that are organization-specific. We developed

a set of behaviors that are entirely discretionary and relevant to universities. Examples of these behaviors are: "I often stay after class time to accommodate students", "I donate money to my college", and "I volunteer to serve as advisor for student groups".

Emotional Intelligence
The 24-item scale developed by Groves, McEnrue, and Shen (2008) was used to measure EI. This scale measures four dimensions of EI: perception and appraisal, facilitating thinking, understanding, and regulation and management of emotion. Responses were on a 7-point Likert-type scale, anchored by "strongly agree" and "strongly disagree". Example perception statements are: "I can usually imagine what another person in feeling," and "I can accurately identify a range of emotions that I feel from day to day". Example facilitating thinking statements are: "I listen to the feelings of other people in establishing priorities," and "In deciding to go forward with a decision, I always consider how other people may feel about it". Example understanding statements are: "I can usually detect subtle changes in the emotions of my coworkers", and "I can watch other people interact and recognize the feelings they hold toward each other". Example management statements are: "I am capable of calming someone down who is angry or frustrated at work", and "I am usually able to transmit a sense of enthusiasm abut a work project to others".

Analysis

The traditional OCBs and university-specific discretionary behavior items were factor analyzed. Factor inclusion criteria were eigenvalue greater than 1, and minimum contribution to the variance of 5%. The 13 traditional OCBs formed four factors accounting for 77% of the variance. These were named altruism, problem prevention, compliance, and sportsmanship. The university-specific discretionary behaviors formed four factors accounting for 69% of the variance: these were named service, spend personal funds, external interaction, and accommodating.

Descriptive statistics were calculated, Cronbach's alpha was calculated for the scale variables, and Person correlation (r) matrices for the variables were developed. The relationships of interest were investigated via multiple regression analysis: each of the discretionary behaviors was regressed by the four EI dimensions.

RESULTS

Our results are presented in aggregate for the combined samples, and for the nursing faculty and business faculty separately.

Combined Sample

Emotional Intelligence and Discretionary Behavior
The scores for EI, on a 1–7 scale ranged from 4.9 to 5.9. The scores, with Groves et al.'s (2008) scores in parentheses, were: 4.9 (5.0) for perceiving emotion; 5.4 (4.9) for thinking with emotion; 5.1 (5.1) for understanding emotion; and 5.9 (5.4) for managing emotion.

The discretionary behavior scores (also on a 1–7 scale) ranged from 4.8 to 6.4. The scores were: 6.4 for altruism; 5.8 for preventing problems; 5.8 for sportsmanship; 5.4 for compliance; 4.8 for accommodating; 5.9 for service; 5.3 for external interactions; and 5.1 for spending personal funds.

Correlations
The significant correlations between EI and discretionary behaviors were positive, as expected, with the exception of sportsmanship. Perception of emotion was correlated with altruism (.32; $p < .05$); sportsmanship (−.51; $p < .001$); and accommodating (.39; $p < .05$). Thinking with emotion was not correlated with any of the discretionary behaviors. Understanding emotion was negatively correlated with sportsmanship (−.49; $p < .001$). Managing emotion was correlated with altruism (.60; $p < .001$); preventing problems (.39; $p < .01$); compliance (.64; $p < .001$); service (.58; $p < .001$); and external (.36; $p < .01$). H_1 and H_4 received some support. H_2 and H_3 were not supported (see Table 1).

Regression Results: Traditional OCB
Regression analysis of the traditional OCBs by the EI dimensions produced a significant equation for altruism with managing emotion ($\beta = .73$; $p = .000$; $R^2 = .41$). The regression model for compliance included only managing emotion ($\beta = .97$; $p = .000$; $R^2 = .42$). The equation for preventing problems included managing emotions ($\beta = .31$; $p = .01$; $R^2 = .21$). These results support H_4.

Regression Equations: University-Specific Discretionary Behaviors
Managing emotions was the only independent variable in the models for service ($\beta = .46$; $p = .003$; $R^2 = .27$) and for external interactions

Table 1. Combined Samples: Means, Standard Deviations, Cronbach Alpha, and Correlations.

	Mean	S.D.	Cronbach Alpha	1	2	3	4	5	6	7	8	9	10	11	12
1. Perception of emotion	4.9	.85	.81	—											
2. Thinking w/emotion	5.4	.85	.69	.38*	—										
3. Understanding emotion	5.1	.88	.72	.60***	.32*	—									
4. Managing emotion	5.9	.65	.86	.18	.37**	.29	—								
5. Altruism	6.4	.84	.84	.34*	.22	.34	.60***	—							
6. Prevent problems	5.8	.74	.76	.31*	.25	.33	.36**	.55***	—						
7. Sportsmanship	5.8	.97	.84	-.33***	-.04	-.23***	.04	.28	.41	—					
8. Compliance	5.4	1.1	.80	.20	.35	.31	.64***	.57**	.54**	.25	—				
9. Accommodating	4.8	.96	.82	.32*	.16	.30	.18	.41	.29*	-.10	.26	—			
10. Service	5.9	.66	.79	.15	.26	.23	.52***	.52***	.50**	.25	.64***	.49	—		
11. External	5.3	.79	.84	.02	.06	.09	.38*	.42	.28*	.16	.64**	.33***	.58	—	
12. Spend personal funds	5.1	1.2	1.0	-.05	-.16	-.01	.18	.13	.04	.10	.42***	.06	.29	.41*	—

*<.05; **<.01; ***<.001.

$(\beta = .52; \; p < .05; \; R^2 = .16)$, providing additional support for H_4. The equations for accommodating and spending personal funds were not significant. The regression equations are set out in Table 2.

Results: Nursing Professors

Correlations

The correlations between EI and discretionary behaviors unexpectedly included negative as well as positive relationships. Perception of emotion was positively correlated with altruism (.32; $p < .05$) and accommodating (.39; $p < .05$); but negatively correlated with sportsmanship ($-.51$; $p < .001$). Thinking with emotion was not correlated with any of the measures of discretionary behavior. Understanding emotion negatively correlated with sportsmanship ($-.49$; $p < .001$). Managing emotion was positively correlated with altruism (.60; $p < .001$); preventing problems (.39; $p < .01$); compliance (.64; $p < .001$); service (.58; $p > 001$); and external interaction (.36; $p < .05$) (see Table 3).

Regression Equations: Traditional OCB

Regression analysis of the traditional OCBs by the EI dimensions produced a significant equation for altruism with managing emotion ($\beta = .74$; $p = .0003$; $R^2 = .43$), supporting H_4. Managing emotion ($\beta = 1.1$; $p = .0001$; $R^2 = .41$) was the only independent variable in the equation for compliance, further supporting H_4. Contrary to H_2 and H_3, the equation for sportsmanship ($p = .001$; $R^2 = .37$) indicated a negative relationship with perception of emotion ($\beta = -.37$) and understanding emotion ($\beta = -.38$), as presented in Table 4.

Regression Equations: University-Specific Discretionary Behaviors

The equations for discretionary accommodating behavior and spending personal funds were not significant. However, the equation for discretionary service behavior was significant with managing emotion ($\beta = .61$; $p = .004$; $R^2 = .34$): also external interactions ($\beta = .63$; $p = .004$; $R^2 = .30$) produced a significant equation with managing emotions, further supporting H_4.

Results: Business Professors

Correlations

The significant business faculty sample correlations were positive, as expected. Perception of emotion was correlated with altruism (.34; $p < .05$), preventing

DAVID L. TURNIPSEED AND ELIZABETH VANDEWAA

Table 2. Combined Samples: Regression Results-Discretionary Behaviors by Emotional Intelligence.

Dependent Variables	Independent Variables: Emotional Intelligence				R^2
	Perception	Thinking	Understanding	Managing	P
Traditional OCB					
Altruism					
β	.25	−.11	.03	.73***	
Full model					$R^2 = .41$
					$P = .0000$
Compliance					
β	.03	.10	.12	. 97***	
Full model					$R^2 = .42$
					$P = .0000$
Prevent problems					
β	.16	.02	.11	.31*	
Full model					$R^2 = .21$
					$P = .01$
Sportsmanship					
β	−.36*	.07	−.08*	.19	
Full model					$R^2 = .12$
					$P = .16$
Organization specific					
Accommodating					
β	.19	−.02	.10	.09	
Full model					$R^2 = .13$
					$P = .13$
Service					
β	.03	.02	.04	.46***	
Full model					$R^2 = .27$
					$P = .003$
External					
β	−.02	−.09	.00	.52**	
Full model					$R^2 = .16$
					$P = .07$
Spend personal funds					
β	−.05	−.33	.01	.49*	
Full model					$R^2 = .08$
					$P = .34$

* $<.05$; ** $<.01$; *** $<.001$.

Table 3. Nursing Faculty Data: Means, Standard Deviations, Cronbach Alpha, and Correlations.

	Mean	S.D.	Cronbach Alpha	1	2	3	4	5	6	7	8	9	10	11	12
1. Perception of emotion	4.9	.83	.81	—											
2. Thinking w/emotion	5.4	.83	.68	.33*	—										
3. Understanding emotion	5.2	.85	.72	.53***	.23	—									
4. Managing emotion	6.1	.65	.85	.18	.41**	.26	—								
5. Altruism	6.4	.78	.84	.32*	.17	.09	.60***	—							
6. Prevent problems	5.9	.57	.76	.08	.11	.10	.39**	.52***	—						
7. Sportsmanship	5.8	.90	.84	-.51***	-.21	-.49***	.04	.25	.35	—					
8. Compliance	5.5	1.1	.80	.06	.24	.18	.64***	.46**	.53**	.22	—				
9. Accommodating	4.8	.96	.82	.39*	.08	.32	.09	.29	-.12	-.34	-.02	—			
10. Service	5.9	.66	.79	.06	.18	.16	.58***	.50***	.43**	.14	.65*	.13	—		
11. External	5.3	.79	.84	-.13	-.15	-.02	.36*	.31	.33*	.23	.59**	.00	.61***	—	
12. Spend personal funds	5.1	1.3	1.0	-.18	.21	-.06	.23	.06	.01	.24	.47***	-.02	.31	.37*	—

*<.05; **<.01; ***<.001.

Table 4. Nurses Data: Regression Results-Discretionary Behaviors by Emotional Intelligence.

Dependent Variables	Independent Variables: Emotional Intelligence				R^2
	Perception	Thinking	Understanding	Managing	P
Traditional OCB					
Altruism					
β	.22	−.16	.05	.75***	
Full model					$R^2 = .43$
					$P = .0003$
Compliance					
β	−.12	−.01	.08	1.1***	
Full model:					$R^2 = .41$
					$P = .0006$
Prevent problems					
β	.02	.05	−.01	.36*	
Full model					$R^2 = .15$
					$P = .18$
Sportsmanship					
β	−.37*	−.14	−.38*	.35	
Full model					$R^2 = .37$
					$P = .001$
Organization specific					
Accommodating					
β	.38	−.06	.17	.01	
Full model					$R^2 = .17$
					$P = .14$
Service					
β	−.04	−.05	.04	.61***	
Full model					$R^2 = .34$
					$P = .003$
External					
β	−.10	−.30	−.22	.63**	
Full model					$R^2 = .30$
					$P = .005$
Spend personal funds					
β	−.21	−.48	.03	.76*	
Full model					$R^2 = .18$
					$P = .11$

*<.05; **<.01; ***<.001.

Table 5. Business Faculty: Means, Standard Deviations, Cronbach Alpha, and Correlations.

	Mean	S.D.	Cronbach Alpha	1	2	3	4	5	6	7	8	9	10	11	12
1. Perception of emotion	5.2	.79	.81	—											
2. Thinking w/emotion	5.3	.77	.69	.64	—										
3. Understanding emotion	5.3	.96	.72	.78***	.61	—									
4. Managing emotion	5.7	.47	.86	.28	.34**	.40	—								
5. Altruism	6.2	.94	.84	.34*	.35	.39	.67***	—							
6. Prevent problems	5.6	1.00	.76	.59	.49	.67	.33**	.59***	—						
7. Sportsmanship	5.7	.99	.84	.11	.38	.37***	.07	.33	.53	—					
8. Compliance	5.1	1.00	.80	.63	.67	.66	.66**	.85**	.62**	.27	—				
9. Accommodating	6.0	.96	.82	.64*	.81	.65	.21	.37	.50	.44	.73	—			
10. Service	5.8	.68	.79	.36	.55	.46	.41**	.61***	.73**	.66	.61***	.56	—		
11. External	5.3	.83	.84	.48	.60	.40	.76*	.76	.28*	-.02	.89**	.55	.44***	—	
12. Spend personal funds	5.8	.99	1.0	.22	-.01	.30	.58	.53	.24	-.30	.52	.09	.20	.56*	—

*<.05; **<.01; ***<.001.

Table 6. Business Faculty Data: Regression Results-Discretionary Behaviors by Emotional Intelligence.

Dependent Variables	Independent Variables: Emotional Intelligence				R^2
	Perception	Thinking	Understanding	Managing	P
Traditional OCB					
Altruism					
β	.39	−.03	−.08	.93**	
Full model					$R^2 = .34$
					$P = .03$
Compliance					
β	.59	.23	.03	.76**	
Full model					$R^2 = .64$
					$P = .002$
Prevent problems					
β	.27	.06	.51	.02	
Full model					$R^2 = .46$
					$P = .14$
Sportsmanship					
β	−.75	.39	.82	−.60	
Full model					$R^2 = .33$
					$P = .36$
Organization specific					
Accommodating					
β	.38	.59	.12	−.78**	
Full model					$R^2 = .59$
					$P = .004$
Service					
β	.13	.19	.07	.10	
Full model					$R^2 = .25$
					$P = .32$
External					
β	.36	.32	.31	1.23***	
Full model					$R^2 = .76$
					$P = .001$
Spend personal funds					
β	.29	−.44	.12	.04	
Full model					$R^2 = .39$
					$P = .25$

* $< .05$; ** $< .01$; *** $< .001$.

problems (.59; $p < .001$), compliance (.63; $p < .001$), service (.36; $p < .05$), and external interaction (.48; $p < .01$). Thinking with emotion correlated with altruism (.35; $p < .05$), preventing problems (.49; $p < .01$), sportsmanship (.38; $p < .05$), compliance (.67; $p < .001$), accommodating (.81; $p < .001$), service (.55; $p < .01$), and external interaction (.60; $p < .001$). Understanding emotion correlated with altruism (.39; $p < .05$), prevent problems (.67; $p < .001$), sportsmanship (.37; $p < .05$), compliance (.66; $p < .001$), accommodating (.65 < .001$), service (.46; $p < .01$), and external interactions (.40; $p < .01$). Managing emotion correlated with altruism (.67; $p < .001$), compliance (.66; $p < .001$), service (.41; $p < .01$), external interactions (.76; $p < .001$), and spending personal funds (.58; $p < .001$) (see Table 5).

Regression Equations: Traditional OCB
The regressions for traditional OCB by EI produced significant models for altruism by managing emotions ($\beta = .93; p = .93; R^2 = .34$), and compliance by managing emotions ($\beta = .76; p = .002; R^2 = .64$), supporting H$_4$ (see Table 6).

Regression Equations: University-Specific Discretionary Behaviors
Consistent with H$_4$, significant regressions for university-specific discretionary behaviors include accommodating by managing emotions ($\beta = -.78; p = .004; R^2 = .59$), and external interactions by managing emotions ($\beta = 1.23; p = .004; R^2 = .76$).

DISCUSSION

EI is linked to discretionary behavior measured both as traditional OCB and as organization-specific behaviors, in this faculty sample. Although universities are facing hard times, and consequently, the affective and cognitive bases of positive discretionary behavior are scarce, most faculty continue to work diligently, going far beyond the minimum. This suggests an individual basis for positive discretionary behavior. This study expands the knowledge by identifying robust linkages between EI and discretionary behaviors, and demonstrating a differential linkage between the four components of EI and various dimensions of OCB and organization-specific discretionary behavior.

Although our results have limitations, they identify highly significant personal ability antecedents to discretionary workplace behaviors. There are several important implications of these results including the idea that OCB and other discretionary behaviors may be more a function of personal ability than previously thought. Our results suggest that some aspects of the work environment may operate as a moderator between EI and discretionary actions. Our results support those of Turnipseed and VandeWaa (2011, in review) who found a greater relationship between EI and traditional OCBs directed at individuals than at the organization.

Combined Sample

The sample of university faculty had EI scores equal to, or slightly higher than the sample used for measure development by Groves et al. (2008). Also the discretionary behavior dimension scores were all above 5 on a 1–7 scale, with the exception of accommodating (4.8). These scores indicate that the faculty sample that was the basis of this study was non-aberrant. The most interesting results were the relationships between the dimensions of EI and discretionary behaviors.

The four-branch model of EI includes dimensions ranging from the perception of emotion, which is the necessary first aspect of EI, to managing emotion. In the combined sample, H_1, H_2, and H_3 were not supported: there were no significant linkages between the discretionary behaviors and perceiving emotion, using emotion to facilitate thinking, and understanding emotions. There were however several linkages between the discretionary behaviors and managing emotions, supporting H_4. This does not suggest that perceiving, thinking with, and understanding emotions are unimportant: rather these first three branches are not directly linked to discretionary behavior. Obviously, only after emotions have been accurately perceived can interpretations be made, and emotion-based responses formulated. Possibly the perception of emotions may be linked to other antecedents of discretionary behavior, rather than to the behaviors themselves.

The absence of a link between thinking with emotion (emotional facilitation of thought) and discretionary behavior has not been identified previously. However, Erez and Isen (2002) report that various types of problem solving are facilitated by some emotions, but not others. This appears to be a function of one's knowledge of a relationship between certain emotions, and thinking, which can be used to direct individual planning (Izard, 2001). Perhaps the absence of a relationship between thinking with emotion and discretionary behavior may be explained as emotions being connected with precursors of behaviors rather than the behaviors themselves. Or, consistent with Erez and Isen (2002), all emotions do not facilitate discretionary behaviors.

Similarly, the absence of a link between understanding emotion and discretionary behavior may be explained, speculatively, as the ability to analyze emotions being focused on the contextual and environmental cues that eventually motivate the discretionary behaviors. Possibly the feelings and emotions triggering discretionary behavior may be appropriate metrics for assessment of the influence of EI on discretionary behaviors. Understanding emotions may lead to emotional management efforts, but have little direct effect on discretionary behaviors.

Although lower branches of EI were not linked to discretionary behavior, management of emotion was linked to five of the eight discretionary behavior measures. As the top branch, management of emotions includes all of the personality: the context of social awareness, self-knowledge, and one's goals influence how emotions are managed (Mayer et al., 2004). Mayer et al. (2004) argues that the ability to manage emotions includes enabling one to avoid negative feelings or to "reframe appraisals to assure oneself or to achieve equanimity" (p. 200). This logic may hold for discretionary behaviors: an individual observing an organizational environment and perceiving negative, disturbing events and relationships may utilize emotional management abilities to avoid, deflect, or alter those perceptions to more cognitively acceptable situation, or attempt to achieve equanimity and composure. However, even with great emotional management ability, such cognitive redefinitions or reframing machinations may have limited success, require constant effort, or an uncomfortable level of effort. Engaging in discretionary behaviors may supplement the effects of emotional management.

Discretionary behavior may operate in a compensatory manner to augment the effects of emotional management. Emotional management is controlling or directing of emotions, which have arisen from some stimulus, whereas engaging in discretionary behavior may be corrective. For example, if one recognizes that a peer is having difficulty at work, negative emotions may result. Depending on the severity, centrality, and personal relevance of the peer's difficulty, the negative emotions may be intense and uncomfortable. One with high EI may decide to engage in emotional management, initially through self-management and psychologically isolating the negative emotions. Subsequently, the emotional management may be extended to the troubled coworker through inquiries about the nature of the problem, attempted fixes, and what can be done to help. Listening to the responses will create a caring, supportive environment, while possibly helping to clarify and ameliorate the workplace difficulties.

These emotional management processes may be temporary, or work only in the presence of others with high EI: an individual with low EI could enter a situation and reverse the positive effects. Therefore, discretionarily engaging in behaviors intended to aid the troubled worker may be the logical next step. Our results indicate that high emotional management abilities are linked to altruistic behaviors (e.g., giving time to help follow employees with work-related problems, taking time to help new employees, "touching base" with other employees before taking actions that may affect them, encouraging other employees when they are down). This same logic of behavior may hold for other discretionary actions. Managers high in EI are known to engage in behaviors supportive of their organization's goals (Côté & Miners, 2006). This study showed that managing emotions was linked to organizationally-compliant, accommodating behaviors, service, and supportive external behaviors. EI is also known to correlate highly with effective interpersonal behaviors (Rosete, 2007, in Mayer, Salovey, & Caruso, 2008).

The Unique Cases of Nursing and Business

The present results suggest that the ability to manage emotions is linked with altruism: in the business faculty sample, accommodating discretionary behaviors, which comprises altruistic interpersonal actions, was linked to managing emotions. Perceiving and understanding emotions were linked with the traditional OCB dimension of sportsmanship in the nursing faculty sample. Considering the components of sportsmanship (complaining, finding fault, focusing on what is wrong, making mountains out of molehills), perceiving the situation is quite relevant to any further actions. Complaining and finding fault, for example, may be quite emotion laden, and an observer or participant in such a climate may wonder what others are feeling. There will likely be worry, anxiety, stress, and anger among individuals in an environment that is causing complaining or fault finding. From a multitude of clues, an individual with the ability to accurately perceive the emotions of others, as well as his/her own emotions, can identify the salient feelings and formulate an appropriate response.

The samples from nursing and business faculty were similar. Two of the traditional OCBs – altruism and compliance – produced significant regression equations with the relationships in the same directions for both samples. Sportsmanship was significant for the nursing sample but not for the business faculty. The organization-specific discretionary behavior of external interaction was significant for the both samples. However, service was significant for the nurses only; and accommodating was significant only for the business faculty.

These differences may reflect a difference in the level of faculty (graduate versus undergraduate), a difference in discipline, or the business faculty's significantly longer time in higher education. Another interesting possibility is gender differences: the nursing sample was 73% female versus the business sample with 53% female. Determination of the differences between the two samples was beyond the scope of this study; however, the relative consistency of the results argues for a fairly stable trait basis for EI, and insensitivity to contextual variances.

SUMMARY

In summary, this study has provided support for the results of prior research showing links between EI and behaviors such as effective interpersonal behaviors, social competency, interpersonal sensitivity, and organizational support. However, we go beyond contributing that support, and demonstrate differential linkages between the four branches of EI and discretionary workplace behaviors. Managing emotion was the branch with the most relationships with the discretionary behaviors: thinking with emotion produced no linkages. This study also indicates – limited by the two samples – that the relationship between EI and discretionary behavior is relatively stable and not contextually responsive. In two different professional schools, the relationships between EI and discretionary behaviors were similar suggesting minimal contextual differences in this study. However just as the contexts may have been similar, the EI–discretionary links may not be sensitive to context: the determination of contextual sensitivity was beyond the scope of this study.

Practical Implications

The results of this study have several practical implications for managers and supervisors. The linkage between EI and positive discretionary behaviors suggests that after measurement of EI improves, employees be screened for EI or their EI developed for jobs in which that trait is desirable. This is especially important in education, service companies, hospitals, and other organizations characterized by a high degree of interpersonal activity. The need for EI increases as the degree of interpersonal activity increases. Individuals having interpersonal difficulties may logically be evaluated for EI.

EI is linked to organizational performance. This is indicated by prior research, and the results of this study. Although we did not measure financial or other metrics of organizational performance and evaluate their linkage with EI, the discretionary behaviors assessed in this study contribute to performance. And these discretionary actions do not add to direct costs: consequently, EI may increase organizational performance by improving the social and interpersonal relationships in the organization.

Limitations

The small sample size and the discipline-specific samples may limit the generalizability of our results. Although our EI metrics provided some robust linkages with discretionary behaviors, EI is likely highly correlated with other personal traits and abilities. Some may criticize the choice of EI and the traditional organizational citizenship instruments. Given the relatively new EI construct, its evolving definition, and the lack of a generally accepted measure, there is the possibility that other measures would produce different results. However, there are no alternative measures that would be a less susceptible to criticism. Analyzing nursing and business faculty and forming any conclusions from the results may be imprudent due to discipline differences and the possible contextual differences in the two colleges (which are likely insignificant when compared to other organizations). Generalizability of the study results may be limited by the single organization sample.

The self-report nature of the study may be a limitation. Individuals who are high in EI are more sensitive, socially competent, and tend to have higher quality relationships: these individuals are more likely to have volunteered to participate in this study than those with lower EI. Also, those prone to engaging in pro-social and pro-organizational discretionary behaviors may be more likely to volunteer to assist. Consequently, our volunteer sample may not represent the population with respect to EI and discretionary behavior.

Future Study

This study presents many potentially fruitful areas for future research. For example, this study should be replicated with a larger sample, other disciplines, and in other organizations. Our study strongly supports the linkage between EI and various behaviors that are, in at least some instances, discretionary. Future study should examine whether there is a discernable point at which one begins to engage in discretionary behaviors to augment emotional management efforts. Alternatively, is there a point at which emotional management efforts are perceived to have maximized their contributions, and behavioral efforts are undertaken? An interesting study would be a multi-discipline comparative study: are the nursing and business results of this study unique? Is there a discipline difference? Also, examination of a possible gender effect on the EI–discretionary behavior link may provide useful data.

A very interesting study would be the examination of the potential moderation of the EI–OCB linkage by management style or quality of management. Possibly very good or very poor management or possibly an autocratic or participatory management style could alter the EI–OCB relationship. The effect of EI as a moderator in the antecedent–behavior link should be investigated. Analysis with a phase model (see Turnipseed, 2000) may provide beneficial results, as EI may have an identifiable temporal progression over some age range.

Our study provides strong support for the assertion that EI is linked to discretionary organization behaviors, and points the way to additional valuable study.

REFERENCES

Abraham, R. (1999). Emotional intelligence in organizations: A conceptualization. *Genetic, Social, and General Psychology Monographs, 125*(2), 209–224.

Barnard, C. I. (1938). *The functions of the executive.* Cambridge, MA: Harvard University Press.

Bateman, T. S., & Organ, D. W. (1983). Job satisfaction and the good soldier: The relationship between affect and employee "citizenship". *Academy of Management Journal, 26*, 587–595.

Beauchamp, M. H., & Anderson, V. (2010). Social: An integrative framework for the development of social skills. *Psychological Bulletin, 136*, 39–64.

Blair, R. J. (2005). Responding to the emotions of others: Dissociating forms of empathy through the study of typical and psychiatric populations. *Consciousness and Cognition, 14*, 698–718.

Bracket, M. A., Rivers, S. E., Shiffman, S., Lerner, N., & Salovey, P. (2006). Relating emotional abilities to social functioning: A comparison of self-report and performance measures of emotional intelligence. *Journal of Personality and Social Psychology, 91*, 780–795.

Cardona, P., Lawrence, B. S., & Bentler, P. M. (2004). The influence of social and work exchange relationships on organizational citizenship behavior. *Group and Organization Management, 29*, 219–247.

Carmeli, A., & Josman, Z. E. (2006). The relationship among emotional intelligence, task performance, and organizational citizenship behaviors. *Human Performance, 19*, 403–419.

Côté, S., & Miners, C. T. H. (2006). Emotional intelligence, cognitive intelligence, and job performance. *Administrative Science Quarterly, 51*, 1–28.

Erez, A., & Isen, A. M. (2002). The influence of positive affect on the components of expectancy motivation. *Journal of Applied Psychology, 87*, 1055–1067.

Groves, K. S., McEnrue, M. P., & Shen, W. (2008). Developing and measuring the emotional intelligence of leaders. *Journal of Management Development, 27*, 225–250.

Herzberg, F., Mausner, B., & Snyderman, B. (1959). *The motivation to work* (2nd ed.). New York, NY: Wiley.

Ilies, R., Scott, B. A., & Judge, T. A. (2006). The interactive effects of personal traits and experienced states on intraindividual patterns of citizenship behavior. *Academy of Management Journal, 49*, 561–575.

Izard, C. E. (2001). Emotional intelligence or adaptive emotions. *Emotion, 1*, 249–257.

Katz, D., & Kahn, R. L. (1966, 1978). *The social psychology of organizations*. New York, NY: Wiley.

Kerr, R., Garvin, J., & Heaton, N. (2006). Emotional intelligence and leadership effectiveness. *Leadership and Organizational Development Journal, 27*, 265–279.

Mayer, J. D., Caruso, D. R., & Salovey, P. (1999). Emotional intelligence meets traditional standards for an intelligence. *Intelligence, 27*, 267–298.

Mayer, J. D., Caruso, D. R., & Salovey, P. (2000). Selecting a measure of emotional intelligence: The case for ability scales. In R. Bar-On & J. D. A. Parker (Eds.), *The handbook of emotional intelligence* (pp. 320–342). New York, NY: Jossey-Bass.

Mayer, J. D., Caruso, D. R., Salovey, P., & Sitarenios. (2001). Emotional intelligence as a standard intelligence. *Emotion, 1*, 232–242.

Mayer, J. D., & Salovey, P. (1997). What is emotional intelligence? In P. Salovey & D. Sluyter (Eds.), *Emotional development and emotional intelligence: Implications for educators* (pp. 3–31). New York, NY: Basic Books.

Mayer, J. D., Salovey, P., & Caruso, D. R. (2004). Emotional intelligence: Theory, findings, and implications. *Psychological Inquiry, 15*, 197–215.

Mayer, J. D., Salovey, P., & Caruso, D. R. (2008). Emotional intelligence: New ability or eclectic traits? *American Psychologist, 63*, 503–517.

Organ, D. W. (1988). *Organizational citizenship behavior: The good soldier syndrome*. Lexington, MA: Lexington Books.

Organ, D. W., Podsakoff, P. M., & MacKenzie, S. B. (2006). *Organizational citizenship behavior: Its nature, antecedents, and consequences*. Thousand Oaks, CA: Sage Publications.

Podsakoff, P. M., Ahearne, M., & MacKenzie, S. B. (1997). Organizational citizenship behavior and the quantity and quality of work group performance. *Journal of Applied Psychology, 83*, 262–270.

Rosete, D., & Ciarrochi, J. (2005). Emotional intelligence and its relationship to workplace performance of leadership effectiveness. *Leadership & Organizational Development Journal, 26*, 388–399.

Salovey, P., & Grewal, D. (2005). The science of emotional intelligence. *Current Directions in Psychological Science, 14*, 281–285.

Salovey, P., & Mayer, J. D. (1990). Emotional intelligence. *Imagination, Cognition, and Personality, 9*, 185–211.

Schnake, M. (1991). Organizational citizenship: A review, proposed model, and research agenda. *Human Relations, 44*, 735–759.

Schutte, N. S., Malouff, J. M., Bobik, C., Cotson, T. D., Greeson, C., Jedlicka, C., ... Wendorf, G. (2001). Emotional intelligence and interpersonal relations. *The Journal of Social Psychology, 141*, 523–536.

Smith, C. A., Organ, D. W., & Near, J. P. (1983). Organizational citizenship behavior: Its nature and antecedents. *Journal of Applied Psychology, 68*, 655–663.

Turnipseed, D. L. (2000). Phase analysis of burnout and other psychological phenomena. *Psychological Reports,* 1530–1542.

Turnipseed, D. L. (2002). Are good soldiers good? Exploring the link between organizational citizenship behavior and personal ethics. *Journal of Business Research, 55*, 1–15.

Turnipseed, D. L., & Rassuli, A. (2005). Performance perceptions of organisational citizenship behaviours at work: A bi-level study among managers and employees. *British Journal of Management, 16*, 231–244.

Turnipseed, D. L. & VandeWaa, E. D. (2011). The relationship between emotional intelligence and organizational citizenship behavior. *Psychological Reports* (in review).

Williams, L., & Anderson, S. (1991). Job satisfaction and organizational commitment as predictors of organizational citizenship and in-role behaviors. *Journal of Management, 17*, 601–617.

Witt, A. (1991). Exchange ideology as a moderator of job attitudes – Organizational citizenship behaviors relationships. *Journal of Applied Social Psychology, 21*, 1490–1501.

CHAPTER 2

TEACHERS' ORGANIZATIONAL CITIZENSHIP BEHAVIOR: AN EMPIRICAL EXAMINATION OF THE SUBJECTIVE AND DYNAMIC NATURE OF THE BOUNDARY BETWEEN IN-ROLE AND EXTRA-ROLE BEHAVIOR ☆

Elena Belogolovsky and Anit Somech

ABSTRACT

The purpose of this research was to explore common conceptions about the underlying nature of teachers' organizational citizenship behaviors (OCBs). Two studies were conducted to examine the dynamic and subjective nature of the boundary between teachers' in-role and extra-role

☆Some parts of this chapter are based on Belogolovsky, E., & Somech, A. (2010). Teachers' organizational citizenship behavior: Examining the boundary between in-role behavior and extra-role behavior from the perspective of teachers, principals, and parents. *Teaching and Teacher Education, 26*, 914–923.

Discretionary Behavior and Performance in Educational Organizations: The Missing Link in Educational Leadership and Management
Advances in Educational Administration, Volume 13, 31–59
Copyright © 2012 by Emerald Group Publishing Limited
ISSN: 1479-3660/doi:10.1108/S1479-3660(2012)0000013007

behavior. Study 1, based on a sample of 205 teachers from 30 elementary schools in Israel, examined this boundary between teachers' in-role and extra-role behaviors through teachers' career stages. Study 2, based on a survey of 29 principals, 245 teachers, and 345 parents from 30 elementary schools in Israel, investigated how different stakeholders in schools (principals, teachers, parents) conceptualized teachers' in-role–extra-role boundary. Results from these two studies attest to its dynamic and subjective nature. Implications for research and practice are discussed.

THEORETICAL BACKGROUND

Organizational citizenship behaviors (OCBs) are those behaviors that go beyond specified role requirements and are directed toward the organization as a unit, the team, and the individual, to promote organizational goals (Somech & Drach-Zahavy, 2000). This definition of teachers' OCBs stresses three main features of extra-role behavior (ERB). First, the behavior must be voluntary, that is, neither role-prescribed nor part of formal job duties. Second, the focus is on behaviors that do not simply happen in an organization but are directed toward or seen as benefiting the organization (Van Dyne, Cummings, & Parks, 1995). Third, by this definition, OCBs are multidimensional by nature. Although most scholars agree on the multidimensionality of this construct, a review of the literature reveals a lack of consensus about its dimensionality. This study adopted the three-dimension construct of Somech and Drach-Zahavy (2000), which was developed specifically for the context of school. The three dimensions are (a) OCB toward the student, pertaining to behaviors directly and intentionally aimed at improving the quality of teaching (e.g., acquiring expertise in new subjects that contribute to teaching); (b) OCB toward the team, that is, behaviors intentionally directed at helping a specific teacher (e.g., helping other teachers who have heavy workloads); and (c) OCB toward the organization as a whole, that is, a more impersonal form of behaviors that are directed to the benefit of the whole organization (e.g., making innovative suggestions to improve the school).

OCBs are essential because schools cannot anticipate the entire array of behaviors needed for achieving goals through formally stated in-role job descriptions (George & Brief, 1992). Moreover, today, as educational systems move into an era of reorganization and are required to work in a competitive and complex environment (Miller, 2002), the success of schools fundamentally depends on teachers who are committed to school goals and values

(Oplatka, 2006; Somech & Ron, 2007) and are more willing to go above and beyond the call of duty to contribute to successful change, that is, to engage in such OCBs. Yet, despite evidence of the contribution of teachers' OCB to school effectiveness, critics have questioned the extent to which OCBs, or ERBs, may be regarded as discretionary, arguing that the distinction between the required behavior, that is, in-role behavior (IRB), and behavior that exceeds one's job requirements, that is, OCB, is ambiguous (Turnipseed & Wilson, 2009), and may differ among people (Coyle-Shapiro, Kessler, & Purcell, 2004; Morrison, 1994), contexts, and over time (Van Dyne et al., 1995). However, although in the school context teachers' OCBs have been examined from principals' and teachers' perspectives (e.g., Somech & Ron, 2007; Vigoda-Gadot, 2007), previous research on teachers' OCBs has neglected the potential dynamic and subjective nature of teachers' OCBs construct. That is, no systematic work has examined whether different role-holders in schools perceive the boundary between IRBs and ERBs differently. In addition, no previous study examined whether teacher's career stages have an impact on this boundary. Finally, to the best of our knowledge, no study has incorporated the client's perspective (parents) in obtaining a more comprehensive picture of the in-role–extra-role boundary.

PURPOSE OF THE RESEARCH

To address the above research gaps, the current research aimed to explore common conceptions about the underlying nature of teachers' OCBs. More specifically, our aim was twofold: first, to clarify the possibly dynamic nature of the teachers' OCBs construct, in our first study we examined the boundary between teachers' IRBs and ERBs through their career stages. Second, to clarify the possible subjectivity of the teachers' OCBs construct, in our second study we examined how different stakeholders in schools (principals, teachers, and parents) conceptualized teachers' OCBs boundary, that is, whether they defined particular behaviors commonly assumed to be teachers' OCBs as their IRBs or ERBs.

CONCEPTUAL FRAMEWORK

By Organ's (1988) definition, that OCBs consist of positive types of behavior that are not part of the formal job description, OCBs should be limited to ERBs and be distinguished from IRBs. This distinction is meant to draw a line between the types of "behaviors which are required or expected as part of performing the duties and responsibilities of the assigned role" (IRB) (Van Dyne et al., 1995, p. 222) and the types of behavior that go beyond the formal contract (ERB).

Yet, as Van Dyne et al. (1995) argued, defining behavior as in-role or extra-role is theoretically important, but empirically, it is difficult to distinguish because of the dynamic and subjective nature of OCBs. According to these researchers, there are three main factors that impede the differentiation of IRBs and ERBs. First, the features deemed to make a certain behavior in-role or extra-role might be a function of the expectation of the observer who does the labeling. This is a typical example of role conflict (Katz & Kahn, 1978) that might develop because two observers have different standards and expectations. The second factor concerns the characteristics of the employees being observed: one observer may have different standards and expectations for different employees, based on their ability, motivation, etc. Third, perceptions can change over time. In sum, OCBs are difficult to follow and measure empirically because they are not stable, hard to quantify, and defined variously by different people (Van Dyne, Grahm, & Dienesh, 1994). Accordingly, we posit that teachers' work roles are socially constructed with a subjective and dynamic boundary between in-role and extra-role work behavior (Morrison, 1994) and therefore subject to multiple interpretations by teachers at different career stages and by different stakeholders in schools.

RESEARCH QUESTIONS

1. How do teachers at different career stages conceptualize their OCB boundary: do they define various behaviors commonly assumed to be teachers' OCBs as in-role or extra-role? (Study 1)
2. How do different stakeholders in schools (principals, teachers, parents) conceptualize teachers' OCBs boundary: do they define various behaviors commonly assumed to be teachers' OCBs as in-role or extra-role? (Study 2)

STUDY 1: THE DYNAMIC NATURE OF TEACHERS' IRB–ERB BOUNDARY

Conceptual Framework

Van Dyne et al. (1995) argue that there is no common perception of OCBs among the same employees over time. Moreover, in accordance with an approach according to which role perception is not static, but rather tends to change over time (Neale & Griffin, 2006), we posit that the teacher's perceptions about the boundary between their IRBs and ERBs are likewise dynamic and vary through career stages.

Morrison (1994) was the first to show that longer tenure is associated with more OCBs (specifically, the "keeping-up" dimension of OCB) being defined as ERBs. However, because age and tenure as measures of career stages have the weaknesses of psychometric properties (i.e., generalizability, validity, and reliability; for review see Cooke, 1994), we employ a more appropriate measure of the dynamic nature of the IRB–ERB boundary, that is, career-stage measurement based on the assessment of career concerns related to career stages through self-reporting.

The Career Cycle Model developed by Fessler and Christensen (1992), which serves as the theoretical framework for this study, based on teachers' self-reported characteristics, posits that teachers "ebb and flow" in their progression through eight career-long stages as described below. The *pre-service stage*, which begins this process, is the period of initial teacher preparation at a college or university. The *induction stage* is defined as the first few years of employment, when the teacher is socialized into the system. During the *competency building stage* of the career cycle, the teacher strives to improve his/her skills and abilities. At the *enthusiastic and growing stage*, teachers have reached a high level of competence in their job but continue to progress as professionals. Key ingredients here are enthusiasm and high levels of job satisfaction. The *career frustration stage* is characterized by frustration and disillusionment with a profession. Much of what is described as teachers' burnout in the literature occurs in this stage. The *stable and stagnant stage* is characterized by stability and contentment with selected enthusiasm. Teachers are interested in their job but do little more than is expected of them. This is the stage when a teacher is preparing to leave the profession. The *career wind-down and exit stage* is the time after a teacher has left the job (Fessler & Christensen, 1992). This study is based on sample of current teachers so it does not focus on teachers in the pre-service and career exit stages of this model.

The literature (Burden, 1990; Lynn, 2002) describes the variability that occurs through career stages in personal awareness, cognitive development, interpersonal development, and theoretical knowledge. It implies that as employees' characteristics change, their needs in professional activities, relationships, and interests will change accordingly. We argue that teacher' perceptions of the in-role–extra-role boundary vary through the career stages as well.

Although researchers have yet to examine whether and how role perceptions may vary through career stages, there are strong theoretical grounds to posit that teachers will define more OCBs as IRBs as they progress through the first three stages (induction, competency building, and enthusiastic and growing), and they will define more OCBs as ERBs in the last three stages (career frustration, stable and stagnant, and career wind-down). Specifically, considerable uncertainty and a lack of understanding of structures and processes in school are likely for beginning teachers at the induction stage. Many of them may interpret their experiences as "random" occurrences. In a new, relatively unfamiliar environment, they are likely to have a diminished sense of personal control (McCormick & Barnett, 2008). Also, they are unlikely to define behaviors that go beyond the established task requirements as in-role because they are focused on fitting in and gathering occupational self-confidence. Nor are these teachers likely to have time and energy to invest in OCBs even if they perceive that to do so would be instrumental in achieving their career goals (Sutton, 2005). Hence, they are likely to define these behaviors as extra-role rather than in-role.

In the mid-career stages (enthusiastic and growing), as teachers reach a high level of competence, their uncertainty lessens and they may start to broaden their role responsibilities for several reasons. First, in these stages, teachers' feelings of obligation may intensify as the level of trust and commitment between themselves and their principals increases (Blau, 1964). Second, they may define more activities as in-role as they try to achieve more variety in their work. Third, these teachers become more knowledgeable and adept at their jobs, which may affect how they cognitively define them (Morrison, 1994). Fourth, individuals who are the most skilled at the technical aspects of work are the most likely to broaden their job because they have a better understanding of the specific tasks associated with it (Morgeson, Delaney-Klinger, & Hemingway, 2005).

Although teachers have higher capabilities in the last career stages (career frustration, stable and stagnant, and career wind-down), we speculate that teachers at these stages may define more OCBs as ERBs because they have reached high levels of stability and disillusionment and their enthusiasm has dissipated. These stages are characterized by frustration with the profession, burnout, and waning of job satisfaction (Fessler & Christensen, 1992). Teachers at these stages might engage in loss-based selection (Freund, Li, & Baltes, 1999) by defining more OCBs as ERBs and choosing to withhold behaviors that are discretionary, such as OCBs, since this would not carry direct consequences for themselves.

On the basis of the arguments above, we suggest that perceived in-role–extra-role boundary differs through teacher's career stages. Teachers at the competency building and enthusiastic and growing stages define more OCBs as IRBs than do teachers in the induction, career frustration, stable and stagnant and career wind-down stages.

Method

Sample and Procedure
Participants were 205 teachers from 30 elementary schools in Israel. 89.8% were women; their average age was 41.55 years (SD = 9). Average number of years of teaching in the current school was 10.7 (SD = 7.5), and the average number of years as teachers was 16.7 (SD = 9.7). In educational background, 60.8% (N = 149) of the respondents held a Bachelor's degree, 15.1% (N = 37) a Master's degree and 21.3% (N = 50) had the equivalent of a junior college diploma with teaching credentials; 3.6% (N = 9) did not answer this question.

Measures
Organizational Citizenship Behavior. Teachers' OCB was assessed by the 24-item questionnaire developed and validated specifically in the context of schools by Somech and Drach-Zahavy (2000).

Teachers' Career Stage. Teachers were asked to fill out the questionnaire developed by Burke, Christensen, Fessler, Mcdonell, and Price (1987) for self-identifying their stage in their professional careers. The teachers were asked to read the descriptions of 6 career stages and mark the stage that best described them.

Level of Analysis
To decide the level of analysis, namely individual (N = 205) or school (N = 30), we ran two tests: inter-rater reliability (r_{wg}) and intra-class correlation (ICC). The mean r_{wg} values were higher than the generally acceptable level of good agreement of .70 (George, 1990). Thus, all scales demonstrated high agreement among organization respondents. Next we performed the ICC test using two measures: ICC(1), that is, an estimate of the reliability of an individual respondent's rating and ICC(2), that is, an estimate of the reliability of mean differences across schools (Bliese & Halverson, 1996). Our results demonstrated that all values were below the median or recommended ICC values reported in

the literature (Liao & Chuang, 2004). Consequently, we concluded that the variables did not show an appropriate level of agreement among respondents in different schools, so treating the data on the individual level of analysis was justified. Therefore, one-way multivariate analysis of variance (MANOVA) was used to test the study question.

Results

Descriptive Statistics
The means and frequencies are presented in Tables 1 and 2.

Tests of the First Research Question
As mentioned above, given that the within-group component was greater than the corresponding between-group component for each OCB dimension, one-way MANOVA was used to test the first research question, that is, how teachers at different career stages conceptualize the boundary between teachers' IRBs and ERBs. The results of MANOVA (see Table 3) indicate significant differences between career stages (Wilks' Λ T $= .88$; $F(20,624.5) = 1.27$, $p > .05$, partial $\eta^2 = .03$). This result suggests that the dependent variables assess independent constructs, so an investigation of the univariate effects was warranted.

Table 1. Teachers' Definitions of Their OCBs as In-Role versus Extra-Role Behaviors: Means and Standard Deviations by Career Stages.

Dependent Variable Career Stage		OCB	OCB toward the School	OCB toward the Team	OCB toward the Student
Induction ($N = 11$)	M	3.25	3.09	3.83	2.7
	(SD)	(.54)	(.64)	(.59)	(.61)
Competency building	M	3.65	3.79	4.11	3.2
($N = 115$)	(SD)	(.47)	(.67)	(.49)	(.57)
Enthusiastic and	M	3.7	3.81	4.21	3.02
growing ($N = 47$)	(SD)	(.45)	(.66)	(.53)	(.58)
Career frustration	M	3.45	3.30	4.03	2.92
($N = 6$)	(SD)	(.56)	(.64)	(.43)	(.92)
Stable and stagnant	M	3.48	3.56	4.01	2.8
($N = 17$)	(SD)	(.45)	(.69)	(.50)	(.55)
Career wind-down	M	3.49	3.51	4.11	2.79
($N = 9$)	(SD)	(.29)	(.37)	(.42)	(.20)

Note: In all cases higher cores reflect a greater perception of OCBs as IRBs.

Table 2. Teachers' Definitions of Their OCBs as In-Role versus Extra-Role Behaviors: Frequencies (%) by Career Stages.

Dependent Variable	OCB		OCB toward the School		OCB toward the Team		OCB toward the Student	
Career Stage	IRB	ERB	IRB	ERB	IRB	ERB	IRB	ERB
1. Induction ($N=11$)	63.6	36.4	63.6	36.4	81.8	18.2	27.3	72.7
2. Competency building ($N=115$)	92.2	7.8	90.4	9.6	95.7	4.3	44.3	55.7
3. Enthusiastic and growing ($N=47$)	93.6	6.4	91.5	8.5	95.7	4.3	44.7	55.3
4. Career frustration ($N=6$)	83.3	16.7	66.7	33.3	100		48	52
5. Stable and stagnant ($N=17$)	94.1	5.9	64.7	35.3	94.1	5.9	29.4	70.6
6. Career wind-down ($N=9$)	100		100		100			100

Table 3. Results of MANOVA, Testing Teachers' Definitions of their OCBs as In-Role versus Extra-Role Behaviors through Career Stages.

	DV	SS	df	MS	Partial η^2	F
	1. OCB	2.57	5	.51	.05	2.36*
	1a. OCB toward the school	7.05	5	1.41	.07	3.21**
	1b. OCB toward the team	1.49	5	.29	.03	1.16
	1c. OCB toward the student	1.81	5	.36	.03	1.09
Error	1. OCB	43.33	199	.22		
	1a. OCB toward the school	87.36	199	.44		
	1b. OCB toward the team	50.98	199	.26		
	1c. OCB toward the student	66.05	199	.33		
Total	1. OCB	2730.97	205			
	1a. OCB toward the school	2922.74	205			
	1b. OCB toward the team	3516.02	205			
	1c. OCB toward the student	1883.69				

Notes: Wilks' Λ T $= .88$; $F(20,651) = 1.32$, $p > .05$, partial $\eta^2 = .03$.
*$p < .05$; **$p < .01$.

Four separate univariate ANOVA analyses were conducted to examine each of the six career stages separately. Significant differences emerged among teachers at different stages concerning their OCBs in general ($F(5,199) = 2.36$, $p < .05$, partial $\eta^2 = .05$) and toward the school ($F(5,199) = 3.21$ $p < .01$, partial

$\eta^2 = .07$). However, as there were six career stages categories, Tukey's Honestly Significant Difference test (HSD) was applied as a post-hoc test to determine the precise nature of the differentiation. Pair-wise comparisons indicate that teachers at the competency building stage ($M = 3.65$, SD $= .47$) were significantly ($p < .01$) more likely to define their *OCBs in general* as IRBs than teachers at the induction stage ($M = 3.25$, SD $= .54$). In addition, teachers at the enthusiastic and growing stage ($M = 3.7$, SD $= .45$) were significantly ($p < .01$) more likely to define their OCBs in general as IRBs than teachers at the Induction stage ($M = 3.25$, SD $= .54$).

Moreover, the Tukey's HSD test showed the differences between teachers at the same career stages in their definitions of their *OCBs toward the school*. Specifically, teachers at the competency building stage ($M = 3.79$, SD $= .67$) were significantly ($p < .01$) more likely to define their OCBs toward the school as IRBs than were teachers at the induction stage ($M = 3.09$, SD $= .64$). Teachers at the enthusiastic and growing stage ($M = 3.81$, SD $= .66$) were significantly ($p < .01$) more likely to define their OCBs toward the school as IRBs than were teachers at the induction stage ($M = 3.09$, SD $= .64$).

In addition, the post-hoc analysis revealed that teachers at the enthusiastic and growing stage ($M = 4.21$, SD $= .53$) were significantly ($p < .01$) more likely to define their *OCBs toward the team* as IRBs than were teachers at the Induction stage ($M = 3.83$, SD $= .59$).

Finally, the groups of teachers at the career frustration, stable and stagnant, and career wind-down stages were quite small ($n = 6$, $n = 17$ and $n = 9$ respectively), which probably accounts for the non-significant differences between these and all the other groups.

Discussion

The findings of this study confirmed the claim in career literature that career stage can affect individual's job perceptions. Our speculations were partially supported: Teachers at the competency building career stage defined more *teachers' OCBs in general and toward the school* as IRBs than did teachers at the induction stage. Teachers at the enthusiasm and growing stage defined more *teachers' OCBs in general, toward the school, and toward the team* as IRBs than did teachers at the Induction stage. The caution needed in interpreting results from a small number of participants at the induction stage notwithstanding, many of the differences in perceived teachers' OCBs boundary were between teachers at that stage and more experienced ones at the competency building and enthusiasm and growing stages. This is not surprising given the considerable literature on differences between novice and veteran teachers (e.g., Berliner, 1987).

The results are also aligned with the career literature on the concerns and problems of early career teachers (Fessler & Christensen, 1992; Hall, 1986; Super, 1992), suggesting that those at the induction stage are likely to define more OCBs as ERBs probably as a result of insufficient knowledge of the school and professional activities, and lack of professional confidence. The transition from preparing to teach to actual teaching in the school is a major step for many beginning teachers, accompanied by uncertainty and self-doubt about the career choice (Hebert & Worthy, 2001). Highly motivated, idealist and enthusiastic in their entry to the profession, novice teachers have to cope with "reality shock" (Corcoran, 1981). Given little time to reflect, they feel overwhelmed and unsure of how to solve their problems, thus often narrowing their job responsibilities. They have limited knowledge of the school environment and job responsibilities, and they do not recognize the complexity of their job. Many teachers at the Induction stage express feelings of inadequacy in every area (Burden, 1982) and consequently are concerned about their success. They prefer to narrow their responsibilities and define more OCBs as ERBs in order not to feel failure. Teachers at this stage are not likely to define OCBs as in-role because they are focused on fitting in and building occupational self-confidence. Nor are they likely to have the time and energy to invest in OCBs even if they perceive that it will be instrumental to achieving their career goals (Sutton, 2005). They prefer not to define these behaviors as a part of their job responsibilities. This finding may also be attributed to the low levels of job involvement and career commitment in this early career stage (DeConinck, 1993), resulting in narrow perceptions of job responsibilities.

Moreover, the findings indicate that as teachers reach the competency building and the enthusiastic and growing stages they define more OCBs as IRBs. There are several possible explanations for this result. First, teachers at these stages become more knowledgeable about the job responsibilities and they are more confident. They have mastered some initial skills and are confident about trying new methods. They know more about their job and are starting to perceive its complexities. At these stages teachers feel that they can handle any situation that may come along. Experience with a particular task has been found to affect how an individual cognitively represents that task (Chi, Glaser, & Farr, 1988), so unlike novices these teachers perceive more task activities as the required part of their job. Individuals who are the most skilled at the technical aspects of work are the most likely to broaden their job because they have a better understanding of its specific associated tasks (Morgeson et al., 2005). This is due to at least two reasons: first, to broaden job responsibilities, teachers must be able to perform the tasks that constitute the broader role. If they cannot, they are unlikely to attempt to integrate them into their job responsibility. The influence of abilities on broad job responsibilities has not been directly examined, yet teachers' self-efficacy has proven an important factor for broadening job responsibilities. Morrison and Phelps (1999) found that self-efficacy was positively related to taking charge at work (an important OCB), and Parker (1998) posited that effective performance of broader roles "requires employees who are sufficiently confident in their abilities" (p. 835). The relationship between self-efficacy and broad job responsibility is relevant because ability is an essential component of self-efficacy (Gist & Mitchell, 1992). Second, principals are likely to have greater job expectations from teachers with higher levels of ability (Graen & Scandura, 1987). If a principal believes teachers are capable, he/she will afford them greater discretion to expand their roles, and indicate that this is expected of them. Absent the requisite ability, principals are likely to minimize their expectations of the range of tasks the teacher is able to perform.

Second, as teachers start to see the complexities of the job at these stages they improve their abilities and subsequently their job performance to meet the job demands better (Burden, 1982). At these stages they are often willing to learn more and to continually develop their skills (Phillips, Blustein, Jobin-Davis, & Finkelberg White, 2002) to become better teachers (Burden, 1982). They expect that a wider repertoire of skills and a high degree of proficiency at them will help advance their careers more rapidly (McEnrue, 1989). Therefore, they broaden their job responsibilities and define a wide variety of OCBs as IRBs. Third, these teachers may broaden their job responsibilities as they try to achieve more variety in their work (Morrison, 1994). Fourth, with increased knowledge and experience, teachers' feelings of obligation deepen and the level of trust and commitment to their principals rises (Blau, 1964); they are then likely to define more OCBs as IRBs (Morrison, 1994).

STUDY 2: THE SUBJECTIVE NATURE OF TEACHERS' IRB–ERB BOUNDARY

Conceptual Framework

The purpose of this study was to explore the subjective nature of teachers' in-role–extra-role boundary by examining how different stakeholders in schools (principals, teachers, parents) define given teachers' OCBs as IRBs or ERBs. Although to the best of our knowledge, this issue has not been examined in the school context, a few studies have probed the differences between employees' job responsibilities rating sources in industrial organizations (Allen, Bernard, Rush, & Russell, 2000; Becker & Vance, 1993; Hsiung & Tsai, 2009; Van Dyne & LePine, 1998). This research (Chiaburu, 2007; Morrison, 1994; Putka & Vancouver, 1999; Vey & Campbell, 2004) suggested that employees' perceptions of their job requirements may differ substantially from their supervisors' perceptions (e.g., Cardona & Espejo, 2002; Lam, Hui, & Law, 1999; Morrison, 1994). Morrison (1994) and Lam et al. (1999) found that supervisors had a broader definition than employees of IRBs. Not surprisingly, these findings matched prior propositions indicating that work roles are simply artificially and continuously enlarged by supervisors, in an attempt to make employees over-fulfill their work obligations (e.g., Vigoda-Gadot, 2007).

A number of different explanations have emerged to account for why the ratings of employees' OCBs obtained from different sources (e.g., subordinates, supervisors) generally do not converge. For example, the modest correspondence among ratings from different organization stakeholders may be due to the different perceptions of what constitutes effective performance in a particular job (Campbell & Lee, 1988). In addition, disagreements in their ratings may be attributed to the fact that different organization stakeholders differ in their opportunity to observe any given individuals' work behavior (Murphy & Cleveland, 1995) and they are exposed to only moderately overlapping sets of employees' behavior (Lance, Teachout, & Donnelly, 1992). Finally, Campbell and Lee (1988), as well as Cardy and Dobbins (1994), described a number of processes that may lead to disagreement in the ratings provided by different types of raters. These processes include well-established attributional tendencies, such as the self-serving attributional bias and the actor–observer effect, as well as motivational and informational differences between rating sources such as self-raters' needs for self-enhancement (Farh & Dobbins, 1989b) and differences in social comparison information available to self-raters and their supervisors (Farh & Dobbins, 1989a).

Drawing on these attributional tendencies, Becker and Vance (1993) compared OCB ratings among self, supervisor, and peers. They provided evidence that job incumbents, supervisors, and peers perceived OCB in different ways. Their results formed a pattern similar to those observed by Harris and Schaubroeck (1988), Allen et al. (2000) and Van Dyne and LePine (1998), demonstrating that ratings made by others (subordinates and superiors) were more similar than ratings made by self and others. Together, these studies highlight the importance of capturing the extent to which different stakeholders in school view teachers' OCB as IRBs or ERBs. From the findings of these studies, which confirm the attribution theory (Gibson & Schroeder, 2003; Kelley, 1967), it seems likely that teachers' (actors) perception of their OCBs will differ from those of principals and parents (others).

However, an alternative perspective might suggest that parents' perceptions of teachers' OCBs will differ from those of teachers and principals. Principals' and teachers' perceptions of teachers' IRB-ERB boundary will be similar as a result of a common professional and educational background (Oplatka, 2006). In other words, principals and teachers as role-holders who share the same profession might adopt similar job behaviors and attitudes as a result of job norms that characterize their profession (Bidwell, 1965). Moreover, according to Schneider's (1987) attraction-selection-attrition (ASA) model, people with similar characteristics tend to be attracted to one another and stay in the same work environment. Principals and teachers working together in schools might find themselves working with colleagues much like themselves, so there might be more similarity in attitudes, values, and personalities between organization members, principals and teachers than between them and their clients – the parents (Somech, 1994). Therefore, given the conflicting theorizing, it was not possible to make any a priori hypotheses regarding the differences among principals, teachers and parents about teachers' OCBs boundary.

Method

Sample and Procedure

Participants were 29 principals, 245 teachers, and 345 parents from 30 elementary schools in Israel. Of the principals, 65.5% ($N = 19$) were female, average age was 48.8 years (SD = 7.4); average tenure in managing a specific school was 7 years (SD = 6), and average tenure in teaching was 24 years (SD = 8.8). Regarding the teachers, 89.8% were women; the teachers' average age was 41.55 years (SD = 9). Average number of years of teaching in the current school was 10.7 (SD = 7.5), and the average number of years as teachers was 16.7 (SD = 9.7). These demographic characteristics are similar to those found in comparable studies on teachers and principals in Israel (Bogler & Somech, 2004; Somech, 2002).

Of the parents, 75.9% ($N = 262$) were women, with average age 39.8 years (SD = 5). Regarding educational background, 35.6% ($N = 123$) completed high school or less, 30.1% ($N = 104$) held a Bachelor's degree, 16.6% ($N = 57$) held a Master's degree, 2.8% ($N = 10$) held a PhD degree or were studying for it, and the rest did not answer this question. 22.3% ($N = 77$) of the respondents were on parents' committees.

Measures
Organizational Citizenship Behavior. Same as in Study 1 with critical exception: because Somech and Drach-Zahavy (2000) developed their OCB questionnaire from interviews with teachers only, we conducted a pretest to examine what items in it were relevant to principals and parents as well. In a semi-structured interview, 3 principals (females), 5 teachers (females), and 8 parents (4 males and 4 females) were asked to list all kinds of behaviors that teachers might perform to benefit the student, the team, or the organization as a unit. The focus was on behaviors exceeding specific role expectations and requirements. In their interviews, all eight parents said that questions about behaviors that teachers may perform to benefit the team were irrelevant to them, so we decided to omit these items from the questionnaire that was distributed to parents.

Level of Analysis
To decide the level of analysis, namely individual ($N = 619$) or school ($N = 30$), we ran two tests: inter-rater reliability (r_{wg}) and ICC. Although the results showed high level of agreement among organization respondents, given that individuals were nested in 30 different schools, we applied Mixed Linear Models procedure, allowing us to analyze the data at the individual level, while taking into account the random effect of the school level.

Results

Descriptive Statistics
Means, standard deviations, reliability coefficients and intercorrelations (Pearson) of the variables calculated for principals, teachers and parents at the individual level ($N = 619$) and at the organizational level ($N = 30$) are displayed in Table 4. On the basis of these results, it appears that all the correlations at the individual level among teachers' OCB in general and its three dimensions (toward the school, the team and the student) from the principals', teachers' and parents' perspective were positive and significant.

Table 4. Means, Standard Deviations, Reliability Coefficients, and Intercorrelations (Pearson) of the Variables Calculated for Principals, Teachers and Parents at the Individual Level ($N = 619$) and at the Organizational Level ($N = 30$).

Variable	Principals					Teachers					Parents				
	M (SD)	1	2	3	4	M (SD)	1	2	3	4	M (SD)	1	2	3	4
1 OCB	3.77 (.36)	1.00	.80***	.81***	.82***	3.65 (.47)	1.00	.84***	.83***	.77***	3.41 (.66)	1.00	.82***	.53***	.87***
2 OCB toward the school	4.05 (.47)	.86	1.00	.54**	.51**	3.84 (.66)	.89	1.00	.61***	.49***	3.59 (.80)	.78	1.00	.39***	.45***
3 OCB toward the team	4.27 (.39)	.78	.53	1.00	.41*	4.10 (.53)	.76	.49	1.00	.37***	—	—	—	—	—
4 OCB toward the student	3.01 (.47)	.82	.59	.41	1.00	3.0 (.57)	.74	.63	.23	1.00	3.18 (.77)	.89	.42	.56	1.00

Notes: Individual-level correlations are above the diagonal. Organizational-level correlations are below the diagonal. Means and standard deviations are reported for the individual level. N(principals) = 29; N(teachers) = 245; N(parents) = 345.
*$p < .05$; **$p < .01$; ***$p < .001$.

Tests of the Second Research Question
Mixed Models Analyses were used to examine the second research question, that is, how different stakeholders in schools (principals, teachers, parents) conceptualize teachers' OCBs in general and its three dimensions as IRBs vs. ERBs. In line with Becker's (2005) recommendation for treating control variables, we ran the mixed model analyses with and without the control variables (i.e., school socio-economic level, school size and school type). This procedure was conducted to rule out the control variables as a potential explanation for the findings. Because the results did not differ, we report only the results *without* the control variables.

The mixed models analyses results for testing the differences among teachers, principals and parents in their definition of teachers' OCB in general and its three dimensions as IRB vs. ERB are reported in Table 5. First, the results in the second column labeled "OCB" of Table 5 show that principals, teachers and parents differed significantly in their definition of *teachers' OCB in general* (F (2, 586) = 14.16, $p < .001$). Specifically, contrast analysis revealed that teachers defined their OCBs in general as IRBs significantly more ($M = 3.65$; $SD = .47$) than parents did ($M = 3.41$; $SD = .66$), t (586) = 4.70, $p < .001$. Also, principals defined teachers' OCBs in general as IRBs significantly more ($M = 3.77$; $SD = .36$) than parents did ($M = 3.41$; $SD = .66$), t (586) = 3.35, $p < .001$. However, we did not find a significant difference between principals and teachers in their definition of teachers' OCBs in general. Therefore, our findings suggest less difference between organizational members (i.e., principals and teachers) than between them and organizational clients (i.e., parents) in how broadly they define teachers' role responsibilities, and consequently in whether they define teachers' OCBs as IRB or ERBs.

Second, the results in the third column labeled "OCB toward the school" of Table 5 show that principals, teachers and parents differed significantly in their definition of *teachers' OCBs toward the school* (F (2, 586) = 9.67, $p < .001$). Contrast analysis showed that teachers defined teachers' OCBs toward the school as IRBs significantly more ($M = 3.84$; $SD = .66$) than parents did ($M = 3.59$; $SD = .80$), t (586) = 3.53, $p < .001$. Also, principals defined teachers' OCBs toward the school as IRBs significantly more ($M = 4.05$; $SD = .47$) than parents did ($M = 3.59$; $SD = .80$), t (586) = 3.24, $p < .001$. We found no significant differences between principals and teachers in their definition of teachers' OCBs toward the school.

Third, the results in the fourth column labeled "OCB toward the team" of Table 5 demonstrate that principals and teachers evinced no significant difference in their perception of *teachers' OCBs toward the team*, suggesting

Table 5. Results of Mixed Models Analyses, Testing Principals', Teachers' and Parents' Definitions of Teachers' OCBs as In-Role versus Extra-Role Behaviors.

Dependent Variables	OCB				OCB toward the School				OCB toward the Team				OCB toward the Student			
Independent Variables	Est.	SE	t	F	Est.	SE	t	F	Est.	SE	t	F	Est.	SE	t	F
Source (principals = 1; teachers = 2; parents = 3)				14.16***				9.67***								5.82**
Differences between teachers and parents	.22	.05	4.70***		.21	.06	3.53***						−.19	.06	−3.34***	
Differences between principals and parents	.36	.11	3.35***		.44	.13	3.24***						−.17	.13	−1.31	
Differences between principals and teachers	.13	.11	1.26		.23	.14	1.66		.16	.10	1.64		.02	.13	.16	
Variance of school level intercept			.03				.05				.001				.03	
Variance of individual level intercept			.30				.50				.26				.43	

** $p < .01$; *** $p < .001$.

that teachers and principals have similar conceptions of teachers' job responsibilities in this regard and define the majority of teachers' OCBs toward the team as IRBs.

Fourth, as evident from the fifth column of Table 5 ("OCB toward the student"), principals, teachers and parents differed significantly in their definition of *teachers' OCBs toward the student* (F (2, 586) = 5.82, $p < .001$). Contrast analysis indicated that teachers defined teachers' OCBs toward the student as IRBs significantly less ($M = 3.0$; $SD = .57$) than parents did ($M = 3.18$; $SD = .77$), t (586) = -3.34, $p < .001$. However, we did not find significant differences between principals and teachers, or between principals and parents, in their definition of teachers' OCBs toward the student.

Discussion

The findings of this study confirmed the suggestion in the literature that the distinction between the required behavior, that is, IRB, and behavior that exceeds one's job requirements, that is, OCB, is ambiguous (Turnipseed & Wilson, 2009), and may differ among people (Coyle-Shapiro et al., 2004; Morrison, 1994). The results of the present study, in line with prior evidence from research conducted in industrial organizations (e.g., Allen et al., 2000; Cardona & Espejo, 2002), indicate that there is no clear, common understanding of the boundary between teachers' OCB and IRB across different stakeholders in school. In other words, our findings suggest that different role-holders perceive differently teachers' work roles and responsibilities. These findings point to the need to take the perceptions of other organization actors into account. Because raters on different levels might observe different aspects of teachers' OCB and also use different standards when judging it (Mount, Judge, Scullen, Sytsma, & Hezlett, 1998), each source has its bias, and it is hard to say that one rating source is more valid than another (Organ, 1990).

In addition, the findings demonstrate that teachers and principals defined the teachers' role responsibilities broadly, and consequently they defined more teachers' OCBs as IRBs than parents did. This finding is not surprising and is consistent with studies conducted in industrial organizations (e.g., Van Dyne & Ellis, 2004; Morrison, 1994). These studies showed that when managers were asked to evaluate their subordinates' performance they took OCBs into account too (e.g., MacKenzie, Podsakoff, & Paine, 1999; Van Scotter & Motowidlo, 1996). Principals apparently tend to define relatively larger teachers' job scopes because they are intent on being effective. From their perspective teachers' OCBs should be related to their own effectiveness and efficiency (Podsakoff, MacKenzie, & Hui, 1993), so it is to the principal's advantage to define more teachers' OCBs as IRB rather than ERBs (Wanxian & Weiwu, 2007). For example, a teacher who is willing to help a new teacher may reduce the time and effort that the principal must put in to guide and train this new teacher. As Vigoda-Gadot (2007) suggests, sometimes principals re-define behaviors previously perceived as extra-role as in-role, or "required," without agreement from the teachers. In doing so, they sometimes extend the definition of formal duties into the informal area of good will and put pressure on teachers to work beyond their formally required duties.

Furthermore, from the teachers' perspective, it might be suggested that by extending the definition of teachers' formal duties, principals cause teachers to define their OCBs as IRBs. In other words, teachers might tend to engage in OCBs as part of their role obligations in response to external pressure by significant others in the workplace (i.e., principals) (Vigoda-Gadot, 2007). Another possible explanation for the finding suggesting that teachers define their role responsibilities broadly relates to the essence of teachers' work in schools. The ethical and humanistic dimensions of teachers' work frequently act as a source of intrinsic motivation for individual teachers, and inspire them to remain committed to the profession (O'Connor, 2008). Moreover, because teaching is characterized as an ambiguous role with vague boundaries and an unclear input-process-outcome connection (Meyer, Scott, & Deal, 1992), teachers may prefer to include many behaviors, defined in research literature as OCBs, in their formal role definition. This process may be as a result of cognitive dissonance (Festinger, Carlsmith, & Bem, 2007) caused by their regularly performing a multitude of unrewarded ERBs because of external pressure and expectations (from principals, parents, the public, etc.). As a result, teachers so obliged feel dissonance, that is, disharmony. To assuage it, they modify their definition of these behaviors from ERBs to IRBs. However, this finding is inconsistent with findings from studies conducted in industrial organizations, which showed that supervisors have a broader definition of job in-roles than employees do (Chiaburu, 2007; Morrison, 1994; Putka & Vancouver, 1999; Vey & Campbell, 2004). It seems that school organizations create a work environment different from those in other types of organizations, thus leading to different findings.

Regarding the dimensions of teachers' OCB, several insights emerge. First, teachers and principals defined *teachers' OCBs toward the school* more broadly than parents did, hence they defined more so-called teachers' OCBs toward the school (e.g., "organize social activities for school"; "organize joint activities with parents") as IRBs. This finding is not surprising, since principals are "school-oriented" in their thinking because they are responsible for the whole school's effectiveness. They have high work performance expectations of teachers– their subordinates, which lead them to broaden teachers' in-role duties. Similarly, teachers as members of the school organization have a variety of responsibilities to the class, but also to the whole school. They define many of their so-called OCBs toward the school as the part of their job, in contrast to parents, who define these behaviors as teachers' ERBs because they don't necessarily see any direct impact of these teachers' behaviors on their children. Moreover, because parents are not exposed to all the variety of teachers' behaviors outside the class, they may not see the relevance of those behaviors to their children's achievements and well-being.

Second, a comparison of teachers' and principals' perceptions of *the teachers' OCB toward the team* only revealed that both groups defined the majority of these behaviors as teachers' in-role activities. We suggest that although in schools, as loosely coupled organizations, teachers work in isolation from their peers, they view their OCBs toward the team as routine and as part of their professional identity (DiPaola & Tschannen-Moran, 2001). From the teacher's perspective, helping his/her colleague is mutually necessary behavior that both sides are interested in (Somech & Ron, 2007). Teachers generally have high social needs, but find themselves in a profession that isolates them from their colleagues. To avoid feelings of loneliness and dissatisfaction, they tend to engage in strong collegial relations, reducing isolation from peers through joint planning and implementation of activities and defining them as a part of their job (Somech & Drach-Zahavy, 2000). We posit that principals likewise broaden teachers' in-role duties toward the team because it is to their advantage to define these so-called teachers' OCBs as IRBs since this broad definition may ensure teachers' performance of these behaviors that are necessary for school effectiveness.

Third, the parents defined more so-called *teachers' OCBs toward the student* as teachers' IRBs than teachers did. The reason, we suggest, is that parents' expectations of the school are naturally individual in character and relate greatly to the child's needs, abilities and interests. These expectations emphasize his/her centrality in all that the school and teachers do, ignoring other aspects of the teacher's role. Interestingly, most principals, teachers and parents defined many teachers' OCBs toward the student involving the social aspect of the teacher's role (e.g., "participate in private celebrations of students") as a teacher's extra-role rather than IRBs. A possible explanation for this is that in the public eye the teachers' role is primarily to promote the student's academic development. Schools, and consequently teachers and principals, are primarily evaluated according to their students' achievements.

Taken as a whole, the results indicate that teachers, principals and parents assign many teachers' OCBs (e.g., innovative and creative instruction, out-of-school activities, etc.), already discussed in the literature as part of the teachers' moral and ethical commitments (e.g., DiPaola & Hoy, 2005; Somech & Drach-Zahavy, 2000), to the prescribed side of teaching. The ideal of service is imbedded in the ideal of teaching and includes responsibility for other people's development and commitment to moral values (Day, 1999), such as helping to co-workers or enhancing the ability to deal with students' special needs. This perception of teacher's role is essential because although principals and teachers do have job descriptions covering teachers' main job responsibilities, schools cannot anticipate through formally stated job descriptions the entire array of behaviors needed for achieving goals (George & Brief, 1992). We suggest, therefore, that the teachers' role may comprise many behaviors commonly assumed to be teachers' OCBs and measured in previous research as extra-role constructs.

GENERAL DISCUSSION AND CONCLUSIONS

The present research fills the gaps in theoretical knowledge about the nature of teachers' OCBs by exploring common conceptions of their underlying nature. First, we set out to clarify the possibly dynamic nature of the teachers' OCB construct by examining the boundary between their IRBs and ERBs through their career stages. Second, to clarify the possible subjectivity of this construct, we tested how different stakeholders in schools conceptualized this boundary.

Overall, the results attest to the dynamic and subjective nature of the boundary between teachers' IRBs and ERBs. They indicate the absence of any clear-cut common understanding of the boundary between OCBs and IRBs across employees at different career stages, as well as across different stakeholders in schools. The definition of a given OCB as in-role or extra-role depends on the rating source and on the employee's assumed career stage. Role theory supports this finding, holding that work roles are likely to be socially constructed (Biddle, 1979; Graen, 1976; Ilgen & Hollenbeck, 1991), namely the boundary between in-role and extra-role work behavior is subjective (Morrison, 1994) and tends to shift over time. We suggest that the lack of a clear definition of teachers' OCB construct, which is a prerequisite for scientific research, may lead to ambiguity of the conclusions of research on this construct. We posit that a clear-cut scientific definition is the premise on which to promote the development of theory and research on teachers' OCB.

Managerial Implications

The results of our research have significance for school effectiveness by contributing to greater understanding of the nature and conceptualization of the teachers' OCB construct. Because effective school functioning is predicated on behavior that goes beyond formal job requirements (Podsakoff, Whiting, Podsakoff, & Blume, 2009), understanding when teachers choose to broaden their role is important for principals. In light of the present findings, we suggest that teachers' career stages and different stakeholders' perceptions of teachers' OCBs be taken into consideration in management practice. It may yield more effective organizational career planning programs, human resource practices including job analysis, recruitment, selection, training, development, performance appraisal, and compensation, and offer principals more accurate explanations for inter-individual changes in teachers' OCBs. For example, knowing when teachers choose to define OCBs as extra-role enables principals to influence teachers' role perceptions through socialization and training processes. Moreover, knowledge of principals', teachers' and parents' perceptions of teachers' role boundary is critical for policy makers when constructing avenues for parents' involvement in school, since the home–school relationship is based primarily on parents' expectations regarding the teacher's job responsibilities. Finally, teachers may prefer to include many behaviors defined in the literature as OCBs in their formal role definition as a result of parents' and principals' expectations. This process may be beneficial in the short run, but might impact teachers' sense of fairness in the long run. Thus, principals should clarify for their teachers the boundaries between formal IRBs and voluntary, spontaneous behaviors.

Limitations and Future Research

Several limitations of our study may offer additional research opportunities. First, given its exploratory nature its results have to be replicated. To generalize our findings we recommend that future studies replicate our methods in schools in other countries and cultural settings. Also, a substantial majority of the sample were women. A future study with a more heterogeneous sample is essential. Second, while the results of the present study provide evidence that perceptions of the teachers' OCB boundary do differ through the career stages and among different stakeholders, the reasons underlying these differences need further investigation. Researchers may wish to explore further the dynamic and subjective nature this boundary through interviews with teachers, principals and parents to gain more insight into these differences. Researchers may also wish to identify factors that predict them. Third, our findings showed that teachers' behaviors commonly defined in literature as OCBs, that is, discretionary, beyond the strict description of job requirements, and not directly rewarded (Organ, 1988; Organ, Podsakoff, & MacKenzie, 2006), are actually dynamic and subjective. We therefore propose in future research to investigate an appropriate measure of teachers' OCB, drawing a distinction between it and other constructs related to it, such as IRBs. Future research may also examine how the dynamic and subjective nature of OCB relates to school effectiveness. Fourth, although recent research suggests that self-reported data are not as limited as was previously believed, and that people often accurately perceive their social environment (Alper, Tjosvold, & Law, 2000), Study 1 has some limitations in terms of the self-report nature of the data. Fifth, another shortcoming of Study 1 is the small number of participants at their last three career stages. It would be helpful to have more of them in future research. Finally, the findings of the Study 2 revealed homogeneity across parents. Presumably, parents who agreed to spend time on completing the questionnaire are those deeply involved in their children's education. Accordingly, they have high expectations from teachers and define their role broadly.

REFERENCES

Allen, T. D., Bernard, S., Rush, M. C., & Russell, J. E. (2000). Ratings of organizational citizenship behavior: Does the source make a difference? *Human Resource Management Review, 10*(1), 97–114.

Alper, S., Tjosvold, D., & Law, K. S. (2000). Conflict management, efficacy, and performance in organizational teams. *Personnel Psychology, 53*, 625–635.

Becker, T. E. (2005). Potential problems in the statistical control of variables in organizational research: A qualitative analysis with recommendations. *Organizational Research Methods, 8*, 274–289.

Becker, T. E., & Vance, R. J. (1993). Construct validity of three types of organizational citizenship behavior: An illustration of the direct product model with refinements. *Journal of Management, 19*, 663–682.

Berliner, D. C. (1987). Ways of thinking about students and classrooms by more or less experienced teachers. In J. Calderhead (Ed.), *Exploring teachers' thinking* (pp. 60–84). London: Cassell Educational Limited.

Biddle, B. J. (1979). *Role theory: Expectations, identities and behaviors.* New York, NY: Academic Press.

Bidwell, C. E. (1965). The school as a formal organization. In J. G. March (Ed.), *Handbook of organizations.* Chicago, IL: Rand McNally.

Blau, P. M. (1964). *Exchange and power in social life.* New York, NY: Wiley.

Bliese, P. D., & Halverson, R. R. (1996). Individual and nomothetic models of job stress: An examination of work hours, cohesion and well being. *Journal of Applied Psychology, 26*(13), 1171–1189.

Bogler, R., & Somech, A. (2004). Influence of teacher empowerment on teachers' organizational commitment, professional commitment and organizational citizenship behavior in schools. *Teaching and Teacher Education, 20,* 277–289.

Burden, P. R. (1982). Implications of teacher career development: New roles for teachers, administrators and professors. *Action in Teacher Education, 4*(4), 21–25.

Burden, P. R. (1990). Teacher development. In W. R. Houston (Ed.), *Handbook of research on teacher education* (pp. 311–328). New York, NY: Macmillan.

Burke, P. J., Christensen, J. C., Fessler, R., Mcdonell, J. H., & Price, J. R. (1987). *The teacher Career cycle: Model development and research report.* Paper presented at the Annual Meeting of the American Educational Research Association, Washington.

Campbell, D. J., & Lee, C. (1988). Self-appraisal in performance evaluation: Development versus evaluation. *Academy of Management Review, 13,* 302–314.

Cardona, P., & Espejo, A. (2002). *The effect of the rating source in organizational citizenship behavior: A multitrait-multimethod analysis.* Research Paper No. 474.

Cardy, R. L., & Dobbins, G. H. (1994). *Performance appraisal: Alternative perspectives.* Cincinnati, OH: South-Western Publishing Co.

Chi, M. T., Glaser, R., & Farr, M. J. (1988). *The nature of expertise.* Hillsdale, NJ: Erlbaum.

Chiaburu, D. (2007). From interactional justice to citizenship behaviors: Role enlargement or role discretion? *Social Justice Research, 20*(2), 207–227.

Cooke, D. K. (1994). Measuring career stage. *Human Resource Management Review, 4,* 383–400.

Corcoran, E. (1981). Transition shock: The beginning teacher's paradox. *Journal of Teacher Education, 32*(3), 19–23.

Coyle-Shapiro, J., Kessler, I., & Purcell, J. (2004). Exploring organizationally directed citizenship behavior: Reciprocity or 'It's my job'? *Journal of Management Studies, 41,* 85–106.

Day, C. (1999). *Developing teachers: The challenge of lifelong learning.* London: Falmer Press.

DeConinck, J. (1993). Managing the real estate salesforce through career stages. *Journal of Professional Services Marketing, 10*(1), 35–44.

DiPaola, M. F., & Hoy, W. K. (2005). School characteristics that foster organizational citizenship behavior. *Journal of School Leadership, 15,* 308–326.

DiPaola, M. F., & Tschannen-Moran, M. (2001). Organizational citizenship behavior in school and its relationship to school climate. *Journal of School Leadership, 11,* 424–447.

Farh, J. L., & Dobbins, G. H. (1989a). Effects of comparative performance information on the accuracy of self-ratings and agreement between self and supervisor ratings. *Journal of Applied Psychology, 74,* 606–610.

Farh, J. L., & Dobbins, G. H. (1989b). Effects of self-esteem on leniency bias in self-reports of performance: A structural equation model analysis. *Personnel Psychology, 42*, 835–850.

Fessler, R., & Christensen, J. C. (1992). *The teacher career cycle: Understanding and guiding the professional development of teachers.* Boston, MA: Allyn and Bacon.

Festinger, L., Carlsmith, J. M., & Bem, D. J. (2007). Does cognitive dissonance explain why behavior can change attitudes? In J. A. Nier (Ed.), *Taking sides: Clashing views in social psychology* (2nd ed., pp. 74–91). New York, NY: McGraw-Hill.

Freund, A. M., Li, K. Z. H., & Baltes, P. B. (1999). Successful development and aging: The role of selection, optimization, and compensation. In J. Brandtstädter & R. M. Lerner (Ed.), *Action and self-development: Theory and research through the life span* (pp. 401–434). Thousand Oaks, CA: Sage.

George, J. M. (1990). Personality, affect, and behavior in groups. *Journal of Applied Psychology, 75*, 107–116.

George, J. M., & Brief, A. P. (1992). Feeling good doing good: A conceptual analysis of the mood at work organizational spontaneity relationship. *Psychological Bulletin, 112*, 310–329.

Gibson, D., & Schroeder, S. (2003). Who ought to be blamed? The effect of organizational roles on blame and credit attributions. *International Journal of Conflict Management, 14*, 95–117.

Gist, M. E., & Mitchell, T. R. (1992). Self-efficacy: A theoretical analysis of it determinants and malleability. *Academy of Management Review, 17*, 183–211.

Graen, G. (1976). Role-making processes within complex organizations. In M. D. Dunnette (Ed.), *Handbook of Industrial and Organizational Psychology.* Chicago, IL: Rand McNally College Publishing Company, 1201–1245.

Graen, G. B., & Scandura, T. A. (1987). Toward a psychology of dyadic organizing. In L. L. Cummings & B. M. Staw (Ed.), *Research in organizational behavior* (pp. 175–208). Greenwich, CT: JAI Press.

Hall, D. T. (1986). *Career development in organizations.* San Francisco, CA: Jossey-Bass.

Harris, M. M., & Schaubroeck, J. (1988). A meta-analysis of self-supervisor, self-peer, and peer-supervisor ratings. *Personnel Psychology, 41*, 43–62.

Hebert, E., & Worthy, T. (2001). Does the first year of teaching have to be a bad one? A case study of success. *Teaching and Teacher Education, 17*, 897–911.

Hsiung, H.-H., & Tsai, W. C. (2009). Job definition discrepancy between supervisors and subordinates: The antecedent role of LMX and outcomes. *Journal of Occupational and Organizational Psychology, 82*, 89–112.

Ilgen, D. R., & Hollenbeck, J. R. (1991). The structure of work: Job design and roles. In M. D. Dunnette & L. M. Hough (Ed.), *Handbook of industrial and organizational psychology* (vol. 2, pp. 165–207). Palo Alto, CA: Consulting Psychologists Press.

Katz, D., & Kahn, R. L. (1978). *The social psychology of organizations* (2nd ed.). New York, NY: Wiley.

Kelley, H. H. (1967). Attribution theory in social psychology. In D. Levine (Ed.), *Nebraska symposium of motivation* (Vol. 15. pp. 192–238). Lincoln: University of Nebraska Press.

Lam, S. S., Hui, C., & Law, S. L. (1999). Organizational citizenship behavior: Comparing perspectives of supervisors and subordinates across four international samples. *Journal of Applied Psychology, 84*(4), 584–601.

Lance, C. E., Teachout, M. S., & Donnelly, T. M. (1992). Specification of the criterion construct space: An application of hierarchical confirmatory factor analysis. *Journal of Applied Psychology, 77*, 437–452.

Liao, H., & Chuang, A. (2004). A multilevel investigation of factors influencing employee service performance and customer outcomes. *Academy of Management Journal, 47*, 41–58.

Lynn, S. K. (2002). The winding path: Understanding the career cycle of teachers. *The Clearing House, 75*(4), 179–182.

MacKenzie, S. B., Podsakoff, P. M., & Paine, J. B. (1999). Do citizenship behaviors matter more for managers than for salespeople? *Journal of the Academy of Marketing Science, 27*, 396–410.

McCormick, J., & Barnett, K. (2008). A multilevel investigation of relationships between Australian teachers' career stages and locus of control. *Journal of Educational Administration, 46*(1), 8–24.

McEnrue, M. P. (1989). Self-development as a career management strategy. *Journal of Vocational Behavior, 34*, 57–68.

Meyer, J. W., Scott, R., & Deal, T. E. (1992). Institutional and technical sources of organizational structure: Explaining the structure of educational organizations. In J. Meyer & R. W. Scott (Ed.), *Organizational Environments* (pp. 45–70). Newbury Park, CA: Sage.

Miller, N. (2002). Insider change leadership in schools. *International Journal of Leadership in Education, 5*, 343–360.

Morgeson, P., Delaney-Klinger, K. A., & Hemingway, M. A. (2005). The importance of job autonomy, cognitive ability, and job-related skill for predicting role breadth and job performance. *Journal of Applied Psychology, 90*, 399–406.

Morrison, E. W. (1994). Role definitions and organizational citizenship behavior: The importance of the employee's perspective. *Academy of Management Journal, 37*, 1543–1567.

Morrison, W., & Phelps, C. C. (1999). Taking charge at work: Extra role efforts to initiate workplace change. *Academy of Management Journal, 42*, 403–419.

Mount, M. K., Judge, T. A., Scullen, S. E., Sytsma, M. R., & Hezlett, S. A. (1998). Trait, rater and level effects in 360-degree performance ratings. *Personnel Psychology, 51*, 557–576.

Murphy, K. R., & Cleveland, J. N. (1995). *Understanding performance appraisal: Social, organizational, and goal based perspectives*. Thousand Oaks, CA: Sage.

Neale, M., & Griffin, M. A. (2006). A model of self-held work roles and role transitions. *Human Performance, 19*(1), 23–41.

Oplatka, I. (2006). Going beyond role expectations: Toward an understanding of the determinants and components of teacher organizational citizenship behavior. *Educational Administration Quarterly, 42*, 385–423.

Organ, D. W. (1988). *Organizational citizenship behaviors: The good soldier syndrome*. Lexington, MA: Lexington Books.

Organ, D. W. (1990). The motivational basis of organizational citizenship behavior. *Research in Organizational Behavior, 12*, 43–72.

Organ, D. W., Podsakoff, P. M., & MacKenzie, S. B. (2006). *Organizational citizenship behavior: Its nature, antecedents and consequences*. Thousand Oaks, CA: Sage Publication.

O'Connor, K. E. (2008). "You choose to care": Teachers, emotions and professional identity. *Teaching and Teacher Education, 24*, 117–126.

Parker, S. K. (1998). Enhancing role breadth self-efficacy: The roles of job enrichment and other organizational interventions. *Journal of Applied Psychology, 83*, 835–853.

Phillips, S. D., Blustein, D. L., Jobin-Davis, K., & Finkelberg White, S. L. (2002). Preparation for the school-to-work transition: The views of high school students. *Journal of Vocational Behavior*, *61*, 1–15.

Podsakoff, N. P., Whiting, S. W., Podsakoff, P. M., & Blume, B. D. (2009). Individual- and organizational-level consequences of organizational citizenship behaviors: A meta-analysis. *Journal of Applied Psychology*, *94*, 122–141.

Podsakoff, P. M., MacKenzie, S. B., & Hui, C. (1993). Organizational citizenship behaviors and managerial evaluations of employee performance: A review and suggestions for future research. In G. R. Ferris & K. M. Rowland (Ed.), *Research in personnel and human resources management* (pp. 1–40). Greenwich, CT: JAI Press.

Putka, D. J., & Vancouver, J. B. (1999, August). The moderating effects of employee perceptions of behavioral discretion on the relationship between OCB and job satisfaction. Paper presented at the annual meeting of the Academy of Management, Chicago, IL.

Schneider, B. (1987). The people make the place. *Personnel Psychology*, *40*, 437–453.

Somech, A. (1994). *The social loafing phenomenon compared to extra role behavior (pro-social behavior) as a function of culture and goal setting*. Unpublished dissertation, Technion: Israel Institute of Technology.

Somech, A. (2002). Explicating the complexity of participative management: An investigation of multiple dimensions. *Educational Administration Quarterly*, *38*, 341–371.

Somech, A., & Drach-Zahavy, A. (2000). Understanding extra-role behavior in schools: The relationships between job satisfaction, sense of efficacy, and teachers' extra-role behavior. *Teaching and Teacher Education*, *16*, 649–659.

Somech, A., & Ron, I. (2007). Promoting organizational citizenship behavior in schools: The impact of individual and organizational characteristics. *Educational Administration Quarterly*, *5*, 1–29.

Super, D. E. (1992). Toward a comprehensive theory of career development. In D. A. Montross & C. J. Shinkman (Ed.), *Career development: Theory and practice*. Illinois, IL: Charles & Thomas Publishers.

Sutton, M. J. (2005). *Organizational citizenship behavior: A career development strategy*. Unpublished dissertation, University of South Florida.

Turnipseed, D. L., & Wilson, G. L. (2009). From discretionary to required: The migration of organizational citizenship behavior. *Journal of Leadership and Organizational Studies*, *15*(3), 201–216.

Van Dyne, L., Cummings, L. L., & Parks, J. (1995). Extra-role behaviors: In pursuit of construct and definitional clarity. *Research in Organizational Behavior*, *17*, 215–285.

Van Dyne, L., & Ellis, B. J. (2004). Job creep: A reactance theory perspective on organizational citizenship behavior as over fulfillment of obligations. In J. Coyle-Shapiro, L. Shore, M. S. Taylor & L. Tetrick (Ed.), *The employment relationship: Examining psychological and contextual perspectives* (pp. 181–205). Oxford: Oxford University Press.

Van Dyne, L., Grahm, J. W., & Dienesh, R. M. (1994). Organizational citizenship behavior: Construct redefinition, measurement and validity. *Academy of Management Journal*, *37*, 765–802.

Van Dyne, L., & LePine, J. A. (1998). Helping and voice extra-role behaviors: Evidence of constructive and predictive validity. *Academy of Management Journal*, *41*, 108–119.

Van Scotter, J. R., & Motowidlo, S. J. (1996). Interpersonal facilitation and job dedication as separate facets of contextual performance. *Academy of Applied Psychology*, *81*, 525–531.

Vey, M. A., & Campbell, J. P. (2004). In-role or extra-role organizational citizenship behavior: Which are we measuring? *Human Performance, 17,* 119–135.

Vigoda-Gadot, E. (2007). Redrawing the boundaries of OCB? An empirical examination of compulsory extra role behavior in the workplace. *Journal of Business and Psychology, 21*(3), 377–405.

Wanxian, L., & Weiwu, W. (2007). A demographic study on citizenship behavior as in-role orientation. *Personality and Individual Differences, 42,* 225–234.

CHAPTER 3

ORGANIZATIONAL CITIZENSHIP BEHAVIORS OF TEACHERS: ANTECEDENTS, TRANSFORMATIONAL LEADERSHIP, AND CONTRADICTIONS ☆

Nancy L. Ras

ABSTRACT

In an educational landscape fraught with demands and limited finances, organizational citizenship behaviors (OCBs) of teachers are a coveted resource. In this regard, transformational leadership (TL) is often attributed with the achievement of such organizational outcomes. This conceptual essay considers the relationship between teacher culture, teacher OCBs, and TL, arguing that the characteristics of teacher culture predispose those who become teachers to perform OCBs. Furthermore,

☆This chapter is partially informed by an earlier unpublished paper entitled Multidisciplinary Reflections on Leadership: Unintended Consequences and Conflicting Paradigms presented at the 2008 AERA conference.

Discretionary Behavior and Performance in Educational Organizations: The Missing Link in Educational Leadership and Management
Advances in Educational Administration, Volume 13, 61–85
Copyright © 2012 by Emerald Group Publishing Limited
ISSN: 1479-3660/doi:10.1108/S1479-3660(2012)0000013008

*due to its participatory style, TL may result in either a motivating or de-
motivating influence on teacher OCBs depending on the perceived values
congruence between teacher culture and leadership goals and behavior.
Implications and suggestions for practice are offered.*

Keywords: Transformational leadership; organizational citizenship
behaviors; teacher culture; collectivism

INTRODUCTION

Increased accountability and reduced resources available to schools demand
the maximization of existing resources. Described as *extra-role behaviors*
(Vigoda-Gadot, 2006), *pro-social behaviors* (McNeely & Meglino, 1994), *role
expansion* (Grant & Hofmann, 2011), and Organ's (1988) organizational
citizenship behavior (OCB), discretionary behaviors beyond formal
recognition or reward, are the focus of attempts to extend existing school
capacities. In 2006, Organ, Podsakoff, and MacKenzie reemphasized the
organizational benefit of such behaviors and two meta-analyses carried out
in 2009 by Podsakoff, Whiting, Podsakoff & Blume, ($n = 168$) and by
Nielsen, Hrivnak & Shaw ($n = 38$) found positive relationships between
OCBs and individual and organizational level performance indicators.
Relationships between the performance of OCBs and job satisfaction
(McNeely & Meglino, 1994), collective efficacy (Somech & Drach-Zahavy,
2000), and commitment (Williamson, Burnett, & Bartol, 2009) have also
been found. Researchers have considered the antecedent motivations
engagement in such behaviors and intended beneficiaries (McNeely &
Meglino, 1994), culture (Wollan, Sully de Luque, & Grünhagen, 2009), job
characteristics (Purvanova, Bono, & Dzieweczynski, 2006), and leadership
(Cho & Dansereau, 2010), are considered salient in its performance.

Teacher OCB has been explored from the perspectives of job satisfaction
and efficacy at both the individual and the group levels of analysis (Somech &
Drach-Zahavy, 2000), participative decision-making (Bogler & Somech,
2005), cultural identification (Cohen, 2007), individual and organizational
characteristics (Somech & Ron, 2007), personality, motivation, and culture
(Chen & Carey, 2009), and antecedent personal and contextual factors
(Oplatka, 2006). Ras (2003; see this volume), suggests a relationship between
extra role behaviors and teachers' perception of shared values and common

goals. Together, these studies suggest a wide array of individual level and organizational level factors that are salient to teacher performance of OCBs.

Oplatka (2006) suggests that OCBs may be emotively-based due to the particular dispositions of teachers such as the assumption that their "OCB has some influence upon students' and graduates' future tendencies to perform OCBs in their workplace and society" (p. 385) suggesting a long term, other-oriented view related to the socialization aspect of teaching. In this chapter OCB, extra-role, discretionary, and role expansion behaviors will be referred to using the language of specific authors' in their respective studies, yet collectively these behaviors will be regarded as within the class of employee behaviors regarded as *organizationally beneficial yet informal.*

In this regard, transformational leadership (TL) has been attributed with influencing extra role behaviors (Purvanova et al., 2006; Wang, Oh, Courtright, & Colbert, 2011) and as negatively related to employee perceptions of organizational politics (Vigoda-Gadot, 2007). TL a "style" of leadership focused on "intrinsic motivation and on the positive development of followers" (Bass & Riggio, 2006, p. xi), and on the attainment of organizational goals. TL is charismatic and serves as a model for identification in idealized influence (II), and exhibits inspirational motivation (IM)-defining purpose and meaning for followers; intellectual stimulation (IS)-challenging follower thinking, and individualized consideration (IC)-support and mentoring of followers (Bass & Riggio, 2006). A transformational leader is a positional authority who utilizes these personal and behavioral competencies to influence followers to achieve specific organizational goals.

In educational organizations, TL has been regarded as influencing teacher perceptions of efficacy and thereby indirectly affecting student outcomes (Ross & Gray, 2006), developing the collective capacity of the school organization (Marks & Printy, 2003), and fostering school climates that support innovation (Moolenaar, Daly, & Sleegers, 2010). However, in a meta-analysis by Leithwood and Jantzi (2005), TL effects were mediated by school culture, teacher commitment, and job satisfaction. It is of value then to consider those particular characteristics of teachers, as a professionally identifiable group, related to the performance of OCBs. No studies to date have explicitly considered the role of *teacher culture*, as distinct from *school culture*, in teacher extra-role behavior, nor has the relationship between teacher culture, the influence of TL, and teacher OCBs been explored. Through the lens of collectivism at the individual level of analysis (Shamir, 1990; Singelis & Brown, 1995), conceptually refined as *psychological collectivism* (Jackson, Wesson, Colquitt, & Zapata-Phelan, 2006), heretofore taken-for-granted aspects of this relationship may be suggested. Although the construct of collectivism is common in organizational analyses (Baker, Carson, & Carson, 2009; Erez & Earley, 1993; Flynn & Chatman, 2001; Ilies, Wagner, & Morgeson, 2007; Moorman & Blakely, 1995), outside of cross cultural research (Alexander, 2000; Hallinger & Leithwood, 1998), it is less utilized. Recently educational researchers are increasing the use of this construct and suggest that a collectivistic organizational culture may predispose members of such an organization to extra role behaviors through norms and shared values (Ras, 2003, 2004; Somech & Ron, 2007; Williams, Prestage, & Bedward, 2001; Williamson et al., 2009), and positive correlations between measures of collectivism and teacher OCBs unrelated to the type of leadership have been reported (Chen & Carey, 2009; Cohen, 2007; Oplatka, 2006; Williams et al., 2001). Cohen (2007) found that collectivism was related to both the altruism and civic virtue dimensions of teacher OCBs and suggested that reduced power distance, in a flattened hierarchical structure, "encourages such behavior" (p. 296).

TL, with its participatory methodologies (Somech & Wenderow, 2006), is suited to such a reduction in power distance. On this very point, however, rests the contradiction that may result in the unintentional *undoing* of teacher OCB which is the focus of this conceptual paper. As TL derives legitimacy from influence and "motivational methods rather than power or authority" (Vigoda Gadot, 2007, p. 661) and teacher culture may be regarded as values-based, with a fundamental long-term, other-focused orientation, TLs flattening of organizational hierarchy and focus on building collectivity (both of which support teacher OCBs), may unin-tentionally validate the values-basis inherent in the culture of teachers. In this way, the positional authority of the TL may be diminished. The purpose then is to suggest how the relationship between teacher culture and TL may result in the withdrawal of teacher OCBs, undermining of precisely what TL sets out to support – improved organizational performance. Positing such a conceptual relationship, suggestions will be made for both policy and praxis.

The chapter begins by considering the salient literature antecedent to teacher OCBs from the perspective of values (Kristof-Brown & Jansen, 2007; Welch, Pitts, Tenini, Kuenlen, & Wood, 2010) and burnout (Friedman, 1991; Kahn, Schneider, Jenkins-Henkelman, & Moyle, 2006; Malach-Pines, 2002; Pines & Kafry, 1978), utilizing the lens of collectivism (Jackson et al., 2006; Triandis, 1995; Shamir, 1990; Singelis & Brown, 1995), and bridging the individual to organizational levels of analysis. The characteristics and methodologies of TL (Bass & Riggio, 2006; Burns, 1978) will then be overviewed and contrasted with teacher culture highlighting the potential for contradictions and unintentional effects on teacher OCBs. Finally, ways to influence and support such behaviors, without detrimental effects to the collectivity that promotes them, will be suggested.

IN PURSUIT OF DISCRETIONARY BEHAVIORS

OCBs are so highly valued that identifying "employees with a propensity to be effective group members" (Jackson et al., 2006, p. 884) and selecting "employees who have a propensity to exhibit OCBs" (Organ, Podsakoff, & Podsakoff, 2011, p. 133) has become an explicit organizational goal, while Grant (2008) suggests that helping behavior is correlated with perceptions of social impact and social worth of the task. Organizational pursuit of OCBs is a means to enhance performance and from the employee side as a reflecting the significance of one's employment – a psychologically existential need (Malach-Pines, 2002). OCBs by teachers have become an organizational imperative as "the work of school is too complex to be clearly delineated in a written contract" (Tschennen-Moran, 2009, p. 242).

Somech (2010) suggests that school-based research place less emphasis on dyadic relations between individual teachers and the principal, due to the active role played by groups of teachers in organizational dynamics and the achievement of organizational goals and is supported by Vigoda-Gadot, Beeri, Birman-Shemesh, and Somech (2007) who suggest that teacher OCBs are determined by group-level norms in which "outcomes and performance are subject to collective-level dynamics that are far beyond individual initiatives and actions" (p. 469). Somech and Ron (2007) investigated the relationships between OCBs and group, dyadic, and context-related influences and found that the normative characteristics of context were most influential suggesting that teacher OCB may be created, promoted, and sustained through group-level norms rather than by dyadic relations with authority figures. The group level of analysis as the locus for understanding OCBs is consistent with organizational research generally (Kark & Shamir, 2000) yet explicit bridging of levels of analysis is necessary as the individual teacher brings with her or himself ideas, beliefs, and opinions when entering the schoolhouse.

TEACHER CULTURAL VALUES

Edwards and Cable (2009) define values as "general beliefs about normatively desirable behaviors or end states" (p. 655). Person organization (P-O) fit literature and Attrition-Selection-Attrition (ASA) theory suggest that when able to choose, people tend to self-select into organizations with which they perceive they share values (Sparrow, 2001) as such choices are regarded to be the fulfillment of personal needs (O'Reilly & Chatman, 1986). If congruence is perceived between individual values and the organizational context, including in goals and actions, desirable organizational outcomes are likely to result (Kammeyer-Mueller, 2007; Kristof-Brown & Jansen, 2007; Ostroff & Schulte, 2007; Schleicher, Hansen, & Fox 2011). Teacher education programs also support characteristics considered desirable in teacher candidates, such as empathy, vision, and humanity – and which were found to be the greatest motivation for teaching – such as the perceived value of the job to society. (Welch et al., 2010). In a cross-cultural study of new teachers, Czerniawski (2009) found that stressors occurred between teachers' values of egalitarianism and authority (Norway), pastoral care and curricular demands (Germany), desire for a humanitarian approach, and perceived need for authoritarianism (England), suggesting teachers' basic, if sometimes frustrated desires were to foster positive, student-centered relationships that would improve students' lives. That teachers have a primarily other-focused, rather than organizationally, or academically focused, orientation is supported by findings that the primary concern of novice teachers is with the social aspects of teaching, noted by Book and Freeman (1986) and again three decades later by Jephcote (2009). This is not to suggest that teachers are disconnected from the curricular work of teaching, but rather that their predisposition is relational and that seems to hold true despite challenging conditions such as in large, urban schools, when they "speak of teaching as love [and] a commitment to social justice – the ideals of democracy, fair play, and equality [which] figure prominently among the reasons why these teachers chose this profession" (Nieto, 2003, p. 15). This "sense of calling" (Farkas, Johnson, & Foleno, 2000, p. 10) has been coined "effective altruism" as it is based in teachers' perceptions that they will be able to create significant change in students' lives (p. 17). Teacher burnout may highlight these values when left unrealized.

Malach-Pines (2002) found that teachers have an existential need "to believe that the things they do are important and significant" (p. 137) and suggested that discipline problems were the primary factor in burnout as the singular factor that places teachers' goal out of reach as teachers cannot carry out their role when disrupted. Indeed, in their early work on social service professionals, Pines and Kafry (1978) noted the "emotional depletion" that can result when the service provider is the "primary instrument" (p. 504) and that the perception of meaningful engagement supported job satisfaction despite challenging conditions. Some 30 years later, positive social support remained central to lower levels of emotional exhaustion and cynicism and increased professional efficacy among teachers (Kahn et al., 2006). Such research suggests shared beliefs common to teachers which reflect the other-orientation and values-bases of their work and depend on the social and relational (both with students as professional meaning is made through this interaction, and with colleagues as mutuality supports them in this endeavor) as foundational and essential. For this reason, teachers may be predisposed to helping behaviors (Welch et al., 2010) with such behaviors an embodiment of teachers' values. This suggests not a *school culture*, but a *teacher culture* at work (Ras, 2004).

Teachers not only fill multiple roles and are answerable to multiple stakeholders, but they also engage as individuals as well as members of organizational and professional cultures within a school. This organizational context also takes place within an externally dynamic context, compounding the content and outcome level demands made on teachers and schools. Love (2007) suggests that under stressful conditions individuals tend more toward relationships with their lateral colleagues to find support through environmental uncertainties, and a meta-analysis carried out by Rasmussen and Jeppesen (2006) ($n = 55$) found positive associations between psychological variables, employee well-being, and teamwork. Tschennen-Moran (2009) expands such positive effects of relationships in suggesting that professional communities, high in trust and commitment, serve the needs of both teachers and students through increased teacher engagement. The pro-social values shared by teachers are antecedent to engagement in extra-role behaviors and have been associated with collectivistic organizational cultures (Jackson et al., 2006; Wollan et al., 2009).

COLLECTIVISM IN ORGANIZATIONS

The construct of individualism/collectivism (I/C) at an individual level of analysis can be regarded as two different and separate continua that exist independently and can be evoked depending on circumstance and experience (Singelis & Brown, 1995) and in the recognition that all people embody "both the calculative and the moral dimensions" (Shamir, 1990, p. 314) – the *I* (individualism), and the *we* (collectivism), respectively.

The evocation of the collectivist aspect, through collective norms and values, is a way of perceiving and reacting to the social world, not a relinquishment of individual thought, as "the mere existence of norms suggests that there is some *conformity* among organizational members ... not that there is also *uniformity* among these members" (Flynn & Chatman, 2001, p. 268) (italics original). Indeed, recent neuropsychological research using *f*MRI scanning suggests that "distinct regions were found to be selectively associated with cooperation and competition ... this pattern reflects the different mental frameworks implicated in being cooperative versus being competitive with another person" (Decety, Jackson, Sommerville, Chaminade, & Meltzoff, 2004, p. 744), which suggests just such an I-C duality. Kâğitçibaşi (1994) suggests that "the common tendency to pit individualism against collectivism and use them as general traits across time and space is not warranted [and] should rather be treated as the likelihood of a person or a group of people behaving in individualistic or collectivistic ways" (p. 56). This evocation of this collectivistic aspect has been equated with higher levels of trust (Fukayama, 1995), higher levels of motivation (Cohen & Prusak, 2001), increased outcome production (Gabbay & Leenders, 1999), pro-social behavior (Dierdorff, Bell, & Belohlav, 2011; Jackson et al., 2006; Wollan et al., 2009), higher levels of cooperation (Baker et al., 2009), and an increased psychological sense of community at work (Love, 2007). Jackson et al., (2006) refined this individual-level collectivistic conceptualization through validation of a measure of *psychological collectivism* specifically for the workplace context.

Collectivistic organizational cultures are characterized by individuals who tend to group-reference rather than self-reference (Erez & Earley, 1993), emphasize and prioritize the perspectives, goals, and needs of others, and behave in a way that is determined by shared norms and beliefs (Triandis, 1995). Such a group-focus mediates organizational behavior and is noted for reflecting collegiality, minimal levels of conflict, a tendency toward compromise, and the willingness to take risks, the confluence of which tend to result in achievement of desired outcomes (Flynn & Chatman, 2001). In such cultures, process emphasis, empathy, and relational issues are prioritized which reflect the collectivist value of effort over that of ability (Triandis, 1995). As collectivistic behavior is characterized by interdependency, understanding such an organizational culture is significant, particularly in collaborative and interdependent task accomplishment (Ramamoorthy & Flood, 2004). Viewing behaviors through the collectivist construct may make explicit otherwise implicit meanings behind teacher behaviors and these seem to be characteristic to the culture of teachers.

Wheelan and Kesselring (2005) found that student achievement could be positively correlated with faculty cooperation as a group when group goals became the point of reference regardless of size of school, socio-economic status of the students, or location. Williams, et al. (2001) note the severe outcomes of individualism on newly qualified teachers (NQTs) and the "significance of collaborative cultures...for the quality of induction practice" (p. 263). The outcomes portended by such cooperative and highly associative organizations have not gone unnoticed by educational researchers and gave rise to the call for the creation of school *communities* (Lieberman, 1996; Sergiovanni, 1994), and *community,* through the lens of collectivism, "is essentially collectivistic interdependence" (Triandis, 1995, p. 40). As Cohen and Keren (2008) found in a collectivist sampling of teachers, higher levels of collectivism reflected increased normative and affective commitment, and high levels of collectivism and feminism (a nurturing, empathetic orientation), combined with low power distance, were positively related to OCBs among teachers. They posit that such feminine values are more closely related to OCBs than to in-role behaviors suggesting that the relationship between pro-social teacher predisposition and OCBs remain distinct from formal task accomplishment.

Such a construct is in stark contrast to the organizational paradigms used by most positional authorities – focused on task completion rather than on task processing, and consistent with quantifiable performance outcomes within known and measurable parameters for student achievement (Seashore Louis, Febey, & Schroeder, 2005) – which are the criteria used in assessing organizational leaders (Moolenaar et al., 2010). When viewed in this way, an educational leader trying to facilitate collaborative processes may unknowingly be walking a tightrope between teacher culture and external measures of success. TL in the school context would seem to fall squarely into this category.

LEADING AND TRANSFORMING

Ashkanasy and Tse (2000) regard TL as emotion management. They suggest that transformational leaders succeed "through enticing their followers to join them in achieving positive and visionary goals" (p. 224) and posit that such leaders need to be high in the dimensions of emotional intelligence to be both sensitive and self-regulatory in this process. The distinction of TL from traditional management through power paradigms is that it suggests purpose-bound leadership rather than leadership-by-hierarchy (Harter, Ziolkowski, & Wyatt, 2006). Such leadership is often distinguished from management, directive leadership (Euwena, Wendt, & Van Emmerik, 2007; Kark & Van Dijk, 2007), or transactional leadership (Burns, 1978), all of which share a focus on "deviations, details, duties, and obligations" (Kark & Van Dijk, 2007, p. 509).

Effects attributed to TL include job satisfaction, (Bono & Judge, 2003), employee OCBs (Purvanova et al., 2006), and higher levels of employee performance (Bass, 1985). The assumption guiding TL is that positive employee attitudes will increase organizational productivity (Vigoda-Gadot, 2007). The influence of transformational leaders, attributed with inspirational and ethical motivation, has been regarded as creating values congruence between leadership visions and organizational goals and then changing the values of followers to suit. The question of values congruence goes to the heart of the discussion of TL in the educational arena (to which we will return momentarily) as Bono and Judge (2003) note self-concordance theory suggests that TL has a positive influence on job satisfaction and P-O fit research also suggests that values congruence between individuals and their organizations garner positive outcomes such as positive attitudes (Kristof-Brown & Jansen, 2007; O'Reilly & Chatman, 1986), support for organizational change (Lamm, Gordon, & Purser, 2010), organizational identification and decreased turnover intentions (Edwards & Cable, 2009). Posner (2010) found that personal and organizational values alignment resulted in job satisfaction among employees, which was not mediated by demographic variables such as education or gender and did not consider leadership style. Studies then suggest that values-based outcomes are not leader or leadership-style dependent.

Leithwood, Begley, and Cousins' (1994) definition of TL for the educational organization suggests the transformational leader should engage in major changes of some form, function, or structure. Ross and Gray (2006) suggest that transformational leader-praxis includes "raising the values of members to go beyond self-interest and redefining their needs to align with organizational preferences" (p. 802) and includes any strategy that can change members' perceptions "to develop organizational capacity for school improvement" (Marks & Printy, 2003, p. 377). Transformational school leaders are then those who are able to employ personal and professional strategies to create leader-defined change. This encapsulates the "impression management" dynamic that is emphasized in TL elicitation of follower commitment (Chemers, 2002, p. 147) and views followers as the means "through" which the work of a transformational leader is done (Moolenaar et al., 2010, p. 657) while supporting and developing followers.

However, OCB research in schools has also suggested teacher performance of OCBs unrelated to leadership style (Christ, van Dick, Wagner, & Stellmacher, 2003; Somech & Drach-Zahavy, 2000). In a meta-analysis

($n = 113$), Wang et al. (2011) found that TL had "a stronger effect on employee attitudes and motivation than on employee performance" (p. 249), in particular, their analysis did not show positive effects on individual level task performance, that is, performance of those formal specifications of an employee's job description. Indeed, they note that TL resulted in increases in contextual performance (social identification and cohesion) as contrasted with task-related performance (Wang et al., 2011). However, as outcomes are what determine the success of the TL, these remain dependent upon follower perceptions and behaviors. The ability of the transformational educational leader to achieve quantifiable teacher performance, including OCBs, would by definition, be garnered through the transformational leader's *realignment* of individual teachers' goals and values to suit organizational priorities – and herein is located the contradiction that may negatively affect teacher OCBs.

DRAWING CONCEPTUAL LINES

It could be argued that teachers are predisposed to valuing certain goals and outcomes which are primarily social and these have been found to support teacher individual and collective efficacy (Ciani, Summers, & Easter, 2008) and assist in the development and support of interpersonal trust (Ali Chughtai, & Buckley, 2009; Erez & Earley, 1993; Triandis, 1995). These factors suggest antecedent characteristics that may predict teachers' willingness to engage in OCBs – as a social, community-building, act. This connection is supported by Somech and Drach-Zahavy (2000) who found positive relationships between teachers' job satisfaction, their collective and self-efficacy, extra-role behavior toward their team, as well as between job satisfaction and extra-role behavior toward the student. The same relationship was not, however, found between collective efficacy and extra role behavior toward the organization. That relationship was defined by *self-efficacy*. Although the authors suggest that this may be the result of a loosely coupled system in demand of "increasing cohesiveness and collegial relationships" (p. 656), an alternative view might posit that teachers do not view *the organization* as a defining and identifying factor, but rather define and identify themselves through their interdependent relationships with students and peers. In this regard Hargreaves (1994) notes that "the relationship between teachers and their colleagues are among the most significant aspects of teachers' lives and work" (pp. 165–166) as these are the group members upon whom they rely.

The suggestion that performance of OCBs both serve as, and reflect, social support is supported by Kahn et al. (2006) who found that emotional social support plays a definitive role in mediating teacher burnout independent of individual affective dispositions. By the same token, Barsade and Gibson (2007) note that organizational environments in which positive affect is present reflect higher levels of pro-social behavior. In this regard, Grant and Hofmann's (2011) theoretical model of the interpersonal dynamics of role expansion suggests that the experiential system of information processing is done in "an intuitive, emotional fashion" (p. 17), is engaged by those with intrinsic values, and results in role expansion when a "strong emotional investment in the role" (p. 18) is tapped. The intrinsic values of teachers have long been recognized, as by Lortie (1975) in his hallmark study which described the "psychic rewards of teaching" (p. 101), and by Hargreaves (1994) who called such intrinsic motivation "internally generated dedication" (p. 127). From this perspective then, it may be posited that teachers' actions are reflective of goals that are "inherently valued in their own right" (Grant & Hofmann, 2011, p. 17) – a process that engages a different motivational system from that of individuals who are extrinsically motivated. Grant and Hofmann (2011) and Joireman, Kamdar, Daniels, and Duell (2006) found that short-term perspectives and extrinsic motivators caused a steep decline in OCBs.

In sum, teachers' OCBs would be pro-socially directed as a result of their individual and collective psychological collectivism – that which brought them to the teaching profession. It cannot then be taken for granted that teacher OCBs are *organizationally* directed; the collective and relational aspects may be the intended *direction* of these behaviors with the organization of school offering the *context* and indirectly harvesting the rewards. Teachers are therefore predisposed to the performance of pro-social behaviors – particularly behaviors that are focused on peers and students – as these are congruent with their values and identities as teachers. Although TL in schools has been attributed with teacher OCBs and organizational outcomes, it is arguably the predisposition of teachers to provide these pro-social behaviors, and indeed collectivists would tend to view these behaviors as in-role as for them actions are reflections of values and so they carry a moral component (Clugston, Howell, & Dorfman, 2000; Oplatka, 2006). However, such a professional culture within an organizational structure creates a confounding duality in purposes, goals, and behaviors, much of which remains taken for granted.

It was the management thinker Peter Drucker (1992) who pointed out this values-based incompatibility when he offered that "an organization is defined by task ... communities are defined by their centers of values, sentiments and beliefs" (cited in Sergiovanni, 1994, p. 13–14). Telling in this regard, and of particular salience to the performance of teacher OCBs, is the work of Friedman (1991), whose comparative study of the characteristics of high and low-burnout schools found that high burnout schools were characterized by strict administrative systems with formal hierarchies, a focus on measurable goals, and stressing academic achievement. In these schools teachers generally did not work in teams, and teacher-principal relations were dyadic. Conversely, in low-burnout schools educational objectives were flexible, the hierarchy was fluid, and teachers were involved in management teams. In these schools teachers were not evaluated only on their students' achievements, but also on their own integration within the staff, and their willingness to give and receive mutual assistance. This latter point suggests a relationship between OCBs and social support that buffers against teacher burnout. However, the administrative side of organizations, including schools, function unlike *communities* and more like prototypical hierarchies.

A school is responsible for the achievement of externally mandated academic standards, and the administrator's role-based responsibility is to attain them. We concurrently assume schools to be and to function as organizations while seeking the positive outcomes afforded by the cohesion of school-as-community. This may ferment dissonance and without the awareness of teacher culture's defining characteristics, an organizational leader may assume that the need to make "efforts to align personal-organizational values" (Posner, 2010, p. 540), and to align teacher cultural characteristics with managerial style (Somech, 2010), endows the positional authority with the prerogative to offer a personal vision and engage in brokering support for it, incurring change to those values already in place (Ross & Grey, 2006). The means used by leaders to attain such goals can have effects on trust (Ali Chughtai & Buckley, 2009; Cartwright & Holmes, 2006; Edwards & Cable, 2009), on teacher motivation and sense of collective efficacy (Ciani et al., 2008), and ultimately on the performance of OCBs (Purvanova et al., 2006).

Kotlyar and Karakowsky (2006) found that transformational leader styles had a "greater propensity for generating functional and dysfunctional conflict in a team context" related to both content-based conflict and socio-emotional conflict (p. 397). They suggest that this may be due to the fact that team members of transformational leaders "fight harder to defend their positions" (p. 397). In light of our understanding of teacher culture and its foundational values, such conflict suggests the defending of strongly held beliefs and values perceived as threatened. Gibson, Cooper and Conger (2009) suggest that perceptual differences between team members and leaders regarding outcomes and their attainment may also promote higher levels of conflict which highlights underlying contradictions that may surface as conflict when a transformational leader attempts to supplant his or her own vision into a school, and onto existing teacher culture. The unintended outcome may be the withdrawal of teacher OCBs.

The ability to legitimize action in a collectivistic professional culture results from the perception of congruence between personal values and organizational goals (Erez & Earley, 1993). In fact, in the famous Asch study of organizational participation it was found that "the effectiveness of participatory practices was moderated by the perceived legitimacy of such an intervention according to existing social structures" (p. 185), so this is hardly a new idea. When we recognize that "vision is likely to be more or less appealing depending on the extent to which it is appears to be relevant to a particular context" (Pawar & Eastman, 1997, p. 429), such cultural legitimacy is then the basis upon which actions will or will not be commenced and from which authentically shared purposes will be sculpted. The term *teacher resistance* has often been used to describe the latter. Tschennen-Moran (2009) notes that "as teachers are socialized into the norms of the profession, their beliefs, attitudes, and actions are expected to evidence a strong sense of accountability to the shared mission of service to students and their families [which] does not rely on a chain of command to enforce the investment of effort" (p. 225), and as Shamir and Lapidot (2003) offer, "teams have greater legitimacy than individuals to represent collective values and identities" (p. 486). Teacher OCBs are then symptomatic of values congruence yet teacher culture is one "of process bound tightly in an organizational structure of product" (Ras, 2004, p. 37).

The conceptual model offered for consideration here (see Fig. 1) suggests the performance of OCBs then is theorized to be based in psychological collectivism (Jackson et al., 2006) aggregated to the group, creating a collectivistic teacher culture and teacher OCBs reflect this collectivism (Wollan et al., 2009). Although TL has been attributed with teacher OCBs (Purvanova et al., 2006), research suggests that such behaviors take place without leader intervention or style of leadership (Chen & Carey, 2009; Oplatka, 2006). In the case of TL, its participatory style and facilitating of collaboration and shared values unintentionally reduces the hierarchical authority of the leader and may serve to legitimize the pro-social, rather

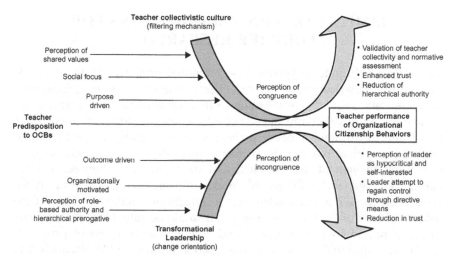

Fig. 1. A Conceptual Model of the Outcomes of Transformational Leadership and Teacher Culture on Teacher Organizational Citizenship Behaviors.

than pro-organizational, predispositions of teachers to perform such behaviors. Such a posit frames TL as indirectly facilitating teacher OCBs only if goals are not perceived as threatening the collective values of teacher culture.

Conversely, a transformational leader may introduce a vision that is perceived as contrary to foundational values and beliefs of teacher culture – those perceived to be short-term and outcome oriented, for example – and these would likely be met with teacher *resistance*. As is taken for granted from an organizational/management perspective, a positional leader takes for granted her/his authority and such *resistance* may then be met with leadership behaviors in which power paradigms are engaged to reassert positional authority (Kark & Van Dijk, 2007; Tschennen-Moran, 2009). The positional authority may be unable to comprehend how subordinates misconstrue the relationship, and teachers to comprehend how hierarchy and goals have shifted away from values assumed to be shared. As collectives have greater legitimacy in representing group values, the positional leader may then be perceived as self-interested (Kark & van Dijk, 2007) or hypocritical (Cha & Edmondson, 2006), further denigrating the positional authority.

LIMITATIONS AND SUGGESTIONS FOR FURTHER RESEARCH

The conceptual model suggested here is limited primarily by the need for supporting empirical data to test these relationships in educational organizations. The data contributing to this model come from a wide array of sources, both within and outside of education, and although an attempt was made to distinguish between these sources, paradigms, and levels of analysis, empirical research is necessary to explore these relationships in education. In light of the complexity of the relationship between teacher culture, TL, and teacher OCBs, this model offers an inviting opportunity for researchers to gain much needed data to inform our understanding. At the individual level of analysis, for example, it would be valuable for researchers to compare and contrast teachers' and administrators' levels of psychological collectivism in different locations, school settings, and levels. Such data might also add to our understanding of longitudinal trends as teachers and administrators progress in tenure, follow new teachers as they become organizationally embedded or indeed leave the profession, as well as suggesting changes to teachers' psychological collectivism as they take on administrative roles, and whether, or in what ways, OCBs are affected by such variables. The question of gender differences in this regard also offers fertile ground for inquiry with regards to teacher pro-social predispositions and their willingness to engage in OCBs, as does the question of how teachers regard their OCB – as in-role or extra-role – as for collectivists, such behaviors are moral imperatives (Erez & Earley, 1993; Triandis, 1995; Wanxian & Weiwu, 2007). Researching such a distinction among teacher OCBs could highlight the ways in which managerially mandated OCBs might affect teacher culture in a specific context.

In addition, the connection between collectivism and psychological sense of community (Love, 2007) should be explored as this relationship, should there be found to be one, may offer valuable insights on the bases for teacher OCBs and the directedness of those behaviors, whether interpersonal, group-related, or organizationally focused. Cha and Edmondson (2006) note that "a strong emphasis on values in organizations may be a double-edged sword" (p. 75). If shared pro-social values are indeed prerequisite to teacher OCBs, as is suggested here, such a sword may be hovering over the organization's literal and figurative head and this too offers fertile ground for further inquiry.

At the organizational level of analysis, we would invite the use of social network analysis (SNA) (Schensul, Le Compte, Trotter, Cromley, & Singer, 1999; Scott, 1991) to frame inquiry regarding dyadic or group based interaction among staff and suggesting the relationship between TL, psychological collectivism, and the performance of OCBs. As SNA offers the ability to traverse the individual to group levels of analysis, it may be of particular value in illumining the relational processes at play (Balkundi, Barsness, & Michael, 2009; Moolenaar et al., 2010). Context too is a central factor of interest. As much of the data regarding teacher OCBs and collectivistic organizational cultures has been researched in the Israeli context (e.g., Belogolovsky & Somech, 2010; Cohen & Keren, 2008; Oplatka, 2006, 2009; Ras, 2004; Somech & Drach-Zahavy, 2000; Somech & Wenderow, 2006; Vigoda-Gadot et al., 2007), it would be valuable for scholars to test these results in other countries, areas, and various educational organizations. It would seem that the lack of such research in the United States reflects some level of reticence to engage with this theoretical lens in what is assumed to be an individualistic country (Kâğitçibaşi, 1994). However, as the work of western scholars has shown outside of education, the use if the I-C lens is indeed valuable and relevant (Erez & Earley, 1993; Flynn & Chatman, 2001; Williamson et al., 2009).

SUMMARY AND CONCLUSION

The conceptual model of the relationship between TL, teacher culture, and teacher suggests an inherent contradiction between the school-as-organization and the school-as-community as may be seen in the predisposing values of those who become teachers and what is identified as teacher culture. As "Goals can be viewed as applications of values to specific situations" (Erez, 1997, p. 205), how these OCBs are effected within a particular school environment will depend on the perceptions of school goals and actions being congruent with teacher cultural norms. Collectivism is characterized by normative legitimacy structures (Erez & Earley, 1993; Triandis, 1995), suggesting that teacher culture will tend to evaluate goals and behaviors through this filter. However, TL, with its goal of changing existing values to coalesce around an organizationally determined one (Bass & Riggio, 2006; Ross & Gray, 2006), sets the stage for dissonance that may adversely affect teacher behaviors generally and OCBs in particular. This dissonance has the potential for becoming a *no-win* situation for transformational leaders as two possible outcomes are immediately evident. The first, that organizational goals will be deemed *illegitimate* based on collectivistic normative assessments (Ras, 2003). This scenario evokes the warning of Adler (cited in Erez & Earley, 1993) that "if beliefs and values are threatened by organizational practices, we can expect dysfunctional work behavior or maladjustment" (p. 43). For the socially oriented and values-based teachers, such *maladjustment* may be reflected in the withholding of OCBs or attrition. Second, and perhaps more unexpected, is the possibility that the transformational leader's goals are deemed *legitimate* and adopted as reflecting collective beliefs and values, and will then unknowingly validate these normative-based filters with the potential of further eroding the hierarchical authority. A well-intended leader attempting transformational methodologies may then be interpreted by teachers either as threatening their beliefs and values on the one hand, or validating their collective cultural assessments of the leader's suggestions or goals, on the other. In both cases, teacher culture remains the normative filter by which goals and behaviors are assessed. As these mechanisms function *under the organizational radar* and only the resulting behaviors are evident, attention to teacher cultural characteristics as underlying causes of behavior offer much in the way of unraveling the complex relationships between teacher beliefs, values, and actions outside of organizational research lenses.

It is important to note that it is a core function of educational organizations, in particular due to their receipt of public funds, to ensure that the mastery of knowledge is achieved and the posits made here regarding teacher culture are not intended to suggest that teachers do not support these aims. However, research on the predisposing characteristics of teachers and their collective values suggests that the acquisition of knowledge rests within a wider, more holistically integrated scope of goals and objectives than those from an administrative perspective. This may also shed light on the large percentage of public school teachers who send their own children to charter and private schools as such choices may be interpreted through the collectivistic lens as the pursuit of values crossing professional and personal lines.

The values-driven culture of teachers may be challenging within an organizational setting yet it is suggested that this foundation and the collectivistic characteristics of teacher culture that portend teacher engagement in OCBs and result in desirable organizational outcomes. To support such characteristics without exacerbating the potential erosion of a leader's positional authority, it is suggested that leaders explicitly engage teacher collectivity and jointly investigate commonly held beliefs and values that are taken for granted such as the purposes of schooling, the function of curriculum, the hierarchical roles of administration and leadership, and the meaning behind and specific understandings of teachers regarding their discretionary behaviors. Such an intentional process is not as "transformational" as it is "inclusive" in that it does not attempt to *transform* another's beliefs but sculpts a collective, culturally legitimate, and organizationally congruent set of values and articulates them as collective agency through authentically and explicitly shared goals. This process of *congruent collectivity* through which valuable organizational outcomes may be attained protects the integrity of hierarchy and public accountability, and although an arguably arduous process, is within the domain of the transformational educational leader. This path places the leader as the organizational interpreter of collective beliefs, and their translator, toward the writing of a collective educational narrative that portends cogent organizational action.

ACKNOWLEDGMENTS

The author would like to thank Dr. Ibrahim Duyar and an anonymous reviewer for their constructive comments in the preparation of this chapter.

REFERENCES

Alexander, R. (2000). *Culture and pedagogy.* Oxford, UK: Blackwell Publishers.

Ali Chugtai, A., & Buckley, F. (2009). Linking trust in the principal to school outcomes. *International Journal of Education, 22*(7), 574–589. doi:10.1108/09513540910990816

Ashkanasy, N. M., & Tse, B. (2000). Transformational leadership as management of emotion: A conceptual review. In N. M. Ashkanasy, C. E. J. Härtel & W. Zerbe (Eds.), *Emotions in the workplace: Research, theory, and practice* (pp. 221–235). Westport, CN: Quorum Books.

Baker, D. S., Carson, K. D., & Carson, P. P. (2009). An individual-level examination of the impact of cultural values on organizational identification. *The Journal of Applied Management and Entrepreneurship, 14*(2), 29–43. Retrieved from ABI/INFORM Global.

Balkundi, P., Barsness, Z., & Michael, J. H. (2009). Unlocking the influence of leadership network structures on team conflict and viability. *Small Group Research, 40*, 301–322. doi:10.1177/1046496409333404

Barsade, S. G., & Gibson, D. E. (2007). Why does affect matter in organizations? *Academy of Management Perspectives, 21*(7), 36–59. Retrieved from *Ebsco*host.

Bass, B. M. (1985). *Leadership beyond expectations.* New York, NY: Free Press.

Bass, B. M., & Riggio, R. E. (2006). *Transformational leadership* (2nd ed.). London: Lawrence Erlbaum.

Belogolovsky, E., & Somech, A. (2010). Teachers' organizational citizenship behavior: Examining the boundary between in-role behavior and extra-role behavior from the perspective of teachers, principals, and parents. *Teaching and Teacher education, 26,* 914–923. doi:10.1016/j.tate.2009.10.032

Bogler, R., & Somech, A. (2005). Organizational citizenship behavior in school: how does it relate to participation in decision making? *Journal of Educational Administration, 43*(4/5), 420–438. doi:10.1108/09578230510615215

Book, C., & Freeman, D. J. (1986). Differences in entry characteristics elementary and secondary teacher candidates. *Journal of Teacher Education, 37*(2), 47–51. doi:10.1177/002248718603700209

Bono, J. E., & Judge, T. A. (2003). Self concordance at work: Toward understanding the motivational effects of transformational leaders. *Academy of Management Journal, 48*(5), 554–571. Retrieved from PsycINFO.

Burns, J. (1978). *Leadership.* New York, NY: Harper and Row.

Cartwright, S., & Holmes, N. (2006). The meaning of work: the challenge of regaining employee engagement and reducing cynicism. *Human Resource Management Review, 16,* 199–208. doi:10.1016/j.hrmr.2006.03.012

Cha, S. E., & Edmondson, A. C. (2006). When values backfire: Leadership, attribution, and disenchantment in a values-driven organization. *The Leadership Quarterly, 17,* 57–78. doi:10.1016/j.leaqua.2005.10.006

Chemers, M. M. (2002). Efficacy and effectiveness: Integrating models of leadership and intelligence. In R. E. Riggio, S. E. Murphy & F. J. Pirozzolo (Eds.), *Multiple intelligences and leadership* (pp. 139–160). Mahwah, NJ: Lawrence Erlbaum Associates.

Chen, S. X., & Carey, T. P. (2009). Assessing citizenship behavior in educational contexts: The role of personality, motivation, culture. *Journal of Psychoeducational Assessment, 27*(2), 125–137. doi:10.1177/073428908325146

Cho, J., & Dansereau, F. (2010). Are transformational leaders fair? A multi-level study of transformational leadership, justice perceptions, and organizational citizenship behaviors. *The Leadership Quarterly, 21,* 409–421. doi:10.1016/j.leaqua.2010.03.006

Christ, O., van Dick, R., Wagner, U., & Stellmacher, J. (2003). When teachers go the extra mile: Foci of organizational identification as determining of different forms of organizational citizenship behaviours among schoolteachers. *British Journal of Educational Psychology, 73,* 329–334. Retrieved from EBSCO*host.*

Ciani, K. D., Summers, J. J., & Easter, M. A. (2008). A "top-down" analysis of high school teacher motivation. *Contemporary Educational Psychology, 33,* 533–560. doi:10.1016/j.cedpsych.2007.04.002

Clugston, M., Howell, J. P., & Dorfman, P. W. (2000). Does cultural socialization predict multiple bases and foci of commitment? *Journal of Management, 26*(1), 5–30. doi:10.1177/014920630002600106

Cohen, A. (2007). One nation, many cultures: A cross-cultural study of the relationship between personal cultural values and commitment in the workplace to in-role performance and organizational citizenship behavior. *Cross Cultural Research, 41*(3), 273–300. doi:10.1177/1069397107302090

Cohen, A., & Keren, D. (2008). Individual value and social exchange variables: examining their relationship to and mutual effect on in-role performance and organizational citizenship behavior. *Group and Organization Management, 33*(4), 425–452. doi:10.1177/1059601108321823

Cohen, D., & Prusak, L. (2001). *In good company.* Boston, MA: Harvard University Press.

Czerniawski, G. (2009). Positioning the values of early career teachers in Norway, Germany and England. *European Journal of Education, 44*(3), 421–440. doi:10.1111/j.1465-3435.2009.01391.x

Decety, J., Jackson, P. L., Sommerville, J. A., Chaminade, T., & Meltzoff, A. N. (2004). The neural bases of cooperation and competition: an ƒMRI investigation. *NeuroImage, 23,* 744–751. doi:10.1016/j.neuroimage.2004.05.025

Dierdorff, E. C., Bell, S. T., & Belohlav, J. A. (2011). The power of "we": Effects of psychological collectivism on team performance over time. *Journal of Applied Psychology, 96*(2), 247–262. doi:10.1037/a0020929

Drucker, P. F. (1992). The new society of organizations. *The Harvard Business Review, 70*(1), 95–103. Retrieved from EBSCO*host.*

Edwards, J. R., & Cable, D. M. (2009). The value of value congruence. *Journal of Applied Psychology, 94*(3), 654–677. doi:10.1037/a0014891

Erez, M. (1997). A culture based model of work motivation. In P. Earley & M. Erez (Eds.), *New perspectives on international industrial/organisational psychology.* San Francisco, CA: Jossey-Bass.

Erez, M., & Earley, P. C. (1993). *Culture, self identity, and work.* New York, NY: Oxford University Press.

Euwena, M., Wendt, H., & Van Emmerik, H. (2007). Leadership styles and group organizational citizenship behavior across cultures. *Journal of Organizational Behavior, 28,* 1035–1057. doi:10.1002/job.496

Farkas, S., Johnson, J., & Foleno, T. (2000). *A sense of calling: Who teaches and why.* New York, NY: Public Agenda.

Flynn, F. J., & Chatman, J. A. (2001). Strong cultures and innovation: Oxymoron or opportunity? In C. L. Cooper, S. Cartwright & P. C. Earley (Eds.), *The international handbook of organizational culture and climate* (pp. 263–287). New York, NY: Wiley.

Friedman, I. A. (1991). High and low burnout schools: School culture aspects of teacher burnout. *Journal of Educational Research, 84*(6), 325–333. Retrieved from EBSCO*host.*

Fukayama, F. (1995). *Trust: the social virtues and the creation of prosperity.* New York, NY: Free Press Paperbacks.

Gabbay, S., & Leenders, R. (1999). *Social capital of organizations.* Oxford: Elsevier Science Ltd.

Gibson, C. B., Cooper, C. D., & Conger, J. A. (2009). Do you see what we see? The complex effects of perceptual distance between leaders and teams. *Journal of Applied Psychology, 94*(1), 62–76. doi:10.1037/a0013073

Grant, A. M. (2008). The significance of task significance: Job performance effects, relational mechanisms, and boundary conditions. *Journal of Applied Psychology, 93*(1), 108–124. doi:10.1037/0021-9010.93.1.108

Grant, A. M., & Hofmann, D. A. (2011). Role expansion as a persuasion process: The interpersonal influence dynamics of role redefinition. *Organizational Psychology Review, 1*(9), 9–31. doi:10.1177/2041386610377228

Hallinger, P. & Leithwood, K. (1998). Unseen forces: The impact of social culture on school leadership. In P. Hallinger & K. Leithwood (Eds.). *Peabody Journal of Education* (Vol. *73*(2), pp. 126–151). Mahwah, NJ: Lawrence Erlbaum Associates.

Hargreaves, A. (1994). *Changing teachers, changing times.* New York, NY: Teachers College Press.

Harter, N., Ziolkowski, F. J., & Wyatt, S. (2006). Leadership and inequality. *Leadership, 2*(3), 275–293. doi:10.1177/1742715006066019

Ilies, R., Wagner, D. T., & Morgeson, F. P. (2007). Explaining affective linkages in teams: Individual differences in susceptibility to contagion and individualism-collectivism. *Journal of Applied Psychology, 92*(4), 1140–1148. doi:10.1037/0021-9010.92.4.1140

Jackson, C. L., Wesson, M. J., Colquitt, J. A., & Zapata-Phelan, C. P. (2006). Psychological collectivism: A measurement validation and linkage to group member performance. *Journal of Applied Psychology, 91*(4), 884–899. doi:10.1037/0021-9010.91.4.884

Jephcote, M. (2009). Teachers' learning: Committed and resilient teachers are more effective practitioners. *The International Journal of Learning, 16*(11), 63–72. Retrieved from EBSCO*host*.

Joireman, J., Kamdar, D., Daniels, D., & Duell, B. (2006). Good citizens to the end? It depends: empathy and concern with future consequences moderate the impact of a short-term horizon on organizational citizenship behaviors. *Journal of Applied Psychology, 91*(6), 1307–1320. doi:10.1037/0021-9010.91.6.1307

Kahn, J. H., Schneider, K. T., Jenkins-Henkelman, T. M., & Moyle, L. L. (2006). Emotional social support and job burnout among high-school teachers: Is it all due to dispositional affectivity? *Journal of Organizational Behavior, 27,* 793–807. doi:10.1002/job.397

Kammeyer-Mueller, E. (2007). The dynamics of newcomer adjustment: Dispositions, context, interaction, and fit. In C. Ostroff & T. A. Judge (Eds.), *Perspectives on organizational Fit* (pp. 99–122). New York, NY: Lawrence Erlbaum Associates.

Kark, R., & Van Dijk, D. (2007). Motivation to lead, motivation to follow: The role of the self-regulatory focus in leadership processes. *Academy of Management Review, 32*(2), 500–528. Retrieved from EBSCO*host*.

Kark, R., & Shamir, B. (2000). The dual effect of transformational leadership: Priming relational and collective selves and further effects on followers. In B. J. Avolio & F. J. Yammarino (Eds.), *Transformational and charismatic leadership: The road ahead* (Vol. 2, pp. 67–91). Amsterdam, NL: JAI Press.

Kâğitçibaşi, Ç. (1994). A critical appraisal of individualism and collectivism: Toward a new formulation. In U. Kim, H. C. Triandis, Ç. Kâğitçibaşi, S. Choi & G. Yoon (Eds.), *Individualism and collectivism: Theory, method, and application* (pp. 52–66). Thousand Oaks, CA: Sage Publications.

Kotlyar, I., & Karakowsky, L. (2006). Leading conflict? Linkages between leader behaviors and group conflict. *Small Group Research, 37*(4), 377–403. doi:10.1177/1046496406291388

Kristof-Brown, E., & Jansen, E. (2007). Issues of person-organization fit. In C. Ostroff & T. A. Judge (Eds.), *Perspectives on organizational fit* (pp. 123–155). New York, NY: Lawrence Erlbaum Associates.

Lamm, E., Gordon, J. R., & Purser, R. E. (2010). The role of values congruence in organizational change. *Organizational Development Journal, 28*(2), 49–64. Retrieved from ABI/INFORM Global.

Leithwood, K. A., Begley, P. T., & Cousins, J. B. (1994). The nature, causes and consequences of principals' practices: An agenda for future research. *Journal of Educational Administration, 28,* 4. doi:10.1108/09578239010001014

Leithwood, K. A., & Jantzi, D. (2005). A review of transformational school leadership research 1996–2005. *Leadership and Policy in Schools, 4,* 177–199. doi:10.1080/15700760500244769

Lieberman, A. (1996). Creating intentional learning communities. *Educational Leadership, 54*(3), 51–55. Retrieved from EBSCO*host*.

Lortie, D. C. (1975). *Schoolteacher: A sociological study*. Chicago, IL: University of Chicago Press.

Love, M. S. (2007). Security in an insecure world: An examination of individualism-collectivism and psychological sense of community at work. *Career Development International, 12*(3), 304–320. doi:10.1108/13620430710745917

Malach Pines, A. (2002). Teacher burnout: A psychodynamic existential perspective. *Teachers and Teaching, 8*(2), 121–140. doi:10.1080/1354060022012733

Marks, H. M., & Printy, S. M. (2003). Principal leadership and school performance: An integration of transformational and instructional leadership. *Educational Administration Quarterly, 39*(3), 370–397. doi:10.1177/0013161X03253412

McNeely, B. L., & Meglino, B. M. (1994). The role of dispositional and situational antecedents in prosocial organizational behavior: An examination of the intended beneficiaries of prosocial behavior. *Journal of Applied Psychology, 79*(6), 836–844. doi:10.1037/0021-9010.79.6.836

Moolenaar, N. N., Daly, A. J., & Sleegers, P. J. (2010). Occupying the principal position: Examining relationships between transformational leadership, social network position, and schools' innovative climate. *Educational Administration Quarterly, 46*(5), 623–670. doi:10.1177/0013161X10378689

Moorman, & Blakely. (1995). Individualism-collectivism as an individual predictor of organizational citizenship behavior. *Journal of Organizational Behavior, 16*, 127–142. Retrieved from EBSCO*host*.

Nieto, S. M. (2003). What keeps teachers going? *Educational Leadership, 60*(8), 14–18. Retrieved from EBSCO*host*.

Oplatka, I. (2006). Going beyond expectations: Toward an understanding of the determinants and components of teacher organizational citizenship behavior. *Educational Administration Quarterly, 42*(3), 385–423. doi:10.1177/0013161X05285987

Oplatka, I. (2009). Organizational citizenship behavior in teaching: The consequences for teachers, pupils, and the school. *International Journal of Educational Management, 23*(5), 375–389. doi:10.1108/09513540910970476

Organ, D. W. (1988). *Organizational citizenship behavior: The good soldier syndrome*. Lexington, MA: Lexington Books.

Organ, D. W., Podsakoff, P. M., & MacKenzie, S. B. (2006). *Organizational citizenship behavior: Its nature, antecedents, and consequences*. Thousand Oaks, CA: Sage.

Organ, D. W., Podsakoff, P. M., & Podsakoff, N. P. (2011). Expanding the criterion domain to include organizational citizenship behavior: Implications for employee selection. In S. Zedeck (Ed.), *APA handbook of industrial and organizational psychology* (Vol. 2, pp. 281–323). Washington, DC: American Psychological Association.

Ostroff, & Schulte. (2007). Multiple perspectives of fit in organizations across levels of analysis. In C. Ostroff & T. A. Judge (Eds.), *Perspectives on organizational fit* (pp. 3–70). New York, NY: Lawrence Erlbaum Associates.

O'Reilly, C. A., & Chatman, J. (1986). Organizational commitment and psychological attachment: The effects of compliance, identification, and internalization on prosocial behavior. *Journal of Applied Psychology, 7*(3), 492–499. doi:10.1037/0021-9010.71.3.492

Pawar, B. S., & Eastman, K. K. (1997). The nature and implications of contextual influences on transformational leadership: A conceptual examination. *The Academy of Management Review, 22*(1), 80–109. Retrieved from http://www.jstor.org/stable/259225.

Pines, A., & Kafry, D. (1978). Occupational tedium in the social services. *Social Work*, 499–507. Retrieved from EBSCOhost.

Podsakoff, N. P., Whiting, S. W., Podsakoff, P. M., & Blume, B. D. (2009). Individual- and organizational-level consequences of organizational citizenship behaviors: A meta-analysis. *Journal of Applied Psychology, 94*(1), 122–141. doi:10.1037/a0013079

Posner, B. Z. (2010). Another look at the impact of personal and organizational values congruency. *Journal of Business Ethics, 97*, 535–571. doi:10.1007/s10551-010-0530-1

Purvanova, R. K., Bono, J. E., & Dzieweczynski, J. (2006). Transformational leadership, job characteristics, and organizational citizenship performance. *Human Performance, 19*(1), 1–22. Retrieved from EBSCO*host*.

Ramamoorthy, N., & Flood, P. C. (2004). Individualism/collectivism, perceived task interdependence and teamwork attitudes among Irish blue-collar employees: A test of the main and moderating effects. Human *Relations, 57*(3), 347–366. doi:10.1177/0018726704043274

Ras, N. L. (2003). *Curriculum change at Hilltop School: A case study of intervention and organisational change at an elementary school in Israel.* Unpublished doctoral dissertation. Brighton, UK: The University of Sussex.

Ras, N. L. (2004). On choosing a theoretical lens in educational change research or the road not taken. *Quarterly Journal of Ideology, 26*(3).

Rasmussen, T. H., & Jeppesen, H. J. (2006). Teamwork and associated psychological factors. *Work & Stress, 20*(2), 105–128. doi:10.1080/02678370600920262

Ross, J. A., & Gray, P. (2006). School leadership and student achievement: The mediating effects of teacher beliefs. *Canadian Journal of Education, 29*(3), 798–822. Retrieved from EBSCO*host*.

Schensul, J. J., LeCompte, M. D., Trotter, R. T., Cromley, E. K., & Singer, M. (1999). *Mapping social networks, spatial data, & hidden populations*. Walnut Creek, CA: Alta Mira Press.

Schleicher, D. J., Hansen, S. D., & Fox, K. E. (2011). Job attitudes and work values. In S. Zedeck (Ed.), *APA handbook of industrial and organizational psychology* (Vol. 3, pp. 137–189). Washington, DC: American Psychological Association.

Scott, J. (1991). *Social network analysis: A handbook* (2d ed.). Los Angeles, CA: Sage.

Seashore Louis, K., Febey, K., & Schroeder, R. (2005). State-mandated accountability in high schools: Teachers' interpretations of a new era. *Educational Evaluation and Policy Analysis, 27*(2), 177–204. doi:10.3102/01623737027002177

Sergiovanni, T. J. (1994). *Building community in schools*. San Francisco, CA: Jossey-Bass.

Shamir, B. (1990). Calculations, values, and identities: The sources of collectivistic work motivation. *Human Relations, 4*(4), 313–332. doi:10.1177/001872679004300402

Shamir, B., & Lapidot, Y. (2003). Trust in organizational superiors: Systemic and collective considerations. *Organization Studies, 24*(3), 463–491. doi:10.1177/0170840603024003912

Singelis, T. M., & Brown, W. J. (1995). Culture, self, and collectivist communication: Linking culture to individual behavior. *Human Communication Research, 21*, 354–389. doi:10.1111/j.1468-2958.1995.tb00351.x

Somech, A. (2010). Participative decision-making in schools: A mediating-moderating analytical framework for understanding school and teacher outcomes. *Educational Administration Quarterly, 46*(2), 174–209. doi:10.1177/1094670510361745

Somech, A., & Drach-Zahavy, A. (2000). Understanding extra-role behavior in schools: The relationships between job satisfaction, sense of efficacy, and teachers' extra-role behavior. *Teaching and Teacher Education, 16*, 649–659. doi:10.1016/S0742-051X(00)00012-3

Somech, A., & Ron, Y. (2007). Promoting organizational citizenship behavior in schools: The impact of individual and organizational characteristics. *Educational Administration Quarterly, 43*(1), 38–66. doi:10.1177/0013161X06291254

Somech, A., & Wenderow, M. (2006). The impact of participative and directive leadership on teachers' performance: The intervening effects of job structuring, decision domain, and leader-member exchange. *Educational Administration Quarterly, 42*(5), 746–772. doi:10.1177/0013161X06290648

Sparrow, P. R. (2001). Developing diagnostics for high performance organizational cultures. In C. L. Cooper, S. Cartwright & P. C. Earley (Eds.), *The international handbook of organizational culture and climate* (pp. 85–106). West Sussex, UK: Wiley.

Triandis, A. C. (1995). *Individualism and collectivism*. Boulder, CO: Westview Press.

Tschennen-Moran, M. (2009). Fostering teacher professionalism in schools: The role of leadership orientation and trust. *Educational Administration Quarterly, 45*(2), 217–247. doi:10.1177/0013161X08330501

Vigoda-Gadot, E. (2006). Compulsory citizenship behavior: Theorizing some dark sides of the good soldier syndrome. *Journal for the Theory of Social Behaviour, 36*(1), 77–93. doi:10.1111/j.1468-5914.2006.00297.x

Vigoda-Gadot, E. (2007). Leadership style, organizational politics, and employees' performance: An empirical examination of two competing models. *Personnel Review, 36*(5), 661–683. doi:10.1108/00483480710773981

Vigoda-Gadot, E., Beeri, I., Birman-Shemesh, T., & Somech, A. (2007). Group-level organizational citizenship behavior in the education system: A scale reconstruction and validation. *Educational Administration Quarterly, 43*(4), 462–493. doi:10.1177/0013161X07299435

Wang, G., Oh, I-S., Courtright, S. H., & Colbert, A. E. (2011). Transformational leadership and performance across criteria and levels: A meta-analytical review of 25 years of research. *Group and Organization Management, 36*(2), 223–270. doi:10.1177/1059601111401017

Wanxian, L., & Weiwu, W. (2007). A demographic study on citizenship behavior as in-role orientation. *Personality and Individual Differences, 42*(2), 225–234. doi:10.1016/j.paid.2006.06.014

Welch, F. C., Pitts, R. E., Tenini, K. J., Kuenlen, M. G., & Wood, S. G. (2010). Significant issues in defining and assessing teacher dispositions. *The Teacher Educator, 45*, 179–201. doi:10.1080/08878730.489992

Wheelan, S. A., & Kesselring, J. (2005). Link between faculty group: Development and elementary student performance on standardized tests. *The Journal of Educational Research, 98*(6), 323–330. doi:10.3200/JOER.98.6.323-330

Williams, A., Prestage, S., & Bedward, J. (2001). Individualism to collaboration: The significance of teacher culture to the induction of newly qualified teachers. *Journal of Education for Teaching, 27*(3), 253–267. doi:10.1080/02607470120091588

Williamson, I. O., Burnett, M. F., & Bartol, K. M. (2009). The interactive effect of collectivism and organizational rewards on affective organizational commitment. *Cross Cultural Management: An International Journal, 16*(1), 28–43. doi:10.1108/13527600910930022

Wollan, M. L., Sully de Luque, M. F., & Grünhagen, M. (2009). Motives for helping: Exploring cultural influences on extra-role behavior. *Multinational Business Review, 17*(1), 99–119. Retrieved from ABI/INFORM Global.

CHAPTER 4

PERFORMANCE BEYOND EXPECTATIONS: A CLOSER LOOK AT TEACHERS' TASK PERFORMANCE, DISCRETIONARY PERFORMANCE, AND CAREER ASPIRATIONS

Ibrahim Duyar and Anthony H. Normore

ABSTRACT

The purpose of this study was to examine factors affecting teachers' work performance (i.e., task performance and discretionary performance) and career aspirations (i.e., remaining a teacher, seeking promotion to a principalship, and career change). Applying an inclusive social-cognitive perspective, the study integrated the personal, organizational, and leadership domains to explain teachers' task performance, discretionary performance, and career aspirations. The three domains, represented by the independent variables of self-efficacy, collective efficacy, perceived organizational support, and principal leadership styles, predicted teachers' work performance and career aspirations. Participants included 897 public

Discretionary Behavior and Performance in Educational Organizations: The Missing Link in Educational Leadership and Management
Advances in Educational Administration, Volume 13, 87–116
Copyright © 2012 by Emerald Group Publishing Limited
All rights of reproduction in any form reserved
ISSN: 1479-3660/doi:10.1108/S1479-3660(2012)0000013009

school teachers in a southern state in the United States. The data gathering instrument incorporated several previously validated scales on study constructs. The analyses indicated that teacher self-efficacy, collective efficacy, POS, and principal transformational leadership all significantly predicted the teachers' task performance, discretionary performance, and career aspirations. Study findings suggest directions for future research on factors influencing teachers' work performance and career aspirations.

Keywords: Task and discretionary performance; self-efficacy; collective efficacy; perceived organizational support; career aspirations

INTRODUCTION

Teachers are undoubtedly the most crucial component of any educational system because they design and directly deliver instruction to future generations. The extant literature links teaching to educational outcomes, particularly student learning and achievement (e.g., Darling Hammond, 2004; Goldhaber & Anthony, 2004; Heck, 2009; Rivkin, Hanushek, & Kain, 2005; Seidel & Shavelson, 2007). Because of the acknowledged importance of teachers, educational systems strive to hire capable and high-quality new teachers and to improve the skills and qualifications of existing teachers to increase effectiveness of their schools (Goldhaber, 2002). In the United States, national, regional, and local efforts to increase teacher quality and capacity abound. However, as Arcaro (1995) has noted, these efforts do not address the educational system as a whole, whereas educational professionals can make the needed improvements only by improving the entire educational system.

Many well-intentioned school improvement efforts fail not because of a lack of will or commitment but because they focus only on certain aspects of the personal, organizational, or leadership domains (Kurt, Duyar, & Calik, 2011). In reality, teachers' work performance is the product of complex interactions among these domains of organizational behavior (Murphy, 1989). The literature on teacher performance also suffers from studies that concentrate only on a particular domain or certain features of a domain and provide only limited guidance to educational policy and practice as a result. To determine how teachers' work performance is related to their career aspirations, more comprehensive studies are needed.

By adopting an inclusive and integrative social-cognitive perspective, this study examined the relation of teachers' work performance to their career aspirations by including measures of organizational behavior that represented the personal domain (self-efficacy), the organizational domain (perceived organizational support (POS) and collective efficacy), and the leadership domain (transformational leadership). The following section reviews the theoretical foundations of the constructs that were included in the study's conceptual framework.

THEORETICAL FOUNDATIONS

Kozlowski and Klein (2000) recommended that researchers developing a conceptual framework start by identifying their dependent (endogenous or criterion) constructs of interest because dependent variables drive the identification of the necessary levels, constructs, and processes within a theory. The current study first identified the dependent variables: two measures of work performance (task performance and discretionary performance) and three measures of teachers' career aspirations (remaining a teacher, promotion to a principalship, or career change). The rest of this section describes the independent variables that are proposed to influence teacher work performance and career aspirations: teacher self-efficacy, collective efficacy, POS, and transformational leadership by principals.

Teachers' Work Performance

Work performance is a key dependent variable that interests educators, businesses, government, and society at large. Researchers, policymakers, and practitioners have attempted to achieve a consensus regarding how to define and conceptualize work performance in organizations at the individual level. Work performance has been defined as employee actions and behaviors that contribute to the goals of the organization (Rotundo & Sackett, 2002). Motowidlo (2003) defined work performance as "the total expected value of discrete behavioral episodes to an organization that an employee carries out over a standard period of time" (p. 39). As a megaconstruct, employee work performance consists of two related but distinct components: *Task performance* includes both employees' direct and indirect support of the organization's core activities, while *contextual performance* consists of employee behaviors that support the organization's broader social and psychological environment (Hoffman, Blair, Meriac, & Woehr, 2007). Van Dyne, Cummings, and Parks (1995) presented a similar distinction between *in-role performance* versus *extra-role performance*. Teachers' task performance can be defined as the performance of the core duties and responsibilities associated with teaching (Chang, Johnson, & Yang, 2007).

Teachers' Task Performance

Teachers' task performance and overall educational productivity are currently hotly debated issues, with increasing demands for accountability in public education in the United States over the past 30 years. Hoxby (2004) has claimed that the productivity of American public schools fell by approximately 50% from 1970 to 2000. American students' scores have continued to be worse than their peers in other developed countries. The American public has noticed this steady decline in the public education and has demanded accountability (Duyar, 2006). Teacher quality and performance are considered to be measures that are directly related to student learning and, thus, the overall productivity of the educational system. The National Council for Accreditation of Teacher Education (NCATE), a consortium of professional organizations, plays a major role in the identification of teachers' responsibilities and task performance in the United States. The professional organizations that make up the NCATE have developed *program standards* for teaching different subjects (e.g., language arts, social studies, and math). The NCATE program standards serve as benchmarks and guide state education agencies in the development of state standards for licensing and assessment of teacher performance. The NCATE and state standards for different programs identify program-specific content knowledge, curriculum, curriculum delivery, and learning assessments. In addition to specific program content, program standards also identify the knowledge, skills, and dispositions with regard to several common elements such as diversity, utilization of technology, and communication skills.

The Council of Chief State School Officers (2011) has recently developed the *Model Core Teaching Standards: A Resource for State Dialogue*, which outline the knowledge, performance, and dispositions that teachers are expected to use to provide effective teaching and learning. These standards update those of the 1992 Interstate New Teacher Assessment and Support Consortium (INTASC), formerly known as the *Model Standards for*

Licensing Beginning Teachers: A Resource for State Dialogue. While the 1992 INTASC standards were designed for "new" teachers, the 2011 Model Core Teaching Standards are intended as professional practice standards that provide a single standard for performance, which takes into account the different developmental stages of the teacher's career. The updated model core standards are grouped into four general categories: The Learner and Learning, Content, Instructional Practice, and Professional Responsibility. These four categories include 10 core teaching standards. It is worth noting that, while maintaining the distinction between knowledge, disposition, and performance, the 2011 Model Core Teaching Standards reframed the relationships among the three concepts to rank the *performance* dimension first (Council of Chief State School Officers, 2010). The current 10 core teaching standards include a total of 84 teacher performance items.

The current study used selected 2011 Model Core Teaching Standards to assess teachers' task performance for a number of reasons. First, the schools included in the study were located in a state that had adopted the Model Core Teaching Standards. In addition, using the Model Core Teaching Standards would also be expected to produce more generalizable results because 38 states have adopted these standards (Council of Chief State School Officers, 2010). Finally, and most importantly, use of the Model Core Teaching Standards provides a methodological advantage because these "common core" standards are comparable across different school settings (i.e., elementary, middle school, high school, or K-8) and subject areas (i.e., social sciences, math, or language arts). This feature of the Model Core Teaching Standards provides educational researchers and policymakers with a *parsimonious* instrument for assessing teachers' task performance.

Teachers' Discretionary Performance

Organizations and researchers have traditionally focused on employees' task performance. However, a number of studies (e.g., Bass, 1985; Borman & Motowidlo, 1993; Organ, Podsakoff, & MacKenzie, 2006) have found that employees also engage in additional activities that are relevant to organizational goals. In his seminal work, Bass (1985) stated that to be competitive, modern organizations need employees who operate "beyond the expectations" of their job descriptions. These employees approach work proactively and willingly adopt additional roles and functions that do not fit narrow, predefined task duties and activities. This strategic aspect of organizational behavior has been variously described in the literature as *discretionary behavior* (Katz & Kahn, 1966), *extra-role behavior* (Van Dyne et al., 1995), *pro-social behavior* (Brief & Motowidlo, 1986), *organizational citizenship behavior* or the *good soldier syndrome* (Organ, 1997), *active performance* (Frese & Fay, 2001), and *contextual performance* (Borman & Motowidlo, 1993).

To some extent, all these different conceptions share the view that discretionary performance is "individual behavior, that is discretionary, not directly or explicitly recognized by the formal reward system, and that in the aggregate promotes the effective functioning of the organization" (Organ, 1988, p. 27). Due to the introduction of this concept, researchers now view employees' work performance as a multidimensional construct that consists of both *task performance* and *discretionary performance*. The current view has validated the *contextual performance* proposed by Borman and Motowidlo (1993), which Organ endorsed within the context of *organizational citizenship behaviors*. Adopting Organ's definition, the current study treated teachers' discretionary behaviors as part of their *work performance* and operationally defined it as *discretionary performance*.

A number of studies have documented that discretionary work behaviors contribute to individual task performance and overall organizational performance in business environments (e.g., Koys, 2001; Podsakoff, Whiting, Podsakoff, & Blume, 2009; Vey & Campbell, 2004). Conway's (1999) meta-analysis of the relationship between discretionary performance and task performance found that the two constructs were empirically related yet distinct. Hoffman et al. (2007) confirmed these findings in their meta-analysis and argued that although discretionary performance and task performance were highly correlated ($p = .74$), they were best viewed as separate constructs.

A comprehensive review of the educational literature has revealed few studies of discretionary performance in educational organizations, particularly with regard to K-12 education. Somech and Drach-Zahavy (2000) investigated the antecedents of teachers' discretionary performance and found that job satisfaction, self-efficacy, and collective efficacy predicted teachers' extra-role behaviors. Belogovsky and Somech (2010) studied teachers' task performance and discretionary performance (referred to as organizational citizenship behavior, OCB) from the perspectives of principals, teachers, and parents and found that the three groups differed in their assessment of teachers' targeted performance toward students, teams, or schools. Somech and Ron (2007) also examined the relative impacts of individual and organizational characteristics on the OCBs of teachers and found that collectivism (an organizational variable) was the most influential predictor of teachers' OCB. Because these studies, while informative, were conducted in other countries, the present study extended this research by examining teachers' discretionary performance in the United States.

Teachers' Career Aspirations

The low levels of job satisfaction and low retention rates among teachers in all K-12 grades continue to confound schools across the country (Hanusek, Kain, & Rivkin, 2004; Rentz, 2007; Stutz, 2004). Replacing public school teachers is financially and academically costly because personnel usually account for 75% of educational expenditures. In 2003, a conservative estimate of the funds spent annually nationwide to replace teachers who dropped out of the profession or transferred schools was $4.9 billion (Alliance for Excellent Education, 2005). In addition, high rates of teacher attrition have been found to negatively affect teacher quality and student achievement (Henke, Chen, & Geis, 2000). Rentz (2007), who found a significant relationship between teacher retention and student achievement levels in reading and math, concluded that schools with more stable teaching staffs had better school achievement outcomes. Each year, more than a million students do not graduate with their peers, and many students graduate without the skills needed for college or work. According to the Alliance for Excellence in Education (2005), teacher quality is critical to stem the tide of the 7,000 high school students who drop out of school every day.

Ingersoll (2003) uses the "revolving door" analogy to describe the low retention of teachers and argues that the main problem is not the shortage of teachers but the short time teachers spend in the classroom before they are replaced by other new teachers. From this perspective, teachers do not stay long enough to develop adequate skills but instead cycle in and out of certain campuses to escape poor working conditions. Teacher preparation programs appear to keep up with demand by graduating 150,000 new teachers annually, and thus, there is an adequate supply of teachers overall (National Commission on Teaching and America's Future, 2003). However, many teachers transfer to other schools, take early retirement, or exit the profession altogether due to frustration with school organizational problems and unsuccessful communication with parents (Johnson, 2004).

Most previous teacher retention studies have focused on the characteristics of individual teachers (rather than school organizations) that often cause high rates of teacher attrition (Ingersoll, 2003; Rentz, 2007). For instance, Belogovsky and Somech (2010) found significant relationships between teachers' different career stages and their OCBs. However, few studies have investigated how teacher characteristics interact with organizational attributes to shape teacher retention or attrition. The current study fills this gap by examining the influence of personal, organizational, and leadership domains on teachers' career aspirations.

Teachers' Self-Efficacy and Collective Efficacy

Teachers possess not only the skills to influence student learning outcomes but also the belief that every child can and will learn. A persuasive body of research has linked teachers' *efficacy beliefs* with student achievement (Buddin & Zamarro, 2009; Goddard, 2002; Hoy, Tarter, & Hoy, 2006; Kane, Rockoff, & Staiger, 2008; Rivkin et al., 2005; Rockoff, 2004). Tschannen-Moran and Hoy (2001) defined a teacher's self-efficacy as the belief that teachers can help even unmotivated students achieve desired outcomes. Teachers with a strong sense of self-efficacy have been found to be more willing to take risks, such as employing new strategies, to be less critical of student behavioral issues, and to work harder with academically struggling students. Students of teachers with high self-efficacy have been found to exhibit higher achievement, motivation, participation, and self-efficacy (Rentz, 2007).

Teachers' collective efficacy within schools, an extension of teacher self-efficacy, also has an impact on student achievement (Bandura, 1997; Goddard, Hoy, & Hoy, 2000). Although they share conceptual roots, collective efficacy and self-efficacy are different constructs. While self-efficacy is the personal belief in the ability to perform a particular task, collective efficacy is a property of the organization (Bandura, 2000). Collective teacher efficacy emerges from teachers' personal efficacy and the organizational environment (Bandura, 1995). Bandura (1997) defined *collective efficacy* as "a group's shared belief in its conjoint capabilities to organize and execute the courses of action required for producing given levels of attainment" (p. 477). In the school environment, collective efficacy is the perception that the faculty as a whole can engage in actions that positively affect student achievement (Goddard et al., 2000).

The relationship of efficacy, effort, and performance is well documented in the behavioral and organizational sciences (Walumbwa, Wang, Lawyer, & Shi, 2004). According to Bandura (2000), efficacy beliefs play an important role in both individual and group motivation because people must often rely on others to accomplish tasks. Bandura (1997) pointed out that self-efficacy plays a significant role in both task performance and discretionary performance. Similarly, Walumbwa et al. (2004) documented significant relationships between collective efficacy and employees' task performance and discretionary performance. Somech and Ron (2007) confirmed that organizational "collectivism" was the most effective predictor of OCB in educational organizations. While earlier studies have identified significant relationships between teachers' self-efficacy or collective efficacy and work performance, there is a need for a study that examines these relationships from a comprehensive perspective that integrates the personal, organizational, and leadership domains.

Transformational Leadership

Public schools' ability to meet the diverse needs of their students rests on the ability and willingness of educational leaders to design and manage systems that produce efficient, adequate, and equitable educational outcomes. The transformational leadership style has evoked great interest in educational and policymaking literature. Burns (2010), the foremost figure in the area of transformational leadership, has argued that exceptional leaders do not base their influence on the exchange relationships that influence the strategies of transactional leaders. Instead, they appeal to organization members' personal goals and values to elevate and transform them into common goals and interests (Duyar, Aydin, & Pehlivan, 2009). In that sense, the transformational approach to leadership emphasizes shared emotions and values to promote the development of the individual's skills and personal commitment to organizational goals (Leithwood & Jantzi, 2005). Bass (1999), a contemporary of Burns, defined *transformational leadership* as "moving the follower beyond self-interests through idealized influence (charisma), inspiration, intellectual stimulation, or individualized consideration" (p. 11). This definition identifies how transformational leaders promote self-efficacy and collective efficacy to enhance organizational performance.

Through visionary, inspirational messages, and confidence in self and others, a transformational leader can enhance efficacy beliefs at both the individual and the group level (Bass, 1999). This type of leader adopts an engaging speaking style, makes direct eye contact, is animated and expressive, and is assertive, confident, and dynamic during interactions. Transformational leaders also enhance others' efficacy beliefs by providing emotional and intellectual reasons that convince others to identify with the organization (Kark & Shamir, 2002). For example, transformational leaders enable organization members to recognize their capabilities through individualized consideration, which then motivates them to *perform beyond expectations*. Kark and Shamir (2002) have further argued that transformational leaders have a dual effect on organization members by influencing them to personally identify with the leader and to socially identify with their work group.

Similarly, the intellectual stimulation provided by a transformational leader can help organization members identify and confront obstacles to develop a better understanding of what needs to be done to be successful. Understanding how to approach problems and challenges would increase their confidence that they can perform exceptionally, resulting in job satisfaction and commitment to the organization (Bass & Avolio, 1994). Transactional leadership, on the other hand, focuses on the task rather than the individual who performs the task. This approach, which separates the task from the employee, reduces employee self-efficacy. Dvir, Eden, Avolio, and Shamir (2002) described transformational leadership as "influencing followers by broadening and elevating followers' goals and providing them with confidence to perform beyond the expectations specified in the implicit or explicit exchange agreement" (p. 735).

Most studies on transformational leadership focus on its relationship to a particular domain or construct. Few studies have examined how transformational leadership practices of principals influence teachers' task and discretionary performance. In addition to assessing the influence of the personal and organizational domains (through self-efficacy, collective efficacy, and POS), the current study also examined the effects of transformational leadership domain on teachers' work performance and career aspirations.

Perceived Organizational Support

Blau (1964) viewed work as a form of social exchange consisting of a series of transactions that consequently obligated both parties involved in the interaction. Employees trade work effort and loyalty for material and social rewards. In this view, employees consider the extent to which the organization values their contributions and well-being when they decide to commit to their organizations. Eisenberger, Huntington, Hutchison, and Sowa (1986) also regarded perceived organizational commitment as a predictor of employees' commitment and effort to their organizations. The authors termed this phenomenon "*perceived organizational support*" and defined it as the "global beliefs about the extent to which the organization cares about their well-being and values their contributions" (p. 501).

Organizational support theory assumes that the obligation that employees feel toward the organization will help it reach its objectives (Rhoades & Eisenberger, 2002). Committed employees help coworkers perform their jobs more effectively, which aids not only fellow employees but also the organization by leading to greater productivity (Bell & Menguc, 2002; Rhoades & Eisenberger, 2002). Wayne, Shore, and Liden (1997) found a positive relationship between POS and extra-role behavior for both managerial and lower level employees. Managers with high POS were more likely to help employees to orient new employees to their jobs and to assist coworkers with their duties, providing preliminary evidence that both managerial and lower level employees respond to POS with task and discretionary performance that benefit the organization.

POS "may be used by employees as an indicator of the organization's benevolent or malevolent intent in the expression of exchange of employee effort for reward and recognition" (Lynch, Eisenberger, & Armeli, 1999, pp. 469–470). POS has a positive impact on several job-related perceptions and outcomes. Employees with high levels of POS missed work less often and were more conscientious in performing their responsibilities (Eisenberger et al., 1986). POS also had positive associations with organizational commitment and OCBs. A meta-analysis by Rhoades and Eisenberger (2002) revealed that POS was modestly related to job performance, leading the authors to argue that high POS creates an obligation to repay the organization for its attention to the individual's socio-emotional needs, which leads to increased effort and greater performance. Studies have also shown that POS is negatively related to the intention to leave and positively related to the intention to remain in the organization (Allen, Shore, & Griffeth, 2003; Wayne et al., 1997). Although the effects of POS have been documented for industrial and business organizations, few studies have examined the role of POS in education. The present study will fill this gap by investigating the relation of POS to teachers' work performance and career aspirations.

The current study attempted to answer the following research questions:

1. Do successive models including teachers' self-efficacy, collective efficacy, and POS add to the prediction of their task performance and discretionary performance?
2. What overall structure and relationship patterns best characterizes the relationships between teacher career aspirations (remaining a teacher, promotion to a principalship, and career change) and the variables of teacher task and discretionary performance, teacher self-efficacy, collective efficacy, principal transformational leadership, and POS?

CONCEPTUAL MODEL

The conceptual model integrated several established theoretical approaches. Teachers' self-efficacy represented the *personal* domain of organizational behavior within the context of social-cognitive theory. *Social psychology* focuses on personal characteristics such as self-efficacy to explain behavior in organizations. *Industrial psychology* treats collective efficacy as a construct that comes to existence during the interaction of the *personal* and *organizational* domains. *Social exchange* and *institutional support* theories view POS as one of the main *organizational* constructs affecting employees' task performance and discretionary performance; these approaches also consider transformational leadership to be an *organizational* construct.

In applying *social-cognitive theory* (Bandura, 2000) and *systems theory*, this study incorporated a number of diverse approaches rather than limiting the focus to a particular domain. The resulting conceptual model hypothesized that employees' work performance was the product of reciprocal relations among the personal domain (self-efficacy), the organizational domain (collective efficacy and POS), and the leadership

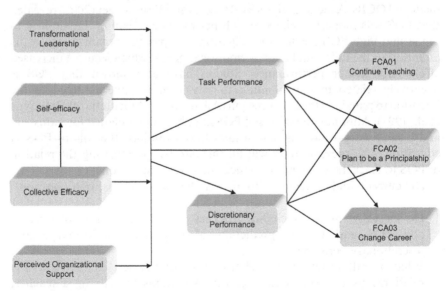

Fig. 1. Conceptual Framework: Work Performance and Future Career Aspirations of Teachers. *Note*: The arrows do not show causal relationship; rather they indicate the direction of association stated in the literature.

domain (transformational leadership). The inclusive nature of study's conceptual framework made it possible to explore how complex organizational behaviors such as teachers' task or discretionary performance were related to their career aspirations. The study focus on integrated aspects of individual and organizational domains that had previously been studied separately to provide a more comprehensive approach to the complexity and interconnectedness of educational processes.

Fig. 1 presents the conceptual framework and the hypothesized relationships among study constructs and variables.

METHODS

The study adopted a causal-comparative design to gather and analyze the survey responses of public school teachers in the southern United States. Random cluster sampling procedures were used, with geographical location and grade level configuration serving as the two sampling criteria. Anderson's (1990) *theoretical sample size table* was used to identify a sample size of 1,600 teachers with a 95% confidence interval. A total of 1,241 surveys were received from participants. Data from the 897 surveys meeting the inclusion criterion were analyzed, resulting in a response rate of 72%. The inclusion criterion for questionnaires was the completion of all items except for items that provided demographic information for participants and their schools. Questionnaires with other missing items were excluded from the analyses.

Instrumentation

Participants responded to an online survey that incorporated several previously developed and validated instruments. The survey was organized into three sections. The first section provided demographic information for participants and their schools. Demographic data for participants and their schools were included as control variables because Farmer, Maslyn, Fedor, and Goodman (1997) have suggested that individual characteristics and contextual factors might shape individual preferences. Personal demographic information included gender, age, educational background, and years of teaching experience. School demographic information included school size, school grade configuration, and the percentage of students qualifying for a free/reduced price lunch.

Items in the second section of the survey measured the independent variables of self-efficacy, collective efficacy, POS, and transformational leadership. The *Teacher Sense of Efficacy Scale Short Form* (2001) measured teachers' self-efficacy; it included items such as "I can always manage to solve difficult problems if I try hard enough." The short version of the *Collective Efficacy Scale* (CE-SCALE; Goddard et al., 2000) measured teachers' collective efficacy; it included items such as "Teachers in my school can produce meaningful student learning." This section also included a revised version of the *Perceived Organizational Support Scale* (Rhoades & Eisenberger, 2002). The eight items of this scale measured the organizational support that teachers felt they received from their schools. It included items such as "My work organization values my contribution to its well-being." Finally, this section included the short version of *The Multifactor Leadership Questionnaire* (MLQ; Bass & Avolio, 1994), which included items such as "My principal stresses the importance of having a strong sense of purpose." Participants indicated the extent to which each statement applied to them or their work environment on a four-point Likert scale ranging from 1 (*never*) to 4 (*almost always*).

Items in the last section of the survey measured the dependent variables of the study: task performance, discretionary performance, and the three career aspirations of teachers. Items from the *Model Core Teaching Standards: A Resource for State Dialogue* (CCSSO, 2011) were used to measure teachers' task performance. A total of 19 representative performance items were chosen by a panel of experts (three university professors and two teachers). The section also included Tschannen-Moran's *School Organizational Citizenship Behavior Scale*. Scale items measured the discretionary performance of teachers and included items such as "Take action that protects the school from risk" and "Spread goodwill and positivity." Participants indicated their level of performance on a four-point Likert scale ranging from 1 (*never*) to 4 (*almost always*). Finally, the section included three items designed to measure the extent to which teachers intended to continue to teach, seek promotion to the principalship, and leave teaching.

Data Analysis

Before performing the statistical analyses, data were screened to determine whether assumptions of normality, homogeneity of variance–covariance matrices, and linearity were met. Although some assumptions were violated, additional tests (e.g., *Wilks' Lambda* for linearity, *Box's test* for equality of covariance matrices, and *Levene's test* for homogeneity of variance) indicated that the violations were not severe. The violations were primarily due to the skewness of the data and hierarchical regression analysis is robust to mild violations of these assumptions.

The mean age of the teachers was 34 years (SD = 1.161); 85% were female (SD = .369). The mean length of teaching experience was 14 years (SD = 1.656); 28% of the teachers had 21 or more years of teaching experience, while 36% had less than 10 years experience. With regard to educational background, 47% of the teachers had a bachelor's degree, 49% had a master's degree, and 3.6% had a doctoral degree. With regard to school grade configuration, 40% of participants taught in elementary schools, 39% taught in middle schools, and 8.6% taught in high schools. The majority of participants (79%) taught in schools with more than 500 but fewer than 1,500 students. In approximately half the schools, 31–45% of the students qualified for a free/reduced lunch, whereas in more than a third of the schools, more than 60% of the students qualified for a free/reduced lunch.

The mean scores for teachers' self-efficacy, collective efficacy, POS, and transformational leadership were 3.5, 3.2, 2.9, and 2.7, respectively. While the mean self-efficacy and collective efficacy scores were high, the mean scores for POS and transformational leadership were considerably lower. Teachers' mean scores for the dependent variables of task performance, discretionary performance, remaining a teacher, seeking promotion to a principalship, and changing career were 3.4, 3.3, 3.6, 1.4, and 1.5, respectively. The mean scores for seeking promotion to a principalship and career change were low. The standard deviations for all the independent and dependent variables were less than 1.0, indicating consistency in scoring.

The alpha coefficients of reliability for the independent variables of self-efficacy, collective efficacy, POS, and transformational leadership were .88, .93, .96, and .96, respectively. The alpha coefficients of reliability for the dependent variables of task performance and discretionary performance were .93 and .87. No reliability coefficients were calculated for the three career aspirations because each was only measured by a single item. The high reliability coefficients for the study variables indicated that both scales and scale items had a high level of internal consistency and each study construct formed a reliable scale.

FINDINGS

The findings of the study were organized to parallel the two research questions.

Research Question 1: Do successive models including teachers' self-efficacy, collective efficacy, and POS add to the prediction of their task performance and discretionary performance?

Two separate hierarchical multiple regression analyses were performed to test the predictive value of the independent variables of self-efficacy, collective efficacy, POS, and transformational leadership for task performance and discretionary performance of teachers. The use of hierarchical regression analysis permitted control over the order in which the predictor variables were entered into the analysis. The regression analysis for task performance included discretionary performance as a predictor variable, and the regression analysis for discretionary performance included task performance as a predictor variable due to the theoretical relationship identified by previous research. Participant and school demographics were also separately entered into the analyses as control variables. Tests of assumptions were performed for both items and the summed (index) variables representing the study constructs (i.e., self-efficacy, collective efficacy, and so on). Variable items with high correlations were eliminated to avoid multicollinearity. Similarly, the variable items with low tolerance $(<1-R^2)$ values were eliminated. Wilks' Lambda and Levene's tests were used to determine whether the summed variables violated assumptions.

The hierarchical multiple regression analysis for teacher task performance produced seven competing models. As Table 1 demonstrates, all the models were significant, indicating that the combination of variables entered into each model significantly contributed to teachers' task performance. However, only Models 1–3 were significant at the .001 level, and only these models produced a meaningful change in R^2. All coefficients were significant only for the first four models. Model 1 included only discretionary performance as the predictor of teacher task performance, $F(1,883) = 570$, $p = .001$, and this variable accounted for 39% of the variance in the teacher task performance $(R^2 = .39)$. Model 2 included both discretionary performance and teachers' self-efficacy, $F(1,882) = 370$, $p = .001$; the adjusted R^2 for this model was .453, and the inclusion of teachers' self-efficacy accounted for an additional 6.2% of the variance in task performance. Model 3 included discretionary performance, teachers' self-efficacy, and collective efficacy, $F(1,881) = 310$, $p = .001$; the adjusted R^2 for this model was .529, and the inclusion of collective efficacy accounted for an additional 5.9% of the variance in teachers' task performance. Although Models 1 and 2 were also significant at the .001 level, Model 3 was the optimal model. Models 4, 5, 6, and 7 produced only marginal changes in R^2, with values of .003, .003, .008, and .008, respectively.

Table 1. Hierarchical Regression Model Summary for Teacher Task Performance.

Model	R	R^2	Adjusted R^2	Std. Error of the Estimate	F	df1	df2	Sig. F Change
1	.626[a]	.392	.391	.32466	569.518	1	883	.000
2	.633[b]	.454	.453	.30782	366.893	1	882	.000
3	.636[c]	.513	.512	.29086	309.600	1	881	.000
4	.649[d]	.516	.514	.29009	234.832	1	880	.018
5	.653[e]	.520	.517	.28923	190.250	1	879	.012
6	.658[f]	.528	.523	.28745	108.669	4	875	.005
7	.661[g]	.536	.529	.28555	83.803	3	872	.002

[a]Predictors: (Constant), DISCAVERAGE.
[b]Predictors: (Constant), DISCAVERAGE, SEAVERAGE.
[c]Predictors: (Constant), DISCAVERAGE, SEAVERAGE, COEAVERAGE.
[d]Predictors: (Constant), DISCAVERAGE, SEAVERAGE, COEAVERAGE, TLAVERAGE.
[e]Predictors: (Constant), DISCAVERAGE, SEAVERAGE, COEAVERAGE, TLAVERAGE, POSAVERAGE.
[f]Predictors: (Constant), DISCAVERAGE, SEAVERAGE, COEAVERAGE, TLAVERAGE, POSAVERAGE, Educational background, Gender, Age, Teaching Experience.
[g]Predictors: (Constant), DISCAVERAGE, SEAVERAGE, COEAVERAGE, TLAVERAGE, POSAVERAGE, Educational background, Gender, Age, Teaching Experience, Enrolment, Free/Reduced lunch percentage, School configuration.

Because the model that included all the independent variables and demographic variables (Model 7) was significant, a simultaneous multiple regression analysis was also performed. Table 2 presents the results of the simultaneous regression analysis for teachers' task performance, which included participant and school demographic characteristics as well as study independent variables as independent variables in the regression equation. In combination, all of these factors significantly predicted teacher task performance ($F(12,872) = 83.803$, $p = .001$). The adjusted R^2 value was .53, indicating that the model explained 53% of the variance in teachers' task performance, a large effect (Cohen, 1988). As Table 2 shows, four independent variables and three demographic variables made significant contributions to the model. The beta weights indicate that discretionary performance was the strongest predictor of teacher task performance ($\beta = .45$), a medium-to-large effect size. In addition to discretionary performance, collective efficacy ($\beta = .31$) and teachers' self-efficacy ($\beta = .22$) also appreciably predicted teachers' task performance. While POS, gender, school configuration, and the percentage of students qualifying for a free/reduced lunch were also significant, their contributions were marginal.

Table 2. Simultaneous Multiple Regression Analysis Summary for
Teacher Task Performance.

Variables	B	SEB	β	p
Discretionary performance	.4.09	.024	.453	.000
Self-efficacy	−.247	.029	.223	.000
Perceived organizational support	−.053	.020	−.096	.009
Collective efficacy	−.264	.028	.311	.000
Transformational leadership	−.005	.025	−.008	.837
Age	−.012	.010	−.033	.239
Gender	−.064	.027	−.057	.018
Teaching experience	.003	.007	.012	.661
Educational background	−.008	.016	−.011	.637
School configuration	−.034	.013	−.074	.008
Enrolment	.004	.009	.011	.671
Free/Reduced lunch percentage	.014	.007	.049	.045

The hierarchical multiple regression analysis of teachers' discretionary performance also produced seven different models. The ANOVAs for all seven models were significant. Significant ANOVAs indicated that combination of variables in each model significantly ($p = .001$) predicted the discretionary performance of teachers. Further review revealed that Models 1–6 produced significant changes in F at the .005 level (see Table 3). Model 1 included only the variable of teachers' task performance; it was significant, $F(1,883) = 570$, $p = .001$, and this variable accounted for 39% of the variance in teacher discretionary performance. However, while Models 2–6 significantly predicted teacher discretionary performance, they did not produce meaningful changes in R^2. Model 6, which included the independent variables and personal demographic characteristics as factors, accounted for only an additional 3.8% of the variance in teachers' discretionary performance.

To better examine the contribution made by each variable, Table 4 presents the results of the simultaneous regression analysis for teacher discretionary performance. The combination of study variables and demographic characteristics significantly predicted teacher discretionary performance, $F(12,872) = 56.383$, $p = .001$. The model accounted for 43% of the variance in teachers' discretionary performance ($R^2 = .429$), a medium-to-large effect (Cohen, 1988). As Table 4 shows, four independent variables and two demographic factors significantly contributed to the prediction of teachers' discretionary performance. The beta weights indicate that task

Table 3. Hierarchical Regression Model Summary for Teacher Discretionary Performance.

Model	R	R^2	Adjusted R^2	Std. Error of the Estimate	F	df1	df2	Sig. F Change
1	.626[a]	.392	.391	.35978	569.518	1	883	.000
2	.633[b]	.401	.400	.35735	295.164	1	882	.000
3	.636[c]	.405	.403	.35632	199.943	1	881	.014
4	.649[d]	.421	.418	.35174	159.921	1	880	.000
5	.653[e]	.427	.424	.35009	131.006	1	879	.002
6	.658[f]	.433	.427	.34895	74.341	4	875	.046
7	.661[g]	.437	.429	.34844	56.383	3	872	.136

[a]Predictors: (Constant), TASKPER.
[b]Predictors: (Constant), TASKPER, SE.
[c]Predictors: (Constant), TASKPER, SE, COE.
[d]Predictors: (Constant), TASKPER SE, COE, TL.
[e]Predictors: (Constant), TASKPER, SE, COE, TL, POS.
[f]Predictors: (Constant), TASKPER, SE, COE, TL, POS, Educational background, Gender, Age, Teaching Experience.
[g]Predictors: (Constant), TASKPER, SE, COE, TL, POS, Educational background, Gender, Age, Teaching Experience, Enrolment, Free/Reduced lunch percentage, School configuration.

Table 4. Simultaneous Regression Analysis for Teacher Discretionary Performance.

Variables	B	SEB	β	p
Task performance	.609	.036	.549	.000
Self-efficacy	.089	.036	.072	.015
Perceived organizational support	.074	.025	.122	.003
Collective efficacy	−.021	.036	−.022	.562
Transformational leadership	.061	.031	.082	.046
Age	.011	.012	.028	.362
Gender	.070	.033	.056	.034
Teaching experience	.000	.009	−.002	.953
Educational background	.023	.020	.030	.242
School configuration	.020	.016	.039	.205
Enrolment	.003	.011	.007	.799
Free/Reduced lunch percentage	.018	.009	.058	.034

performance was the strongest predictor of teachers' task performance ($\beta = .55$), a medium-to-large effect size. POS ($\beta = .12$), transformational leadership ($\beta = .08$), and teacher self-efficacy ($\beta = .07$) also significantly contributed at the .05 level, although the effects were modest in size. Gender

($\beta = .06$) and the percentage of students qualifying for a free/reduced lunch ($\beta = .06$) were the only two significant demographic factors, but their contributions were also modest.

Research Question 2: What overall structure and relationship patterns best characterize the relationships between teacher career aspirations (remaining a teacher, promotion to a principalship, and career change) and the variables of teacher task and discretionary performance, teacher self-efficacy, collective efficacy, principal transformational leadership, and POS?

To answer the second research question, a standard linear canonical correlation analysis was performed. This type of analysis was appropriate since the dependent variable (teachers' career aspirations) was not a single variable but included three variables, the extent to which an individual intended to (a) remain a teacher, (b) seek promotion to a principalship, and (c) change careers. A canonical correlation analysis is appropriate when analyzing the relationship between two sets of variables. The first set included the independent variables of task performance, discretionary performance, self-efficacy, collective efficacy, transformational leadership, and POS. The second set included the dependent variables of remaining a teacher, seeking promotion to a principalship, and changing careers.

The correlations and canonical coefficients are presented in Table 5. The analysis produced three canonical correlations. The first canonical

Table 5. Correlation and Standardized Canonical Coefficients between Teacher Future Career Aspirations and Predicting Variables.

Set Variables	First Canonical Correlation		Second Canonical Correlation	
	Loading	Coefficient	Loading	Coefficient
Predicting variables				
Self-efficacy	−.624	**−.263**	−.138	−.065
Perceived organizational support	−.755	−.242	**.448**	**.410**
Collective efficacy	−.773	.239	−.334	.296
Transformational leadership	−.737	−.196	**.431**	.278
Task performance	−.693	−.089	−.233	.036
Discretionary performance	−.750	**−.350**	**−.616**	**−.970**
Career aspirations				
Staying in teaching	**−.992**	**.−993**	.111	−.071
Promotion to principalship	−.134	−.125	**−.853**	**−.753**
Changing career	.310	−.005	**−.664**	**−.551**

Note: Redundant canonical covariates are in bold fonts.

correlation was .499 (25% overlapping variance); the second was .205 (4% overlapping variance); and the third was .090 (1% overlapping variance). The first two canonical correlations were significant; the third canonical correlation was not significant. With all three canonical correlations included, $\chi^2(18) = 299.96$, $p < .001$; with the first canonical correlation removed, $\chi^2(10) = 45.48$, $p < .001$. Examination of the canonical loadings suggests that first canonical correlation represents a relationship between almost all the predictor variables and remaining a teacher. High structure coefficients (canonical loadings) for all predictor variables in set 1 indicate high correlations between each of these variables and the linear composites of predicting variables. Discretionary performance (−.350), self-efficacy (−.263), POS (−.242), and collective efficacy (−.239) appeared to have the highest loadings on the linear composite canonically correlated with remaining a teacher. Similarly, examination of the canonical loadings suggests that the second canonical correlation captured a relationship between three predictive variables (discretionary performance, POS, and transformational leadership) and two aspirations (seeking promotion to a principalship and career change). Discretionary performance (−.970) and POS (.410) had the highest loadings on the linear composite canonically correlated with the two career aspirations involving changing career and promoting principalship.

A supplementary general multivariate model procedure was conducted to examine the relationships between the predictor variables and the three career aspirations. The results complemented the results of the canonical correlation analysis. The significant sources for discriminating the three career aspirations are presented in Table 6. Self-efficacy significantly discriminated remaining a teacher at the .001 level, with a small effect size

Table 6. Linear Combination of Coefficients Distinguishing Future Career Aspirations of Teachers.

Dependent Variable	Source	B	β	$\acute{\eta}$
Remaining teacher	Self-efficacy	.998	.128	.13**
Changing career	Perceived organizational support	−.175	−.159	.10**
Remaining teacher	Collective efficacy	.148	.121	.10**
Remaining teacher	Transformational leadership	.110	.113	.08*
Remaining teacher	Discretionary performance	.195	.150	.13**
Promotion to principalship	Discretionary performance	.389	.197	.16**

Note: Nonsignificant sources are not shown in the table.
*$p < .05$; **$p < .01$.

($\acute{\eta} = .13$). POS discriminated career change at the .002 level, with a small effect size ($\acute{\eta} = .10$). Collective efficacy discriminated remaining a teacher at the .002 level, with $\acute{\eta} = .10$. Transformational leadership discriminated remaining a teacher at the .002 level, with $\acute{\eta} = .08$. Finally, discretionary performance predicted both remaining a teacher and seeking promotion to a principalship at the .001 levels, with etas of $\acute{\eta} = .13$ and $\acute{\eta} = .16$, respectively.

CONCLUSIONS, IMPLICATIONS, AND LIMITATIONS

The purpose of this study was to examine the factors affecting teachers' work performance (task performance and discretionary performance) and career aspirations (remaining a teacher, seeking promotion to a principalship, and changing careers). By applying an inclusive social-cognitive perspective, the study integrated the personal, organizational, and leadership domains to explain teachers' task performance, discretionary performance, and career aspirations. The independent variables of self-efficacy, collective efficacy, POS, and principal leadership styles predicted the work performance and career aspirations of teachers. The study expanded on previous research by combining the previously disparate elements in the personal, organizational, and leadership domains to provide a more comprehensive and dynamic perspective on the relation between teachers' work performance and career aspirations.

In addition to adopting a broader perspective, the study also applied typologies from the literature on work performance (Rotundo & Sackett, 2002) to reconceptualize teachers' work performance as the product of two related but distinct constructs: task performance and discretionary performance.

To overcome the methodological limitations in the assessment of teachers' task performance due to the lack of a parsimonious measure of professional standards, the present study used the 2011 Model Core Teaching Standards (CCSSO, 2010) as a measure of teacher task performance that was comparable across different school configurations and subject areas.

In the face of the ever increasing and diversified expectations, schools need teachers who go beyond their formal job descriptions. Unfortunately, in the United States, practitioners, policymakers, and the scholarly community have tended to neglect teachers' discretionary performance.

A major contribution of this study was its focus on this unexplored aspect of teachers' work performance.

The current study's finding of a strong relationship between teacher task performance and discretionary performance was consistent with findings in other fields (Hoffman et al., 2007; Niehoff, 2006; Podsakoff et al., 2009). Both hierarchical and simultaneous regression analyses confirmed that the strongest relationship was between task performance and discretionary performance. The regression model that included only the factor of discretionary performance accounted for 39% of the variance in the teacher task performance. Conversely, the regression model that included only the factor of task performance also accounted for 39% of the variance in discretionary performance. The beta weights for task performance ($\beta = .55$) and discretionary performance ($\beta = .45$) in the simultaneous regression analyses confirmed the existence of a strong relationship.

The current study also found that teacher self-efficacy ($\beta = .223$), collective efficacy ($\beta = .311$), and POS ($-.096$) predicted teachers' task performance, results that were consistent with previous research findings (Honingh & Oort, 2009; Kurt et al., 2011; Rhoades & Eisenberger, 2002). However, the present study did not find that principals' transformational leadership influenced teachers' task performance. The current study also found that the demographic variables of participant gender, school configuration, and percentage of students qualifying for a free/reduced lunch contributed significantly to teachers' task performance. Teachers' self-efficacy ($\beta = .072$), POS ($\beta = .122$), and principals' transformational leadership ($\beta - .082$) predicted teachers' discretionary performance, confirming the results of previous research (Podsakoff et al., 2009; Rhoades & Eisenberger, 2002). The present study's finding of a significant relationship between teachers' discretionary performance and principals' transformational leadership was also consistent with prior research (Tschannen-Moran, 2003). However, contrary to relevant research and expectations, collective efficacy did not appear as a significant predictor of teacher discretionary performance in the current study. Paralleling the relationship of demographic variables to teachers' task performance, study findings also indicated that teachers' gender and the percentage of students qualifying for a free/reduced lunch were significantly related to teachers' discretionary performance. It is worthwhile to note that the significant relationship between the percentage of students qualifying for a free/reduced lunch and both teachers' task and discretionary performance has been a common finding in educational research.

As Hanusek et al. (2004) have noted, hiring better teachers, improving their professional skills, and retaining them in the system are essential for improving academic processes and achieving educational outcomes. Rather than focusing solely on either organizational factors or personal characteristics (Heck, 2009), the present study incorporated measures from the personal domain (self-efficacy), organizational domain (collective efficacy and POS), and leadership domain (transformational leadership) to identify factors influencing teachers' career aspirations. The study also included teacher task and discretionary performance as independent variables. The study findings indicated that for the career aspirations of remaining a teacher, seeking promotion to a principalship, and career change, different independent variables influenced different career aspirations. While the factors contributing to remaining a teacher were easy to determine, it was more difficult to identify factors influencing the desire for a principalship or career change. Teacher self-efficacy ($\beta = .128$), collective efficacy ($\beta = .121$), transformational leadership ($\beta = .113$), and discretionary performance ($\beta = .150$) significantly predicted and discriminated teachers' desire to remain a teacher. This finding has practical significance when one considers that the field of education has an attrition rate of 150,000 teachers a year (Alliance for Excellent Education, 2005). Thus, this finding offers policy-makers clear guidance for the development of teacher retention policies. Interestingly, discretionary performance ($\beta = .197$) was the only variable that significantly predicted and discriminated the career aspiration of seeking promotion to a principalship; it was also the only independent variable that predicted and discriminated two different teacher career aspirations (remaining a teacher and seeking promotion to a principalship). However, it was POS ($\beta = -.159$) rather than teachers' discretionary performance that predicted the desire to change careers. In this respect, the study did not support Chen's (2006) finding that OCB significantly predicted the intent to leave and employee turnover. Nevertheless, discretionary performance appeared to be one of the more influential variables with regard to teachers' career aspirations, and it was the only variable whose canonical loadings and coefficients were high in the canonical correlation redundancy analysis of teacher career aspirations. This finding shows that discretionary performance of teachers is a relevant factor when assessing teacher retention or discussing promotion.

Study findings that are not consistent with prior research require further exploration. For instance, future research should investigate why transformational leadership did not significantly contribute to teachers' task performance; why collective efficacy did not significantly contribute to teachers' discretionary performance; and why POS induced changing career.

The current study was not without a number of limitations. The broad perspective on the factors affecting teacher work performance and career aspirations provided by the current study also unfortunately precluded an in-depth examination of study variables. Because each study variable was a composite index based on different scale items, it was not possible to examine the underlying dimensions and/or items composing each study variable. For instance, although the analysis found that principals' transformational leadership was significantly related to teachers' discretionary performance, it was impossible to identify the relative contribution of the different dimensions of transformational leadership (individual consideration, intellectual stimulation, inspirational motivation, or idealized influence) to teachers' discretionary performance. Conversely, it was impossible to identify which aspects of discretionary performance (toward students, toward the group, or toward families) were affected by the transformational leadership of principals. Future research should investigate the in-depth relationships holding between study constructs.

Another methodological limitation of the current study was the reliance on accepted definitions of constructs and readily available instruments to measure these constructs. Future studies should undertake construct cleanups and ensure that measurement instruments are valid in educational settings. For example, construct cleanup efforts are relevant for the evolving concept of discretionary performance (Podsakoff, MacKenzie, Paine, & Bacrach, 2000). While discretionary performance was once defined as activities that were "not formally recognized or encouraged by organizations" (Organ, 1988), the boundaries between task performance and discretionary performance are currently disputed. There may be crossover between discretionary performance and task performance (Kwantes, Karam, Kuo, & Towson, 2008; Turnipseed, 2006). Further, discretionary performance that was initially unrewarded may be acknowledged, encouraged, and rewarded by the administration or organization at a later date. Employees and administrators may define the same employee performance differently (Turnipseed, 2006). Kwantes et al. (2008) have noted that discretionary performance may be affected by unique organizational cultures and situations. In this regard, future research might investigate both antecedents and outcomes of teacher work performance in different school settings. For instance, a comparative study of teacher task and discretionary performance in public schools, charter schools, and private schools could determine the extent to which organizational context and specific situations shape teacher work performance.

Another construct cleanup issue involves the positive and negative dimensions of discretionary performance. Even though discretionary performance was initially defined as *positive* behaviors that ultimately benefit the organization, other research has identified *negative* or *counterproductive* discretionary behaviors (Miles, Borman, Spector, & Fox, 2002). Future research must be cognizant of the emergent aspects of discretionary performance. Finally, future research might also resolve the extent to which the conceptual definitions of discretionary performance converge into OCB.

The current study only examined the influence of teachers work performance at the individual level in the context of teachers' career aspirations. Future research might investigate the effects of teachers' task and discretionary performance on school effectiveness. This type of study would have practical implications for the current movement toward accountability.

From the standpoint of methodology, this study did not employ a truly multilevel analysis of teachers' work performance and career aspirations. Future studies of this topic should investigate both within- and between-school differences.

Two other aspects of the study methodology are worth noting. First was the reliance on quantitative methods. While studies of the antecedents and outcomes of employee performance tend to employ quantitative methods, qualitative studies are also relevant to methodologically disentangle the complex relationships underlying study constructs. The second methodological limitation of the study was its reliance on self-reported teacher attitudes. Future research should include data from different sources to reduce bias.

REFERENCES

Allen, D. G., Shore, L. M., & Griffeth, R. W. (2003). The role of POS in the voluntary turnover process. *Journal of Management, 29,* 99–118.

Alliance for Excellent Education. (2005, August). *Teacher attrition: A costly loss to the nation and to the states.* Issue Brief. Retrieved from http://www.all4ed.org. Accessed on June 2, 2011.

Anderson, G. (1990). *The fundamentals of educational administration.* Bristol, PA: Falmer.

Arcaro, J. S. (1995). *Quality in education.* Delray, FL: St Lucie Press.

Bandura, A. (1995). *Self-efficacy in changing societies.* New York, NY: Cambridge University Press.

Bandura, A. (1997). *Self-efficacy: The exercise of control.* New York, NY: W. H. Freeman and Company.

Bandura, A. (2000). Cultivate self-efficacy for personal and organizational effectiveness. In E. A. Locke (Ed.), *The Blackwell handbook of principles of organizational behavior* (pp. 120–136). Oxford, UK: Blackwell.

Bass, B. M. (1985). *Leadership and performance beyond expectations.* New York, NY: Free Press.

Bass, B. M. (1999). Two decades of research and development in transformational leadership. *European Journal of Work and Organizational Psychology, 8*(1), 9–32.

Bass, B. M., & Avolio, B. J. (1994). *Improving organizational effectiveness through transformational leadership.* Thousand Oaks, CA: Sage.

Bell, S. J., & Menguc, B. (2002). The employee–organization relationship, organizational citizenship behaviors, and superior service quality. *Journal of Retailing, 78*, 131–146.

Belogovsky, E., & Somech, A. (2010). Teachers' organizational citizenship behavior: Examining the boundary between in-role behavior and extra-role behavior from the perspective of teachers, principals and parents. *Teaching and Teacher Education, 26*, 914–923.

Blau, P. M. (1964). *Exchange and power in social life.* New York, NY: Wiley.

Borman, W. C., & Motowidlo, S. J. (1993). Expanding the criterion domain to include elements of contextual performance. In N. Schmitt & C. Borman (Eds.), *Personality selection* (pp. 71–98). San Francisco, CA: Jossey-Bass.

Brief, A. P., & Motowidlo, S. J. (1986). Prosocial organizational behaviors. *The Academy of Management Review, 11*(4), 710–725.

Buddin, R., & Zamarro, G. (2009). Teacher qualifications and student achievement in urban elementary schools. *Journal of Urban Economics, 66*, 103–115.

Burns, J. M. (2010). *Leadership* (Harper perennial political classics). New York, NY: Harper Torchbooks.

Chang, C. H., Johnson, R. E., & Yang, L. Q. (2007). Emotional strain and organizational citizenship behaviors: A meta-analytic review. *Work & Stress, 21*, 312–332.

Chen, X.-P. (2006). Organizational citizenship behavior: A predictor of employee voluntary turnover. In D. L. Turnipseed (Ed.), *Handbook of organizational citizenship behavior: A review of "good soldier" activity in organizations* (pp. 435–454). Hauppauge, NY: Nova Science Publishers.

Cohen, J. (1988). *Statistical power analysis for the behavioral sciences* (2nd ed.). Hillsdale, NJ: Erlbaum.

Conway, J. M. (1999). Distinguishing contextual performance from task performance for managerial jobs. *Journal of Applied Psychology, 84*(1), 3–13.

Council of Chief State School Officers. (2010). Interstate Teacher Assessment and Support Consortium (InTASC) Model Core Teaching Standards: A Resource for State Dialogue (Draft for Public Comment). Council of Chief State School Officers, Washington, DC.

Council of Chief State School Officers. (2011). *Interstate Teacher Assessment and Support Consortium (InTASC) Model Core Teaching Standards: A Resource for State Dialogue.*

Darling Hammond, L. (2004). The color line in American education: Race, resources, and student achievement. *W.E.B. Du Bois Review: Social Science Research on Race, 1*(2), 213–246.

Duyar, I. (2006). Analyzing education productivity. *Education Review, 9*(4). Retrieved from http://edrev.asu.edu/essays/v9n4/. Accessed on July 2011.

Duyar, I., Aydin, I., & Pehlivan, Z. (2009). Analyzing principal influence tactics from a cross-cultural perspective: Do preferred influence tactics and targeted goals differ by national culture? In *Educational leadership: Global context and international comparisons* (pp. 191–220). Bingley, UK: Emerald.

Dvir, T., Eden, D., Avolio, B. J., & Shamir, B. (2002). Impact of transformational leadership on follower development and performance: A field experiment. *Academy of Management Journal, 45*(4), 735–744.

Eisenberger, R., Huntington, R., Hutchison, S., & Sowa, D. (1986). Perceived organizational support. *Journal of Applied Psychology, 71*(3), 500–507.

Farmer, S. M., Maslyn, J. M., Fedor, D. B., & Goodman, J. S. (1997). Putting upward influence strategies in context. *Journal of Organizational Behavior, 18*(1), 17–42.

Frese, M., & Fay, D. (2001). Personal initiative: An active performance concept for work in the 21st century. *Research in Organizational Behavior, 23*, 133–187.

Goddard, R. D. (2002). Collective efficacy and school organization: A multilevel analysis of teacher influence in schools. In W. K. Hoy & C. G. Miskel (Eds.), *Theory and research in educational administration* (pp. 171–185). Charlotte, NC: Information Age.

Goddard, R. D., Hoy, W. K., & Hoy, A. W. (2000). Collective teacher efficacy: Its meaning, measure, and effect on student achievement. *American Education Research Journal, 37*(2), 479–507.

Goldhaber, D. D. (2002). The mystery of good teaching. *Education Next, 2*(1), 50–55.

Goldhaber, D., & Anthony, E. (2004). Can teacher quality be effectively assessed? Urban Institute. Retrieved from http://www.urban.org/UploadedPDF/410958_NBPTSOut comes.pdf. Accessed on June 29.

Hanusek, E. A., Kain, J. F., & Rivkin, S. G. (2004). Why public schools lose teachers? *Journal of Human Resources, 39*, 326–354.

Heck, R. H. (2009). Teacher effectiveness and student achievement: Investigating a multilevel cross-classified model. *Journal of Educational Administration, 47*(2), 227–249.

Henke, R. R., Chen, X., & Geis, S. (2000). *Progress through the teacher pipeline: 1992–1993 college graduate and elementary/secondary school teaching as of 1997.* Statistical Analysis Report. Washington, DC: National Center for Education Statistics.

Hoffman, B., Blair, C., Meriac, J., & Woehr, D. J. (2007). Expanding the criterion domain? A quantitative review of the OCB literature. *Journal of Applied Psychology, 92*, 555–566.

Honingh, M. E., & Oort, F. J. (2009). Teachers' organisational behaviour in public and private funded schools. *International Journal of Educational Management, 23*(2), 172–184.

Hoxby, C. C. (2004). Productivity in education: The quintessential upstream industry. *Southern Economic Journal, 71*(2), 209–231.

Hoy, W. K., Tarter, C. J., & Hoy, A. W. (2006). Academic optimism of schools: A force for student achievement. *American Educational Research Journal, 43*(3), 425–446.

Ingersoll, R. M. (2003). *Who controls teachers' work?* Cambridge, MA: Harvard University Press.

Johnson, S. M. (2004). *Finders and keepers: Helping new teachers survive and thrive in our schools.* San Francisco, CA: Jossey-Bass.

Kane, T. J., Rockoff, J. E., & Staiger, D. O. (2008). What does certification tell us about teacher effectiveness? Evidence from New York City. *Economics of Education Review, 27*(2), 615–631.

Kark, R., & Shamir, B. (2002). The dual effect of transformational leadership: Priming relational and collective selves and further effects on followers. In B. J. Avolio & F. J. Yammarino (Eds.), *Transformational and charismatic leadership: The road ahead* (Vol. 2, pp. 67–91). Amsterdam: JAI Press.

Katz, D., & Kahn, R. (1966). *The social psychology of organizations.* New York, NY: Wiley.

Klein, K. J., & Kozlowski, S. W. J. (2000). *Multilevel theory, research, and methods in organizations.* San Francisco, CA: Jossey-Bass.

Koys, D. J. (2001). The effects of employee satisfaction, organizational citizenship behaviour and turnover on organizational effectiveness: A unit-level, longitudinal study. *Personnel Psychology, 54*, 101–114.

Kozlowski, S. W. J., & Klein, K. J. (2000). A multilevel approach to theory and research in organizations: Contextual, temporal, and emergent processes. Multilevel theory, research, and methods in organizations: Foundations, extensions, and new directions. In K. J. Klein & S. W. J. Kozlowski (Eds.), *Multilevel theory, research, and methods in organizations: Foundations, extensions, and new directions* (pp. 3–90). San Francisco, CA: Jossey-Bass.

Kurt, T., Duyar, I., & Calik, T. (2011). Are we legitimate yet? A closer look at the mechanisms the leadership of principals affecting collective efficacy and self-efficacy of teachers. *Current Issues of Educational Management and Leadership*, Special Issue of the *Journal of Management Development*, *31*(1), 71–86.

Kwantes, C. T., Karam, C. M., Kuo, B. C. H., & Towson, S. (2008). Culture's influence on the perception of OCB as in-role or extra-role. *International Journal of Intercultural Relations*, *32*, 229–243.

Leithwood, K., & Jantzi, D. (2005). A review of transformational school leadership research 1996–2005. *Leadership and Policy in Schools*, *4*(3), 177–199.

Lynch, P. D., Eisenberger, R., & Armeli, S. (1999). Perceived organizational support: Inferior-versus-superior performance by wary employees. *Journal of Applied Psychology*, *84*, 467–483.

Miles, D. E., Borman, W. C., Spector, P. E., & Fox, S. (2002). Building an integrative model of extra role work behaviors: A comparison of counterproductive work behavior with organizational citizenship behavior. *International Journal of Selection and Assessment*, *10*(2), 51–57.

Motowidlo, S. J. (2003). Job performance. In W. C. Borman, D. R. Ilgen, R. J. Klimonski & I. B. Weiner (Eds.), *Handbook of psychology, Volume 12: Industrial and organizational psychology* (pp. 39–53). Hoboken, NJ: Wiley.

Murphy, K. R. (1989). Dimensions of job performance. In R. Dillon & J. Pellingrino (Eds.), *Testing: Applied and theoretical perspectives* (pp. 218–247). New York, NY: Praeger.

National Commission on Teaching and America's Future. (2003). *No dream denied: A pledge to America's children*. Washington, DC. Retrieved from http://www.nctaf.org/documents/no-dream-denied_full-report.pdf. Accessed on June 27, 2003.

Niehoff, B. P. (2006). A theoretical model of the influence of organizational citizenship behaviors on organizational effectiveness. In D. L. Turnipseed (Ed.), *Handbook of organizational citizenship behavior: A review of "good soldier" activity in organizations* (pp. 385–397). Hauppauge, NY: Nova Science Publishers.

Organ, D. W. (1988). *Organizational citizenship behavior: The good soldier syndrome*. Lexington, MA: Lexington Books.

Organ, D. W. (1997). Organizational citizenship behavior: It's construct clean-up time. *Human Performance*, *10*(2), 85–97.

Organ, D. W., Podsakoff, P. M., & MacKenzie, S. (2006). *Organizational citizenship: Its nature, antecedents, and consequences*. Thousand Oaks, CA: Sage.

Podsakoff, N. P., Whiting, S. W., Podsakoff, P. M., & Blume, B. D. (2009). Individual- and organizational-level consequences of organizational citizenship behaviors: A meta-analysis. *Journal of Applied Psychology*, *94*(1), 122–141.

Podsakoff, P. M., MacKenzie, S. B., Paine, J. B., & Bacrach, D. G. (2000). Organizational citizenship behaviors: A critical review of the theoretical and empirical literature and suggestions for future research. *Journal of Management*, *26*(3), 513–563.

Rentz, N. L. (2007). *The influence of positive behavior support on collective teacher efficacy*. Unpublished doctoral dissertation, Baylor University.

Rhoades, L., & Eisenberger, R. (2002). Perceived organizational support: A review of the literature. *Journal of Applied Psychology*, *87*(4), 698–714.

Rivkin, S. G., Hanushek, E. A., & Kain, J. F. (2005). Teachers, schools, and academic achievement. *Econometrica*, *73*(2), 417–458.

Rockoff, J. E. (2004). The impact of individual teachers on student achievement: Evidence from panel data. *American Economic Review*, *94*(2), 247–252.

Rotundo, M., & Sackett, P. R. (2002). The relative importance of task, citizenship, and counterproductive performance to global ratings of job performance: A policy capturing approach. *Journal of Applied Psychology*, *87*(1), 66–80.

Seidel, T., & Shavelson, R. J. (2007). Teaching effectiveness research in the past decade: The role of theory and research design in disentangling meta-analysis results. *Review of Educational Research*, *77*(4), 454–499.

Somech, A., & Drach-Zahavy, A. (2000). Understanding extra-role behavior in schools: The relationships between job satisfaction, sense of efficacy, and teachers' extra-role behavior. *Teaching and Teacher Education*, *16*, 649–659.

Somech, A., & Ron, I. (2007). Promoting organizational citizenship behavior in schools: The impact of individual and organizational characteristics. *Educational Administration Quarterly*, *43*(1), 38–66.

Stutz, T. (2004). Revolving door. *Dallas Morning News*, June 12, p. A1.

Tschannen-Moran, M. (2003). Fostering organizational leadership: Transformational leadership and trust. In W. K. Hoy & C. G. Miskel (Eds.), *Studies in leading and organizing schools* (pp. 157–179). Greenwich, CT: Information Age.

Tschannen-Moran, M., & Hoy, A. (2001). Teacher efficacy: Capturing and elusive construct. *Teaching and Teacher Education*, *17*, 783–805.

Turnipseed, D. L. (2006). *Handbook of organizational citizenship behavior: A review of "good soldier" activity in organizations.* Hauppauge, NY: Nova Science Publishers.

Van Dyne, L., Cummings, L. L., & Parks, J. M. (1995). Extra-role behaviors: In pursuit of construct and definitional clarity (A bridge over muddied waters). In B. M. Staw & L. L. Cummings (Eds.), *Research in organizational behavior* (Vol. 17, pp. 215–285). Greenwich, CT: JAI Press.

Vey, M. A., & Campbell, J. P. (2004). In-role or extra-role organizational citizenship behavior: Which are we measuring? *Human Performance*, *17*(1), 119–135.

Walumbwa, F., Wang, P., Lawyer, J., & Shi, K. (2004). The role of collective efficacy in the relations between transformational leadership and work outcomes. *Journal of Occupational and Organizational Psychology*, *77*, 515–530.

Wayne, S. J., Shore, L. M., & Liden, R. C. (1997). Perceived organizational support and leader–member exchange: A social exchange perspective. *Academy of Management Journal*, *40*, 82–111.

CHAPTER 5

RELATIONSHIP BETWEEN DEMOGRAPHIC VARIABLES AND ORGANIZATIONAL CITIZENSHIP BEHAVIOR AMONG COMMUNITY COLLEGE LECTURERS

Noriah Abdul Malek and Fatt Hee Tie

ABSTRACT

Organizational citizenship behavior involves behaviors that support an organization. However, such behaviors are not normally set out in an individual's job description. These behaviors normally exceed the minimum role requirements of the job and are not easily enforceable, thus performing them is usually at the discretion of the individual (Organ, 1997). This study seeks to examine the relationship between the demographic variables and organizational citizenship behavior among lecturers in community colleges that have been established by the Ministry of Higher Education in Malaysia. The variables consist of gender, age, educational level, recruitment status, length of service with the organization, tenure, job classification, and intention to leave the service.

Discretionary Behavior and Performance in Educational Organizations: The Missing
Link in Educational Leadership and Management
Advances in Educational Administration, Volume 13, 117–138
Copyright © 2012 by Emerald Group Publishing Limited
All rights of reproduction in any form reserved
ISSN: 1479-3660/doi:10.1108/S1479-3660(2012)0000013010

A review of literature produced a list of 59 organizational citizenship behaviors. This list was then sent to 10 educational experts in the community colleges. After identifying the most important organizational citizenship behaviors, the experts then ranked the importance of each of the behaviors. This resulted in 36 organizational citizenship behaviors being selected for the formulation and development of the questionnaire. A pilot test of the questionnaire showed a Cronbach's alpha value of .93. The questionnaire was then distributed to 762 lecturers in 14 community colleges throughout Malaysia. A factor analysis showed three important dimensions of organizational citizenship behaviors emerged from the study. It includes: helping behavior, sportsmanship, and organizational compliance. Next, the study examined the impact of demography on organizational citizenship behavior. The findings of the study are discussed along with implications and directions for future research.

INTRODUCTION

Organizational citizenship behavior is discretionary individual behavior that is not directly or explicitly recognized by the formal reward system although it promotes the effective functioning of an organization (Organ, 1988). It contributes to maintenance and enhancement of the social and psychological context which supports task performance (Organ, 1997). In general, organizational citizenship behavior represents an "extra effort" by employees in their job performance that is essential for the effective functioning of an organization, especially where organizational performance is dependent on the interconnectedness and social networks of its people. Furthermore, it can provide a source of long-term competitive advantage (McBain, 2004; Schneider, 1996). The extra-role behavior, which does not form part of the specific job description, is voluntary in nature. Unfortunately, many employers and the reward system in the organizations do not formally recognize the contribution of organizational citizenship behavior to the success of the organization.

BACKGROUND TO THE STUDY

In Malaysia, community colleges are established by the Ministry of Higher Education to conduct mid-level technical and professional courses. The job performance of the lecturers, as employees of the public civil service, is assessed under the Malaysian Remuneration System, a performance management system that was introduced in 2002 to reward public employees for excellent job performance. The quality of work produced determines the employee's annual increase in income. The Malaysian Remuneration System is perceived as an organizational control system (Nagarajah, 2008; Norhayati & Nabiha, 2009) that guides and encourages employees to exhibit appropriate behavior at the workplace. At the beginning of the year, the lecturers set an annual job performance target. The directors of the community colleges evaluate the lecturers' job performance at the end of the year. The directors are former lecturers who have been promoted based on their experience and job performance. The annual job performance is assessed based on four areas, that is, job outcome (forming 50% of the marks), knowledge and skill (25%), personal qualities (20%), and contribution outside the scope of the formal job requirements (5%). It is observed that only a small percentage of the marks are allocated for contribution toward activities such as, innovative ideas to improve the work procedure and process in the office, or even preparation of working papers for national and international seminars (Public Service Department, 2007a).

In January 2009, the Ministry of Higher Education introduced a new salary scheme for community college lecturers. The scheme, which is known as the Higher Education Officer Scheme, provided due recognition where extra marks are given for the additional contribution or organizational citizenship behavior exhibited by the staff when they apply for a promotion. This form of recognition encourages the community college lecturers to exhibit the appropriate organizational citizenship behavior at their workplace. Additional marks would be awarded by the directors during the annual performance assessment if the lecturers' organizational citizenship behavior brings benefits and added value to the organization. The reward system motivates the lecturers to go the extra mile as they are deemed to be an invaluable asset in contributing to the success of the organization. Further, organizations are inclined to hire individuals who are able to exhibit organizational citizenship behavior as well as adapt in a flexible manner to changes at the work environment. However, even though organizational citizenship behavior may improve the performance of the organization and is desired, employers cannot enforce these behaviors on their employees (Motowidlo, 2000).

PURPOSE OF THE STUDY

This study attempts to identify the type of organizational citizenship behavior among community colleges that is perceived to be important by the community colleges directors. It would also investigate the relationship between the demographic variables of the lecturers and organizational citizenship behavior.

Research Questions

Specifically, the study seeks to answer the following research questions:

1. What are the organizational citizenship behaviors that the panel of community college directors considers to be most important?
2. Is there a relationship between the demographic variables of the community college lecturers and their organizational citizenship behaviors?

Significance of the Study

Community colleges, like any other educational institutions, are constantly facing new challenges to meet the requirements of the current job market. As a result, the job performance of the lecturers has become more challenging. Society places high expectation on the lecturers to provide quality education. Lecturers must be willing to assume responsibilities outside their formal job requirement to ensure the success of their organization (Somech & Drach-Zahavy, 2000). A clear understanding of the importance of organizational citizenship behavior is important for the survival of the organization. As Bolino and Turnley (2003) observed the one reason that companies like Southwest Airlines are so successful is that they have dedicated employees whose effort surpasses what is formally required of them. Similarly, the community colleges need committed and dedicated lecturers who are willing to contribute to the extra work.

Employees that exhibit organizational citizenship behavior and are rewarded during the annual performance evaluation tend to be more motivated (Longenecker, Sims, & Gioia, 1987). If the management provides recognition for the organizational citizenship behavior, it will motivate the staff to perform better in the future by doing extra work that benefits the organization. It is vital for the management to appraise the employees in an objective and fair manner as organizational citizenship behavior does help an organization to achieve its goals (Organ, Podsakoff, & MacKenzie, 2006). Prior to this, the management needs to discuss and agree with the employees about the boundaries between formal tasks and voluntary and spontaneous behaviors. This could be set out in the formal contract between the employer and the employee.

The incorporation of organizational citizenship behavior into the organizational control system acknowledges that working in an organizational setting is different from working alone as an individual as the employees also perform in ways beyond their job descriptions (Van Scotter & Motowidlo, 1996).

If the Ministry of Higher Education attempts to foster organizational citizenship behavior among the college lecturers, it should explicitly recognize organizational citizenship behavior as part of the individual performance and should link it to the performance appraisal system. The study could be useful in helping to design and develop a more effective performance evaluation system that incorporates organizational citizenship behavior in the community colleges.

Research on organizational citizenship behavior among higher educational institutions in Malaysia is limited. It is hoped that the findings of the study could provide some useful guidelines and constructive feedback to education managers in Malaysia, especially the job performance and organizational citizenship behavior of the employee.

Review of Literature

Research shows that organizational citizenship behavior has been recognized and rewarded by most organizations (Allen & Rush, 1998; Becton, Giles, & Schraeder, 2008; Werner, 1994). Accordingly, Organ (1997) suggested that organizational citizenship behavior should be redefined to reflect its contribution to the effectiveness of the organization. Organ (1997) proposed using Borman and Motowidlo's (1993, p. 73) definition of contextual performance as activities that "do not support the technical core itself as much as they support the organizational, social, and psychological environment in which the technical core must function."

On the other hand, Organ and Ryan (1995) observed that there is limited research on the relationship between demographic variables of the respondents and organizational citizenship behavior. The general direction of organizational citizenship behavior research seems to focus either on the antecedents of organizational citizenship behavior or its consequent variables. Research that incorporates both the antecedents of organizational citizenship behavior and the consequent organizational citizenship behavior is, however, lacking.

Organ's (1988) concept of organizational citizenship behavior has been continuously researched in many settings and levels of analysis. Lievens and Anseel (2004) demonstrate how organizational citizenship behavior has been studied in a number of disciplines that ranges from human resource management, marketing, economics, health care, education, local governance, to the public sector at various levels of analysis that encompasses the individual, the group, or the organization as a whole (Schnake & Dumler, 2003).

Since then, researchers had investigated the occurrence of these behaviors in various organizations and had used a variety of scales to measure organizational citizenship behavior (Organ et al., 2006). One main finding from the studies is that the dimensions of organizational citizenship behavior appear to vary according to the nature of the organization, the beneficiary, the target of the behavior, as well as the sources of organizational citizenship behavior. This means that even though organizational citizenship behavior may prevail in different organizations, yet its uniqueness remains dependent on the particular setting.

In a university setting, Bateman and Organ (1983) administered a questionnaire among 77 superiors to evaluate the subordinates' organizational citizenship behavior. The sample comprises 62% male and 38% female respondents. The average tenure was 6.8 years. The results of the study showed that there is no significant relationship between the respondents' demographic variables and organizational citizenship behavior. Bateman and Organ's (1983) organizational citizenship behavior scale which consists of 30 items was tested for the factor structure and found that many of the items had substantial loadings on the first factor. They decided to treat the scale as a composite measure of organizational citizenship behavior. The test–retest reliability was .80.

Other researchers have found the different types of Organizational Citizenship Behavior (OCB) as well. Organ et al. (2006) pointed out that many different forms of organizational citizenship behavior have been identified and measured in the literature. Podsakoff, MacKenzie, Paine, and Bachrach's (2000) examination of the literature revealed a lack of consensus about the dimensionality of the organizational citizenship behavior construct. The 30 different forms of citizenship behavior found in the analyses were categorized according to the following 7 common themes: helping behavior, sportsmanship, organizational loyalty, organizational compliance, individual initiative, civic virtue, and self-development.

In another study, Farh, Zhong, and Organ (2004) identified 10 dimensions of organizational citizenship behavior in China and found

4 common OCB dimensions that were similar to Podsakoff et al. (2000). These were helping coworkers, loyalty, taking initiative, and civic virtue. The helping and loyalty dimensions were similar to Moorman and Blakely (1995) interpersonal helping and loyal boosterism. Such behaviors include "go out of the way to help co-workers with work-related problems," "actively promote the organization's products and services to potential users," and "defend the organization when other employees criticize it."

In Van Dyne et al.'s (1994) study, they reconceptualized organizational citizenship behavior in China in term of civic citizenship as described by Graham (1991). From this perspective, civic citizenship was viewed as including all positive community-relevant behaviors of individual citizens. It includes all positive organizationally relevant behaviors of individual organization members.

The multidimensionality of organizational citizenship behavior in organizations as supported by findings from Van Dyne et al.'s (1994) study has led some researchers to use the organizational citizenship behavior instrument in their studies. For examples, Bienstock, DeMoranville, and Smith (2003) adapted the organizational citizenship behavior scale developed by Van Dyne et al. (1994) and pretested to undergraduate students at a southeastern university. The revised organizational citizenship behavior scale contained 15 items measuring loyalty behaviors, obedience behaviors, and participation behaviors was administered to 535 restaurant employees. The coefficient alphas were .80 for loyalty, .51 for obedience, and .77 for participation.

Podsakoff and MacKenzie (1994) found three dimensions of organizational citizenship behavior in their studies namely helping, civic virtue, and sportsmanship. They developed the organizational citizenship behavior construct based on the conceptual work of Organ (1988), and empirical studies of Podsakoff, MacKenzie, Moorman, and Fetter (1990), Podsakoff et al. (2000), and MacKenzie, Podsakoff, and Fetter (1991, 1993).

The instrument used by Netemeyer, James, McKee, and McMurrian's (1997) study was also used by other researchers in different settings and samples such as Ackfeldt and Coote (2005), Castro, Armario, and Ruiz (2004), and Piercy, Lane, and Cravens (2002). For example, in a retail setting, Ackfeldt and Coote (2005) collected data from 211 frontline employees. Seventy percent of the respondents were women. The average age was 29 years. The average company tenure was 4 years. Forty-five percent of the respondents had completed high school. The sources for the organizational citizenship behavior construct used in the study were from Netemeyer et al. (1997), Organ and Konovsky (1989), and Williams and Anderson (1991). The dimensions included helping behavior, civic virtue, and sportsmanship. Some of the examples for helping behavior dimension were: "give time to help employees with work-related problems," "support employees who have problems at work," "help train new employees," and "share knowledge and expertise with other employees." Some examples for civic virtue dimension were: "attend work-related information sessions," "attend and participate in meetings," "make suggestions for improving the company's policies and practices," and "keep up with changes in the workplace." Some examples of the sportsmanship dimensions were: "keep trivial complaints to oneself," "try not to find fault with other employees," and "focus on the positive aspects of the work." The reliability for organizational citizenship behavior as measured by Cronbach's alpha was .76.

In a school context, DiPaola, Tarter, and Hoy (2004) replicated and confirmed the factor analysis of DiPaola and Tschannen-Moran (2001) scale measure of organizational citizenship behavior among three samples of teachers. All the organizational citizenship behavior items loaded strongly on a single first-order factor and the factor structure was almost the same and stable in all three samples. For middle school teachers, the alpha coefficient of reliability was .93, for the elementary and middle school teachers, the alpha coefficient of reliability was the same, a value of .93, while for the high school sample, the reliability was .86.

In summary, the above studies have treated organizational citizenship behavior as a constructive, self-initiated, spontaneous, or voluntary behavior aimed at enhancing the productivity of the workplace. Organizational citizenship behavior is important as it contributes to organizational effectiveness (Organ et al., 2006). The definition has "evolved from one that encompassed behavior that is not monitored or rewarded to one in which the observation and rewarding of behavior plays a significant role" (Korsgaard, Meglino, Lester, & Jeong, 2010, p. 277).

Demographic Variables and Organizational Citizenship Behavior

Research shows that the relationship between demographic variables and organizational citizenship behavior is inconclusive (Burton, 2003; Organ & Ryan, 1995). In a meta-analyses study, Organ and Ryan (1995) found that many studies used descriptive statistics and reported the mean and standard deviation of the demographic variables. However, they revealed that many researchers did not report the relationship of the demographic variables with organizational citizenship behavior.

In another study, Rego, Ribeiro, and Cunha (2010) found that gender correlates negatively with sportsmanship, with males showing lower scores. The research also showed that age correlates negatively with sportsmanship, but positively with conscientiousness. Further, organizational tenure correlates negatively with sportsmanship and positively with conscientiousness and civic virtue.

Ng and Feldman (2008) conducted a meta-analysis study on the relationship between age and job performance from 380 empirical studies which contained 438 independent samples. The age of the sample ranged from 17 to 59 years with a standard deviation of 8.8. The average age across the entire sample was 36.6 years. They found that age demonstrated significant and positive relationships with self-ratings organizational citizenship behavior ($r = .08$). This suggests that older workers tend to demonstrate more citizenship behaviors than younger workers. The study also found that age was related to job performance ($r = .02$). Both researchers also found that education level is positively related to organizational citizenship behavior.

Deckop, Mangel, and Cirka (1999) studied the effect of behavioral and output control systems on organizational citizenship behaviors among 146 utilities employees across the United States. The demographic variables used in the study in relation to organizational citizenship behavior were age, education, and gender. They found that there were no significant correlations between age, education and gender, and organizational citizenship behavior. The Pearson correlation values were $-.09$, .08, and .01 respectively.

METHOD

The study used a survey research design which allows the researcher to make inferences about some characteristics, attitudes, or behaviors of a population. This research design is well-suited for measuring attitudes and orientations in a large population (Babbie, 2007) and is appropriate for research questions about self-reported beliefs or behaviors (Neuman, 2006).

Subjects

A stratified sampling technique was utilized. The number of subjects involved in the study consists of 465 lecturers.

Development of the Organizational Citizenship Behavior Instrument

The instrument was a modified version of the instruments developed by other researchers (MacKenzie et al., 1991, 1993; Netemeyer et al., 1997; Turnipseed, 2002; Werner, 1994).

The researchers replicated the procedure used by Griffin (1992) to develop the organizational citizenship behavior instrument. First, the researchers reviewed the relevant literature on organizational citizenship behavior. This resulted in a list of 46 identified organizational citizenship behaviors. Besides the 46 identified behaviors, the researchers also included 13 additional items in the questionnaire based on the criteria set up in the Higher Education Scheme (Public Service Department, 2007b).

Second, content validity was established by asking qualified experts to rate the questionnaire items. In order to validate these items and determine which would be judged to be most important in community colleges, the 59 items were sent to experienced personnel in the field. The qualifications of the experts include: (a) having a postgraduate degree, (b) responsible for community college activities in current position, (c) have teaching experience, (d) experience in holding a community college director position, and (e) know the nature, concept, and implementation of the community colleges. Any person who fulfilled at least four of the five criteria mentioned above was selected to be an expert in the study.

The process of identifying the important behaviors consists of two phases. During the first phase, the questionnaire was sent to the 10 experts via e-mail. All 10 experts returned the questionnaire. The experts were asked to rate each of the behaviors according to the degree of importance on a 5-point scale. It ranges from "not important" with a value of 1 and 2; "important" with a value of 3 and 4; to "most important" with a value of 5. Once the experts returned the questionnaire, the identification of "most important" behavior was identified by the researcher following the procedure adopted by Griffin (1992). From the returned questionnaires, it was possible to select the 38 behaviors that were judged by the experts to be most important as organizational citizenship behavior. The mean value was obtained for each identified organizational citizenship behavior from the instrument that was sent to the panel experts. The results of the questionnaire to the experts were analyzed by determining the mean value and the standard deviation of each item. Items receiving a mean rating of 4.05 or higher were included in the final questionnaire.

From these results, it was possible to identify the "most important" organizational citizenship behavior as judged by the experts. The final list of "most important" organizational citizenship behavior according to the mean ranking consists of 36 items. The Cronbach's alpha for the 36 items was .93. This instrument was included in Section A of the questionnaire. The subjects respond according to a 5-point Likert scale with a range of 1 (strongly disagree) to 5 (strongly agree). Higher scores reflect higher levels of exhibited organizational citizenship behavior.

Finally, the instrument which also seeks information on the demographic background of the respondents was sent to all lecturers in the 14 community colleges.

RESULTS

The subjects were lecturers at the community colleges set up by the Ministry of Higher Education. Table 1 presents the profile of the subjects.

As Table 1 shows, the majority of the subjects are female lecturers (54.6%), married (78.9%), has a first degree (60.2%), joins the public service after Malaysian Remuneration System, MRS (76.6%), has worked in the organization between 3 and 6 years (38.1%), from the Grade 41 (68.8%), has never received a promotion (92.9%), has not received a service award (74.2%), does not intend to apply for a transfer to another organization (63.0%), and has no intention to leave the service (95.5%). The data indicated that the subjects were educated, relatively young in terms of years of service, and intend to remain in the service even though they have yet to receive a promotion or a service award.

Table 2 presents the descriptive statistics of the variables. The overall measure of organizational citizenship behavior was obtained by totaling all the 36 items. The mean for the overall measure of organizational citizenship behavior was 4.35.

Organizational citizenship behavior comprised of three dimensions: individual initiative, sportsmanship and organizational compliance. The organizational compliance dimension has the highest mean value (4.45) compared to the sportsmanship dimension (4.43) and the individual initiative dimension (4.25).

Exploratory factor analysis was performed to examine the relationships between the various items of the OCB instrument. The 36 items of organizational citizenship behavior scale were subjected to principal component analysis (PCA) using SPSS Version 16. Prior to performing the PCA, the suitability of data for factor analysis was assessed. Inspection of the correlation matrix revealed the presence of many coefficients of .3 and

Table 1. Profile of Respondents ($N = 465$).

Profile	Category	N	%
Gender	Male	209	44.9
	Female	256	54.6
Marital status	Single	95	20.4
	Married	367	78.9
	Widowed	3	.6
Educational level	Diploma	115	24.7
	Bachelor's degree	280	60.2
	Postgraduate	70	15.0
Recruitment status	Join public sector before MRS	109	23.4
	Join public sector after MRS	356	76.6
Length of service	Below 3 years	172	37.0
	3–6 years	177	38.1
	More than 6 years	116	24.9
Job classification	Grade 32 and below	121	25.9
	Grade 41	320	68.8
	Grade 44 and above	24	5.2
Promotion received	Yes	33	7.1
	Never	432	92.9
Award received	Yes	120	25.8
	No	345	74.2
Intention to transfer	Yes	172	37.0
to another organization	No	293	63.0
Intention to leave the service	Yes	21	4.5
	No	444	95.5

Table 2. Descriptive Statistics for the Variables.

	Mean	Standard Deviation
Overall OCB	4.35	.39
Individual initiative	4.25	.47
Sportsmanship	4.43	.45
Organizational compliance	4.45	.43

Table 3. The Component Correlation Matrix Table (Organizational Citizenship Behavior).

Component	1	2	3
a. Individual initiative	–		
b. Sportsmanship	.352	–	
c. Organizational compliance	−.490	−.366	–

above. The Kaiser-Meyer-Olkin value was .936, exceeding the recommended value of .6 (Pallant, 2005) and the Bartlett's test of sphericity (Pallant, 2005) reached statistical significance, supporting the factorability of the correlation matrix.

A factor analysis with principal components analysis was conducted on OCB items to determine the dimensions measured by the instrument. Items that are closely related tend to cluster into one factor or component. The analysis revealed the presence of several factors. Items that do not fall into a factor may be deleted.

The analysis revealed the presence of eight components with eigenvalues exceeding 1, explaining 33.99%, 6.34%, 4.11%, 3.73%, 3.39%, 3.35%, 3.01%, and 2.86% of the variance respectively. To confirm the number of components retained, a parallel analysis was done (Pallant, 2005). The results resulted in only three components with eigenvalues which exceeded the corresponding criterion values for a randomly generated data matrix of the same size (36 variables × 465 respondents).

To aid in the interpretation of these three components, direct oblimin rotation with Kaizer normalization was used, given that the components were more strongly correlated (Pallant, 2005) as shown in Table 3.

The three components showed a number of strong loadings. The eigenvalues for the organizational citizenship dimensions were individual initiative (12.23), sportsmanship (2.28), and organizational compliance (1.48).

Reliability

Table 4 presents the internal consistency estimates for the variables. It ranged from .81 (sportsmanship) to .93 (overall OCB). In general, these estimates indicate that adequate reliability was observed for each measure.

Table 4.   Scale Reliability of Study Variables.

Variable	Coefficient
Overall OCB	.93
Individual initiative	.87
Sportsmanship	.81
Organizational compliance	.85

Correlations among the Variables

The correlations among the variables are presented in Table 5.

The 10 experts identified 38 organizational citizenship behaviors that were the most important. Table 6 shows the mean ranking of each of the organizational citizenship behavior. Item 1 has the highest mean value of 4.8 ("keep up" with the development in the organization) together with item 2 (produce as much as capable at all times). This is followed by four items with a mean of 4.7. The items are: item 3 (actively promote the organization's products and services to potential users), item 4 (always come to work on time), item 14 (do not miss work without a valid reason), and item 29 (make innovative suggestions to improve the overall quality of the organization). The rest of the six items have a similar mean of 4.6.

Further analysis of the behaviors using factor analysis identified three dimensions of organizational citizenship behaviors. The three dimensions are: individual initiative, sportsmanship and organizational compliance. These three dimensions are similar to those identified by Organ et al. (2006).

Relationship between Demographic Variables and Organizational Citizenship Behavior

Table 7 shows that there is a significant relationship between age and overall organizational citizenship behavior ($r = .25, p < .01$). The findings also show a significant relationship between tenure and overall organizational citizenship behavior ($r = .21, p < .01$).

There was a significant relationship between age and each of the three dimensions of organizational citizenship behavior dimensions respectively (individual initiative, $r = .20$, $p < .01$; sportsmanship, $r = .15$, $p < .01$; organizational compliance, $r = .27, p < .01$).

Table 5. Intercorrelations of the Study Variables.

	1	2	3	4	5	6	7	8	9
1. Overall OCB	.14**	.10*	.15**	(.93)					
2. Individual initiative	.17**	.13**	.16**	.88**	(.87)				
3. Sportsmanship	.08	.03	.12**	.78**	.53**	(.81)			
4. Organizational compliance	.07	.05	.08	.88**	.66**	.66**	(.85)		

*Correlation is significant at the .05 level (two tailed).
**Correlation is significant at the .01 level (two tailed).

Table 6. Community College Experts' Rating of Organizational Citizenship Behaviors by Mean and Standard Deviation.

No.	Item	Mean	Standard Deviation
1.	"Keep up" with developments in the organization	4.8	.42
2.	Produce as much as capable at all times	4.8	.42
3.	Actively promote the organization's products and services to potential users	4.7	.48
4.	Always come to work on time	4.7	.48
5.	Do not miss work without a valid reason	4.7	.67
6.	Make innovative suggestions to improve the overall quality of the organization	4.7	.48
7.	Conscientiously follow organization regulations and procedures	4.6	.70
8.	Defend the organization when other employees criticize it	4.6	.52
9.	Follow all necessary rules, regulations, policies, and procedures	4.6	.70
10.	Keep informed about products and services and tell others	4.6	.70
11.	Keeping workplace clean	4.6	.84
12.	Represent organization favorably to outsiders	4.6	.70

The findings also show a significant relationship between tenure and the three dimensions of organizational citizenship behavior (individual initiative, $r = .16$, $p < .01$; sportsmanship, $r = .13$, $p < .01$; organizational compliance, $r = .21$, $p < .01$).

Gender was only significantly and negatively related to individual initiative ($r = -.11$, $p < .05$). Recruitment status showed a significant and negative relationships to overall organizational citizenship behavior ($r = -.10$, $p < .05$) and sportsmanship ($r = -.10$, $p < .05$). The grade was significantly related to overall organizational citizenship behavior ($r = .11$, $p < .05$) and organizational compliance ($r = .12$, $p < .01$).

Table 7. Demographics and OCB Correlation Matrix.

Demographic elements	OCB Dimensions			
	Overall OCB	Individual initiative	Sportsmanship	Organizational compliance
Sex	$-.07, p = .15$ ns	$-.11^*, p = .01$	$-.02, p = .69$ ns	$-.01, p = .83$ ns
Marital status	$.06, p = .22$ ns	$.04, p = .37$ ns	$.02, p = .72$ ns	$.04, p = .45$ ns
Age	$.25^{**}, p = .000$	$.20^{**}, p = .000$	$.15^{**}, p = .001$	$.28^{**}, p = .000$
Educational level	$.03, p = .52$ ns	$-.01, p = .78$ ns	$.02, p = .64$ ns	$.06, p = .17$ ns
Recruitment status	$-.10^*, p = .04$	$-.08, p = .10$ ns	$-.10^*, p = .03$	$-.08, p = .08$ ns
Length of service with the organization	$.03, p = .49$ ns	$-.01, p = .84$ ns	$.01, p = .81$ ns	$.06, p = .22$ ns
Tenure	$.21^{**}, p = .000$	$.16^{**}, p = .000$	$.13^{**}, p = .004$	$.21^{**}, p = .000$
Job classification	$.11^*, p = .02$	$.06, p = .17$ ns	$.07, p = .16$ ns	$.12^*, p = .007$
Promotion received	$-.16^{**}, p = .001$	$-.15^{**}, p = .002$	$-.08, p = .08$ ns	$-.13^{**}, p = .004$
Award received	$-.13^{**}, p = .004$	$-.07, p = .11$ ns	$-.12^*, p = .01$	$-.16^{**}, p = .000$
Intention to transfer	$.05, p = .05$ ns	$.04, p = .37$ ns	$.05, p = .33$ ns	$.02, p = .65$ ns
Intention to leave public service	$.03, p = .53$ ns	$-.02, p = .63$ ns	$-.04, p = .43$ ns	$.08, p = .07$ ns

*Correlation significant at $p < .05$.
**Correlation significant at $p < .01$, ns = not significant.

Promotion received by the lecturers was also significantly and negatively related to overall organizational citizenship behavior ($r = -.16$, $p < .01$), individual initiative ($r = -.13$, $p < .01$), and organizational compliance ($r = -.13$, $p < .01$). Significant and negative relationships were also observed between award received and overall organizational citizenship behavior ($r = -.13$, $p < .01$), sportsmanship ($r = -.11$, $p < .05$), and organizational compliance ($r = -.16$, $p < .01$). The other demographic variables were not significantly related to organizational citizenship behavior.

t-Tests and one-way analysis of variance (ANOVA) were performed to determine if demographic factors contributed to differences in organizational citizenship behavior.

The independent samples *t*-test procedure was used to test for significant differences between two means if the independent variables have only two categories. The variables were gender, marital status, recruitment status, promotion, and award, intention to transfer and intention to leave the public sector.

The one-way ANOVA was used to test for significant differences in means if the independent variables have more than two categories. The variables were age, educational level, length of service with the current organization, tenure, and grade. When the results indicated that the group means were significantly different, the Tukey post hoc test was carried out to determine which pair of groups had significantly different means. The alpha values for the independent samples *t*-test, the one-way ANOVA, and the post hoc test were set at .05 level.

The results of the subsequent analyses indicate that there is a significant relationship between gender, recruitment status, promotion and award received, age, tenure, grade, and overall organizational citizenship behavior, as well as the different dimensions of organizational citizenship behavior.

CONCLUSION AND IMPLICATIONS

The results of the study suggest that the community college directors perceived that the identified organizational citizenship behaviors were important for organizational success. The 38 identified organizational citizenship behaviors were factor analyzed and resulted in 3 dimensions namely individual initiative, sportsmanship, and organizational compliance. These dimensions were among the three dimensions identified by Podsakoff et al. (2000). An interesting finding was that more than half of the main organizational citizenship behaviors identified by community college experts fall into the third factor in the factor analysis namely organizational compliance. For examples, "'keep up' with developments in the organization," "produce as much as capable at all times," "actively promote the organization's products and services to potential users," "conscientiously follow organization regulations and procedures," "follow all necessary rules, regulations, policies, and procedures," "keep informed about products and services and tell others," and "keeping workplace clean" were loaded on the third factor.

This suggests that both the employers and employees have common understanding of the kind of behaviors that are important for the organization.

The results also showed that gender, recruitment status, job grade, promotion, and excellence award received were related to some dimensions of organizational citizenship behavior. Gender was only related to individual initiative. Recruitment status was related to overall organizational citizenship behavior and sportsmanship. Job grade was related to overall organizational citizenship behavior, individual initiative, and organizational compliance. Both promotion and excellence award received were related to overall organizational citizenship behavior and organizational compliance. Promotion received was related to individual initiative and not related to sportsmanship while excellence award received was related to sportsmanship and not individual initiative. Tenure and age showed consistent results to overall organizational citizenship behavior and all of the three dimensions of individual initiative, sportsmanship, and organizational compliance.

Traditionally, the majority of the lecturers are granted continuous tenure after a probation period of between 1 and 3 years. By exhibiting continuous organizational citizenship behavior at the workplace, the chances of lecturers being granted tenure increases as these behaviors are recommended by the administrators. Indirectly, the culture of exhibiting organizational citizenship behavior has been embedded in the organization.

In the current study, senior or older lecturers tend to demonstrate more organizational citizenship behavior than younger lecturers, supporting results of previous research (Ng & Feldman, 2008). Further research concerning organizational citizenship behavior and lecturer experience and award received would be valuable to practitioners. The experience of the lecturer and giving recognition for excellent service in the form of a service award can further improve job performance. It is possible that there exist other dimensions of organizational citizenship behavior that might be applicable to community colleges. Hence, the second recommendation is that to explore this area in depth.

Although there is justification in the research literature to use the lecturer survey as the sole method of evaluating the lecturers' organizational citizenship behavior, relying on one evaluation score does not provide as comprehensive assessment of lecturers' organizational citizenship behavior as would be available with the use of multiple evaluation tools. Therefore, the third recommendation is that lecturer evaluation of organizational citizenship behavior should include student evaluation, coworker evaluation, and head of department evaluation in addition to self-evaluation of organizational citizenship behavior.

The number of lecturers varies among the 14 community colleges. It ranges from 16 to 92 lecturers per college. In this respect, it is possible that fewer lecturers may create a closer relationship between the administrator and the lecturers. This could result in a natural bias as to how administrators evaluate lecturer job performance. The study, as designed, does not allow for the control of a possible confounding variable based on the number of lecturers in the college. Consequently, it is recommended that a quasi-experimental study that compares job performance based exclusively on number of lecturers be conducted.

The requirements for evaluation of job performance may vary from college to college. In this study, job performance is based on the annual performance appraisal marks of the lecturers. The evaluation is done by taking the average marks from two evaluators in which the head of department as the first evaluator and the director of the college as the second evaluator. Since in the study, the average for 3 years was taken, it is possible some lecturers might have been evaluated by different administrators. This is possible because during the period of the study, some of the directors' and head of department posts were yet to be filled by the Ministry of Higher Education. Without taking these differences in requirements into account, it is impossible to determine whether differences in job performance are the result of organizational citizenship behavior or a covariate based on time being administrators and having less experience being administrators. Therefore, the sixth recommendation is that the requirements for job performance be identified for each sampled college prior to data collection.

The limitations of this study should cause the practitioner to take vital action. High performance among the lecturers is a result to be considered very important by administrators. As discussed earlier, lecturers in community colleges should strive for excellence. Organizational citizenship behavior as a construct seems ripe with opportunities to accomplish the organizational goals. Developing an environment that increases job performance without additional cost, as organizational citizenship behavior by nature is voluntary, would be an important goal for administrators' consideration. Specifically, it is recommended that administrators understand the relatively consistent results from this and studies already existing in the literature outside the educational setting.

REFERENCES

Ackfeldt, A. L., & Coote, L. V. (2005). A study of organizational citizenship behaviors in a retail setting. *Journal of Business Research*, *58*(1), 151–159.

Allen, T. D., & Rush, M. C. (1998). The effects of citizenship behavior on performance judgments: A field study and a laboratory experiment. *Journal of Applied Psychology*, *83*, 247–260.

Babbie, E. (2007). *The practice of social research* (11th ed.). Belmont, CA: Thomson Wadsworth.

Bateman, T. S., & Organ, D. W. (1983). Job satisfaction and the good soldier: The relationship between affect and employee "citizenship". *Academy of Management Journal*, *26*, 587–595.

Becton, J. B., Giles, W. F., & Schraeder, M. (2008). Evaluating and rewarding OCBs: Potential consequences of formally incorporating organizational citizenship behaviour in performance appraisal and reward systems. *Employee Relations*, *30*(5), 494–514.

Bienstock, C. C., DeMoranville, C. W., & Smith, R. K. (2003). Organizational citizenship behavior and service quality. *The Journal of Services Marketing*, *17*(4/5), 357–378.

Bolino, M. C., & Turnley, W. H. (2003). Going the extra mile: Cultivating and managing employee citizenship behavior. *Academy of Management Executive*, *17*, 60–71.

Borman, W. C., & Motowidlo, S. J. (1993). Expanding the criterion domain to include elements of contextual performance. In W. C. Borman (Ed.), *Personnel selection in organizations* (pp. 71–98). San Francisco, CA: Jossey-Bass.

Burton, C. H. (2003). *An empirical investigation of the interrelationships of organizational culture, managerial values, and organizational citizenship behaviors*. Unpublished doctor of education dissertation. The George Washington University, District of Columbia.

Castro, C. B., Armario, E. M., & Ruiz, D. M. (2004). The influence of employee citizenship behavior on customer loyalty. *International Journal of Service Industry Management*, *15*(1), 27–54.

Deckop, J. R., Mangel, R., & Cirka, C. C. (1999). Getting more than you pay for: Organizational citizenship behavior and pay for performance plans. *Academy of Management Journal*, *42*, 420–428.

DiPaola, M. F., Tarter, C. J., & Hoy, W. K. (2004). Measuring organizational citizenship: The OCB scale. In W. K. Hoy & C. Miskel (Eds.), *Educational leadership and reform* (pp. 319–342). Greenwich, CT: Information Age.

DiPaola, M. F., & Tschannen-Moran, M. (2001). Organizational citizenship behavior in schools and its relationship to school climate. *Journal of School Leadership*, *11*, 424–447.

Farh, J. L., Zhong, C. B., & Organ, D. W. (2004). Organizational citizenship behavior in the People's Republic of China. *Organization Science*, *15*, 241–253.

Graham, J. W. (1991). An essay on organizational citizenship behavior. *Employee Responsibilities and Rights Journal, 4,* 249–270.

Griffin, G. (1992). *Principals' and superintendents' perceptions of superintendent behaviors and activities which are linked to school effectiveness.* Unpublished doctoral dissertation. The University of Oklahoma.

Korsgaard, M. A., Meglino, B. M., Lester, S. W., & Jeong, S. S. (2010). Paying you back or paying me forward: Understanding rewarded and unrewarded organizational citizenship behavior. *Journal of Applied Psychology, 95*(2), 277–290.

Lievens, F., & Anseel, F. (2004). Confirmatory factor analysis and invariance of an organizational citizenship behavior measure across samples in a Dutch-speaking context. *Journal of Occupational and Organizational Psychology, 77,* 299–306.

Longenecker, C. O., Sims, H. P., & Gioia, D. A. (1987). Behind the mask: The politics of employee appraisal. *The Academy of Management Executive, 1*(3), 183–193.

MacKenzie, S. B., Podsakoff, P. M., & Fetter, R. (1991). Organizational citizenship behavior and objective productivity as determinants of managerial evaluations of salespersons' performance. *Organizational Behavior and Human Decision Processes, 50,* 123–150.

MacKenzie, S. B., Podsakoff, P. M., & Fetter, R. (1993). The impact of organizational citizenship behavior on evaluations of sales performance. *Journal of Marketing, 57,* 70–80.

McBain, R. (2004). Developing organisational citizenship behaviour. *Henley Manager Update, 16,* 26–33.

Moorman, R. H., & Blakely, G. L. (1995). Individualism-collectivism as an individual difference predictor of organizational citizenship behavior. *Journal of Organizational Behavior, 16,* 127–142.

Motowidlo, S. J. (2000). Some basic issues related to contextual performance and organizational citizenship behavior in human resource management. *Human Resource Management Review, 10*(1), 115–126.

Nagarajah, L. (2008). Developing and validating an instrument to assess performance of public sector organizations: A case study of Malaysian schools. *Measuring Business Excellence, 12*(3), 56–75.

Netemeyer, R. G., James, S. B., McKee, D. O., & McMurrian, R. C. (1997). An investigation into the antecedents of organizational citizenship behaviors in a personal selling context. *Journal of Marketing, 61*(July), 85–98.

Neuman, W. L. (2006). *Social research methods: Qualitative and quantitative approaches* (6th ed.). Boston, MA: Pearson Education, Inc.

Ng, T. W. H., & Feldman, D. C. (2008). The relationship of age to ten dimensions of job performance. *Journal of Applied Psychology, 93,* 392–423.

Norhayati, M. A., & Siti Nabiha, A. K. (2009). A case study of performance management system in a Malaysian government-linked company. *Journal of Accounting and Organizational Change, 5*(2), 243–276.

Organ, D. W. (1988). *Organizational citizenship behavior: The good soldier syndrome.* Lexington, MA: Lexington Books.

Organ, D. W. (1997). Organizational citizenship behavior: It's construct clean-up time. *Human Performance, 10,* 85–97.

Organ, D. W., & Konovsky, M. A. (1989). Cognitive versus affective determinants of organizational citizenship behavior. *Journal of Applied Psychology, 74*(1), 157–164.

Organ, D. W., Podsakoff, P. M., & MacKenzie, S. B. (2006). *Organizational citizenship behavior. Its nature, antecedents and consequences.* Thousand Oaks, CA: Sage Publications.

Organ, D. W., & Ryan, K. (1995). A meta-analytic review of attitudinal and dispositional predictors of organizational citizenship behavior. *Personnel Psychology, 48,* 775–802.

Pallant, J. (2005). *SPSS survival manual* (2nd ed.). New York, NY: McGraw-Hill.

Piercy, N. P., Lane, N., & Cravens, D. W. (2002). Sales manager gender and salesperson organizational citizenship behavior. *Women in Management Review, 17*(8), 373–391.

Podsakoff, P. M., & MacKenzie, S. B. (1994). Organizational citizenship behaviors and sales unit effectiveness. *Journal of Marketing Research, 31,* 351–363.

Podsakoff, P. M., MacKenzie, S. B., Moorman, R. H., & Fetter, R. (1990). Transformational leader behaviors and their effects on followers' trust in leader, satisfaction, and organizational citizenship behaviors. *Leadership Quarterly, 1,* 107–142.

Podsakoff, P. M., MacKenzie, S. B., Paine, J. B., & Bachrach, D. G. (2000). Organizational citizenship behaviors: A critical review of the theoretical and empirical literature and suggestions for future research. *Journal of Management, 26,* 513–563.

Public Service Department, Malaysia. (2007a). Surat Pekeliling Bilangan 12 Tahun 2007. Dated 13 December 2007.

Public Service Department, Malaysia. (2007b). *Pekeliling Bilangan 33 Tahun 2007. Skim Perkhidmatan Pegawai Pendidikan Pengajian Tinggi.* Putrajaya: Jabatan Perkhidmatan.

Rego, A., Ribeiro, N., & Cunha, M. (2010). Perceptions of organizational virtuousness and happiness as predictors of organizational citizenship behaviors. *Journal of Business Ethics, 93*(2), 215–235.

Schnake, M. E., & Dumler, M. P. (2003). Levels of measurement and analysis issues in organizational citizenship behavior research. *Journal of Occupational and Organizational Psychology, 76,* 283–301.

Schneider, B. (1996). Whither goest personality at work? *Applied Psychology: An International Review, 45,* 289–296.

Somech, A., & Drach-Zahavy, A. (2000). Understanding extra-role behavior in schools: The relationships between job satisfaction, sense of efficacy and teachers' extra-role behavior. *Teaching and Teacher Education, 16,* 649–659.

Turnipseed, D. L. (2002). Are good soldiers good? Exploring the link between organizational citizenship behavior and personal ethics. *Journal of Business Research, 55,* 1–15.

Van Dyne, L., Graham, J. G., & Dienesch, R. M. (1994). Organizational citizenship behavior: Construct redefinition, operationalization, and validation. *Academy of Management Journal, 37,* 765–802.

Van Scotter, J. R., & Motowidlo, S. J. (1996). Interpersonal facilitation and job dedication as separate facets of contextual performance. *Journal of Applied Psychology, 81,* 525–531.

Werner, J. M. (1994). Dimensions that make a difference: Examining the impact of in-role and extra-role behaviors on supervisory ratings. *Journal of Applied Psychology, 94,* 98–107.

Williams, L. J., & Anderson, S. E. (1991). Job satisfaction and organizational commitment as predictors of organizational citizenship and in-role behaviors. *Journal of Management, 17,* 601–617.

PART II
APPLICATIONS OF DISCRETIONARY BEHAVIOR IN EDUCATIONAL ORGANIZATIONS

CHAPTER 6

NATURE OF LEADERSHIP DISCRETIONS AND SUSTAINABILITY OF EDUCATIONAL INNOVATIONS: CRITICAL CONNECTIONS

Tamara Savelyeva and Yeung Lee

ABSTRACT

The inherit complexity of an educational system further complicates the challenge of introducing technology-based educational initiatives into a school environment. Once introduced, the initiative has the potential to become self-sustaining or to cease once the term is over. Such uncertainty makes the use of expensive information technology (IT) in schools "risky business," which requires school leaders go above and beyond their current routine to extend the system's capacity to sustain the innovation. A discretionary behavior of school leaders and teachers is one of key factors that contribute to or prevent the sustainability of an innovation. A lack of understanding of what encourages an individual's discretionary behavior and how discretion is fostered in school practices contribute to the challenge of innovation's sustainability. If the individuals' discretion is required to sustain a technology-based educational program within a school, do their actions

Discretionary Behavior and Performance in Educational Organizations: The Missing Link in Educational Leadership and Management
Advances in Educational Administration, Volume 13, 141–168
ISSN: 1479-3660/doi:10.1108/S1479-3660(2012)0000013011

dwell outside or inside of the school environment? More importantly, how does a discretionary chain of command operate and can it be aligned? In this chapter we use an "ecological model" approach to describe the influential factors, which affect project's sustainability by transforming effective discretionary approaches of school leaders and teachers from policy to practice. We draw our description of the model on the results of the empirical study of Hong Kong schools involved in the design and strategic IT implementation of the e-Leadership Enhancement Project *(*eLEP*)*.

BACKGROUND OF THE STUDY AND LITERATURE REVIEW

This study highlights aspects of research on discretionary behavior (DB) and how it relates to the applications in sustaining information technology (IT) innovations in schools. To gain a comprehensive picture of this broad topic, we divided the following review in two parts: the use of discretion in educational studies and ecological approaches to educational leadership research. In the first part, we define our meanings of discretion and provide background information on various generalizations about discretion and IT innovations. The second part contains review of literature related to ecological approaches in leadership studies.

Discretion and Innovation

Defined as the "latitude of action" of an individual (Hambrick & Frankelstein, 1987), the concept of professional discretion is recognized as a major factor, which contributes to sustaining a technological innovation in educational settings (Banathy, 2010; Fullan, 2007; Law, 2008). When the level of discretionary behavior is low, the adaptation of innovation within schools becomes constrained by the formalized chain of command and organizational rules. When discretion is given to principals and teachers, they become relatively free in choosing their actions, which can cause an innovation to become self-sustaining or to fail outright. Following in line with Kiser and Hogan (2006), we view discretion as a situational variable that moderates the degree of organizational processes and outcomes.

The literature on discretion behavior has yielded three generalizations relevant to our discussion of sustaining innovations in schools. The first rule of thumb is that discretion includes three aspects – environment, organization, and personal attributes – that allow educational theorists to comprehensively view the dynamics of change brought about by introduction of technology. This combination of aspects leads to a second generalization: discretion is important for getting the job done in "situations for which conventional administrative authority and methods are ineffective" (Cilo, 1994, p. 91). Cilo's (1994) work illustrated the importance of discretion by school principals in implementing change through bridged management and influence on micro-politics at the leadership level. Third, discretion is a characteristic of not just leadership behavior, but it is also a descriptor of a teacher's actions. Crowson and Porter-Gehrie (1980) reflected on discretionary "rule bending" by both principals and teachers. Their work showed the power of discretion was spread throughout the school hierarchy of command and provided a concept of the multileveled application. Crowson and Porter-Gehrie indicated a potential conflict between different discretionary mechanisms of school leaders and teachers: "the actions taken by one … may be at odds with … [discretionary] mechanism that is considered necessary by the other" (p. 67). Thus, an accurate understanding of the discretionary behavior mechanisms at work is central to identifying the appropriate ways of aligning behavior of both school leaders and teachers and ensuring the educational innovation sustain itself.

We argue that an alignment of discretionary behavior of both principals and teachers is the key to successful technology introduction in schools. Discretion can only work when all the participants are empowered with the complete responsibility for success or failure. When they are only partly in charge or responsible, discretion becomes directly limited by their proportion of authority and accountability. Yet, when specific behaviors are made mandatory this decreases the innovativeness, and thus principals and teachers alike lose motivation and professional satisfaction for the overall project. Most individuals, more often than not, would prefer freedom to succeed with the chance to failure compare with dictated behaviors for guaranteed success. However, the biggest challenge to this argument for individual freedom is the interdependence of the defining aspects of discretion (environment, organization, and personal attributes), which requires us to use a nonlinear approach for understanding the role of discretion in innovation's introduction across different levels of school organizations and their dynamics. To address this challenge, we apply ecological approaches to frame and analyze the power of discretion that influences the introduction of an innovation in the selected educational settings.

Ecological Frameworks and Approaches

Multiple ecological frameworks are present in the educational research literature to provide structures for leadership studies on the multifaceted process of IT innovation and its introductions to school systems. In these studies, the term *ecological* is used quite loosely, as an alternative to the conventional approach that focuses primarily on the three aspects of discretion and their role in the innovation's introduction. The studies that employ conventional approaches (Kozma, 2003; Law, Pelgrum, & Plomp, 2008; Stein & Coburn, 2008; Yeung, Lee, & Yue, 2006) investigated different characteristics and dimensions of school interactive behavior, organization, functioning across micro- and macro-levels of teaching practices. In contrast, our use of ecological frameworks meets the challenge for creating a synergetic understanding of the multiple factors, players, and phenomenon that make an innovation self-sustaining or doomed to extinction. Ecological approaches allow researchers like ourselves to explore, modify, and evaluate the dynamics and impacts of discretionary behavior in a nonlinear way.

Applications of ecological frameworks to educational studies are built upon the assumption that schools are interactive, complex, and adaptive systems (Morrison, 2002), which display all the characteristics of system behavior, including self-perpetuation. There are multiple ecosystem approaches that focus on different aspects of complexity, including: ecological metaphors, population ecology approach, and ecological modeling.

The ecological metaphors are often used in scientific discourses to reflect the wide array of processes and interactions within educational environments. Eco-metaphors usually make a case for a general application of an ecosystem approach through the analysis of an educational system without actually guiding the research. In their study of educational innovation and change in schools, Law, Yuen, and Fox (2011) use a set of eco-metaphors recognizing the importance of a "total educational ecology and ... all factors that need to be considered when planning for continuous change and innovation" (2011, p. 196). Viewing classroom as an "ecosystem" where "different species" of technological innovations are introduced, they provided a detailed description of the introduction process based on the responses of school principals, teachers, and university researchers involved.

Although Law et al.'s (2011) study draws on a more general picture of educational change in schools and not discretionary behavior, there are a few studies in the literature that list specific factors of discretionary behavior. Marcovitz (2006) points out the importance of external rewards and incentives in sustaining innovative projects. He argues for the removal of disincentives and allow teachers to learn from failure rather than "punishing people who try innovative things that fail" (cited in Marcovitz, 2006, p. 12). Other factors related to discretion and cited in the literature include but are not limited to the role of job position/authority, professional ambition, decision mechanisms, and barriers to/liabilities for overstepping professional boundaries.

A "population ecology" approach is often used in studies of organizational change. Hannan and Freeman (1977) used this framework to argue for change being a result of natural environmental selection rather than managerial action. The opposite of "population ecology" is the "strategic-choice" view that acknowledges the role of administrators in organizational actions and outcomes, yet denies the influence of environmental factors. Following these ideas, Hambrick and Frankelstein (1987) applied a construct of discretion for uniting the polar opposite "population ecology" and "strategic-choice" views together by explaining the nature of social dynamics at the top administrative level. They argued that potential variations in executive discretionary behavior are determined in part by the appropriateness of the ecological and strategic-choice views within a specific organizational system.

In contrast to these eco-metaphors, eco-modeling has been used as a research tool in educational studies. Eco-modeling draws on the ideas of interconnectedness and nonlinearity of innovative models in education (Savelyeva, 2009, 2011; Savelyeva & McKenna, 2011). Bethany (1991) and Fullan (2007) considered structural alignment of all the elements across different levels of an education system as very important for constructing a model. This was also described in the works of Biggs and Tang (2003) and Meyer (2000).

THE RESEARCH SCOPE

Our research provides a detailed description of the ecological model of several Hong Kong schools, involved in the design and implementation of the *e-Leadership Enhancement Project* (*eLEP*). Using approaches of the ecological framework in this study, we integrate three ecological principles with discretionary behavior and the process of innovation introduction; specifically we examined the principles of emergence, spatial relationships and disturbances, and diversity.

(1) The *emergent nature* of innovation sustained by the discretionary behavior of school leaders and teachers, where change is the norm and is driven by a multitude of interacting factors and conditions;
(2) The roles of *spatial relationships* and *disturbances* in sustaining the innovation through discretionary behavior; and
(3) The *diversity* of influences within a school setting which can advance the system overall, not just a composition of multiple levels, components, and fluxes.

Overall, these ecological principles allow for a more holistic and systemic investigation of the discretionary behavior phenomena among teachers and principals that is essential for understanding the process of discretion alignment. This ecological framework is best suited for the study of discretion and educational innovations, because it can encompass a wide range of perspectives that reflect on the paradigmatic breadth of discretion mechanisms and innovation as two interrelated phenomena. It allows for the incorporation of a full range of discretionary factors that influence the longevity of innovation's introduction.

PURPOSE

The purpose of our study was to explore the role of discretion and the mechanism of discretionary behavior alignment across school levels during the process of introducing a technology-based educational innovation within a school environment.

Our guiding research questions are:

1. How does the discretionary behavior of school leaders and teachers influences and sustains the new practices within the *eLEP* initiative?
2. What aspects of discretionary behavior encourage the self-sustaining nature of innovation within an educational environment?

CONCEPTUAL FRAMEWORK

At the principal level, we will use a framework of the transformative leader (TL) (Davis, 2008; Hallinger & Heck, 1998; Stewart, 2006) that views change as a result of strategically distributed, cross-level guidance within a specific educational environment. Among multiple leadership theories found in the literature, TL provides the most prominent and empirically grounded theoretical lens for understanding the role of leadership behavior to initiate change and sustain a new project in schools (Bass & Avolio, 1994). TL emphasizes the ability of a leader to boost commitment, capacity, and engagement of his/her employees to meet strategic goals (Leithwood & Jantzi, 2000; Marks & Printy, 2003). Transformative leadership can be thought of as a form of positive discretionary behavior which "motivates followers to do more than they originally expected and often even more than they thought possible, resulting in extra effort and greater productivity" (Bass, 1985; Bass & Avolio, 1994; cited in Moolenaar, Daly, & Sleegers, 2010). A transformational leader, according to Jung and Avolio (2000), can create an environment that will motivate his/her employees to exceed initial expectations.

The following aspects of the TL concept are particularly relevant to our study of discretion and innovation: building school vision and establishing school goals, providing intellectual stimulation, offering individualized support, modeling best practices and important organizational values, demonstrating high-performance expectations, creating a productive school culture, and developing structures to foster participation in school decisions (cited in Leithwood & Jantzi, 2000, p. 114). Among those aspects, the challenge of building organizational culture that fosters the continual improvement of programs and teachers' professional capacities is considered the most significant (Stewart, 2006). Because many leaders are often insufficient in meeting this challenge, we might consider the dispersal of leadership authority (Harris, 2004; Harris & Chapman, 2002; Lambert, 2002; Sergiovanni, 2007) as the separate aspect known as employee empowerment.

At the teachers' level where school culture has its greatest influence, we assess discretionary behavior and the process of sustaining an innovation through teacher empowerment and self-evaluation, where teachers' actions are guided by their "tacit knowledge" of education, formed in response to personal and contextual factors. Within this framework, teachers' fundamental beliefs are a focal point for the analysis of teacher's positive discretion and its influences sustain innovation. According to findings from the field (Efron & Joseph, 2001; Fischer & Kiefer, 2001; Ryan, 2005; Sugrue, 1998) these fundamental beliefs shape teachers' implicit knowledge and may affect their discretionary behavior during the introduction of any new project. The ideas of empowerment and self-reflective action assisted our discovery of other hidden factors that guided teachers' discretion behavior and influence their innovative practices together within the overt dimensions of administration.

All together, the ecological principles, TL, and self-reflective action frameworks will guide our understanding of the alignment process between principal and teacher discretion practices in a school environment.

E-LEADERSHIP ENHANCEMENT PROJECT

eLEP was launched by the Education and Manpower Bureau of Hong Kong in 2005. It aimed to support and evaluate the long-term impact of an IT implementation in Hong Kong schools. The series of pilot training were performed in 10 schools, including 3 primary, 6 secondary, and 1 special education school. School leaders, teachers, and university researchers worked together to (1) create and implement strategic IT adaptation plans in their participating schools and (2) to overcome challenges of IT introduction and provide support to participating schools. The schools were selected based on a quality of their initial proposals, which each school submitted in order to participate in *eLEP*. At the end of the project, schools reported on their progress at the final *eLEP* meeting and shared their future plans. For more information on this project visit http://elep.cite.hku.hk/casestories.

METHODS

We utilized a qualitative research design methodology with a case study approach (Yin, 2004) in order to develop an ecosystem model for evaluating the role of discretion in sustaining technology-based projects in schools. We applied a purposeful sampling method in selecting three information-rich cases of the *eLEP*, which involved primary, secondary, and special schools' principals and teachers. The selection criteria for the case study schools included (1) participation and enthusiasm of the principals in the *eLEP* project and (2) quality of school-based strategic development plans submitted after a pilot *eLEP* trial.

Data Collection and Instrumentation

We employed three forms of data collection: (1) focus group interviews of the school principals and teachers involved in the development and implementation of the *eLEP* projects to identify the aspects of the discretionary behavior that affect innovation's introduction, adaptation, and longevity, (2) textual narratives, documents, and artifacts, which were available to and created by the *eLEP* projects' participants to design, introduce, and adapt the innovation within their schools, and (3) observations of a classroom practice/field work. The combination of these three data collection methods ensured dependability of the study and the trustworthiness of its results.

This study was a two-step project, which involved separate model building at the levels of school leadership and teacher practice. Separating the participants by their level of involvement provided us with two independent images of discretionary behaviors, from the development to implementation, and across different dimensions of school environments. The merging of these models developed at "policy" and "praxis" levels provided a fuller, "3D" vision of a sustainable educational environment.

The focus group method is best suited for our study as it combines elements of both interviewing and participant observation. It provided an opportunity to probe the participants' responses while also observing underlying group dynamics (Vaughn, Schumm, & Sinagub, 1996). The focus group interview instrument consisted of open-ended questions, created upon the data on educational leadership, innovation, and change available in the literature.

We conducted a set of field observations where possible and appropriate to examine how a discretionary chain of command operates in the *eLEP* schools. We videotaped all observations and used the field notes that resulted from observations to supplement focus group recordings. We employed an analysis of textual narratives, documents, and artifacts, which were available to and created by the *eLEP*'s participants to design, introduce, and adapt the innovation within their schools. For the document and artifact analysis, we used a document summary form, adapted from Miles and Huberman (1994). The documentation included a complete set of the 10 *eLEP* case studies. The school's *e-Confidence* matrixes, action plans, schedules, schemes of work, policy, and professional development plans were collected during and after the *eLEP* project.

Data Analysis

The resulted data was analyzed using the QSR NUD_IST (Qualitative Software for Non-numerical Unstructured Data Indexing Searching and Theorizing) Vivo (v.2), also called NVivo®. NVivo is a qualitative data analysis program, which provides various tools for holistic reflective-interpretive approaches to data analyses. With the use of the NVivo software package, we employed a thematic approach to latent data analysis performed across its articulated, attributional, and emergent levels of interpretation. This ensured the clarity of the interpretation and made analysis more transparent to research stakeholders.

The data analysis consisted of three parts. First, we identified themes and generated codes with the coding feature of the software. Second, we cross-analyzed codes for potential relationships and mapped over the themes and theoretical memos, created with the "memo" feature of the software. We also analyzed the available textual narratives, field notes, and recordings resulted from document/artifacts collection together in the cross-case analysis of potential relationships among research constructs. Third, we derived the desired model using the "union" feature of the software.

RESULTS

The types of innovations introduced in participating schools included: use of Internet and pocket PCs for students' project-based learning, use of PowerPoint® software in class, and Learning Management platform® and e-Class® system for school management and administration. Several themes emerged through the process of data analysis, which we performed using a constant comparative method[1] (Lincoln & Guba, 1985). The analyses revealed the following domains of a discretionary behavior model: shared vision, empowerment, institutional commitment, collaboration, and school culture. The analysis also revealed a major criterion, which we called a "focus on students' needs," which bonded the five domains and ensured instances of positive discretionary behavior by school leaders and their teachers. Both the discovered criteria and five domains comprised a model of discretionary behavior that influenced the successful innovation introduction for the schools within the study (see Fig. 1). In the light of these findings, discretionary behavior appeared as a construct of each participant's willingness to expand their efforts above and beyond their formal requirements and duties in order to sustain the innovation within their classroom (see Table 1 for examples of discretionary behaviors, their facilitators, and obstacles).

Domain One: Shared Vision

Shared vision refers to the process of creating a group image of positive change for the whole school which will be created by the innovation's

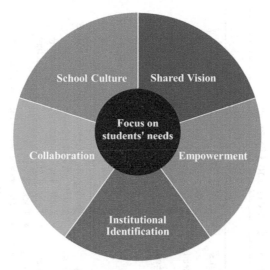

Fig. 1. Discretionary Behavior Model.

introduction. For the schools in our study, shared vision was initially molded by the school mission statements (Table 2). Guiding all school actions, each mission statement provided a common focus and supported the co-constructed vision for the dynamic change of individuals and their schools.

The indicators of discretionary behavior within the shared vision's domain included (a) alternation of personal preferences for the purpose of the common good and (b) focus on the same goals across all participants.

Willingness to alter one's own belief and sacrifice individual preferences in order to meet needs of other school members was an important part of the process. Shared vision required participants' to shift from individual to group thinking and involved the gradual alternation of their personal beliefs about the potential value of innovation. To initiate this process, principals provided a comprehensive description of IT innovation and a general direction for its introduction within the school and established opportunities for communication among participants.

Setting a general direction rather than providing a preset plan for introduction was strategically empowering to all participants and gave them a sense of ownership within the process. The absence of a strict plan invited all school members to share their ideas about how the innovation could be

Table 1. Observed Discretionary Behaviors, Their Facilitators and Obstacles.

Discretionary Behaviors	Facilitators	Obstacles
Teachers: • Volunteer for non-mandatory roles and tasks • Collaborate with other teachers on planning, reflecting, and reporting • Offer lesson materials prepared for the class to other group members • Assign tasks to the class for a substituted teacher • Attend non-mandatory meetings • Stay after school hours to help project members with planning materials • Seek professional development opportunities • Stay in class during breaks • Participate in functions which help the projects' image • Organize separate displays for project-related information • Stay back at lunch to assist project members with IT • Fill out additional project-related forms and evaluations	• Willingness to take on new roles • High engagement of school members in planning and reflections • High degree of initiative • Group-led decision-making teams • A sense of distributed accountability for meeting project goals • Acceptance of personal responsibility for the success of the project team • Everyone has a strong knowledge of the school vision • Equal accountability for project success and for students' learning • Teachers view themselves as leaders • Delegation of authentic powers • Making ongoing professional development a priority • A sense of professional community that are empowered to make decisions	• Lack of willingness to invest in a participative leadership model • Personalized decision-making • Unequal efforts of teachers and principals • Poorly distributed leadership roles • Lack of acceptance for new ideas and suggestions • Perception that a school is great as it is and don't need change • Strong top-down power structure • Inadequate information about the project and its implementation • Lack of infrastructure for info-sharing • Lack of IT maintenance infrastructure • Lack of time • Teachers are placed on a periphery of the process • Lack of trust • Fault-finding approach to communication • Self-oriented and uncooperative behaviors • Senior-teacher's resistance to a leadership style of a new principal

Teachers and Principals:

- Organize joint activities with project investigators
- Make suggestions to improve the project
- Check on group members who have problems implementing IT in their lessons
- Take time to listen to group members, reflect on their stories, and address their concerns
- Assist school members in adapting an IT innovation
- Participate actively in project meetings
- Make an effort to tolerate individual differences
- Arrive to work earlier than required
- Attend out-of-school project meetings
- Come to school on free days
- Participate in celebrations of project's milestones
- Organize project showcases for parents

- Trabnsparent decision-making
- Clear goals and expectations
- Timely reflection on the process
- Principal ensures reciprocal communication
- The school and project structure support continues learning opportunities
- Teamwork and work in committees
- Collaboration is both intentional and unintentional
- Agreement on common goals
- School members have a sense of identification
- Resources support goals
- Public access to the project data
- Recognition of different views and opinions
- Individual and group recognition of project contributors
- School-wide effective and frequent communication
- Common and clear vision
- Leaders' support for trying new and taking risks

Table 2.   School Mission Statements.

School	Mission Statements
Case school A	A special school provides high quality education services to children with special needs. It aims to provide students with all-round education and help them to develop lifelong learning abilities to become independent, confident, active, and contributive citizens.
Case school B	With the love of Christ, compassion for humanity, and a progressive attitude, we strive to deliver a quality education, to develop students' potential to the fullest, to share with them the Gospel, and to cultivate in them a sense of good citizenship which will benefit our society and nation.
Case school C	The school aims to build a team that is open and ready to learn new knowledge and skills. In short, leading a high-performance team by means of providing an effective communication channel to the teachers is part of the vision of school C for the 2005–2006 school year.
Case school D	The "Reading School, Thinking Community" school strives to provide a positive learning environment that enhances each student's opportunity to learn and develop at his/her own rate through a balanced educational program, which recognizes the need for growth in attitude, knowledge, and skills through moral, intellectual, social, physical, spiritual, and aesthetic development. The schools' long-term goal is to groom dynamic, caring, goal-directed, and self-motivated students for the third millennium.

introduced in a school and thus contributed significantly to the creation of a shared vision which all participants could believe in.

Domain Two: Empowerment

Empowerment is the participants' perception of having a voice and a stake in all decisions and resolutions, which influenced the success or failure of the innovation's introduction. By pulling toward a common ground together, a sense of renewed power and reliance was created for many participants. The three indicators of discretionary behavior related to the empowerment of participants were revealed and included (a) all participants taking an active role in the innovation's introduction, (b) teachers voicing their own ideas within the decision-making process, and (c) willingness of a school leader to give up some control while monitoring the effectiveness of decisions through results.

By involving all the participants and not simply seeking the opinions of the most experienced teachers or administrators, we observed that successful innovation's introduction utilized the strengths of the entire group and fostered a personal commitment to the school. Participants used a word "we" to describe their experiences with the introduction process and indicate professional empowerment with the authority to finalize resolutions together. Voicing their opinions more openly, participants also changed the conversational style from a top-down administrator lecture to a participatory discussion by the end of a project. A strong sense of empowerment was perceived by the teachers when principals delegated control over the process for monitoring success to subordinate members, and thus the leaders instilled a group commitment to the process, project, and to the school as whole.

Domain Three: Institutional Commitment

Institutional commitment refers to the self-identification of participants with their schools and their personal awareness of a linked future together. The participants' commitment was expressed as a degree of individual attachment and identification with various school goals that directed their specific acts of discretionary behavior. Instances of positive discretionary behavior observed related to this domain included: (a) teachers voluntarily taking on new roles while implementing the new technologies, (b) leaders delegating decision-making, (c) principals remaining open to trying new ideas, (d) teachers not being afraid to make mistakes, and (e) administrators allowing participants to learn through trial and error.

Time working in a particular school and participants' level of experience affected their level of commitment to their institution. Schools with an experienced, yet newly assigned school leaders were prone to embracing dynamic change and showed more flexibility while experimenting with different leadership strategies. On the other hand, schools with an experienced and internally promoted leader showed dedication to the "tried and true" leadership style of predecessors while adopting new technologies.

Domain Four: Collaboration

Collaboration refers to a sense of team building and mutual learning which will propel the school ahead with introduction of an innovation. Widespread and open communication was key to the process of collaboration. The observed instances of collaborative discretionary behavior included: (a) discussing information openly and gathering feedback from all participants, (b) attending regular meetings to share information and discuss it with all participants, and (c) encouraging each individual to take an active role in the innovation introduction, for example, volunteering. Principals and teachers acted together as a group to incorporate an innovation within their school. They used their own ideas and abilities to be united in the one effort as a group, who normally do their teaching and administrative work as isolated individuals. Collaboration served as a foundation for building togetherness and team spirit. This team approach gave participants opportunities to communicate their concerns, openly discuss information about implementation process, and exchange pertinent data concerning innovation introduction.

Domain Five: School Culture

School culture refers to the basic assumptions that drive school businesses and typical patterns of interactions among teachers and administrators. The data showed that school culture which promoted positive discretionary behavior was built on mutual respect among its participants and respect for traditions of the school. The instances of discretionary behavior related to school culture included (a) acknowledging individual and group contributions toward innovation introduction and dedication to the goals, (b) principals supporting decisions of the teachers, and (c) mutual support of all the participants. School culture defined the level of participants' openness to implementing new innovations and their flexibility with accepting new practices. Schools that exhibited an established climate of mutual respect and cultivated a sense of trust among all the participants had wider discretionary latitude to sustain an innovation.

Criterion One: Focusing on Students' Needs

The criterion of focusing on students' needs refers to both teachers and principals placing their foremost attention on what is beneficial for students above all else. Instances of this focus included: (a) holding high expectations for results, (b) considering different students' cognitive levels and the specifics of a class' curriculum while choosing technology, (c) committing to the goals of a group, and (d) looking for different strategies to promote learning within a class.

The overarching focus on students' needs suggested that improvement was possible in both teaching and learning practices with the introduction of a new technology. Academic improvement of students, as well as change in their skills, behavior, performance, and comprehension, was a major motivator for teachers and administrators that generated acts of discretionary behavior. The demand for successful teaching and amplified by the innovation created benefits for students and their education.

DISCUSSION

Sustainability of Innovation and Discretionary Behavior

By using an ecological framework to translate the general meaning of sustaining innovations in schools into specific research measures, our study is expected to aid public discourse by advancing discretionary behavior through creating a model of its informed decision-making process. The ecological framework in our study (1) helped to identify the structural, social, and other emerging realms of the educational phenomena so they can be described with precision and accuracy, (2) extract useful generalizations about the role of discretionary behavior in an innovation's introduction process, and (3) define the mechanisms for the alignment of the discretionary mechanisms across all system levels.

In this study, we utilized three principles of an ecosystem's organization: emergence, spatial relationships and disturbance, and diversity. We applied these principles to the DB model in order to understand the underlining mechanisms which sustain the educational phenomena we observed. It is important to perceive the principles of emergence, spatial relationships, and diversity all together and simultaneously. Individually, they represent sustaining powers of the system that can only work when all other ecological principles are fulfilled.

What is significant here is that discretionary behavior is sustained in terms of principles, and not entities. This is important to understand for the two reasons. First, the analysis of discretionary behavior requires a methodological reduction and comparative analysis: (a) deriving components and factors influencing its instances, (b) composing a comprehensive model, and (c) making connections among its parts. This step-by-step approach to creating a model of DB provided us some insights into the nature of DB in terms of its structure and connectivity with different educational aspects (i.e., individual, social, and environmental). However, to understand what sustains the model, it is also helpful to know the ways the three aspects of the model behave when they formed as a complex system. In other words, what holds the individual, social, and environmental aspects of the model together in comparison their behavior isolation will not necessarily sustain the system they comprise. Second, the significance of the dependence on ecosystem principles (i.e., emergency, spatial relationships, and diversity) for a discretionary behavior model to work is that the accuracy of the results will be higher and therefore more applicable to different educational settings. This means, a model of *how* DB occurs might be entirely different from our proposed model. However, this will not affect the connections derived from the use of ecological principles themselves. The application of ecological principles does not suggest dismissing comparative and reductionist approaches to analyze the DB phenomenon. We need to be aware of their limitations and refrain from excusing possible methodological discrepancies.

Principle of Emergence
The principle of emergence addresses one of the major limitations of applying an ecological framework to educational modeling; specifically it is difficult to derive exact results from a model's generalizations. Modeling, as the way to explain the observed educational phenomena, provides us with explanatory details describing the functioning mechanisms within the system. However, it fails to explain the exact sustaining connections associated with a "transitory" phenomenon, such as introduction of a new IT in schools and the discretionary behavior of participants. While the phenomena in the study displayed connective properties among the different domains of the model, innovation introduction and discretionary behavior are emergent in nature and difficult to model. This simply means that they arise from but are not necessarily dependent on the educational processes and entities involved in our study. Although high approximations and precise predictions about instances of discretionary behavior during an innovation introduction follow the model, more generally they arise from the ideas that (a) this model exhibits spontaneous attributes and (b) the sustaining power of the model goes beyond the connectivity among its parts. This kind of synergic evolution and asymmetry in the model's properties suggests that the whole becomes more than and very different from the sum of its parts.

Principle of Spatial Relationships and Disturbances
In a natural ecosystem, all elements of the system relate to each other in a spatial manner: they are linked in a non-direct, proximate fashion, which affects ecosystem function in a nonlinear way (Krohne, 1998; Townsend,

Begon, & Harper, 2008). Disturbances refer to a temporary change in average environmental conditions that causes a pronounced change in an entire system. As natural part of an ecosystem cycle, disturbances enable the system to change either by adaptation or through transformation (Beeby & Brennan, 2008).

Instances of DB during innovation introduction in schools occurred neither uniformly nor randomly. They rather created some sort of a "patchy" distribution pattern due to various influencing factors and interactions of participants. These internal and external factors are temporary changes, or disturbances in a regular school dynamics that have a potential to create larger changes within a school system. We selected the spatial relationships principle for the DB model so to understand its underlining patterns of distribution within participants' discretionary behavior. It helped to focus our study on the functional relationships, rather than the immediate or short-term effectiveness of the model to describe our observations.

The instances of DB are a result of multiple educational processes, which often operate at different spatial scales. Spatial scale refers to the size, location, and to what extent DB occurred and its interpretation by participants. Using the spatial principle not only allows us to place the occurrences of DB within a particular educational setting (classroom, school, regional, or global educational setting), but also to determine the appropriate spatial scale in order to accurately estimate the DB instances. Detecting an appropriate scale helped to specify underlying disturbances, which are distinct for generating DBs at different educational levels. The incorporation of spatial principle provided a more flexible means for representing behavioral mechanisms of the DB model.

The DB model, which is focused on spatial relationships, has an ability to consider the nonlinear interacting processes with minimal pre-assumptions about the nature of what is generating interactions. This brought our attention to the sustaining quality of relationships among model's aspects and disturbances, instead of the short-term effectiveness of the model. The emphasis on the relationships benefited our understanding of its sustaining qualities in two ways: (1) it allowed for viewing change as a set of discrete steps, and not as a continuous process and (2) it allowed for incorporating different parameters to the analysis of underlying factors, specifically disturbances, which continue to evolve over time. Thus, by applying the spatial relationships principle to the DB model, it provided prospects for flexible assimilation of the different leadership patterns within different levels of an educational system.

Principle of Diversity

In social sciences, the value of diversity is generally understood in terms of forming a strong network of many different relationships with people who have many different approaches to solve the same problem. The value of diverse perspectives, the application of multiple resources and strategies, and diversity of school structures trigger a variety of processes that can potentially embrace or interfere with DB. A vibrant network of relationships among diverse players and influential factors can positively contribute to DB when the connections within the network are supported by a strong flow of communication. This increases the sustaining role of DB, as networks contribute to the overall resilience of school functions. On the other hand, an absence of communication makes diversity a disturbance, which may interfere with DB in some circumstances. The demographic diversity (Jackson & Joshi, 2004) within a school's team of teachers and administrators, for example, might lead to social categorization of particular individuals. As a result, the broken communication often triggers stereotypes and favoritism among participants that prevents positive DB. In this light, the diversity principle brings our attention to the importance of establishing interconnectedness among all participants and the flow of information between them.

A state of interconnectedness within a school team will improve the sustaining power of DB model by increasing team's collaborative ability. Together, the participants consider alternative methods for successful innovation introduction that integrate their diverse perspectives. Generating creative solutions and considering different implementation options allows them to foresee many possible advantages and disadvantages of an innovation. Another sustaining feature of our DB is its potential to enhance a team's network by expanding its relationships. The participants diversify their connections among themselves and share access to the valuable external resources and expertise of each individual to sustain innovation introduction.

Leadership Environment and Discretionary Behavior

The breakdown of school DB model into five parts – shared vision, empowerment, institutional commitment, collaboration, and school culture, connected by a focus of students' needs – reflects a general tendency of educational systems to develop effective leadership structures. A traditional hierarchical and bureaucratic organization of a school system (Darling-Hammond, 2000) promotes a top-down leadership style: principals carry on tasks of school management and teachers focus on learning within their classrooms. The top-down approach to innovation introduction provides very little opportunity for change in schools. An initial *eLEP* structure relied on a top-down leadership approach to innovation introduction in schools: school principals competed for schools' participation in the project and only 10 winners negotiated their terms with a donor. At the same time, the project implementation relied on a bottom-up strategy of creating a leadership environment that sustains innovation and inspires acts of DB in the participating schools. Using the transformative leadership framework as a theoretical underpinning for our study, we envisioned characteristics of a TL (Bass & Avolio, 1994) among *eLEP* leaders, who facilitated change and sustained innovation in schools. Our focus was on a principal's ability to inspire commitment toward shared goals, transcend self-interests, and generate extra effort for lasting change in school practices. However, our findings show that leadership goes beyond principals' performance as TLs and single "know-how" engines for a strategic school change.

In addition to the transformative leadership framework, the DB model incorporates elements of different school leadership practices that consider moral (Duke, 1987; Sergiovanni, 2007) and participative (Murphy & Beck, 1995; Yukl, 1994) frameworks. The combination of different frameworks suggests a multi-concept approach to DB studies to fully incorporate different categories of a leadership practice[2] (Leithwood & Duke, 1999). The emphasis on a moral leadership style in *eLEP* schools positioned participants' values and virtues in the center of their decision-making about innovation introduction. Under the moral framework, principals modeled values and appealed to participants' virtues throughout the process. The participative leadership style emerged through the practice of distributing leadership tasks in the participating schools and engaging a whole group in decision-making.

The five domains of the DB model (shared vision, empowerment, institutional commitment, collaboration, and school culture) emphasized the importance of learning for creating an effective learning environment. This conclusion supported Lambert's (2002) premise of a constructivist principle, which views leadership through the process of mutual learning of all school members. They challenge group belief systems and facilitate reflective dialogues across all levels of a school community. Defining leadership as a right, responsibility, and capability of each school member, the constructivist principle places learning in the center of creating an effective leadership environment. In light of this concept, DB model illustrates conditions for a custom-built school leadership environment, based on how school members participate in roles of leadership, where, when, and how leadership actually happens.

Discretionary Alignment

The alignment of teachers' and principals' discretionary behavior is an intricate mechanism and not a straightforward product of the decision process. We view discretionary alignment as a continual process to reach the desired condition for enhancing sustainability of innovation. However, our results suggest that the alignment is rather an ideal state than an achievable condition that can be maintained. We are inclined to believe that discretionary alignment can only be expressed in terms of degrees of synergistic behavior limited by the individual capacity of each school for implementing IT innovations and differences within a school's culture. Clearly, the degree of discretionary alignment achieved requires careful consideration of multivariate factors and application of multidimensional perspectives, such as an ecological framework. The consistency in leaders' and teachers' goals and underlying assumptions about their capabilities, potentials, impacts, and benefits of an innovation often control the degree of alignment. Alignment works much the way dancing works: teachers and principals must first want to dance together, both must know the steps, and then perform together. The limits of alignment is thought of as being similar to dancing with a beginner: one is learning the steps, becoming familiar with the beat, and being comfortable with a partner. The reactive nature of discretionary alignment is closely connected to the quality of relationships between principals and members of the school faculty.

Developing sound principal–teacher relationships is a basic organizational principle of any school environment (Hoerr, 2005; Sergiovanni, 2007). The significance of relationships in sustaining innovations is evident across the five domains of the DB model and is reflected in the descriptors of the DB processes and procedures for creating shared vision, fostering collaboration, maintaining a unique school culture, and cultivating senses of empowerment and institutional commitment among school members. Both individual and group relationships involve many components. Trust is one of the most significant relational components that affects the process of sustaining innovation. In this sense, we view DB as a trust-promoting behavior, which enhances principal–teacher relationships and aids discretionary alignment. An atmosphere of trust and cooperation is essential for the alignment to take place in a school. As a reciprocal process, alignment also requires a sense of connectedness to be developed in all members. It helps principals and teachers to learn together and from each other through a process of innovation introduction. Because relationships are built on a fundamental value of trust, leadership roles become dispersed across different school levels. Any member makes discretionary alignment an open process. Commonsense seems to suggest discretionary alignment would be easier for schools with long-established relationships between the principal and teacher: a new principal may be more flexible, but a tenured one is predictable.

Discretion as Phronesis

By accepting the same vision, goals, values, and expectations, school faculty and administrators created a shared vision for the process of innovation introduction. This shared vision underlined a process of principal–teachers' discretionary alignment and served as a framework for a collaborative action of the entire school team. This conveys that collaboration might elevate a degree of the alignment in schools. Collaboration creates an open flow of discretion across all school levels, when individual discretionary actions empower other members of the group, stimulate discretion across an entire team, and sustain an innovation. A central criterion of the DB model – a common focus on students' needs – ensures that everyone learns to prioritize the important long-term goal rather than the daily urgencies of a school. Conzemius and O'Neill's (2001) also viewed a common focus, reflective knowledge, and collaboration of all school members as the essential elements of an effective school leadership. The collaborative dynamics of a group help maintain individual and team efforts on behalf of students rather than on personal agendas. Reflective practices of a group contribute a sense of collective responsibility and raise a degree of discretion in school community.

Although studies of discretion rest heavily on the managerial tradition of leadership in the western world, the morals and virtues of leaders and teachers remain "silent" drivers for discretionary actions. Following other findings in the field (Macfarlane & Ottewill, 2005; Park, 2009), discretionary alignment can be best understood via a non-managerial lens of Aristotelian phronesis. Discretion as phronesis is a "process of deliberation that anticipates an ending in excellence ... of choice and action to attain the highest level possible of reciprocity and mutuality" (Park, 2009, p. 3). Stressing the importance of ethical decision-making, the phronesis-discretion is specifically applicable for *eLEP* school environments, which practice moral and participative leadership styles. In the environments influenced by these two leadership styles, the institutional commitment of an individual rises to a high level. The stronger the commitment, the stronger probability that teachers' and leaders' actions are guided by the internalized rules and visions rather than outcomes of his or her actions. Thus, committed leaders and teachers may exhibit DB due to their internalized beliefs, because they think it is the "right and moral thing to do" (Weiner, 1982, p. 421).

Although the influence of rewards on DB in schools with moral leadership styles appears secondary, we suggest that rewards strengthen the domains of the DB model and benefit DB actions. Rewarding all school members provides opportunities for encouragement and celebration of achievements and reflections on backslappings. Nonstrategic rewarding is a type of DB that provides the school faculty and leaders with stimulation of their shared values. Rewarding as DB also emphasizes the importance of an individual effort in introducing innovations introduction and sustaining change in schools.

It is important to note that DB can be measured in both positive and negative markers. Our DB model is derived on the positive examples exhibited by principals and teachers in the *eLEP* case schools. Although not a part of our study, the examples of negative DB (Brief & Motowidl, 1986; Kaiser & Hogan, 2006) may include individual actions of a school member who helps a team member to achieve a personal goal, inconsistent with a shared vision of organization, covers up documentation mismatch or mistakes to protect the organization, and unequally distributes rewards toward a higher end of the hierarchical system to express respect. Negative in their measures, these DB actions are sustaining in their function and contribute to the greater good of an individual and, to some degree, the school organization. However, it would be a mistake to design an innovation introduction exclusively around a sense that all kinds of DB should be encouraged for the sake of sustaining a new practice. Despite the overall focus on a collaborative action for the processes of implementing and sustaining an innovation in schools, an emphasis on teacher and principal as individual players is important for the success of a project. We recognize a diversity of DB, and believe that including DB practices that reflect human sensitivity and concern for the welfare of an individual is highly desirable.

While not necessarily part of our description of the DB in schools, it may be helpful to link DB with an idea of discretionary effort (Daniels & Daniels, 2007) defined as the energy that a person has control over for exercising his or her discretion. Discretionary effort may serve as a possible relational measure of DB. However, we claim our descriptive DB model to be more insightful, less linear, and more comprehensive.

CONCLUSION

The domains of the DB model paint the "big image" of the process of sustaining IT innovations in secondary schools. It is the actual examples of DB performed by teachers and principals within and across the domains of the model that add the significant strokes to the picture and clarify leadership practices. The complexity of the goals and means of IT introduction necessitates a nonlinear ecological approach to a study of DB and its role in igniting and sustaining change in different leadership environments. The shared vision, empowerment, institutional commitment, collaboration, and school culture, connected by a focus of students' needs need to be present for goals of sustaining innovation to be met through discretionary attitude and actions of all school members. Expressed in terms of degrees of synergistic behavior the discretionary alignment of principal's and teachers' behaviors appears in this study more of an ideal state than an achievable goal. The degree of alignment depends on differences in individual capacities of participating schools and their unique cultures.

Innovation introduction, however, does not depend on discretionary or heroic actions and efforts of school members within a set project timeline. As observed, the acts of discretion support can sustain change through a systemic process.

As open systems, schools incorporate innovations that are advantageous for their students, and often do not introduce innovations in a precise manner. The ecological principles of systems' organization that we applied in our study – emergence, spatial relationships and disturbance, and diversity – help us understand the underlining mechanisms that sustain the educational phenomena. Observed together, these principles represent the sustaining powers of the school system and frame important connections between schools' sustainability and DB. The DB model provides us the capacity to believe that most difficult, and even impossible, barriers to innovation introduction in a complex school system can be hurdled at the right time when school members are up to the task and conditions are favorable for change.

NOTES

1. Constant comparative method involves four stages: (1) comparing incidents applicable to each category, (2) integrating categories and their properties, (3) delimiting the theory, and (4) writing the theory.

2. The six leadership categories proposed by Leithwood and Duke included contingency, instructional, managerial, moral, participative, and transformational leadership models.

REFERENCES

Banathy, B. (2010). *Guided evolution of society: A systems view (contemporary systems thinking)*. New York, NY: Springer.

Bass, B. (1985). *Leadership and performance beyond expectations*. New York, NY: Free Press.

Bass, B., & Avolio, B. (1994). *Improving organizational effectiveness through transformational leadership*. Thousand Oaks, CA: Sage.

Beeby, A., & Brennan, A. (2008). *First ecology: Ecological principles and environmental issues* (3rd ed.). Oxford: Oxford University.

Bethany, B. (1991). *Systems design of education*. Englewood Cliffs, NJ: Educational Technology Publications.

Biggs, J., & Tang, C. (2003). *Teaching for quality learning at university*. Buckingham, UK: Open University.

Brief, A., & Motowidl, S. (1986). Prosocial organizational behaviors. *Academy of Management Review, 11*(4), 710–725.

Cilo, D. (1994). Micropolitics: Empowering principals to accomplish goals. *NASSP Bulletin, 78*, 89–96. doi:10.1177/019263659407856418

Conzemius, A., & O'Neill, J. (2001). *Building shared responsibility for student learning*. Alexandria, VA: ASCD.

Crowson, R., & Porter-Gehrie, C. (1980). The discretionary behavior of principles in large-city schools. *Educational Administration Quarterly, 16*(10), 45–69. doi:10.1177/0013161X8001600106

Daniels, A., & Daniels, J. (2007). *Measure of a leader: The legendary leadership formula for producing exceptional performers and outstanding results*. New York, NY: McGraw-Hill.

Darling-Hammond, L. (2000). Futures of teaching in American education. *Journal of Educational Change, 1*(4), 353–373.

Davis, N. (2008). How may teacher learning be promoted for educational renewal with IT? In J. Voogt & G. Knezek (Eds.), *International handbook of information technology in primary and secondary education*. New York, NY: Springer.

Duke, D. (1987). *School leadership and instructional improvement*. New York, NY: Random House.

Efron, S., & Joseph, P. (2001). Reflections in a mirror: Metaphors of teachers and teaching. In P. Joseph & G. Burnaford (Eds.), *Images of school teachers in America* (2nd ed., pp. 75–92). Mahwah, NJ: Lawrence Erlbaum.

Fischer, J., & Kiefer, A. (2001). Constructing and discovering images of your teaching. In P. Joseph & G. Burnaford (Eds.), *Images of school teachers in America* (2nd ed., pp. 93–114). Mahwah, NJ: Lawrence Erlbaum.

Fullan, M. (2007). *The new meaning of educational change* (4th ed.). Washington, DC: Teachers College.

Hallinger, P., & Heck, R. (1998). Exploring the principal's contribution to school effectiveness: 1980–1995. *School Effectiveness and School Improvement, 9*, 157–191.

Hambrick, D., & Frankelstein, S. (1987). Managerial discretion: A bridge between polar views of organizational outcomes. *Research and Organizational Behavior, 9*, 369–406.

Hannan, M., & Freeman, J. (1977). The population ecology of organizations. *American Journal of Sociology, 82*, 929–964.

Harris, A. (2004). Distributed leadership and school improvement. *Educational management administration and leadership, 32*, 11–24.

Harris, A., & Chapman, C. (2002). *Effective leadership in schools facing challenging circumstances.* Nottingham, UK: NCSL.

Hoerr, T. (2005). *The art of school leadership.* Alexandria, VA: Association for Supervision and Curriculum Development.

Jackson, S., & Joshi, A. (2004). Diversity in social context: A multi-attribute, multi-level analysis of team diversity and sales performance. *Journal of organizational Behavior, 25*, 675–702.

Jung, D., & Avolio, B. (2000). Opening the black box: An experimental investigation of the mediating effects of trust and value congruence on transformational and transactional leadership. *Journal of Organizational Behavior, 21*(8), 949–964.

Kaiser, R., & Hogan, R. (2006). *The dark side of discretion: Leader personality and organizational decline.* Retrieved from http://www.hoganassessments.com/_hoganweb/documents/dark%20side%20of%20discretion.pdf

Kiser, R., & Hogan, R. (2006). The dark side of discretion: Leader personality and organizational decline. In J. Antonakis, R. Hooijberg, J. Hunt, K. Boal & W. Macey (Eds.), *Strategic leadership of organizations.* Tulsa, OK: Hogan Assessment Systems.

Kozma, R. (Ed.). (2003). *Technology, innovation, and educational change: A Global perspective.* Eugene, OR: ISTE.

Krohne, D. (1998). *General ecology.* Belmont, CA: Wadsworth.

Lambert, L. (2002). A framework for shared leadership. *Educational Leadership, 59*(8), 37–40.

Law, N. (2008). Technology-supported pedagogical innovations: The challenge of sustainability and scalability in the information age. In C. Ng & P. Renshaw (Eds.), *Reforming learning: Issues, concepts and practices in the Asia-pacific region* (pp. 319–343). New York, NY: Springer.

Law, N., Pelgrum, W., & Plomp, T. (Eds.). (2008). *Pedagogy and ICT in schools around the world: Findings from the SITES 2006 study.* Hong Kong: CERC and Springer.

Law, N., Yuen, A., & Fox, R. (2011). *Educational innovations beyond technology: Nurturing leadership and establishing learning organizations.* New York, NY: Springer.

Leithwood, K., & Duke, D. (1999). A century's quest to understand school leadership. In J. Murphy & K. Louis (Eds.), *Handbook of research on educational administration.* San Francisco, CA: Jossey-Bass.

Leithwood, K., & Jantzi, D. (2000). The effects of transformational leadership on organizational conditions and student engagement with school. *Journal of Educational Administration, 38*(2), 112–129.

Lincoln, Y., & Guba, E. (1985). *Naturalistic inquiry.* Newbury Park, CA: Sage.

Macfarlane, B., & Ottewill, R. (2005). A 'special' context? Identifying the professional values associated with teaching in higher education. *International Journal of Ethics, 4*(1), 89–100.

Marcovitz, D. (2006). Changing schools with technology: What every school should know about innovation. *Advances in Educational Administration, 8,* 3–15. doi:10.1016/S1479.3660(05)08001

Marks, H., & Printy, S. (2003). Principal leadership and school performance: An integration of transformational and instructional leadership. *Educational Administration Quarterly, 39*(3), 370–397.

Meyer, J. (2000). The modeling of a "dissonant" study orchestration in higher education. *European Journal of Psychology in Education, 15*(1), 5–18.

Miles, M. B., & Huberman, A. M. (1994). *Qualitative data analysis* (2nd ed.). Thousand Oaks, CA: Sage.

Moolenaar, N., Daly, A., & Sleegers, P. (2010). Occupying the principal position: Examining relationships between innovative climate, transformational leadership, social network position, and schools' innovative climate. *Educational Administration Quarterly, 46*(5), 623–670. doi:10.1177/0013161X10378689

Morrison, K. (2002). *School leadership and complexity theory.* New York, NY: Routledge.

Murphy, J., & Beck, L. (1995). *School-based management as school reform: Taking stock.* Thousand Oaks, CA: Corwin.

Park, J. (2009). *Leadership of recognition: A philosophical study.* Saarbrücken: VDM Verlag.

Ryan, A. (2005). Teacher development and educational change: Empowerment through structured reflection. *Irish Educational Studies, 24*(2/3), 179–198.

Savelyeva, T. (2009). *Global learning environment: Innovative concept and interactive model for changing academia and academics.* Saarbrücken: VDM Verlag.

Savelyeva, T. (2011). Escaping the "structural trap" of sustainability in academia through global learning environment. In K. Bartels & K. Parker (Eds.), *Teaching sustainability/Teaching sustainably.* New York, NY: Routledge.

Savelyeva, T., & McKenna, J. (2011). Campus sustainability: Emerging curricula models in higher education. *International Journal of Sustainability in Higher Education, 12*(1), 55–66.

Sergiovanni, T. (2007). *Rethinking leadership.* Thousand Oaks, CA: Corwin.

Stein, M., & Coburn, C. (2008). Architectures for learning: A comparative analysis of two urban school districts. *American Journal of Education, 114*(4), 583–626.

Stewart, J. (2006). Transformational leadership: An evolving concept examined through the works of Burns, Bass, Avolio, and Leithwood. *Canadian Journal of Educational Administration and Policy, 54.* Retrieved from http://www.umanitoba.ca/publications/cjeap. Accessed on October 26, 2010.

Sugrue, C. (1998). Confronting student teachers' lay theories and culturally embedded archetypes of teaching: Implications for professional development. In C. Sugrue (Ed.), *Teaching curriculum and educational research* (pp. 118–141). Dublin: St. Patrick's College.

Townsend, C., Begon, M., & Harper, J. (2008). *Essentials of ecology* (3rd ed.). Oxford: Blackwell.

Vaughn, S., Schumm, J., & Sinagub, J. (1996). *Focus group interviews in education and psychology.* Thousand Oaks, CA: Sage.

Wiener, Y. (1982). Commitment in organizations. A normative view. *Academy of Management Review, 7*(3), 418–428.

Yeung, A., Lee, Y., & Yue, K. W. R. (2006). Multicultural leadership for a sustainable total school environment. *Education Research Policy Practice* (5), 121–131.

Yin, R. (2004). *The case study anthology.* Thousand Oaks, CA: Sage.

Yukl, G. (1994). *Leadership in organizations* (3rd ed.). Englewood Cliffs, NJ: Prentice-Hall.

CHAPTER 7

COALFACE ACADEMIC LEADERSHIP IN AUSTRALIAN HIGHER EDUCATION: DISCRETIONARY BEHAVIOUR THROUGH EMPOWERMENT

Judy Nagy

ABSTRACT

The contemporary life of an Australian academic has changed in almost every way imaginable in response to the challenges and opportunities emerging from global and national policy agendas. In this context, the subject coordinator[1] represents the frontline of a move towards increasingly distributed forms of leading and learning. The knowledge that managing teaching responsibilities does not provide a clear route to promotion (with active research status providing a more well established path) means that academics may proactively minimise the time they spend on the discretionary tasks of leading and managing teaching well. Tasks that include adopting a proactive longer term of curriculum development, team building and teaching innovation, in addition to the more immediate needs for compliance and measurable outcomes. Research from an

Discretionary Behavior and Performance in Educational Organizations: The Missing Link in Educational Leadership and Management
Advances in Educational Administration, Volume 13, 169–196
Copyright © 2012 by Emerald Group Publishing Limited
ISSN: 1479-3660/doi:10.1108/S1479-3660(2012)0000013012

Australian Learning and Teaching Council (ALTC) project provides evidence that despite lack of formal recognition for many of the discretionary responsibilities of subject coordination, coordinators believe they are executing their job well. This chapter discusses factors that impede discretionary academic leadership behaviours in Australian higher education and suggests strategies to empower leadership and thus improve engagement with discretionary teaching and learning responsibilities.

Keywords: Academic leadership; higher education; subject coordinators; discretionary behaviour; professional development

BACKGROUND TO THE STUDY

There are a number of macro and micro pressures that have significantly impacted the global learning and teaching environment, particularly over the past decade. Currie and Vidovich (2009) note a number of macro influences in the nature of academic work. These include:

> diminished government funding concurrent with the massification of higher education, work intensification, pressures towards privatisation, marketisation and instrumentalism (in learning and teaching), importation of corporate managerial structures and cultures, increased accountability, new demands associated with accelerated internationalisation, dwindling collegiality and trust, decreased autonomy and challenges to academic freedom (p. 450)

The changing context was noted by Coaldrake and Stedman (1999) in their seminal work on changing roles and policies related to academic work in the 21st century. This work forms a useful baseline identifying a period of change for institutional operations with implications for the roles of university staff members and leaders. The impact of external forces on Australian universities that may lead universities to 'play the role of brokers in distributed knowledge systems' is acknowledged (p. 16). Coaldrake and Stedman (1999) point to a juxtaposition of new student expectations for professional training and career credentials with traditional academic values of critical thinking and disciplinary study. Such expectations have been fuelled by generational change and the changed identity of students in the knowledge society.

Coates and Goedegebuure (2010) confirm this viewpoint identifying that in Australia (and elsewhere) government funding per student has declined radically over the past 20 years, and second, that a sharp increase in the number of students has occurred without a matching increase in teaching staff (p. 384). Although there has been a doubling of student numbers, teaching staff numbers have only increased by about one-third overall. In addition to rising staff to student ratios, the following have also added pressures to academic workloads:

- increasing student diversity resulting from equity and diversity policies;
- the special needs of growing cohorts of international students;
- the need to inculcate graduate attributes in courses and units of study;
- increasing flexibility for both learners and learning through enabling technologies;
- increasing administrative and management responsibilities managing casual teaching staff; and
- management styles moving from collegial to corporate models.

The current reliance on the goodwill of academics (often to the detriment of careers) to perform roles that have been conceptualised within an 'old world view' of faculty life are unsuited to the current hybrid, open and distributed forms of learning. Coates and Goedegebuure (2010) observed that there was a remarkable stretchability of academic work (p. 9) that was now unsustainable. Interestingly this same point was made almost a decade earlier where Anderson, Johnson, and Saha (2002) noted that 'new tasks, new technologies, and new accountability and bureaucratic procedures have added to the traditional academic responsibilities. Nothing has been taken away' (p. 8). Increasing accountability and standardisation through stakeholder influences (particularly through professional accreditation) has removed much academic freedom and discretion about what students are taught. One of the remaining freedoms is the discretion to choose how students can be taught, how resources are provided and how much time will be allocated to the task of leading and managing the teaching domain.

The subject coordinator essentially represents the lowest rung on the academic leadership ladder where the changes in academe have had their most impact. This is particularly true in relation to the influences on academic workloads, academic freedom and how academic identities have consequently evolved. For many Australian university academics, a typical workload is reflected by a 40:40:20 division of time. This means equal time for teaching and research with 20 per cent for service related tasks. While the split between teaching and research is theoretically equal, research activity has hegemony as a performance indicator (perceived by some as an under-valuing of academic teaching activity), with promotion and career advancement criteria emphasising research output indicators. This new academic context has produced a pressured academic work environment with little time for reflection or collaboration.

Academic employment is significantly predicated on subject expertise evidenced by a discipline related doctorate and research capability. This is confirmed by Hemmings and Kay (2010) who suggest that,

> (t)here is no indication that the pressure to perform in research and other scholarly endeavours in Australia will lessen in the short term, particularly with the advent of the federal government's Excellence in Research in Australia (ERA) initiative.... Consequently, experienced and neophyte academics will be expected to produce quality output, and those considering entering the academy will also need to be aware of these expectations. (p. 186)

It is not unusual for pedagogical knowledge and evidence of the ability to teach to be given scant, if any, significant weight in selection processes and yet those employed are required to teach. Scott, Bell, Coates, and Grebennikov (2010) confirm that selection processes for appointment of higher education leaders are often unrelated to the skills and competencies required to 'negotiate the daily realities of their work' (p. 402). Anderson et al. (2002, p. 5) ask whether the PhD that equips an academic for a research career is 'an adequate preparation for an academic career, with all the varied abilities that are now expected of an academic. Do we need something other than a PhD, or more than the PhD?' It is not unusual for academics to become subject co-ordinators in their first year of work (often in first year core units with large student numbers) and then be faced with the need to lead and manage staff and infrastructure resources to effectively discharge their role. However, little (if any) skills development is provided to such staff before they assume roles that have become influential and complex. Anderson et al. (2002, p. 107) also note that, 'casual staff, who can be a relief to a hard-pressed teacher, can also be a burden to be recruited, organised, supervised and encouraged'. The increasing casualisation of academe over the past 10 years means that increasingly subject co-ordinators have significant influence and impact on the academic work practices of others.

Micro pressures are reliant on institutional operational contexts and significantly impact how academics deal with implied, expected and elective aspects of their role. Subject Coordinators confront a number of challenges that include both formal and informal role requirements. These include:

- recruiting, inducting and developing casual/sessional teaching staff to form a cohesive teaching team;

- the establishment and maintenance of teaching and assessment standards often across large teaching teams in geographically distributed, multi-campus and offshore environments;
- the design and operation of ICT-enabled, flexible teaching and learning environments;
- the need to work collaboratively with other subject teams and course coordinators/leaders in designing and delivering coherent and integrated courses/programs of study;
- the need to respond constructively to various forms of feedback (most notably student feedback) both to assure and to improve the quality of the subject offering over time;
- integrating learning support services seamlessly into the teaching and learning environment; and
- understanding and managing infrastructure and administrative systems to achieve desired student learning outcomes.

Effective subject coordination requires leadership capabilities and yet subject coordinator roles are regarded as 'informal leadership' with little support and acknowledgment of the wider responsibilities involved. And yet subject coordinators surveyed as part of an Australian study actively engage in what can be described as discretionary behaviours beyond taking classes, marking, processing results and attending to administrative requirements. The provision of considered informative feedback, being flexible about how and when to be available to answer student queries, providing dynamic and contemporary material for learning, being proactive in the use of new technologies to engage learners, recruiting casual staff and managing human resources, are all features of engaging learning and teaching contexts. It is within these types of activities that academics have the discretion to spend more or less of their time with little immediate visibility for minimalist endeavours.

There are many aspects of a typical academic's role that are not clearly articulated, contextualised or made clear, within a complex environment of competing interests. When considering discretionary behaviour by academics at the subject coordinator level, there are some important dimensions and questions that are particularly relevant to the discussion. In particular,

- what part of formal roles and functions can be considered discretionary?
- are there any informally articulated discretionary role behaviours expected? and
- are there discretionary behaviours that are not expected as part of the role but assist organisational efficiencies?

Roles and responsibilities of subject coordinators are presented in Table 1. Formal job descriptions for subject coordinators are not common as the role represents only a portion of a typical academic's roles and responsibilities. However, research discussed later in this chapter noted that, job descriptions generally do not contain the items identified in columns 2 and 3 of the table.

Academic loyalty tends to be affiliated with the academic unit/subject or discipline, not the interests of the university as a whole. In addition, much academic work, especially research, is individual rather than collective. Hemmings and Kay (2010, p. 197) confirm that '(a) recurring theme within the literature pertaining to academic output is the need for time to plan and conduct research', and studies confirm ' that academics devoting more of their time to teaching and service activities produced less output' (p. 188). Thus, it is not surprising, that research output acts as a very powerful force against time that is devoted to discretionary tasks associated with subject coordination. The focus on accountability and performance hinges on what is countable. Power's (1997) rituals of verification supports the view that in higher education a compliance culture is preoccupied with what can be counted, teaching hours, articles written, projects planned, grants awarded, conferences attended, papers given, assessments marked, theses supervised, and meetings attended. The tasks noted in Table 1 are not visible and assessing compliance or improving capabilities is problematic.

Table 1. Subject Coordinator Discretionary Behaviours.

Formal Discretionary	Informal Discretionary (Expected)	Unexpected (Institutionally Useful)
Effective coordination of staff for teaching	Team building	Leadership
	Recruitment of sessional staff Human Resource Management	Succession planning
Curriculum renewal and development	Innovative use of technologies	Development of new subjects
	Dynamic subject content	Taking a long term development view
High-quality teaching effectiveness	Collegial benchmarking of teaching practice Innovative assessment that builds graduate competencies	Innovative teaching practice

PURPOSE

A gap has been identified in current leadership strategies that points to a need to focus attention on developing skills at the coalface as part of the first rungs of leadership frameworks in Australian higher education. The gap acknowledges that role definition and responsibilities have become much more complex and are not matched with authority, workload support and leadership competencies. The Australian Learning and Teaching Council (ALTC) recognises that academic leadership is a highly specialised and professional activity. Such academic leadership is incompatible with the development of generic leadership capacities for administrative and general staff usually dealt with by many universities within human resources departments. The role of subject co-ordinators is critical to quality teaching and learning and contributes substantially to funding through student enrolments and to organisational reputations. In addition, little work has been done nationally that focuses on the role and capabilities required to lead and manage effectively at the unit/subject level. This study represents a critical extension to the leadership domains investigated in other ALTC leadership work. The professional learning needs of this level of leadership and management have also been relatively neglected in comparison with middle and higher ranking academic leaders and managers. Given the significant numbers of staff who are required to fulfil this role, this group of emerging academic leaders are worthy of particular attention.

Conflicting roles, mismatched recognition and varying reward structures suggest that academics need to make strategic choices in relation to time management. It is reasonable to suggest that tasks within personal capabilities and that have defined measurable outcomes are more likely to be undertaken. Building additional capabilities may contribute to broadening involvement as previously challenging tasks can be undertaken with a measure of confidence. This has consequences for the time allocated to formal and informal discretionary tasks with engagement being brokered through the building of capacities and competencies. The need to lead and manage resources is an increasingly assumed role for subject coordinators and, the performance (or underperformance) of 'leadership' at the subject coordinator level has little visibility. The discretionary behaviours noted in Table 1 are strongly associated with leadership skills. Accordingly, the purpose of the study is to identify how leadership capabilities and competencies can be developed to make engagement with leadership less challenging. This pathway reflects an empowerment objective as a way of providing a foundation for increased discretionary behaviours.

Research findings have highlighted a number of areas where subject coordinators consider they would substantially benefit from some form of professional development to build capacities for the responsibilities they have in contemporary academe. Academic identities are often characterised within concepts of academic freedom, a subject that has a long lineage and continues to be debated. While the degree of empowerment may have changed over time, academics still have a level of choice about the depth and breadth of immersion they may apply to their various roles. Empowerment by building capabilities is likely to encourage academics to undertake discretionary tasks previously avoided and to build efficiencies that will subsequently lead to a rise in teaching engagement.

CONCEPTUAL FRAMEWORK

In many ways, it is difficult to differentiate between tasks that can be identified as management and tasks that can be identified as leadership. The suggestion that management involves specifically identifiable separate behaviours such as managing, communicating, controlling and leading is repudiated by Mintzberg (1994) who assumes leadership into his holistic conceptualisation of the nature of management. For the purposes of this study, a combined perspective to management and leadership is used, as deeper discussion about the merits (or otherwise) of bifurcation is not the intention of this chapter. Thus, literature from academic leadership and organisational management provide the conceptual foundations for the research articulated within this chapter.

Academic Leadership

Academic leadership is critical in higher education because it has an impact on the quality of student learning (Ramsden, Prosser, Trigwell, & Martin, 2007). We believe that these largely informal leadership roles of subject coordinators require formal recognition and development to provide a strong foundation for further leadership capacity building. Leadership is defined as a:

> set of characteristic and behaviours that together enable organizations, and the individuals in them, to create optimal organizations conditions for realizing organizational goals. (Cleveland-Innes & Sandgra, 2010, p. 235)

The form of leadership proposed equates with the 'contingency perspective' of Marshall (2006), described as a process as much about 'developing the organisation as it is of developing the professional knowledge and skills of those called to leadership positions' (p. 3). The development of intellectual capacity and interpersonal skills to lead is crucial to the empowerment and enabling of knowledge workers. One of the challenges for leadership development in learning and teaching is the current 'absence of a culture within the academy that recognises leadership and management as *a part* of teaching, learning and research' (Marshall, 2006, p. 12). This means that academics will need to be encouraged and convinced of the value of pursuing professional development in learning and teaching leadership. Consequently, Marshall sees a focus on 'developing the organisational environment within which leadership for learning and teaching is to occur' as critical (p. 12).

The subject coordinator, at the intersection of teaching, research, administration and implementation of institutional strategic directions for teaching and learning, can be expected to feel conflicting tensions most keenly. In the context of leadership in distance education, Cleveland-Innes and Sandgra (2010) claim that 'adjustment in the way of doing business and producing newly identified outcome in higher education will not proceed smoothly without new types of leadership: that is, leadership is a key ingredient in the successful addressing of significant challenges and transformation to a new higher education' (p. 234). Fullan and Scott (2009, p. 70) agree that new approaches to leadership involve establishing and developing leaders at all levels. Kempster (2009) presents a big picture view of leadership development suggesting that 'the complexity of the idiosyncratic and often invisible nature of informal leadership learning necessitates a qualitative contextualised approach' (p. 441). Vilkinas, Leask, and Lady-shewsky (2009) also note that many academics may not see themselves as leaders in the traditional sense and that 'this often stems from a lack of formal authority or line management over other academics' (p. viii). The absence of positional authority means that leadership necessitates persuasive skills and significant emotional intelligences to manage and motivate teams that often comprise more senior colleagues as well as casual and support staff.

Organisational Management

Within the bounds of contemporary academic freedom, as knowledge workers academics have a degree of choice about how much/how well they engage with each aspect of their formal and informal roles. Mintzberg (1994, p. 23) describes academics as 'autonomous professionals' and suggests that managing such groups involves significant challenges as they come to their work naturally empowered. Kelloway and Barling (2000, pp. 289–291) discuss three thematic definitions of knowledge workers. The first considers knowledge work *as a profession* based on past delineations and notions of skilled versus unskilled work. The second considers knowledge work *as an individual* characteristic with an emphasis on creativity and innovation. The third emerging thematic considers knowledge work is *an individual activity* in terms of a balance between activities that are 'thinking or doing'. It is within this third thematic that Kelloway and Barling (p. 292) place their own definition of knowledge work as discretionary behaviour focussed on the use of knowledge and where the work is in four parts:

• the acquisition of existing knowledge
• the application of existing knowledge to problems
• the creation of new knowledge
• the knowledge transmission

These four parts define well the concept of academic work practices as does the notion of discretionary behaviour in the definition of knowledge work. It is the issue of discretion combined with autonomy that provides the basis for suggesting that empowering academics has the capacity to generate organisational benefits.

In an environment of competing agendas, subject coordinators that actively pursue discretionary behaviours (of the type outlined in Table 1) do so at the risk of reduced time to engage in research that counts towards promotion. Organisational management literature refers to organisational citizenship behaviour (OCB) or extra-role behaviours as becoming increasingly important for organisational effectiveness. Such behaviours are characterised as discretionary and beyond the strict bounds of job requirements and not directly rewarded. Turnipseed and Wilson (2009) also note that 'although OCB is not required by formal job descriptions, one's actual work role and job description may be different' (p. 202). At the coalface of academe, academics are expected to teach and yet not all academics embrace the task of teaching with equal enthusiasm. Sharrock (2010) suggests that 'the requisite skills and outlooks … [for academic and administrative leaders] … are still for the most part learned informally, on the job. Scholars who move from a teaching or research role into a management role often find the transition difficult' (Sharrock, 2010, p. 366). There is no doubt that the skills required to be a 'good' academic are acquired through a process of action learning. However, Sharrock suggests that there is a different logic between the type of professionalism required by those that engage in scholarly work and those engaged in managerial work. Managerialism, accountability and the need to be able to demonstrate performance pervades all university structures and functions with the need for academics to make strategic choices about how to manage their time well. Thus, any tasks perceived as being elective, or that could be reasonably avoided without adverse impacts on career progression, are likely to be given little time. The exercise of role-related leadership has limited visibility and has many discretionary components.

Using a conceptual lens proposed by Belogolovsky and Somech (2010) OCB behaviours are unbundled and considered from a beneficiary viewpoint. Based on research in schools, Belogolovsky and Somech (2010) describe OCB as being multidimensional including OCB towards the school (institution), towards a team and towards students. In the academy, the nature of assumed rather than clearly articulated role expectations, combined with the disconnection between organisational goals, and personal goals are likely to have significant impacts on OCBs. A brief discussion of the three dimensions of OCB proposed by Belogolovsky and Somech follows as applied to Australian higher education.

OCB towards the Institution

Characteristics of 'new managerialism' in organisations include: empha-sising the primacy of management above all other activities; monitoring employee performance (and encouraging self-monitoring); the attainment of financial and other targets, devising means of publicly auditing quality of service delivery and the development of internal markets for services on a user pays system. Often there is a concerted effort to devise mechanisms of quantification for the sake of numerical needs rather than the value of the information generated. In this way a calculative priority can be given to economic factors. Costs, benefits and consequences can be divided into the defined and known and the imprecise and intangible. Emphasis can then be given to the known with a suitable chain of visibility to justify, or give support to, particular actions taken. The decoupling of organisational-self from practice is further perpetuated by increasingly homogenised institu-tional control procedures perpetuated through government audit process controls in the Australian Higher Education Assurance Framework (AUQA) (which will become the Tertiary Education Quality Standards

Association in 2011). The decoupling of institutional structures from practice is also evident in the misalignment of the organisational goals and objectives of universities with the mechanisms by which individual academic effort is rewarded. The kudos garnered by individual academic achievement through publication may have little direct link to a university's institutional mission and objectives. Similarly, improvements in university rankings, student enrolments and university financial outcomes have little impact on individual staff.

Unlike corporations, the public focus and drive for profitability has little presence on a stage that values, international ranking, increasing student numbers and beacons of research to attract corporate investments. Buried amongst an increasingly similar rhetoric of excellence, those at lower level of the academic hierarchy are generally motivated by issues more closely aligned with their immediate work environment.

OCB towards a Team

Subject coordinators operate in complex and dispersed teaching and learning contexts that are increasingly multi-campus, multi-city and multi-modal. The management of teaching teams in such contexts is increasingly challenging and has been exacerbated by the casualisation of the academy. Casual staff are generally remunerated for actual student contact hours and assessment activities and often have no dedicated campus space to work from when they may otherwise be on campus. While they may have significant subject expertise and experience, casual staff are often not paid to contribute to subject and resource development. This leaves fewer full-time academic colleagues to contribute to team meetings and to share the administrative workload, particularly as team members are likely to also coordinate other subjects with their own broader leadership issues. Notwithstanding, many subjects do have a dedicated team of casual and full-time teaching staff that operate well. Such teams often have a shared sense of purpose and contribute time 'above and beyond' from an altruistic perspective. As educators, they care about 'good teaching and have a strong intrinsic motivation to provide an engaging learning environment'. Leading such a team can be very satisfying and act as a motivator for OCB activities towards a team. However, where the team consists of those who do not share an enthusiasm for teaching and the leader lacks the skills and emotional intelligences required to manage a disparate team, engagement with OCBs are likely to be less prevalent.

OCB towards Students

A strong intrinsic motivation can also motivate OCB towards students from either and altruistic or personal viewpoint. As the performance of academics is increasingly measured with reference to student evaluation surveys, academics are increasingly obliged to meet the needs of the 'purchaser' in an environment where staff/student ratios continue to rise. Responsiveness to certain aspects of student needs may be motivated by a genuine desire to assist learning or alternatively to secure favourable evaluation statistics.

An altruistic viewpoint would decry the demise of specific time to spend with and get to know individual students as class numbers rise and online learning places distance and a keyboard between the teacher and students. Anderson et al. (2002, p. 28) noted that, 'teaching is as much a social activity as it is a cognitive one'. In an increasingly performance driven accountability system caring about a strong affinity with teaching needs to be balanced against competing agendas.

Responsibilities towards students also encompass subject development and the need to scaffold and embed graduate attributes as part of a program of study. Learning couched in this broader context requires a longer-term perspective that contemporary academe conspires against. The rotation of teaching allocations in relation to sabbaticals, research agendas, and the time limitations already noted, can conspire against close affinity with cutting-edge development and technology needs.

The above three conceptualisations of OCB activity as applied to higher education, point towards subject coordinators being less motivated by institutional concerns and more by personal drivers. This is cause for concern at the institutional level as subject coordinators represent the coalface where institutional teaching and learning policy agendas (after interpretation and practice alignment strategies have been determined) are implemented.

METHODS

The research findings reported in this study are outcomes of a collaborative study conducted across four, multi campus, multi-modal university campuses from three states in Australia. The research design incorporated triangulation of qualitative and quantitative methods across multiple universities to obtain a more complete understanding of the broad area of subject coordination. The use of multiple procedures to gather information has a long history in the social and behavioural sciences (Silverman, 2006) and allows for a combination of different data collection sources to compare the results obtained from each. The use of triangulation or multiple measures helps to reduce the deficiencies and biases of one particular method and to overcome any problem of validity (Liamputtong & Ezzy, 2005).

The use of both quantitative and qualitative research approaches are not mutually exclusive and are regarded as complementary methods providing a more complete picture of the phenomenon under investigation. It is also used to obtain a more complete understanding of the broad area of unit coordination by revealing different aspects of the participant's responses as well as providing an in depth explanation of the different aspects of the unit coordination. The methodological framework encompasses a more holistic approach to studying the substantive domain of unit coordination. The research consisted of multiple stages each providing more detail and specificity moving from the macro to the micro level of inquiry. This study reports on two particular stages of research. The first involves semi-structured interviews with staff occupying formal teaching and learning leadership positions across various seniority levels within university hierarchies. The second stage (informed by issues raised in the first stage) involved administering a survey to 'in role' subject coordinators. Both stages provided useful data about the complexities and challenges of subject coordination and informed a series of professional development initiatives for building subject coordinator capacities.

Interviews

Fifty senior academics in formal teaching-related leadership roles at four multi-campus Australian universities representing three states were inter-viewed as part of the study. The senior academics involved had a professional interest in work undertaken by subject coordinators and were keen to assist in investigating the key role(s) of subject coordinators and any perceived needs for leadership capacity building. The sample selection ensured that all faculties were represented across the four collaborating institutions, at each level of leadership. Preliminary project team discussions identified that the role of subject coordination is significantly shaped by institutional policy and administrative structures, and the interviews provided a snapshot and overview of the thoughts of senior academic leaders on the role of the subject coordinator.

The sample included Deputy/Pro Vice-Chancellors (Academic), Deans, Associate Deans of Teaching and Learning (ADTL), Heads of School/ Department, and Course/Program Coordinators with 13 academics from each university interviewed. Table 2 shows the 50 interviewees' level of academic appointment.

Each senior academic leader participated in a face-to-face interview with semi-structured questions. The questions examined the complexities of the subject coordinator leadership role, including participant beliefs about the nature of the 'leadership' role, the responsibilities undertaken by subject coordinators, the skills required by them, whether subject coordinator capabilities match the skills needed to complete their duties, and the function of professional development in equipping subject coordinators to complete their work.

All interviews were digitally recorded and transcribed. Interview responses were electronically coded to match interview questions (Bazeley & Richards, 2000) and thematically coded to reveal major themes and sub-themes. Data were tabulated and manually cross-matched to individual interviewees, themes and sub-themes, and institutions. These levels of coding provided a means of separating and combing data, and finding similarities and differences across and within the participants and institutions.

Interview Findings and Discussion

Forty-six interviewees revealed ideas regarding the static ($n = 4$) or changing ($n = 42$) nature of subject coordinator responsibilities. Thirteen of them believed that the subject coordinator's 'core responsibilities' were to design subject content and assessment and prepare, manage and deliver disciplinary knowledge. 'Good teaching is good teaching', an ADTL stressed. These basic elements of subject coordinator work had not changed substantially over the last decade. What had changed, nine interviewees stated, were the

Table 2. Sample, Level of Academic Appointment.

Level of Academic Appointment	Sample Number
Deputy/Pro Vice-Chancellor (Academic)	4
Dean	8
Associate Dean of Teaching and Learning	7
Head of School/Department	15
Course/Program Coordinator	16
Total	*50*

increased number of off-campus students (e.g. offshore and distance); the inclusion of partner institutions and/or industry stakeholders; the need to meet partner requirements; and the technological complexities associated with teaching online and organising and electronically posting materials prior to student contact. A Dean noted: 'the basics of subject coordination hasn't changed – the sophistication of it has'. Some of the key changes to subject coordinator responsibilities included:

- increased use of technology ($n = 22$)
- compliance issues ($n = 18$)
- academic workload ($n = 16$)
- teaching duties ($n = 14$)
- administrative duties ($n = 12$).

Key findings from the data showed that subject coordinators were considered managers or low-level leaders. There was a lack of consensus about what aspects of roles and responsibilities involved management, administration or leadership capabilities. However, there was general agreement that the subject coordinator required disciplinary expertise and advanced learning and teaching capabilities above that of research ability. Findings also revealed a wide range of institutional and role-based factors that impacted on a subject coordinator's work and how the increased scope and scale of the subject coordinator's role had expanded associated workloads and responsibilities. In particular, data showed that:

- The subject coordinator role was often the first stage in an academic's career path;
- The work undertaken by subject coordinators was context-specific;
- The amount of authority given to subject coordinators did not match the level of responsibility asked of them; and
- The scope and scale of subject coordinator responsibilities had broadened with the increasing numbers of sessional academics to supervise; advancements in online learning; and greater student expectations. Subject coordinators needed to comply with university policy; quality teaching and learning principles; and have current discipline knowledge about theory and practice and, in some instances, industry standards.

Interviewees described the role of subject coordinators, as including the management of the teaching team and subject curricula; ensuring the relevance and consistency of subject curricula and practices; maintaining the quality of the subject and leading the teaching team and students. These roles were considered 'leadership' roles by over two-thirds ($n = 34$) of the interviewees. The leadership ideas put forward by them suggested that the subject coordinator 'leads from behind' as she/he motivates, shares ideas, works collegially and encourages the teaching team to develop their individual strengths.

Forty-two of the 48 responding interviewees (88 per cent) perceived the subject coordinator position as fitting into the following levels of leadership:

- low level leadership ($n = 17$)
- team leadership ($n = 16$)
- management ($n = 12$)
- academic leadership ($n = 11$)
- discipline-specific ($n = 5$).

The idea that 'the subject coordinator is the lowest level of leadership an academic would take as part of their career path' was expressed in various ways by 17 interviewees (35 per cent). Responsibilities of subject coordination were considered to be part of the normal work program of a lecturer and that they attended to the day-to-day work in delivering a program of study. One Dean explained: 'their day-to-day responsibility is to make sure our bread and butter business works as well as we hope'. Nine interviewees believed that this role was at 'the bottom of the pyramid' of a hierarchical structure. Interviewees were quick to praise the work of subject coordinators in organising subject content and delivery and maintaining a cohesive teaching team. At the same time, they positioned the subject coordinator as a low-level leadership role because they lacked the authority to employ or question staff, or negotiate with colleagues about subject content and processes.

Interviewees' responses could not be generalised to a specific group (e.g. Dean, Head of School [HoS]). Crude matching of results to home universities suggested that 69 per cent of interviewees from one university and 38 per cent of interviewees from another university believed that the subject coordinator fits into a low level leadership role. Thirty-eight per cent of interviewees from a third university considered the subject coordinator matched a managerial role. Interviewees from the fourth university yielded a broad spread of results. These findings suggested that the positioning of a subject coordinator as a low level leader was influenced by the culture and/or practices of individual universities, possibly a top-down, hierarchical culture.

Some interviewees expressed a concern about the lack of authority subject coordinators had when managing teaching teams and one interviewee expressed this as 'a lack of teeth'. This issue is open to debate as a subject coordinator may be required to supervise tutors at an administrative/ operational level but lacks authority 'to question difficult staff'. The line of authority in this case often rested with a more senior academic. An Associate Dean Teaching and Learning explained: 'subject coordinators have lots of responsibility but no authority because schools have flat structures where everybody just reports to the Head of School'.

Leading the teaching team, requires subject coordinators to take responsibility for establishing and maintaining a cohesive and collaborative team; liaising with and coordinating others and dealing with subject, staff and student issues. Academic leadership is also provided in the form of 'support' for sessional and casual teaching staff. The growing number and turnover of sessional and causal academics now teaching in degree courses have increased subject coordinators' responsibility to ensure that all lecturers and tutors had the required disciplinary knowledge to teach a subject and had an understanding of the university's culture and practices. Nineteen interviewees stressed the importance for the subject coordinator to create a unified and effective teaching team. This organiser/coordinator role could extend beyond the lecture or tutorial classroom to include practicum and/or laboratory work. The subject coordinator was considered a role model for staff and students and someone who guided their teaching and learning.

The idea that the subject coordinator 'leads' separate groups within a collective of lecturers, tutors and students was held by 14 interviewees (44 per cent), all of whom believed that the subject coordinator was a leadership role. This leadership role, a Course/Program Coordinator suggested, was linked to their management of curriculum development responsibilities where they led the students 'through a path of learning knowledge; a learning process about a particular area'. Echoing this belief, an ADTL stated that the subject coordinator led 'the students' learning journeys' and the role occurred regardless of the number of students or staff involved in a subject. The subject coordinator was the 'link person' between the students, teaching team and colleagues working in the course. In the words of a Dean:

> Subject coordinators are critical because, in a way, they often lead the coalface work, they often lead, they ultimately take the responsibility for student learning, so, if anyone's going to lead innovation change, flexibility, student sensitiveness, that's the person who's going to have those conversations with more teams or colleagues. They're the ones that I think have the closest link to students probably through their colleagues but also through their own work and should be driving up how we behave as an organisation or a course, you know. That's where you should be getting the students' sentiments driven up from.

There was an assumption that subject coordinators had the professional background and capabilities to undertake the role and a tacit expectation that they would fulfil their duties. Interviewees believed that the subject coordinator required disciplinary expertise and advanced learning and teaching capabilities above that of research ability. Whilst there were differences of opinion about the exact manager or leader roles and responsibilities of subject coordinators, interviewees agreed on:

- the interpersonal, management, teaching and learning and information technology skills required by subject coordinators;
- the changing nature of subject coordinator responsibilities due to advances in information technology; and
- the increased workload demanded of subject coordinators that stems from increased student enrolments, diverse and flexible modes of delivery, increased compliance to quality/best practice teaching and learning inputs and outcomes, increased number of sessional staff and reduced administrative support.

Survey

The design of an online survey for subject coordinators built on a previous survey at one of the partner institutions and was significantly modified using evidence obtained from interviews (noted above). The final questionnaire contained measures of the main constructs, that is, the themes and sub-themes identified from the analysis of the qualitative interviews. A number of questions employed a multidimensional scale measuring importance and satisfaction for a range of roles and competencies derived from Aigbedo and Parameswaran (2004). Survey respondents were asked to provide an importance rating that was plotted on the vertical axis and the satisfaction rating was plotted on the horizontal axis providing a four-quadrant grid that allowed determination of items of high/low satisfaction and impor-tance. Because the data were nonparametric, further statistical analyses (analysis of variance, t-tests and multiple regression) were unwarranted and not valid given that all the data are frequencies and percentages. In addition, survey participants were invited to respond qualitatively and their comments are embedded into the analysis below.

Overall, there were 445 completed surveys. It was difficult to ascertain the overall response rate as a percentage as information about total numbers of subject coordinators from all four universities was unavailable. It should be noted however, that University protocols and policy contexts contributed to a data set that favoured two particular partner universities. At one university the ability to centrally access and specifically target subject coordinators was not possible, making the task of inviting participation very difficult. This university experienced a low response rate. In another university new protocols concerning the issue of global emails to academic staff prevented use of a central mechanism for inviting participation to complete the survey. Individual appeals to faculty based teaching and learning staff proved to have limited effectiveness resulting in poor response rates at this second institution. These issues are noted to make transparent the logistical challenges encountered in the data collection and as limitations for data interpretation.

Survey Findings and Discussion
The survey data highlighted key findings through the eyes of those serving in the role of subject coordinator across the four different university policy contexts and faculties. The survey also included questions not relevant to the specific focus of this chapter and thus a selective reporting approach has been adopted to ensure relevance. In essence, the results suggested that respondents regarded themselves as experienced academics who manage curriculum development, and teams of permanent and casual colleagues in addition to diverse cohorts of students. To be effective in their role, subject coordinators are required to clearly demonstrate competencies and capabilities of leadership and management. Evidence suggested that acting as a subject coordinator was an integral part of an academic's duties, and yet it was perceived that the role of subject coordinator was not well supported. The skills and competencies required to be a coordinator were generally believed to be acquired through role execution rather than requirements expected in employment selection criteria. In general, the data obtained from this survey suggested that subject coordinators believed:

- the importance and positioning of the role at the 'coalface' was poorly understood;
- the leadership aspects of the role were poorly recognised;
- institutional support for the role was insufficient;
- they have not always had the appropriate skills and capabilities required to effectively discharge their role; and
- collegiate and peer support substituted for formal institutional support frameworks.

The following key findings represent an overview of the data obtained from all partner institutions.

1. The background and demographic information supplied by respondents provided the following generalised portrait of subject coordinators. The typical respondent was described as:
   - having more than 10 years of experience teaching in tertiary education;
   - employed at Level B (Lecturer) or Level C (Senior Lecturer) aged over 46 years; and
   - with more than six years experience as a subject coordinator.
2. Respondents were asked to answer questions in relation to their most challenging subject as many respondents coordinated more than one subject. It was noted that the subject coordinators surveyed taught units across various modes of delivery including on and off-campus, international and online and, in the majority, were responsible for:
   - between 51 and 500 enrolled students per subject (55 per cent)
   - coordinating between one and five academic staff (53 per cent)
3. While the majority of subject coordinators (54.4 per cent) received a workload allocation for their subject coordination duties, 31.2 per cent of respondents received no specific support or recognition for their subject coordination role. Most significantly 96.6 per cent of subject coordinators received no additional administrative support in their role. As a result, subject coordinators considered that their role was not sufficiently valued or supported by university hierarchy. When they did receive support, it came from their academic colleagues (38.7 per cent) or course/program coordinators (18.2 per cent).
4. Using a multidimensional scale to examine factors that subject coordinators found important in their role and their level of satisfaction in being competent for those factors, data indicated that subject coordinators:
   - considered that building and/or leading a successful team of colleagues was of high importance, though they were not satisfied in how effectively they had executed this part of their role;
   - counselling or advising students about subject requirements was considered important and staff were satisfied with their performance for this part of their role; and
   - rated highly the importance of designing relevant assessments and ensuring currency of subject knowledge in their courses and, overall, were highly satisfied with how this outcome had been achieved.

5. Again using a multidimensional scale, this time to examine the
   relationships that subject coordinators had with their colleagues (in
   various positions within the university hierarchy) and their level of
   satisfaction with those relationships, data indicated that subject
   coordinators considered that their relationships with:
   - academic developers (central and/or faculty-based) and members of
     their universities' teaching and learning centres were fairly important,
     yet they were not satisfied with these relationships;
   - Course and Program Coordinators and Heads of School were
     important and they were satisfied with these relationships; and
   - the Deputy-Vice Chancellor (Academic)/Pro Vice-Chancellor (or
     equivalent in the university hierarchy) were of low importance and
     that they were not satisfied with these relationships.
6. Respondents were also asked to rate the importance of various
   professional development and learning opportunities for enhancing their
   performance as a subject coordinator. In other words, how did they
   'learn the ropes' of their role. The results indicated that the three most
   important professional and development opportunities were:
   - learning on the job;
   - ad hoc conversations with other subject coordinators;
   - targeted formal professional development; and
   - informal mentoring/coaching.

The survey included a number of open-ended questions inviting
respondents to make qualitative comments about the most time consuming
aspects of their role, any assistance they believed would facilitate their role
and to share how they dealt with challenges in their role. The following
comments highlighted workload and time management issues:

> At the cost of reduced research activity, they were doing less work that 'counts' for
> promotion or career advancement, 'I just deal with things as best I can – but my research
> time is greatly impacted upon which has serious consequences for me, at a personal
> professional level.
>
> It's always hard to know how the demands of this role are valued in the overall mix of
> demands and expectations upon which my performance evaluation is based.
>
> I am very choosy about sessional staff as having good sessionals makes life much
> easier, ... recruiting known sessional staff,' and 'you fully utilise (exploit) the skills and
> goodwill of the reliable staff members in the team.

Survey evidence suggests that subject coordinators require specific skills
and competencies to be effective in their role and that there is little relevant
professional development to build their leadership capacities.

RESULTS AND DISCUSSION

It is not surprising that the viewpoints expressed by the interviewed academic leaders differed from the views of surveyed subject coordinators. It was evident that the more senior an interviewee was, the more subject coordination was considered to involve management, with a nuanced undertone suggesting that regarding subject coordinators as leaders was not quite appropriate. It was also interesting to note that both interviewees and survey respondents acknowledged the very significant contextual changes that have shaped the current context in which subject coordinators operate. Yet academic leaders struggled with articulating how this may impact role performance as it was perceived that the role had evolved rather than had become more onerous.

This presents a challenge for the promotion of discretionary behaviours towards an institution. While institutional and coalface staff do not hold shared views about role definition, capabilities and competencies, motivation to engage in OCB for the institutions benefit is less likely. While self-interest and organisational interests remain de-coupled individuals are more likely to follow behaviours that create personal benefits rather than support institutional goals. As an illustration of this point, subject coordinators articulated the pressures they felt to engage in research that generated promotion pathways while being burdened with increasing teaching and administrative responsibilities. Research is formally part of job descriptions with measurable outputs and quality indicators in the form of journal rankings. The demonstration of quality teaching and leadership is less obvious and may be broadly and narrowly conceived. This demonstrates what Turnipseed and Wilson (2009) describe as inconsistencies as to which behaviours are expected, valued and rewarded. While research has hegemony in the value and reward stakes, investment of time in teaching quality and leadership can be traded off against high performance in research.

The role of subject coordinators in relation to team building and as part of collegial teams was considered by both interview and survey respondents to be important. Notably however, subject coordinators were not satisfied with their performance of this aspect of their roles. This expressed dissatisfaction provides the most significant opportunities for empowerment through professional development. Team building and team leadership have immediate and medium term elements that span informal expected and informal unexpected behaviours. For example, junior or less experienced subject coordinators would be expected to manage the teaching team and more experienced subject coordinators would, in addition, be expected to plan for curriculum development and be innovative in approaches to modes of teaching. It was noted above (section 4 of survey findings) that surveyed staff were satisfied with their currency of subject knowledge and their ability to design relevant assessment tasks. However, questions about the more medium term needs for subject development are informal role requirements and did not feature among the questions asked.

Jones, Ladyshewsky, Oliver, and Flavell (2009), in their study of those holding formal teaching and learning leadership positions, describe the required academic leadership capabilities as including:

- interpersonal and communication skills;
- problem-solving skills;
- confliction-resolution capabilities;
- cultural management;
- coaching; and
- change management (p. 1).

Empowerment through building such capabilities has the capacity to build confidence and promote OCBs. This will be particularly important as higher education evolves further in response to pressure from stakeholder groups. Turnipseed and Wilson (2009) credit Organ (1997) with refining concepts of OCB in response to such pressures by suggesting that the trend towards team teaching and 'a mandate from accrediting agencies to integrate the curriculum and remove historical silos' (p. 212) suggests that this will see 'a wider breadth of job duties and increased breath of psychological contracts' (p. 212). Those subject coordinators with the skills to manage this increased diversity will make a stronger contribution to effective team and curriculum leadership. However, the problem lies in the current mechanisms prevalent in developing such skills. As noted in the qualitative survey comments, learning on the job or action learning was how subject coordinators acquired skills with support from colleagues that was typically informal or 'self arranged', 'help from other faculty in my corridor,' and 'through informal discussion with colleagues and on-the-job experience.' While Kempster (2009) points out the importance of this style of learning, arguing that vicarious learning makes valuable contributions to learning through experience, it is appropriate to add more formal structured programs of professional development to both recognise and acknowledge such skills and provide a pathway for academic career development.

Survey questions did not specifically aim to collect data about subject coordinator relationships with students. However, a well-designed and managed subject, with a cohesive teaching team providing engaging subject material that reflects contemporary knowledge, has great potential to provide a rich learning experience for students. One aspect of student learning relates to how staff interact with students and, as noted above (in section 4 of survey key findings), survey respondents considered relationships with students to be important and were satisfied with their performance for this part of their role. However, those academics who approach teaching and learning tasks with limited enthusiasm are unlikely to have completed the voluntary survey. This potential limitation needs to be considered when interpreting the data.

CONCLUSIONS AND IMPLICATIONS

The role of subject coordination represents 'the coalface of educational leadership' and the widespread acceptance in academia that it is appropriate to entrust resources and staff to untrained academic leaders and managers is not supported in industry contexts. The subject coordinator is differentiated from staff that have formal leadership responsibility for course/program-wide curriculum development and delivery. The term 'leader' is seldom applied to the subject coordinator position and rarely has the Australian higher education sector provided leadership training for this group – yet they are required to manage and lead staff and students.

The realities of growing student numbers and the increasing use of technologies and initiatives related to 'flexible education' often mean that new academics become coordinators very quickly. Subject co-ordination roles are now common at lecturer and senior lecturer levels with little (if any) skills development provided to such staff as they assume roles that have become influential and complex. The luxury of an apprentice-like initiation in academe with a more experienced academic, allowing competencies to develop are rare opportunities in the contemporary academic environment.

A typical job description for subject coordinators does not articulate many informal role expectations (including OCBs) and where such expectations have little visibility and reward associated with them it is possible to strategically plan to limit the time committed to certain role expectations; particularly when personal competencies mean certain tasks are challenging. Building confidence and self-efficacy through targeted professional development initiatives can contribute to a sense of empowerment with challenging tasks made easier and less time consuming. Developing leadership skills for subject coordinators represents one key area of capacity building that has great potential to contribute to greater engagement with OCB.

Senior academic leaders have suggested professional development topics should include those related to teaching, learning and assessment; duty of care for students; time and priority management; and management and leadership responsibilities. They also considered that the preferred professional development approach was peer mentoring, including whole school in-service, one-to-one mentoring and linking new subject coordinators with experienced colleagues. This same viewpoint was expressed by survey respondents who valued peer support and on the job learning whilst also acknowledging that formal professional development had a place in building capabilities and competencies within a diverse program of academic development.

As a future initiative, it will be important to embed such academic development initiatives within a program of development opportunities to ensure that staff are empowered to engage in all dimensions of discretionary behaviours; that is, toward institutions, teams and students. This remains problematic while the institutional and individual goals are mismatched. However, Fullan and Scott (2009) have also identified a number of more nuanced aspects of leadership and utilise Berbquist and Pawlak's 'six cultures of the academy' as a way of identifying the types of competencies that academic leader require to be effective. The six cultures of the academy include collegial, managerial, developmental, advocacy, virtual and tangible cultures. While these clearly relate to formal and more senior leadership roles, building confidence and empowering leaders across all leadership levels will continue to be important for encouraging discretionary behaviours.

NOTE

1. A subject coordinator may also be referred to as a Unit Chair, Unit Coordinator or Course Coordinator at different universities.

ACKNOWLEDGMENTS

Support for this publication has been provided by the Australian Learning and Teaching Council Ltd, an initiative of the Australian Government's Department of Education, Employment and Workplace Relations. The views expressed in this publication do not necessarily reflect the views of

ALTC. The contributions of the following team members, Dale Holt, Jacquie McDonald, Lynne Cohen, Paul Chang, Glenda Campbell-Evans, Ian Macdonald and Kim Atkinson to the research reported in this study, are also acknowledged.

REFERENCES

Aigbedo, H., & Parameswaran, P. (2004). Importance-performance analysis for improving quality of campus food service. *International Journal of Quality & Reliability Management, 21*(8), 876–896.

Anderson, D., Johnson, R., & Saha, L. (2002). *Changes in academic work, implications for universities of the changing age distribution and work roles of academic.* Department of Education Science and Training, canberra, Australia.

Bazeley, P., & Richards, L. (2000). *The NVivo qualitative project book.* London: Sage.

Belogolovsky, E., & Somech, A. (2010). Teachers' organisational citizenship behaviour: Examining the boundary between in-role behaviour and extra-role behaviour form the perspective of teachers, principals and parents. *Teaching and Teacher Education, 26,* 914–923.

Cleveland-Innes, M., & Sandgra, A. (2010). Leadership in a new era of higher distance education. In M. Cleveland-Innes & D. Garrison (Eds.), *An introduction to distance education: Understanding teaching and learning in a new era.* New York, NY: Routledge.

Coaldrake, P., & Stedman, L. (1999). *Academic work in the twenty-first century: Changing roles and practices.* Occasional Paper Series. Higher Education Division, Department of Education, Training and Youth Affairs, pp. 1–35.

Coates, H., & Goedegebuure, L. (2010). *The real academic revolution.* Research Briefing Report, LHMartin Institute.

Currie, J., & Vidovich, L. M. (2009). The changing nature of academic work. In M. Tight, K. H. Mok, J. Huisman & C. C. Morphew (Eds.), *The Routledge International Handbook of Higher Education* (pp. 441–452). New York, NY: Routledge/Taylor & Francis Group.

Fullan, M., & Scott, G. (2009). *Turnaround leadership for higher education.* San Francisco, CA: Jossey-Bass.

Hemmings, B., & Kay, R. (2010). University lecturer publication output: Qualifications, time and confidence count. *Journal of Higher Education Policy and Management, 32*(2), 185–197.

Jones, S., Ladyshewsky, R., Oliver, B., & Flavell, H. (2009). *Leading courses: Academic leadership for course coordinators,* ALTC final report. Retrieved from http://academi cleadership.curtin.edu.au/course_coordinator/local/docs/leadingcourses_report1.pdf. Accessed on August 28, 2010.

Kelloway, E., & Barling, J. (2000). Knowledge work as organizational behaviour. *International Journal of Management Reviews, 2*(3), 287–304.

Kempster, S. J. (2009). Observing the invisible: Examining the role of observational learning in the development of leadership practice. *Journal of Management Development, 28*(5), 439–456.

Liamputtong, P., & Ezzy, D. (2005). *Qualitative research methods.* Melbourne, Victoria: Oxford University Press.

Marshall, S. J. (2006). *Issues in the development of leadership for learning and teaching in higher education*. Carrick Institute for Learning and Teaching in Higher Education Occasional Paper.

Mintzberg, H. (1994). Rounding out the manager's job. *Sloan Management Review, Fall*, 11–26.

Organ, D. W. (1997). Organisational citizenship behaviour: It's construct clean up time. *Human Performance, 10*(2), 85–97.

Power, M. (1997). *The audit society. Rituals of verification*. New York, NY: Oxford University Press.

Ramsden, P., Prosser, M., Trigwell, K., & Martin, E. (2007). University teachers' experiences of academic leadership and their approaches to teaching. *Learning and Instruction, 17*(2), 140–155.

Scott, G., Bell, S., Coates, H., & Grebennikov, L. (2010). Australian higher education leaders in times of change: The role of pro Vice chancellor and deputy vice-chancellor. *Journal of Higher Education Policy and Management, 32*(4), 401–418.

Sharrock, G. (2010). Two hippocratic oaths for higher education. *Journal of Higher Education Policy and Management, 32*(4), 365–377.

Silverman, D. (2006). *Interpreting qualitative data*. London: Sage Publications.

Turnipseed, D. L., & Wilson, G. L. (2009). From discretionary to required, the migration of organisational citizenship behaviour. *Journal of Leadership and Organisational Studies, 15*(3), 201–216.

Vilkinas, T., Leask, B., & Ladyshewsky, R. (2009). *Academic leadership: Fundamental building blocks* [Resource book]. Strawberry Hills, New South Wales: Australian Learning and Teaching Council. Retrieved from http://www.altc.edu.au/resource-academic-leadership-unisa. Accessed on August 12, 2010.

CHAPTER 8

WHAT WE DO HERE IS WHO WE ARE: TEACHER DISCRETIONARY BEHAVIOR AS SOCIAL IDENTIFICATION [*]

Nancy L. Ras

ABSTRACT

Teacher discretionary behaviors are considered to be organizationally beneficial and ways to develop and support such behaviors are sought after. Discretionary behaviors have, in the main, been considered from an individual level of analysis. However, using the group as the level of analysis, and viewed through Social Identity/Social Categorization theory (SIT/SCT) respectively, data from this longitudinal, mixed-method, case study of teachers during a curricular reform suggest that teacher discretionary behaviors may be the means to teacher socialization and

---

[*] This chapter is partially informed by the author's dissertation research entitled *Curriculum Change at Hilltop School: A Case Study of Intervention and Organisational Change at an Elementary School in Israel*, under the supervision of Professor Harry Torrance.

Discretionary Behavior and Performance in Educational Organizations: The Missing Link in Educational Leadership and Management
Advances in Educational Administration, Volume 13, 197–222
Copyright © 2012 by Emerald Group Publishing Limited
All rights of reproduction in any form reserved
ISSN: 1479-3660/doi:10.1108/S1479-3660(2012)0000013013

*the outcome of teacher social identification. Implications and applicability
of the findings to other settings are discussed.*

Keywords: Teacher discretionary behavior; social identity; teacher
culture; teacher socialization; curricular reform

INTRODUCTION

Discretionary behaviors by teachers, in this study defined as "behaviors
that are neither formally required nor formally assessed and are valuable
to the performer in pursuit of valued outcomes," become even more
important as they may provide support mechanisms that reduce stress
(Haslam & Reicher, 2007) and help to make the many dimensions and
demands of school functioning possible (Burnett, Williamson, & Bartol,
2000; Vigoda-Gadot, Beeri, Birman-Shemesh, & Somech, 2007). The
value of such behaviors is both personal and organizational (Burnett,
Williamson, & Bartol, 2009; McNeely & Meglino, 1994; Podsakoff,
Whiting, Podsakoff, & Blume, 2009; Williamson, Burnett, & Bartol, 2009).
Described as pro-social (McNeely & Meglino, 1994), organizational
citizenship (Organ, 1988), and extra role (Vigoda-Gadot, 2006), in this
chapter will be referred to as discretionary behaviors, but will adhere to
the language used in each particular study.

Discretionary behaviors have generally been considered at an individual
level of analysis using social exchange models (Blau, 1964) and the antecedent
motivations to perform such behaviors including commitment (Meyer &
Allen, 1997), psychological contracts (LePine & Van Dyne, 2001; van den
Heuvel & Schalk, 2009), and actor attributes such as affect, cognition, and
disposition (Ellemers, de Gilder, & van den Heuvel, 1998). Haslam, Powell,
and Turner (2000), however, point to the growing body of research in
organizations at the group level of analysis. The social identity approach
(Haslam, 2004), including social identification theory (SIT) (Tajfel, 1982) and
social categorization theory (SCT) (Turner & Haslam, 2001), suggests that
organizational citizenship behavior, rather than being grounded in
personality, is influenced by group dynamics. Van Knippenberg, van Dick,
and Tavares (2007) note that social exchange and social identification have
different antecedents, with the former focused on person-dependent
calculations of rewards and losses, and the latter on context-dependent
perceptions of self. Van Dick (2004) defines social identification as "the extent
to which *the group membership is incorporated in the self-concept*" (p. 178)

(italics original) and the results dependent upon the degree to which "an individual defines him- or herself in terms of membership in an organizational group ... the more his or her attitudes are governed by this group membership should result in greater performance, lower absenteeism, and turnover, and more extra role behaviors" (van Dick, Wagner, Stellmacher, Christ, & Tissington, 2005, p. 192). In this way social identification answers the question "Who am I?" through group membership. In educational research, however, there is little such research (see Christ, van Dick, Wagner, & Stellmacher, 2003; van Dick, Grojean, Christ, & Wieseke, 2006; van Dick & Wagner, 2002; van Dick, Wagner, Stellmacher, & Christ, 2005; van Dick et al., 2005 for noteworthy exceptions).

This chapter answers the call of Haslam and Reicher (2007) to use the case study approach to investigate organizational identity and self-categorization in organizations – illumining the relationship between social identity and the teacher discretionary behavior. The social identity approach will be presented, followed by presentation of the case, and concluding with implications and suggestions for further research.

THE SOCIAL IDENTITY APPROACH

The origins of SIT can be attributed to Tajfel's "minimal conditions" experiments in which attitudes were affected by membership in even the most contrived groups. Tajfel concluded that identification with an in-group answers the existential question "Who am I?" and has both emotional- and values-based significance. Identifying with a group offers the individual positive self-esteem and empowered distinctiveness as a member of *we*. Van Dick (2004) suggests that social identity is made up of three components – a cognitive component which is the awareness and knowledge of group membership, an affective component which is the emotional attachment to the group, and an evaluative component which is the perceived value of group membership.

SCT (Turner & Haslam, 2001) refined the cognitive aspects of social identity salience and its consequences on individual psychology. SCT offers a broader view than SIT and suggests self-concept is based on self-categorization. As individuals regard themselves as members of groups, they categorize themselves as *prototypes* with those attributes, thoughts, and feelings that are held by other group members. As Hogg (2001) posits "Self-conceptualization is firmly grounded in collectivities: It contains a set of self-definitions (social identities) corresponding to the group prototypes of all the groups to which we feel we belong" (p. 134). SCT suggests the cognitive processes associated with SIT and these complementary theories are referred to as the social identity approach (Haslam, 2004, p. 29). In distinguishing between the salience of personal and social identities, Moreland and Levine (2001) offer "A sense of *social identity* develops when people categorize themselves as members of one group rather than another. In contrast, a sense of *personal identity* develops when people categorize themselves as unique individuals within a group" (p. 95) (italics original). Therefore, when a person's social identity is salient, s/he is motivated less by personal gain than the prospect of contributing to group goals (Ellemers, de Gilder, & Haslam, 2004; Worchel, Rothberger, Day, Hart, & Butemeyer, 1998). In their seminal work on social identity, Ashforth and Mael (1989) offered that social identity was a sense of *belongingness* (p. 135) suggesting that the *self* is dependent on its social connectedness for identity and meaning. Haslam (2004) suggests that "the ability to think in terms of 'we' and 'us,' not just 'I' and 'me' " (p. 17) enables meaningful, integrated, and collaborative engagements in the organizational context.

Grant (2007) notes that when the social identity is salient employees are motivated to make a pro-social difference, particularly when there is a clear connection between behavior and its impact and suggests that the salience of the pro-social identity is "concerned with helping and contributing" (p. 403). When this identity is activated, people are more likely to help others and engage in helping behaviors that fall outside of their job descriptions. Attainment of such outcomes may suggest the reason that individuals are willing to circumscribe their personal will to, and make pronounced efforts for in-groups (Boen, Vanbeselaere, & Cool, 2006; Ellemers et al., 2004; Seyle & Swann, 2007). If an individual's identity as well as her/his ability to achieve desirable goals is group-dependent, social identity serves valuable personal ends, congruent behaviors would support these aims, and the *self* would identify through group membership (Ellemers et al., 1998).

ENCULTURATION – A SOCIAL IDENTITY APPROACH TO TEACHER SOCIALIZATION

Organizational socialization is defined as the process by which individuals learn about and adjust to the work context. Ashforth and Mael (1989) argue "Socialization affects identification and identification in turn affects internalization" (p. 144) of values, beliefs, and behaviors adopted as the prototypical behaviors of the group. "Identification induces the individual to engage in, and derive satisfaction from, activities congruent with the identity, to view him- or herself as an exemplar of the group and to reinforce factors conventionally associated with group formation" (p. 154). Van Dick and Wagner (2002) found that social identity increased aspects of behavior relative to group norms, that the salience of social identity related not only to work behaviors but also to attitudes, and that the emotional component of social identification was the best predictor of group performance. The relationship between social identification through processes of socialization has a profound effect on the ways in which a new group member thinks and behaves and to a great degree this is influenced by the group of which s/he is becoming a part and prototype of a group member.

Kramer (2001) suggests that one of the characteristics of in-groups is in *presumptive* trust, that is, trust accorded to group members on an assumption of trustworthiness based on group membership. This is a way for group members to "affirm the importance they associate with their membership" (p. 171) and to provide organizational members with the opportunity to communicate to others the symbolic value they attach to membership. Indeed, "coworkers are an important source of encouragement, advice, and help for people who seek social support" (Moreland & Levine, 2001, p. 90), and work group norms are good predictors of workers' behaviors – often better than organizational norms or feelings of organizational commitment among workers. This may be explained by the suggestion that organizational commitment is considered to be based on calculative exchange relationships and as such *I* oriented (Van Knippenberg, 2000). Conceptually similar to affective commitment, social identification is based on the perception of shared fate, similarity, and belongingness and are "empirically distinguishable concepts" (Ashforth & Mael, 1989, p. 179), although affective commitment may be the result of social identification (Haslam, 2004). Prentice, Miller, and Lightdale (1994) found that common purpose was of greater importance than homogeneity in predicting group attachment suggesting the salience of social identity may be activated based on the ability of the group to promote a vision that supersedes individual characteristics as binding agents. Van Dick et al. (2006) suggest that this produces "a climate for citizenship in which group norms, shared values and understanding contribute to the development of an environment in which OCB is the norm" (p. 292). Socialization then can be considered to promote role-specific identities that affect individual behavior.

In a study of German schoolteachers, Van Dick and Wagner (2002) found that affective social identification was predictive of OCBs. A study by Somech and Ron (2007) related teachers' organizational citizenship behaviors to school-level collectivism, while social identity processes described above suggest the means to the creation of such an environment. Oplatka (2006) argues that teacher OCBs are the result of affective relationships between teachers and principals – a dyadic and arguably calculative view, whereas the case presented here suggests otherwise, as does the predisposition of teachers to pro-social behaviors (see Ras, this volume). Indeed Chen and Carey's (2009) description of OCB as "not just a function of being a conscientious, responsible person, but ... a complex social psychological phenomenon. It arises in part from one's interdependence, a sensitivity to one's relationships with others and a concern with in-group membership, and cooperation to achieve social goals" (p. 135) – is arguably a process of social identification.

Data and Methods

Data were collected by the author as part of her dissertation research. She had been introduced to the site through a colleague who had identified the school as involved in a self-directed curricular change process which was to unify the school curriculum under the theoretical and methodological lens of multiple intelligences (MI) (Gardner, 1983). After securing entrance to the site through the local municipality (under whose auspices the school was located) and by the principal and faculty, and having been struck by the site's contradiction of what has seemingly become an assumption of teacher *resistance* to change, the study was undertaken to explore the process and meaning of this change through the eyes of the participants. Although by definition a particularistic study, it was structured as an inquiry instrumental to the understanding of the process of educational change more generally through a longitudinal design which utilized mixed methods. Taking place within the context of a curricular change, the study utilized an emergent design to capture those aspects of salience to the participants which then became the foci of the research.

Organizational Context

Hilltop School had been founded as a rural community school which was in suburban transition. In the nine years since its founding, the school had grown from 40 pupils to over 460 serving 10 local communities in the Galilee region of northern Israel. Of the 34 faculty members at Hilltop, including the principal, and the vice-principal, 30 of 34 were female, and most lived in the small local communities served by the school. The school was in its ninth year at the time of the study and this principal, its second. Eight faculty members remained from its founding and faculty experience spanned 2–22 years with 99% holding B.Ed. degrees and elementary level teaching licenses.

During the period of the study, the faculty was beginning implementation of a curricular change that had been developed on-site over the previous three years and which was based in the desire to find ways for a more inclusive classroom experience for all students, including the 20% who were receiving specialized assistance for learning disabilities (LD) (dyslexia, dysgraphia, attention deficit disorder (ADD), and attention deficit hyperactivity disorder (ADHD)). Such students were mainstreamed into regular classes for part of the day, also receiving individualized support by an LD specialist for 1–3 periods daily. There remained an overall feeling by the faculty that "… too many students were being left out, and left behind" (IA). Many meetings were focused on these issues.

The school faculty worked together in two formal working-group capacities: The first was at *grade-level clusters* of two or three classes for each grade level-homeroom teachers (generalists) worked with subject specialists on curricular matters for the grade-level cluster and the second was *area-interest clusters* – bringing subsets of teachers across grade levels together focused on school-wide thematic topics developed twice yearly for the upper grades (4–6), and once yearly for the lower grades (1–3). Teachers met in each of these two capacities weekly for at least two hours after school in addition to whole-school staff meetings held for at least 2 hours weekly. Each working group also provided a representative to the School Steering Committee (SSC). Membership was held on a yearly and rotating basis and was comprised of eight faculty members and the principal and vice-principal. All of these formal meetings had been institutionalized by the new principal and were not part of the teachers' formal duties.

Full time teachers were financially remunerated for between 25 and 30 hours of work per week, while, when including the time spent on-site in meetings and other endeavors, they averaged 45 hours of at-school tasks weekly. This difference reflects one aspect of their discretionary behavior – a more institutionalized aspect thereof – while time and effort spent helping each other before and after classes, taking another's yard duty, assisting students during breaks, and time outside of regular school hours planning and carrying out joint projects increased this amount by some 15–20%, particularly in preparation and culminating activities of school-wide thematic projects. Yet such occurrences were routine at Hilltop and no one seemed to feel imposed to work without financial compensation. RF expressed the consensus regarding this when she related "If we were that interested in money, we should never have become teachers."

At the beginning of her second year on-site, the principal formally introduced the faculty to the theory of MI (Gardner, 1983), and with the faculty explored the possibility of its adoption as an overarching theoretical framework for the curriculum. Over a period of two additional years, meetings, discussions, and staff development workshops were held, and the following year MI was adopted as Hilltop School's curricular framework.

Data Sources
The initial interviewee pool consisted of nine generalists (homeroom teachers at all grade levels), four subject-specific specialists (pedagogical facilitator, music, special education, and school counselor), the school secretary, vice-principal, and the principal. Subsequently, one teacher who had been an interviewee resigned from Hilltop School and one first-year Generalist (see Vignette – LT), as well as an Art teacher who was also a founding teacher, a Special Education teacher who was also a founding teacher, and a Generalist who was beginning her second year at the school were added, bringing the new total number of interviewees to 19. The new teacher to Hilltop was solicited and agreed to participate in the study, whereas the other three teachers had requested to be added to the research. As these additions increased the number of Specialists relative to generalists being interviewed, the research was served by their addition enabling the interviewee pool to more closely reflect the Generalist to Specialist ratio of the Hilltop faculty that was divided at 55%–45% respectively.

Interviews
Interviews were held at approximately 6-week intervals for one hour with each interviewee. Excluding holidays, school breaks, and with sensitivity for beginning of the year and end of the year pressures, this schedule totaled 8 interviews for the core group of 16 interviewees, and 3 interviews for those three who began later joined the pool. Interviews were tape-recorded with participant permission, and subsequently resulted in over 3,000 transcribed pages.

Interviews were held in Hebrew and as necessary, translated into English for excerpting into the final text. Two examples of such translated passages were reviewed by two bilingual colleagues, one a native English speaker and the other a native Hebrew speaker, who validated translations. Where necessary, these reviewers made recommendations regarding vocabulary and tenses as participle forms of verbs, for example, do not exist in Hebrew, yet were utilized for clarity in the English language translations.

Observation
Observation was carried out on those days when interviews were held (approximately 3 days each week of two weeks each month), as well as on 50 additional days during the entire period when, without prior notification, the author appeared at school. These days included, for example, observation in the morning on a day when she also observed afternoon staff meetings, as well as random appearances when no other explicit function was involved. Including interviewing, the total number of research hours at Hilltop School surpassed 400.

Documentary Analysis
Analysis of both documents and records comprised the documentary analysis of this study and included school-based documentation, both historical, focusing on the first years of Hilltop School and its founding, as well as documents related to precursors of the adoption and implementation of MI as the guiding theoretical and curricular framework. These documents were the minutes of meetings held since the new principal had arrived and initiated the process of creating a school-wide *vision statement*. Additionally, "local archival data" (Schensul, Schensul, & LeCompte, 1999) from the local municipality were compared to school-based records.

Questionnaire
The case study approach does not preclude the use of measurement tools and this research utilized "structured ethnographic data" (Schensul et al., 1999, p. 165), collected in questionnaire form or in the structured interview to "measure constructs that the study population understands and has identified as relevant" (p. 169) to show "the generality of specific observation ... verifying or casting new light on qualitative findings" (Miles & Huberman, 1994, p. 41). The use of such data in this study was intended to (1) test developing conceptualizations based on interview data and (2) verify the generality of data gathered through interviews as reflective of the wider organization. The instrument, a prioritization of Teaching Goals (Fig. 2), focused on faculty curricular priorities, exploring the shared values and common purpose articulated in the interviews.

Social Network Analysis (SNA)
The creation of school communities focuses attention on social relationships within schools and among faculty as a valuable resource of support (Tschannen-Moran, 2009). Social network analysis enables organizational and social connections to be made explicit as they bridge individual and group

levels of analysis (Flap & Volker, 2001; Ibarra, Kilduff, & Tsai, 2005; Sparrowe, Liden, Wayne, & Kraimer, 2001). As Degenne and Forse (1999) explain, "Network analysis analyzes overall relations in an inductive attempt to identify behavior patterns and the group or social strata that correlate with those patterns" (p. 2). This is what Scott (1991) calls "relational data ... the contacts, ties, connections, the group attachments and meetings, which relate one agent to another and so cannot be reduced to the properties of the individual agents themselves" (p. 3), and allows a distinction to be made between workplace collegiality and friendship-based relations as driving factors in organizational behavior. Social configurations can be achieved for small samples by calculating the absolute number of connections, or "direct socio-metric choice data" (Scott, 1991, p. 42), which is then graphically presented.

The sociometric instrument *Sociometric Name Generators Used to Ellicit CoWorkers Advice and Friendship Networks* (Lazega, 2001, pp. 263–264) (Fig. 2) was utilized in order to explore the influence of social networks on the relational dynamics as affected by six, not mutually exclusive, subgroups found to be salient in both the educational change and organizational behavior literature (Organizational Founders, generalists, Veterans (≥ 5 years), New teachers (≤ 4 years), Subject specialists, and Kibbutz (personal antecedent)).

DATA AND ANALYSIS

The need to expend additional effort for curricular change did not seem to trouble the teachers. Their language reflected their affective identification as they stated that any extra hours at school were minimal in comparison to "what awaits us at home later" (IA), and "we spend hours and hours on school-related tasks, at home, at school, on Saturdays, and evenings, anyway, because Hilltop is our home too" (YG). This identification seemed to be directly related to the issue of trust and connected to counting on others and feelings of safety. "I know that no matter what happens I can count on these teachers. We care about each other. We take care of each other. When one of us needs help, someone is always there – before we ask" (IA). RF further illumined this in terms of the teaching profession when she stated that "It's hard to be a teacher. And it's impossible unless we work together. Peace of mind and security come from knowing that everyone here cares about the other – that no one is without support. How could we do everything we do if we couldn't count on each other? That's what I expect from my family, and that's what we give and get here, and this is a value we want the children to learn – with us and with each other." The feeling of support also intersected with the expression of that support through helping behaviors. Trusting, therefore, was connected both to helping behaviors and working together.

This aspect of their work was also reflected in the use of the word "we" rather than "I." Despite attempts to unravel the specific teacher from her counterparts, all teachers consistently used "we" and "our" and seldom, if ever, spoke of what "I did," rather about "our" ideas, actions, and plans and "what we think and the way we see it." The all-encompassing parameters of *we* were related to by YG who spoke of

> ... what suits our framework, or what doesn't suit our framework. If we think something is suitable then we should "connect" it to ourselves, and if it isn't, it needs to change. (YG)

SA was even more explicit in that

> This isn't some sort of a vacuum that you enter and exit. It's not. There is a whole here and you are a part of it. Every person in this school is a part of that whole. In each person's small contribution, in some way, each one does something for the good of the whole – together we are creating something here. It cannot be ... there is no, 'I do this or that and they do or do not like it, are or are not partners to it' ... If someone is not part of the whole, then they are not part of the school. And we are the school, and our desire is to create something together. To create our special something, our special school, and that is only in our together, in that whole. (SA)

There was little doubt then that the teachers at Hilltop perceived their school culture as unique and that the culture of the school was reflected in the way that they ensured that uniqueness.

An outward manifestation of the *we* was the rather uniform mode of attire – jeans or other khaki trousers, button-down shirts or tricot tops and sports shoes or other flat footwear. No skirts, no jackets, no dresses, no form-fitting attire of any kind – few, if any hints of makeup or jewelry. When asked, one of the teachers responded jovially

> You noticed, did you? Nobody here wears those tailored outfits. [Looking at mine] You know, we once had a teacher trainer here doing an in-service workshop and the teachers gave her a terrible time because of her clothes. She was so foreign. It's surprising that you've got away with it for this long. It says a lot about the relationship you're building with us if no one has said anything. (ZB)

Hilltop seemed to be bounded (and bonded) by a strong sense of *how it is here, how we act, and work together*. There were definite expectations and unwritten guidelines for those who were a part of Hilltop. Interestingly, RF noted an awareness of these issues when she offered, "There is an atmosphere and a language here and a specific direction that those of us who work here together understand, and I'm not referring to new concepts, like 'the [multiple] intelligences,' we've always had that sort of understanding about learning anyway, but you see, it's something else ... in our substance – something that would make me feel very ... [deleted] ... if I were a new teacher here" (RF). Permeability was determined using the sieve of *suitability* that set a high standard for persons and ideas that desired to become part of the Hilltop School setting. This was articulated by faculty members when the interviewees were requested to "teach me what and who a Hilltop teacher is." The answers were surprisingly similar without regard for the tenure of the interviewee:

> A Hilltop teacher is someone who accepts what we are trying to do here and is willing to learn how to best do it. (IA)

> Being a Hilltop teacher is more than just giving a lesson and going home. It's something that defines how you think and how much you're willing to give and contribute in order for everyone to achieve the results. (RC)

> A Hilltop teacher is willing to spend all the time and effort it takes to get it done right. We are responsible and we don't forget who we are and what we are trying to accomplish when we leave school. What we do here is who we are. (SA)

This together, this whole, required new teachers to accept and learn the rules of engagement and Hilltop suitability standards.

VIGNETTE – LT

LT had been a teacher for 19 years before coming to Hilltop School and as the school year began she was conspicuous as she made her way down the halls wearing flowing skirts, heels, and jewelry. She could be heard before she was seen as her jingling necklaces presaged her arrival. She had joined the interviewee pool when requested and she related that despite her long tenure and teaching experience, there were many things about *being a Hilltop teacher* that she needed to learn.

> I've been very lucky. The two teachers who teach parallel classes to mine have spent a lot of time teaching me how to do things here, how to look at what I do through the eyes of Hilltop teachers. The bottom line is buying into the beliefs that are the basis for all the work here and basically I had no problem with that. Once everyone realized that I was willing to play my part, and I was willing to listen and

learn, I found that it was fine. I came here wanting to be a part of this place, so I
let myself learn how to do that. (LT)

LT reflected that her process of socialization to Hilltop was "easier
because everyone helps each other and everything is done in
conjunction with others. No one is left alone and without support.
Once I too was able to contribute, I felt I belonged here" (LT).

Some two months after the school year had begun, LT was walking
down the hall with a mug of herbal tea when I asked, "Have you
always liked that kind of drink?" "No," she replied. "But it's really
good." Five paces later, she stopped, turned and smiled, and then
wagged a scolding finger at me. Half an hour earlier, during her
interview, I had asked her whether she had changed any routines after
coming to work at Hilltop; things she perhaps did differently here than
in her previous school. She had related a number of such changes as
working in conjunction with other teachers, creating lesson plans
together, and mutual supportiveness, but had not mentioned the
beverage. "I didn't even think of it." "What did you drink before?" I
asked. "Coffee," she replied thoughtfully, "Strong black coffee" (LT).

As herbal tea was the standard fare for all faculty – none of the
teachers drank coffee – this seemed to be symbolic of the process she was
undergoing. I also noted that she was only wearing a single bracelet, flat
shoes, and khaki trousers. Her transformation was complete.

LT was reflective of the *suitability standard* at Hilltop School which
permeated all areas including materials and methods and determined
legitimate or *contextually congruent* beliefs. In this respect, anything
considered incongruent with "our common goals for the children," would
"need to be changed so it suits us and what we are trying to achieve" (IR).
There was little, if any, attention paid to the "how" of teaching in terms of
the methods, yet long, and heated debates about what this topic or
perspective would *mean,* and whether it would be *valuable* for the children,
took place. Once choices had been made regarding questions of value,
however, just how each pair or trio of teachers would present or access the
material was of far less concern. "As long as we all know what it is that we
are doing, where it is we are going, what our goals are, it doesn't matter
much what methods different teachers use. We trust each other to be
professional enough to do the right things, and we help each other too"
(NB). As YG retorted incredulously when asked why individual teachers

expended so much time and effort for each other, "We help each other because that's how we work here. We don't know any other way. How else could it be?" (YG).

In an attempt to understand whether such staff relations were calculative ("I'll scratch his back so that at some later date he'll scratch mine"), or a social norm of behavior, the interviewees were questioned in relation to actual and hypothetical events. The questions asked in this semi-structured interview attempted to retrieve information from the interviewees regarding past events of helping behaviors having been withheld "... when, perhaps, assistance was requested but not rendered." Of the 16 interviewees queried, none could recall such an event occurring between faculty members, since, as IR put it, "We don't think about it, we just do it. That's the way it is" (IR). The follow-up question inquired about a hypothetical situation, "in the teachers' lounge, someone asked for help, and it is refused," and answers were of two types:

> No, that wouldn't happen here. No one would do such a thing. It's unheard of. Why would someone do that? (IA)

and

> Well, it wouldn't be a popular thing to do – everyone would immediately ask "Why aren't you helping?" And people would generally make faces and whisper, but yeah, it could happen. There would be a lot of talk afterward, if it did. Somebody would take that person aside and talk to her. And somebody else would certainly help the person who needed help. (SA)

Interestingly, the *former* response was common among teachers who had been at Hilltop for four years or fewer; the latter response reflected teachers who were veterans.

It appeared that newer teachers had internalized the identity of *a Hilltop teacher* including clearly defined behavior and requiring the rendering of assistance, whereas veteran teachers felt that such a scenario could arise, and that they would respond as needed. Veteran teachers were attentive to ensuring the continuation of normative assistance patterns and from the responses of the newer teachers, the veterans were to a great degree successful in this role – the newer teachers could hardly contemplate such a situation arising.

The seeming imperative toward suitability between the prototype *Hilltop teacher* necessitated constant dialogue and reflection regarding the congruence between beliefs and behaviors, or as SA put it

> First and foremost we are people – students and teachers – people. We bring our *selves* here and I want my students to do the same. We are here for them if they need us and

that goes beyond subject matter. We must *be* before we *do*. If we don't care about the human being, support the qualities and values of being human to each other, there is no meaning in teaching material. That's what teachers who don't know how to teach children do – they teach material, not children. (SA)

The language used by the teachers here was substantially *relationship-centric* and reflected identification with each other, their work, goals, and intentions.

The teachers also used the words *home* and *family* to describe Hilltop School, and I sought to uncover to what extent such identification was generalized among interviewees. The qualitative data was overwhelming as 15 of 16 interviewees during three initial interviews had referred to the school in these terms *at least three times*. When asked "What do you mean, this is your *home* and these teachers are your *family* – you have a home and family outside school – what is *home* and *family* to you?" IA was representative when she offered:

... nothing could get done around here, and no one would want to be here, if we couldn't trust one other to be here and support and help each other, and do the right thing, and to be safe, and to be able to count on each other without question – it's like what you expect from your family. (IA)

The interviewees made clear that there were unwritten expectations of staff members including the willingness to learn from others, the acceptance that the achievement of goals was dependent on the entire staff, the acceptance of the whole staff as an egalitarian entity, including joint decision making, and an acceptance that *education* was not reflected by grades achieved or curricular concepts covered in a classroom lesson plan. The interviewees tended to frame their responses in their *uniqueness*, and their having a *deeper understanding* of what children needed. These could be categorized as a willingness to share common values and behave in accordance with such an understanding that would then be reflected in discretionary behaviors.

Qualitative data were examined inductively and then revisited in different formats with each interviewee. Initial data analysis was carried out through extraction and color-coding of recurring topics, phrases, and vocabulary (Miles & Huberman, 1994), then first-level coded segments were gathered and pattern coding was revealed. This inductive processing of data enabled initial sense-making and categories and themes to emerge, and subsequently revisited through further inquiry. These themes were then addressed in a whole-school questionnaire (see Fig. 1), and using social network analysis (SNA) (see Fig. 2) to interrogate internal validity and relational density, respectively. Upon saturation of the categories, that is, when all coded bits, numbering nearly 500 by the conclusion of 18 months of interviewing, found inclusion and coherence within one of 16 general categories, conceptualization of themes began. The themes of Permeability and Trust which paralleled *if it suits us, or doesn't suit us*, and the characterization of Hilltop School as *home and family,* respectively, reflected the social identification process at Hilltop School.

Instrument #1: Teaching Goals

Qualitative data suggested that *the social* was central to the adoption of MI as the theoretical framework for curricula. To explore the generalizability of this focus, a school-wide survey was utilized to reflect the salience of *the social* to the operative goals of faculty. Drawn from interview data, a list of 12 goals entitled *Teaching Goals at Hilltop School* (to prime operative classroom outcomes rather than educational values) was created. The list included three assessable, content area goals, to augment the eight exclusive social goals reflected by the data. One goal (tolerance) was added to explore the influence of antecedent connections to the kibbutz agricultural collective. Instructions requested that each staff member "choose those 3 goals she wished to ensure pupils achieved *in her classroom*." This tool was a questionnaire sent to the entire faculty by mail, for which the return rate was 70%.

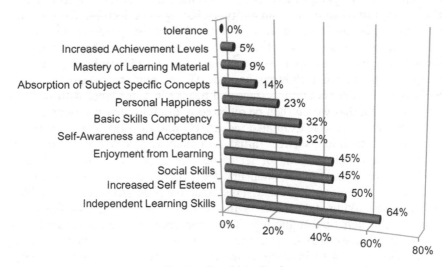

Fig. 1. Teaching Goals.

Findings (See Fig. 1)

As evident, the majority of faculty ranks social goals as of highest priority. The first curricular/content goal (Basic Skills Competency) shares #5 with Self-Awareness and Acceptance. The goal of Self Discipline, which Erez and Earley (1993) posit is not congruent with the collectivist orientation (as group norms rather than individual discipline determine behavior), was not chosen. Results suggest a connection between the individual, curricular, and organizational priorities of the context. The high level of consensus regarding *social* goals, suggests congruence between beliefs and behaviors.

Instrument #2: Social Network Analysis

The interviewees were presented with individual stickers corresponding to the names of each of the staff members at Hilltop School (excluding their own), 33 for each interviewee and presented with three envelopes labeled "*Friendnet*," "*Advicenet*," and "*Neednet*." A fourth envelope was later labeled "*Nevernet*" and would contain stickers left out of the other envelopes.

First, interviewees separated the names of those with whom they had social relations outside of the school without connection to school-related tasks or events and these were placed into the *Friendnet* envelope. Of the remaining names, those with whom they met often, solicited advice from or gave advice to, were put in the "*Advicenet*" envelope. Next was the placement of names of those with whom they had interactions of *necessity*, interaction in meetings, for example, but not sought out were placed into the "*Neednet*" envelope. The interviewees were then asked to look at the remaining names and describe their relations with these persons. These were placed in the remaining envelope and later comprised the "*Nevernet*" category.

Analysis was through the creation of a matrix counting the number of *hits* each staff member had and charting results for each faculty member. Fig. 2 reflects a comparison of the social network of the entire staff as represented by the interviewees, and separates the responses using the Subgroups. Subgroups were related to those variables suggested in the literature to be salient to organizational culture – Founders (tenure as influential); generalists (role as influential); Veterans (past leadership as influential); New Teachers (new leadership as influential); Subject Specialists (role as influential); and Kibbutz (individual antecedents as influential). The *x-axis* reflects the absolute number of choices made, and the *y-axis*, the Subgroups. For each Subgroup, the number of choices for each network is shown.

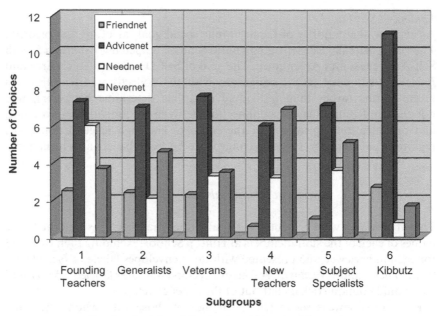

Fig. 2.   Social and Institutional Density Networks.

Findings (See Fig. 2)
Qualitative data gave rise to questions regarding the basis of extra role and helping behaviors among faculty. Sociometric Name Generators (Lazega, 2001) were adapted to explore the social networks and whether personal relationships, such as friendships might be basis for such behaviors. Results support qualitative data regarding interviewee perceptions of staff interdependency and socially dense, but not friendship-based networks as social interaction is primarily located in the *Advicenet* parameter. Faculty ties are therefore not based primarily on personal relationships and findings reflect that Founders (Subgroup 1) and Veterans (Subgroup 3) were not those with the densest networks, suggesting that length of tenure is not the overriding factor with regards to the density of social ties.

The greatest density of social ties is located in Subgroup 6 (Kibbutz). This Subgroup reflected both the highest levels in the *Friendnet* and *Advicenet* parameters and the lowest results on the *Neednet* and *Nevernet* parameters. These results support the social connectedness of this group to other staff members and given that this sociocultural orientation was an antecedent property of a significant number of the founding staff (some of whom are no longer at Hilltop), it could be posited that this social identification provided the basis for the culture that evolved at the school and has been maintained through teacher socialization and identification processes.

DISCUSSION

Teacher discretionary behaviors are a valuable resource in schools. Such behaviors can be particularly valuable when the school is undergoing a change process which by all accounts is a stressful and resource-intensive undertaking for individuals and organizations. The ability to rely on mutual and supportive like-minded others can build trust and commitment to the organization and its members (Lamm & Singer, 2010) such as recounted in this study.

Initial qualitative data suggested that an unfamiliar cohesion unified this group's work habits and behaviors. The taken for granted aspects of interdependent work norms, even on ostensibly independent, within-classroom tasks, belied the dual functions of such interdependence and support discretionary behavior as a mechanism of socialization on the one hand and symbolic of group membership on the other. As the social identity approach (Haslam, 2004) suggests, such a perspective solidifies one's identity through association and identification with a social group (van Knippenberg, 2000), and the relationship between social identification and discretionary behavior has been supported in a number of studies (van Dick et al., 2006; van Dick et al., 2005; Van Knippenberg et al., 2007; Worchel et al., 1998). Group-directed behavior is therefore valuable to the individual as it enables both a positive self-concept and engages an existential question, as well as providing organizational benefits.

The specific context of this study found teachers who had been partners in the creation of a school in an area in which they lived. Research suggests that founders can leave an imprint on the organizational culture of an organization. In this case, a group of teachers sculpted their educational goals in the school and supported that vision through nearly a decade of growth, and the arrival of a new principal. Feelings of ownership reflected not an issue of power, but rather, "a means of extending one's identity to incorporate things outside of the physical body ... and similarly issue ownership provides a means of extending one's social identity (e.g., organizational identity) to encompass issues that may be outside of the organization's corporate "body" " (Pratt & Dutton, 2000, p. 114). It could be argued that in promoting their vision, ownership reflected the desire to extend their control over the communities in which the majority of the teachers lived.

Teachers emphasized the social aspects of schooling and worried about the next generation that they perceived they were preparing. They made clear in their statements and actions that *teaching material* was far less important than *teaching children*. Grades and test scores were secondary to values and building of character, as they perceived the goals of public education and their public service as they saw it started in their own communities. As Haslam and Reicher (2007) note, "social identity should not be considered simply as a set of ideas, values, and beliefs, but rather as a model of how the world should be organized. Thus group members seek to transform the social world into the terms of their social identity" (p. 157). Behaviors defined the school and the teachers and were dependent on mutual trust which was perceived as imperative to attainment of goals. The ability to work together, to agree on meaning, and to work through disagreements was rooted in trust. That this trust would not be misused, as it provided security and promised rewards for all groups, was implicit. Inclusion into this social network was predicated on acceptance of *the social* as the core value at Hilltop and there was little discord between the "Hilltop teacher" *prototype* and new teachers. In the few cases that a lack of fit was perceived, teachers had left. In this way, socialization of new teachers to behavioral norms was secured.

Haslam (2004) relates that salience of an individual's social identity promotes group interests over personal ones and motivates efforts for the benefit of the group whose identity has been internalized. To promote such identification "the worker displays greater sensitivity to the quality of social relations, is more responsive to the views of other ingroup members and conforms more to group norms … this form of motivation is actually uniquely associated with a range of potentially positive organizational behaviour … including helping behaviour" (p. 79). The expression of such behaviors then may both be an expression of identification reflecting the salience of the in-group identity and the fulfilment of in-group behavioral expectations. Organizational socialization processes suggest that "critical decisions are being made by the group about who can belong … which group members can be trusted … and what it takes to be a full group member, with the privileges and duties of that role" (Moreland & Levine, 2001). Social resources were available yet predicated on reflecting group membership and the way in which one did so was to dedicate oneself to the group through performance of discretionary behaviors. These behaviors signaled one's willingness to be a part of the *we/us* – in other words, the prototype *Hilltop teacher*.

In sum, the behavioral norm of discretionary behaviors reflected two concurrent organizational outcomes at Hilltop School, both of which are suggestive of social identification. First, discretionary behaviors as a socialization mechanism for new organizational members, and second, a way for organizational members to exhibit their group membership, promoting and further solidifying these behaviors as organizational norms.

LIMITATIONS AND AVENUES FOR FUTURE RESEARCH

The study at hand was carried out in a specific location at a time of curricular change comprising its foremost limitations as it cannot be replicated and limitations of case study and qualitative research, including, but not limited to the relationship between the researcher and researched, may also be regarded as limitations. Yet as in most such research, it is precisely these limitations that provide the greatest strengths in the depth of access achieved.

This study suggests a number of opportunities for further enquiry: First, an exploration of discretionary behaviors as mechanisms of socialization, and subsequently as expected behavioral symbols of group membership. Can discretionary behaviors under these conditions be regarded as *discretionary*? Vigoda-Gadot (2006) and Turnipseed and Wilson (2009) have engaged with the transformation of discretionary behaviors from "discretionary" to "required" yet have done so from the perspective of management edicts or unspoken managerial expectations. No studies to date have considered teacher discretionary behaviors as obligatory *proof of group membership*. It would be valuable to engage in research that explores relationships in other locations, and whether teachers who do not engage in such behaviors are less satisfied, how this affects teacher turnover, burnout, etc. If social support and teacher stress, burnout, and attrition are indeed inversely related, as research has suggested (Friedman, 1991; Kahn, Schnieder, Jenkins-Henkelman, & Moyle, 2006), might lack of such identification prevent access to social support that might reduce teacher attrition?

In the study of Hilltop School there were predisposing historical and psychosocial factors that may have played a role in the creation of the culture of the school. A particularly interesting aspect that should be examined is the role of teacher education programs and whether different programs affect new teachers' discretionary behaviors. Additionally, the relationship between psychological collectivism (Jackson, Wesson, Colquitt, & Zapata-Phelan, 2006) and social identification (Tajfel & Turner, 1979) may provide an interesting avenue for inquiry. Might the former be antecedent to the latter? Finally, it would be of great value to test the conclusions of this study in larger schools, middle schools and high schools, and schools in which the staff is more equally divided among male and female faculty. Relationships between size, demographics, locations, and gender would all offer valuable insights as would the use of longitudinal and/or mixed method designs enable deeper engagement and exploration of the meanings of, and our understandings about, teacher discretionary behaviors.

Although the specifics of this case are certainly particularistic, the behaviors displayed are common among teachers generally. That teachers exert much effort in unpaid and unrecognized hours is not limited to the case of this school on this hilltop in the Galilee but echoes of many other locations and the efforts and experiences of teachers the world over. As it should, it also raises more questions than it answers.

EPILOGUE

Two points are noteworthy here. First, the role of leadership is conspicuously absent from this discussion and is due to the limitations of space in a single chapter. To read, First, although leadership was a focal point in the change process at Hilltop, any discussion of its impact would not have altered the conclusions regarding social identification and teacher discretionary behavior. Second, this case study was undertaken as a study of educational change and congruent with its emergent design, shifted to an inquiry of the school culture as were highlighted by faculty as central to their meanings. The conclusions offered here regarding discretionary behaviors then is but one of the conclusions drawn from this longitudinal research. For further detail see Ras (2003).

ACKNOWLEDGMENT

The author would like to thank Dr. Ibrahim Duyar and an anonymous reviewer for their constructive comments in the preparation of this chapter.

REFERENCES

Ashforth, B. E., & Mael, F. (1989). Social identity theory and the organization. In M. J. Hatch & M. Schultz (Eds.), *Organizational identity* (pp. 134–160). Oxford, UK: Oxford University Press.

Blau, P. (1964). *Exchange and power in social life*. New York, NY: Wiley.

Boen, F., Vanbeselaere, N., & Cool, M. (2006). Group status as a determinant of organizational identification after a takeover: A social identity perspective. *Group Processes and Intergroup Relations, 9*(4), 547–560. doi:10.1177/1368430206067555

Burnett, M. F., Williamson, I. O., & Bartol, K. M. (2009). The moderating effect of personality on employee fairness and outcome favorability. *Journal of Business and Psychology, 24*(4), 469–484. doi:10.1007/s10869-009-9120-6

Chen, X. S., & Carey, T. P. (2009). Assessing citizenship behavior in educational contexts: The role of personality, motivation, and culture. *Journal of Psychoeducational Assessment, 27*(2), 125–137. doi:10.1177/0734282908325146

Christ, O., van Dick, R., Wagner, U., & Stellmacher, J. (2003). When teachers go the extra mile: Foci of organisational identification as determinants of different forms of organisational citizenship behaviour among schoolteachers. *British Journal of Educational Psychology, 73*, 329–341. Retrieved from EBSCO*host*. doi:10.1348/096317905X71831

Degenne, A., & Forse, M. (1999). *Introducing social networks* (English ed.). London: Sage.

Ellemers, N., de Gilder, D., & Haslam, S. A. (2004). Motivating individuals and groups at work: A social identity perspective on leadership and group performance. *Academy of Management Review, 29*(3), 459–478. doi:10.2307/20159054

Ellemers, N., de Gilder, D., & van den Heuvel, H. (1998). Career versus team-oriented commitment and behavior at work. *Journal of Applied Psychology, 83*(5), 717–730. doi:10.1037/0021-9010.83.5.717

Flap, H., & Volker, B. (2001). Goal specific social capital and job satisfaction: Effects of different types of networks on instrumental and social aspects of work. *Social Networks, 23*, 297–320. doi:10.1016/S0378-8733(01)00044-2

Friedman, I. A. (1991). High and low burnout schools: School culture aspects of teacher burnout. *Journal of Educational Research, 84*(6), 325–333. Retrieved from EBSCO*host*. Available at http://www.jstor.org/stable/27541987

Gardner, H. (1983). *Frames of mind: The theory of multiple intelligences*. New York, NY: Harper & Row.

Grant, A. M. (2007). Relational job design and the motivation to make a prosocial difference. *Academy of Management Review, 32*(2), 393–417. doi:10.2307/20159308

Haslam, S. A. (2004). *Psychology in organizations: A social identity approach* (2nd ed.). London: Sage.

Haslam, S. A., Powell, C., & Turner, J. (2000). Social identity, self-categorization, and work motivation: Rethinking the contribution of the group to positive and sustainable organisational outcomes. *Applied Psychology, 49*(3), 319–339. doi:10.1111/1464-0597.00018.

Haslam, S. A., & Reicher, S. (2007). Social identity and the dynamics of organizational life: Insights from the BBC prison study. In C. A. Bartel, S. Blader & A. Wrzesniewski (Eds.), *Identity and the modern organization* (pp. 135–166). Mahwah, NJ: Lawrence Erlbaum.

Hogg, M. A. (2001). Social identity and the sovereignty of the group. In C. Sedikides & M. B. Brewer (Eds.), *Individual self, relational self, collective self* (pp. 123–143). Philadelphia, PA: Psychology Press.

Ibarra, H., Kilduff, M., & Tsai, W. (2005). Zooming in and out: Connecting individuals and collectivities at the frontiers of organizational network research. *Organization Science*, *16*(4), 359–371. doi:10.1287/orsc.1050.0129

Jackson, C. L., Wesson, M. J., Colquitt, J. A., & Zapata-Phelan, C. P. (2006). Psychological collectivism: A measurement validation and linkage to group member performance. *Journal of Applied Psychology*, *91*(4), 884–899. doi:10.1037/0021-9010.91.4.884

Kahn, J. H., Schnieder, K. T., Jenkins-Henkelman, T. M., & Moyle, L. L. (2006). Emotional social support and job burnout among high-school teachers: Is it all due to dispositional affectivity? *Journal of Organizational Behavior*, *27*, 793–807. doi:10.1002/job.397

Kramer, R. (2001). Identity and trust in organizations: One anatomy of a productive but problematic relationship. In M. A. Hogg & D. J. Terry (Eds.), *Social identity processes in organizational contexts* (pp. 167–179). Philadelphia, PA: Psychology Press.

Lamm, C., & Singer, T. (2010). The role of values congruence in organizational change. *Organization Development Journal*, *28*(2), 49–64. Retrieved from ABI/INFORM Global. doi:10.1007/s00429-010-0251-3

Lazega, E. (2001). *The collegial phenomenon*. Oxford, UK: Oxford University Press.

LePine, J. A., & Van Dyne, L. (2001). Peer responses to low performers: An attributional model of helping in the context of groups. *Academy of Management Review*, *26*(1), 67–84. Retrieved from EBSCO*host*. doi:10.2307/259395

McNeely, B. L., & Meglino, B. M. (1994). The role of dispositional and situational antecedents in prosocial organizational behavior: An examination of the intended beneficiaries of prosocial behavior. *Journal of Applied Psychology*, *79*(6), 836–844. doi:10.1037/0021-9010.79.6.836

Meyer, J. P., & Allen, N. J. (1997). *Commitment in the workplace: Theory, research, and application*. Thousand Oaks, CA: Sage.

Miles, M., & Huberman, A. (1994). *Qualitative data analysis*. Thousand Oaks, CA: Sage.

Moreland, R. L., & Levine, J. M. (2001). Socialization in organizations and work groups. In M. E. Turner (Ed.), *Groups at work: Theory and research* (pp. 25–65). Mahwah, NJ: Lawrence Erlbaum.

Oplatka, I. (2006). Going beyond role expectations: Toward an understanding of the determinants and components of teacher organizational citizenship behavior. *Educational Administration Quarterly*, *42*(3), 385–423. doi:10.1177/0013161X05285987

Organ, D. W. (1988). *Organizational citizenship behavior: The good soldier syndrome*. Lexington, MA: Lexington Books.

Podsakoff, N. P., Whiting, S. W., Podsakoff, P. M., & Blume, B. D. (2009). Individual- and organizational-level consequences of organizational citizenship behaviors: A meta-analysis. *Journal of Applied Psychology*, *94*(1), 122–141. doi:10.1037/a0013079

Pratt, M. G., & Dutton, J. E. (2000). Owning up or opting out: The role of emotions and identities in issue ownership. In N. M. Ashkenasy, C. E. Härtel & W. J. Zerbe (Eds.), *Emotions in the workplace: Research, theory, and practice* (pp. 103–129). Westport, CT: Quorum Books.

Prentice, D. A., Miller, D. T., & Lightdale, J. R. (1994). Asymmetries in attachment to groups and to their members: Distinguishing between common-identity and common-bond groups. *Personality and Social Psychology Bulletin*, *20*, 484–493. doi:10.1177/0146167294205005

Ras, N. L. (2003). *Curriculum change at Hilltop school: A case study of intervention and organisational change at an elementary school in Israel*. Unpublished doctoral dissertation, University of Sussex, Falmer, Brighton, UK.

Schensul, S., Schensul, J., & LeCompte, M. (1999). *Essential ethnographic methods*. Walnut Creek, CA: AltaMira Press.

Scott, J. (1991). *Social network analysis*. London: Sage.

Seyle, D. C., & Swann, W. B. (2007). In C. A. Bartel, S. Blader, & A. Wrzesniewski (Eds.), *Identity and the modern organization* (pp. 177–200). Mahwah, NJ: Lawrence Erlbaum.

Somech, A., & Drach-Zahavy, Z. (2000). Understanding extra-role behavior in schools: The relationships between job satisfaction, sense of efficacy, and teachers' extra-role behavior. *Teaching and Teacher Education, 16*, 649–659. doi:10.1016/S0742-051X(00)00012-3

Somech, A., & Ron, Y. (2007). Promoting organizational citizenship behavior in schools: The impact of individual and organizational characteristics. *Educational Administration Quarterly, 43*(1), 38–66. doi:10.1177/0013161X06291254

Sparrowe, R. E., Liden, R. C., Wayne, S. J., & Kraimer, M. L. (2001). Social networks and the performance of individuals and groups. *Academy of Management Journal, 44*(2), 316–325. doi:10.2307/3069458

Tajfel, H. (1982). Social psychology of intergroup relations. *Annual Review of Psychology, 33*, 1–39. doi:10.1146/annurev.ps.33.020182.000245

Tajfel, H., & Turner, J. C. (1979). An integrative theory of intergroup conflict. In W. G. Austin & S. Worchel (Eds.), *The social psychology of intergroup relations* (pp. 33–47). Monterey, CA: Brooks.

Tschannen-Moran, M. (2009). Fostering teacher professionalism in schools: The role of leadership orientation and trust. *Educational Administration Quarterly, 45*(2), 217–247. doi:10.1177/0013161X08330501

Turner, J. C., & Haslam, S. A. (2001). Social identity, organizations, and leadership. In M. E. Turner (Ed.), *Groups at work: Theory and research* (pp. 25–65). Mahwah, NJ: Lawrence Erlbaum.

Turnipseed, D. L., & Wilson, G. L. (2009). From discretionary to required: The migration of organizational citizenship behavior. *Journal of Leadership and Organizational Studies, 15*(3), 201–216. doi:10.1177/1548051808326037

van den Heuvel, S., & Schalk, R. (2009). The relationship between fulfillment of the psychological contract and resistance to change during organizational transformations. *Social Science Information, 48*(2), 283–313. doi:10.1177/0539018409012415

Van Dick, R. (2004). My job is my castle: Identification in organizational contexts. In C. L. Cooper & I. T. Robertson (Eds.), *International review of industrial and organizational psychology* (Vol. 19, pp. 171–204). West Sussex, UK: Wiley.

Van Dick, R., Grojean, M. W., Christ, O., & Wieseke, J. (2006). Identity and the extra mile: Relationships between organizational identification and organizational citizenship behavior. *British Journal of Management, 17*, 283–301. doi:10.1111/j.1467-8551.2006.00520.x

Van Dick, R., & Wagner, U. (2002). Social identification among school teachers: Dimensions, foci, and correlates. *European Journal of Work and Organizational Psychology, 11*(2), 129–149. doi:10.1080/13594320143000889

Van Dick, R., Wagner, U., Stellmacher, J., & Christ, O. (2005). Category salience and organizational identification. *Journal of Occupational and Organizational Psychology, 78*, 273–285. doi:10.1348/096317905X25779

Van Dick, R., Wagner, U., Stellmacher, J., Christ, O., & Tissington, P. A. (2005). To be(long) or not to be(long): Social identification in organizational contexts. *Genetic, Social, and General Psychology Monographs, 131*(3), 189–218. doi:10.3200/MONO.131.3.189-218

Van Knippenberg, D. (2000). Work motivation and performance: A social identity perspective. *Applied Psychology: An International Review, 49*(3), 357–371. doi:10.1111/1464-0597.00020

Van Knippenberg, D., van Dick, R., & Tavares, S. (2007). Social identity and social exchange: Identification, support, and withdrawal from the job. *Journal of Applied Social Psychology, 37*(3), 457–477. doi:10.1111/j.1559-1816.2007.00168.x

Vigoda-Gadot, E. (2006). Compulsory citizenship behavior: Theorizing some dark sides of the good soldier syndrome. *Journal for the Theory of Social Behaviour, 36*(1), 77–93. doi:10.1111/j.1468-5914.2006.00297.x

Vigoda-Gadot, E., Beeri, I., Birman-Shemesh, T., & Somech, A. (2007). Group-level organizational citizenship behavior in the education system: A scale reconstruction and validation. *Educational Administration Quarterly, 43*(4), 462–493. doi:10.1177/0013161X07299435

Williamson, I. O., Burnett, M. F., & Bartol, K. M. (2009). The interactive effect of collectivism and organizational rewards on affective organizational commitment. *Cross Cultural Management: An International Journal, 16*(1), 28–43. doi:10.1108/13527600910930022

Worchel, S., Rothberger, H., Day, E. A., Hart, D., & Butemeyer, J. (1998). Social identity and individual productivity within groups. *British Journal of Social Psychology, 37*, 389–413. Retrieved from APA PsycNET. doi:10.1111/j.2044-8309.1998.tb01181.x

CHAPTER 9

THE RELATIONSHIP BETWEEN ORGANIZATIONAL JUSTICE, ORGANIZATIONAL TRUST AND ORGANIZATIONAL CITIZENSHIP BEHAVIORS IN SECONDARY SCHOOLS IN TURKEY

Kursad Yılmaz and Yahya Altınkurt

ABSTRACT

This chapter examined the relationships between organizational justice, organizational trust, and organizational citizenship behaviors in Turkish secondary schools. Specifically, the study investigated whether, and to what extent, organizational justice and organizational trust predict variation in the organizational citizenship behaviors of teachers. A survey research methodology was employed in the study. The sample included 466 secondary school teachers in Kutahya, a city in western Turkey. The study adopted pre-developed respective scales for gathering the data. The data gathering instrument of the study incorporated the Organizational Justice Scale (Hoy & Tarter, 2004), the Organizational Trust Scale (Yılmaz, 2006), and

Discretionary Behavior and Performance in Educational Organizations: The Missing Link in Educational Leadership and Management
Advances in Educational Administration, Volume 13, 223–248
ISSN: 1479-3660/doi:10.1108/S1479-3660(2012)0000013014

the Organizational Citizenship Behavior Scale (DiPaola, Tarter, & Hoy, 2005). Analysis of the data through the use of hierarchical multiple regression analysis yielded a significant effect of organizational justice and significant effects for two of the three types of organizational trust. There is a positive and moderate level relationship between organizational citizenship on the one hand, and organizational justice, trust in the principal, trust in colleagues, and trust in stakeholders on the other. Predictor variables are ranked in terms of the size of their effect on organizational citizenship as trust in colleagues, trust in the principal, trust in stakeholders, and organizational justice. Organizational justice is a significant predictor of organizational citizenship behavior when considered in isolation, but becomes insignificant when organizational trust is controlled for. Organizational trust and organizational justice explain around two fifths of the total variance in organizational citizenship behavior.

INTRODUCTION

Recently, organizational citizenship behaviors became an important research focus in studies on educational organization, as witnessed by the increase in the number of publications on the subject. Organizational citizenship behaviors include voluntary behaviors of employees without any official pressure (Organ, 1988). Employees are not obliged to display such behaviors. Furthermore, they do not get punished when they do not display these behaviors. However, organizations might award such behaviors because organizational citizenship behaviors make significant contributions, such as extra efforts by employees for successful task fulfillment, help and collaboration with others, reasonable organizational rule and procedure following, and maintenance, support and confirmation of organizational goals (Borman, 2004). The organizational citizenship behaviors of employees play an important role in analyzing and understanding individual attitudes and behaviors in organizations. In this context, the relationship between organizational citizenship behaviors and various variables has been widely studied. Organizational justice and organizational trust are two such prominent variables. However, to the best of our knowledge, no study has been conducted to examine whether these two variables significantly predict organizational citizenship behavior. This study aims to examine the effects of organizational justice and organizational trust on the organizational citizenship behaviors of employees.

LITERATURE REVIEW

This section first reviews the concepts of organizational justice, organizational trust, and organizational citizenship. Then, it provides background information about secondary schools in Turkey, and the way school principals are trained and appointed.

Organizational Justice

The roots of the concept of organizational justice are found in studies by Homans (1961), Adams (1965), Deutsch (1975), Sampson (1975), Leventhal (1976), and Thibaut and Walker (1978) (Cited in: Greenberg, 1990). Of these, Homans' (1961) Social Exchange Theory (Greenberg, 1990) and Adams' (1965) Equity Theory are particularly important in that they lay the foundations for later studies on organizational justice (Cited in: Greenberg, 1990, 1993; Paterson, Green, & Cary, 2002; Roch & Shanock, 2006).

According to Homans' (1961) Social Exchange Theory, individuals in a relationship of exchange expect returns on the basis of the amount of investment they make, and believe justice is achieved when these expectations are met. In Adams' (1965) Equity Theory, the individual compares himself/herself with others on the basis of the "investments made and outcomes received." Investments denote the contributions, effort and skills of the individual, whereas outcomes denote resources, rewards, pay, and the like (Cited in: Colquitt, Greenberg, & Zapata-Phelan, 2005).

Greenberg (1996) defines organizational justice as a concept that denotes the perceptions of employees concerning how justly they are treated in an organization, with implications for organizational loyalty and job satisfaction. In this sense, organizational justice is about how the decisions and practices of organizational management are perceived by the employees, and the employee perceptions concerning justice in work, and thus, about employee attitudes and behaviors (Eskew, 1993). Organizational justice is about the distribution of tasks, property, rewards, sanctions, pay, organizational positions, opportunities, roles, and the like within an organization, the rules by which decisions concerning these distributions are made, and the social norms on which these rules are based (Folger & Cropanzano, 1998). Earlier studies focus on the dimensions of *distributive justice* and *procedural justice* (Greenberg, 1996; Roch & Shanock, 2006), whereas more recent studies (Bies & Moag, 1986) include the dimension of *interactional justice* as well.

Distributive justice refers to employee perceptions concerning whether benefits are distributed fairly or not (Folger & Cropanzano, 1998). Distributive justice requires that rights, benefits and responsibilities are distributed on the basis of skills and contributions. The main issue in distributive justice is whether gains made are right, appropriate, and ethical (Özen, 2003).

Procedural justice is about how distribution decisions are made, and about subjective and objective conditions (Konovsky, 2000). Procedural justice refers to the perception of an individual concerning whether the procedures or methods used in the making of a decision about himself/ herself or a third person are appropriate (Greenberg, 1996). If the employees perceive that the procedures followed are fair, the results are perceived to be fair as well, regardless of whether they are positive or negative (Greenberg, 1990).

Interactional justice can be defined as the way recipients of justice are treated by management in terms of humane organizational practices (Cohen-Charash & Spector, 2001). Interactional justice is about how the behaviors of the decision makers are perceived (Bies & Moag, 1986). According to Bies and Moag (1986), individuals evaluate justice, to a large extent, on the basis of the way people treat each other. They argue that interactional justice is separate from procedural justice.

Some studies distinguish between the dimensions explained above (Greenberg, 1996; Alexander & Ruderman, 1987; Bies, 2005). Yet, a theoretical framework that encompasses all types of justice has not been developed in the literature on organizational justice, despite the presence of various justice typologies (Roch & Shanock, 2006). Colquitt et al. (2005) observe that researchers are now focusing their attention on developing holistic models or theories that would cover all aspects of organizational justice. Meta-analyses conducted show that relationships between different aspects of organizational justice are not well examined (Colquitt et al., 2005). For all these reasons, this study has a holistic perspective on organizational justice.

Organizational Trust

Organizational trust refers to an individual's perception concerning the support provided by the organization and a belief held by the individual that the managers will always tell the truth and stand by their word. It also reflects the desire of the individual that the organization be open, caring, honest and trustworthy in its relations, interaction, and communication with the individuals. According to Mishra (1996), organizational trust refers to a desire that individuals be open, honest, caring and realistic towards each other in their organizational relations and interactions, and be informed about basic goals, norms, and values. Organizational trust is also defined as the lack of fear, hesitation, or doubt when employees interact with each other within the organization (Hoy & Miskel, 2010; Lewicki & Bunker, 1996).

Organizational trust reflects employee perceptions concerning trust in managers, colleagues and stakeholders. In this sense, organizational trust functions as some sort of glue that holds the organization together (Tschannen-Moran & Hoy, 1998). When organization trust is high, there is an open and participatory environment and less resistance to change, employees internalize their responsibilities, productivity and organizational commitment are higher, the prevailing culture is one of consensus; teamwork and cooperation are the norm, job satisfaction is high, employees participate in decision making, there is less friction between employees, motivation and productivity are high, employee turnover and absenteeism rates are low, and creativity is widespread.

When organizational trust is low, on the contrary, there is more resistance to change, employees blame each other, constantly develop defense mechanisms, avoid taking responsibility, become skeptical and jealous, engage in gossip, try to avoid hard work, and do not support the organization's goals. What is more, employee loyalty decreases, job satisfaction declines, performance descends to minimum levels, employees become unhappy, the general atmosphere in the organization is quiet, complaints result in punishments and firing, and people feel locked into their jobs.

It is possible to extend the lists of benefits of trust and costs of non-trust. In general, it would be fair to say that high organizational trust is a desirable quality, and low organizational trust is one to be avoided. Having high organizational trust plays a very important role in the creation and maintenance of healthy and sustainable organizational relations (Çokluk-Bökeoğlu & Yılmaz, 2008), and organization managements can easily create or destroy this trust among employees by their behaviors. A number of studies find that employee trust is associated with the leadership behaviors of the principals (Hoy & Tschannen-Moran, 1999; Yılmaz, 2004).

Trust is very important in educational organizations, like in any other organization. Trust is also additionally important for schools because schools are where education takes place (Hoy & Tschannen-Moran, 2003).

Trust plays a critical in the development of productive group relations and interpersonal relations (Hoy & Tarter, 2004) and in the improvement of the academic efficiency (Bryk & Schneider, 2003) in schools.

Organizational trust is not a one-dimensional concept. Employee trust in an organization is shaped by the behaviors of people in groups with which the employee comes into direct or indirect contact. Thus, studies on the subject usually treat organizational trust as a multi-dimensional concept. The present study employs the sub-dimensions of "trust in the principal, trust in colleagues, and trust in stakeholders" to study organizational trust. These sub-dimensions were created on the basis of Hoy's studies (Hoy, Gage, & Tarter, 2006; Hoy & Tarter, 2004; Hoy & Tschannen-Moran, 1999, 2003; Tschannen-Moran & Hoy, 1998, 2000). However, organizational concept can also be treated as a single entity, for organizational trust is a whole that consists of employee trust in managers and in the organization itself (Nyhan & Marlowe, 1997).

When there is *trust in the principal*, teachers trust the honesty and integrity of the school principal and expect him/her to stand by his/her word, teacher–principal relations are consistent, the principal cares about the problems of the employees, and avoids disclosing personal and private information about teachers to third parties, among others. *Trust in colleagues* entails, among others, attitudes and behaviors such as teacher trust in other colleagues, communication among teachers that is character-ized by openness, consistency and loyalty, keeping one's word and having faith that others in the organization will do so as well, and having faith that private conversations will remain private. *Trust in stakeholders* entails trust held by teachers in their students, the families of their students, the tasks and homework students are assigned to do, support from families, and the words of their students and families, and so on (Yılmaz, 2009).

Organizational Citizenship

Voluntary behaviors of the employees are defined in the literature as pro-social organizational behaviors (Brief & Motowidlo, 1986), extra-role behaviors (Katz & Kahn, 1977), or organizational citizenship behaviors (Bateman & Organ, 1983; Smith, Organ, & Near, 1983). Many studies are conducted on organizational citizenship because of the critical role they play in the analysis and understanding of individual attitudes and behaviors within an organization (Farh, Podsakoff, & Organ, 1990; Moorman & Blakely, 1995; Organ & Ryan, 1995).

The concept of organizational citizenship was first used in the literature by Bateman and Organ (1983). According to Bateman and Organ (1983), organization citizenship entails behaviors like helping colleagues solve job-related problems; accepting orders without any resistance; performing unexpected tasks that pop up at inconvenient times without complaining; keeping the working environment clean and tidy; talking positively about the business, organization, and managers when having conversations with people outside the organization; creating a work environment where conflicts and distractions are kept to a minimum, and protecting organizational resources (Bateman & Organ, 1983).

In later studies, Organ (1988) defines organizational citizenship behaviors as those voluntary individual behaviors that are not specifically mentioned by the formal reward system of the organization but nevertheless support the efficient functioning of the organization. Organ's (1988) definition is the one that has gained the most widespread acceptance in the literature because it captures the essence of the concept of organizational citizenship by covering all voluntary behavior not officially sanctioned and not specifically ordered.

According to Organ (1988), organizational citizenship behaviors have three basic characteristics: (1) The behaviors in question are voluntary, (2) they are not directly or explicitly rewarded by the formal reward system of the organization, and (3) as a whole, they contribute to the effective functioning of the organization. In sum, organizational citizenship behaviors are those behaviors that benefit the organization and that the employees willingly do without any expectation of formal rewards (Yılmaz & Çokluk-Bökeoğlu, 2008).

Early conceptualizations about organizational citizenship (Smith et al., 1983) tended to study organizational citizenship behaviors under the two headings of "altruism" and "generalized compliance," whereas later studies (Organ, 1988) examined the concept under five separate headings: altruism, conscientiousness, sportsmanship, courtesy, and civic virtue. However, there does not seem to be consensus in the literature on the definitions and sub-dimensions of organizational citizenship behaviors, and different studies (Van Dyne, Graham, & Dienesch, 1994; Graham, 1991) provide different classifications. Still, Organ's (1988) classification, briefly explained in what follows, is the one most commonly used.

Altruism refers to all direct or indirect voluntary behaviors displayed by employees with the purpose of assisting colleagues in organization-related tasks or problems.

Conscientiousness dimension involves what can be termed personal effort as well. Conscientiousness is the case when employees show extra effort exceeding what is expected of them to perform certain roles. It means going beyond what is required, and respecting and internalizing the rules of the organization.

Sportsmanship refers to avoiding making complaints or expressing discontent when faced with problems. It means avoiding displaying negative behaviors.

Courtesy is the case when the employee is in constant communication with people who are likely to be affected by his/her decisions and acts. It is about accepting responsibility and acting responsibly when working in cooperation with colleagues.

Civic virtue refers to taking an interest in what is going on within the organization, in new developments and new policies, and making an effort to improve oneself in these respects. Civic virtue is a measure of employee reactions that lead the organization management to take the right course of action.

Although organizational citizenship behaviors are studied under these headings, some studies report encountering problems in trying to use these dimensions, failing to identify them as separate dimensions (DiPaola & Hoy, 2005). In DiPaola and Tschannen-Moran's (2001) study, which is the first study applying the concept of organizational citizenship in the context of schools, these dimensions were not observed and the concept was treated as a one-dimensional one. DiPaola and Hoy (2005) attribute this to two factors: first, organizational citizenship behaviors have a specific content, and second, state-run schools are very different from private sector schools. The present study also employs a one-dimensional perspective in examining organizational citizenship behaviors.

THE SECONDARY EDUCATION SYSTEM IN TURKEY

The Turkish education system is run by the Ministry of National Education (MoNE). It is an overly centralized system where all practices are planned, implemented, and evaluated by the Ministry itself. The Turkish education system is governed by the Basic Law of National Education, No 1739, and consists of the two main components of "formal education" and "non-formal education." Formal education covers pre-school education, primary education, secondary education and higher education. Non-formal education covers all other educational activities that either support or are independent of formal education. The secondary education level in the Turkish Education System encompasses all general, vocational, and technical education institutions offering a minimum four-year education based on primary education. The age category for secondary education encompasses ages 14–17 (MoNE, 2009). All pupils who graduated from primary education and attained the right to attend secondary education are entitled to benefit from upper secondary education (MoNE, 1973).

SCHOOL ADMINISTRATION IN TURKISH CONTEXT

School principals serving in secondary schools are appointed by the MoNE. Principals are not required to have received any education related or school management related training to be appointed. School management in Turkey is not treated as a separate profession, and there is a lack of institutionalization in the area of training and appointing school principals. School principals are usually appointed from among the teachers on the basis of seniority, which creates numerous problems in school management.

Teachers to be employed in state run schools are also hired and appointed by the Ministry itself. That is to say, school principals are not in a position to select and hire teachers who will serve in their schools. They have to work with the teachers appointed by the Ministry. In this context, organizational citizenship behaviors of the teachers, and the effects of organizational justice and organizational trust on their organizational citizenship behaviors acquire a special importance; for teachers have to work with principals who have no school administration training, and principals have to work with teachers they have not chosen.

Lack of professionalization is identified as the root cause of many problems in numerous studies (Balcı, 2004; Işık, 2003; Şimşek, 2004). In addition, the policy for training educational administrators lacked a scientific foundation for almost 30 years. Turkey still does not have an institution specializing in training educational administrators, in part due to a lack of coordination between the MoNE and the universities. Although it can be argued that universities in Turkey have achieved a certain standard in training educational administrators, this view is criticized by many. For example, Şimşek (2004) argues that university programs supposed to train administrators are currently not capable of performing this function. According to Şimşek (2004), educational administration M.A. programs offered by some faculties of education in Turkish universities, content wise, are far from meeting the needs of the education system. As a result, educational administration in Turkey remains non-professionalized.

THEORETICAL AND CONCEPTUAL FRAMEWORK

The literature on organizational justice, organizational trust, and organizational citizenship contains many studies that examine the relationships between these variables. Studies on the relationship between *organizational justice* and *organizational citizenship* (Greenberg, 1993; Yılmaz & Taşdan, 2009); between *organizational trust* and *organizational citizenship* (Deluga, 1995; Kamer, 2001; Yılmaz, 2009); and between *organizational justice* and *organizational trust* (Hoy & Tarter, 2004; Özen, 2003; Saunders & Thornhill, 2003) abound. Yet, to the best of our knowledge, no study has examined whether *organizational justice* and *organizational trust* significantly predict organizational citizenship when considered in isolation and when controlled for each other.

Özen (2000) fails to find a significant relationship between trust in managers and the four dimensions of citizenship behaviors, and finds a significant but low-level relationship with one dimension. What is more, the study in question was conducted in a tourism company. Another study that fails to find a significant relationship between trust in principals and organizational citizenship behavior was conducted by Yılmaz (2009). Both of these studies are carried out in contexts other than educational organizations.

Previous studies show that organizational trust and organizational justice are among the important predictors of organizational citizenship behaviors. However, in all of these studies organizational trust and organizational justice were used as single predictors. This study aims to examine whether organizational justice and organizational trust are still significant as predictors of organizational citizenship behavior after controlling for each other.

PURPOSE OF THE STUDY

This chapter examined the relationships between organizational justice, organizational trust, and organizational citizenship behaviors in Turkish secondary schools. Specifically, the study investigated whether and to what extent organizational justice and organizational trust predict the variation on organizational citizenship behaviors of teachers. With this purpose, answers to the following research questions were sought:

Q1. What are the views of the participants on organizational justice and organizational trust?

Q2. Are organizational justice and organizational trust significant predictors of organizational citizenship behaviors?

RESEARCH DESIGN AND METHODOLOGY

A survey research methodology was employed in the study. A common goal of survey research is to collect data representative of a population. Survey research is a non-experimental, descriptive research method. Surveys can be useful when a researcher wants to collect data on phenomena that cannot be directly observed. Surveys are used extensively to assess attitudes and characteristics on a wide range of subjects.

Sampling Procedures and Participants

The participants of the study were 466 secondary school teachers in Kutahya, a city in western Turkey. A total of 651 secondary school teachers are employed in secondary schools in Kutahya city center. Because contacting all teachers who constitute the population of the study was not an issue, no sampling was used in the study, and the questionnaire was sent to all the teachers who constitute the population. Of these, 492 (76%) were returned. Questionnaires that were not filled out in line with the instructions provided were also left out, which left 466 (72%) forms to be considered. Of the participants, 49.4% were female ($n = 230$) and 50.6% were male ($n = 236$). The age of the participants varied between 25 and 56, and their professional experience varied between 1 and 32 years. The study aimed to include teachers from different types of secondary schools, and all the different types of secondary schools present in Kutahya were included.

Data Gathering Tools

The data gathering instrument of the study incorporated the Organizational Justice Scale (Hoy & Tarter, 2004), Organizational Trust Scale (Yılmaz, 2006), and Organizational Citizenship Behavior Scale (DiPaola, Tarter, & Hoy, 2005).

The Organizational Justice Scale developed by Hoy and Tarter (2004) was adapted to Turkish by Taşdan and Yılmaz (2008). The original questionnaire for Organizational Justice Scale consists of 10 Likert-type items. The total score is calculated by adding up the scores for individual items. In its original, the scale consists of a single strong dimension. Factor loadings of the items in the scale are larger than 0.77, and the total variance explained by the scale is 78%. Reliability coefficient of the scale is reported to be $\alpha = 0.97$. Items on the scale have the following response types: 1 – strongly disagree to 5 – strongly agree. The higher the score received from the scale, the more positive organizational justice perception is (Hoy & Tarter, 2004). The Turkish version of the scale is also one-dimensional and total variance explained by this single dimension is 53%. Factor loadings of the items in the scale vary between 0.39 and 0.87. In factor analysis, the minimum acceptable factor loading was taken as ".30." The Cronbach's alpha reliability coefficient of the scale is $\alpha = 0.88$ (Yılmaz, 2010a). The scale contains statements such as "The school principal is always fair to everyone," and "Teachers in this school receive equal treatment." In the present study, Cronbach's alpha reliability coefficient of the scale was found to be $\alpha = 0.95$.

The *Organizational Trust Scale* consists of 22 Likert-type items with the responses 1 – never to 5 – always. The scale consists of three dimensions: "Trust in the Principal," "Trust in Colleagues," and "Trust in Stakeholders." The total score received by the respondents from this scale is a measure of their views concerning organizational trust in their institutions. In each factor, higher scores represent higher trust, and lower scores represent lower trust (Yılmaz, 2006). Trust in the principal dimension consists of seven items and the Cronbach's alpha reliability coefficient for this dimension is $\alpha = 0.73$. The Trust in Colleagues dimension consists of seven items and the Cronbach's alpha reliability coefficient for this dimension is $\alpha = 0.90$. The Trust in stakeholders dimension consists of seven items and the Cronbach's alpha reliability coefficient for this dimension is $\alpha = 0.79$. Factor loadings of the items in the scale vary between 0.31 and 0.74. The total variance explained by the whole scale is 56.46%, and the Cronbach's alpha coefficient for the scale is $\alpha = 0.88$ (Yılmaz, 2009). The scale consists of statements such as "I trust the honesty of the school principal" (trust in the principal); "I trust the word of other teachers in this school" (trust in colleagues); "I trust the work of the students in this school" (trust in stakeholders). In the present study, Cronbach's alpha reliability coefficient was found to be $\alpha = 0.90$ for the "Trust in Principal" sub-dimension, $\alpha = 0.88$ for the "Trust in Colleagues" sub-dimension, $\alpha = 0.83$ for the "Trust in Shareholders" sub-dimension, and $\alpha = 0.93$ for the whole scale.

The *Organizational Citizenship Behavior Scale* (DiPaola et al., 2005) consists of 12 items, 10 of them positively worded and two negatively worded, and is one-dimensional. In its original form, there are six responses from "strongly agree" to "strongly disagree," which are assigned scores 1 to 6. In its Turkish adaptation, however, there are five responses, scored as follows: 1 – strongly disagree to 5 – strongly agree. The scale was adapted to Turkish by Taşdan and Yılmaz (2008). Higher scores mean more organizational citizenship behavior. Factor loadings of the items in the Turkish version of the scale vary between 0.30 and 0.78. Total variance explained by the scale 46.39%. Reliability analysis of the organizational citizenship scale shows that the scale has a Cronbach's alpha reliability coefficient of $\alpha = 0.85$ (Yılmaz, 2010b). The scale consists of statements such as "Teachers help students in their free time," and "Teachers volunteer to support extra-curricular activities." In the present study, Cronbach's alpha reliability coefficient of the scale was found to be $\alpha = 0.84$.

Data Analysis

Descriptive statistics were used to examine participants' views on organizational trust, organizational justice, and organizational citizenship behaviors. To analyze the relationship between organizational trust, organizational justice and organizational citizenship behaviors, hierarchical multiple regression analysis was used. Similarly, to see whether organizational justice and organizational trust are significant predictors of organizational citizenship behaviors, hierarchical multiple regression analysis was used. Multiple regression analyses are generally used to predict a dependent variable (in this case, organizational citizenship behaviors) on the basis of two or more independent variables (predictor variables, in this case organizational trust and organizational justice). Multiple regression analysis allows inferences on the basis of the significance of the explained variance, and the direction of the relationship between predictor variables and the dependent variable. In hierarchical regression analysis, on the contrary, variables are entered into the model in stages: first, a group of independent variables are evaluated in terms of how much information they provide about the independent variable, and then, another group of variables are entered into the model, and a statistical test of whether we gain any more information about the dependent variable with their inclusion is conducted. Because it fits the purposes of the present study better, a hierarchical multiple regression analysis was used in the study. A correlation coefficient, as an absolute value, 0.70–1.00: high correlation, 0.69–0.30: moderate correlation, 0.29–0.00: low correlation.

RESULTS

This section first presents the views of secondary school teachers on organizational justice, organizational trust, and organizational citizenship behaviors. Then, it presents findings on whether and to what degree organizational citizenship behaviors are predicted by organizational trust and organizational justice.

Secondary school teachers' perceptions of organizational justice are high. The mean score received for this scale ($M = 3.88$, $S = 0.70$) is closest to the "I agree" response. The item most agreed upon by the participants was "The school principal values everyone and treats everyone with respect" ($M = 4.09$, $S = 0.80$), and the item with the lowest level of agreement was "No one gets privileged treatment in this school" ($M = 3.63$, $S = 1.07$).

Participating teachers' views on organizational trust was closest to the "frequently" response for the dimensions of trust in colleagues ($M = 3.85$, $S = 0.67$) and trust in the principal ($M = 3.79$, $S = 0.55$), whereas it was closest to the "sometimes" response for the dimension of trust in stakeholders ($M = 3.55$, $S = 0.65$) The mean total score received by the teachers for organizational trust ($M = 3.74$, $S = 0.52$) was closest to the "frequently" response.

In the dimension of trust in the principal, the item with the highest level of agreement was "I trust the honesty of the school principal" ($M = 4.20$, $S = 0.75$), and the one with the lowest level of agreement was "The principal openly shares personal information with the teachers" ($M = 2.48$, $S = 1.04$). In the dimension of trust in colleagues, the item with the highest level of agreement was "I trust other teachers in this school" ($M = 4.06$, $S = 0.77$), and the one with the lowest level of agreement was "I trust that what is spoken in the teachers' hall remains private" ($M = 3.55$, $S = 1.03$). In the dimension of trust in colleagues, on the contrary, the item with the highest level of agreement was "I trust the work of the students in this school" ($M = 3.70$, $S = 0.85$), and the one with the lowest level of agreement was "Students in this school would not cheat even if they knew they would not be caught" ($M = 3.30$, $S = 1.04$).

Teachers participating in the study display high levels of organizational citizenship behavior. The mean score of the participants for this scale ($M = 3.95$, $S = 0.51$) is closest to the "I agree" response. The item with the highest level of agreement from the participants was "Teachers do not waste class time" ($M = 4.39$, $S = 1.00$), and the item with the lowest level of agreement was "Teachers volunteer to work in new councils formed at the school" ($M = 3.57$, $S = 0.89$).

The second purpose of the study was to find out whether organizational justice and organizational trust are significant predictors of organizational citizenship behaviors. In the model used, the variable of organizational citizenship behaviors was treated as the dependent variable to be predicted, and a hierarchical multiple regression analysis was conducted. Variables were entered into the analysis in three stages. The first model tested the relationship between organizational justice and organizational citizenship behaviors, and the second model tested the relationship between organizational trust and organizational citizenship behaviors. In the third model, all variables of the two previous models were included in the analysis. Table 1 reports the results of the hierarchical regression analysis concerning the variables that predict organizational citizenship behavior.

Table 1 shows that both Model 1 ($R = 0.43$, $R^2 = 0.19$, $p < 0.01$) and Model 2 ($R = 0.63$, $R^2 = 0.40$, $p < 0.01$) are significant predictors of organizational citizenship. By themselves, Model 1 explains 19% of the variation in organizational citizenship, and Model 2 explains 40% of the variation. Model 3, which predicts organizational citizenship on the basis of both organizational trust and organizational justice, is also significant ($R = 0.63$, $R^2 = 0.40$, $p < 0.01$). Models 1 and 2 together explain 40% of the variation in organizational citizenship behavior. Positive, moderate level, and significant relationships were found to exist between organizational citizenship behavior on the one hand, and organizational justice ($r = 0.43$), trust in the principal ($r = 0.47$), trust in colleagues ($r = 0.61$), and trust in stakeholders ($r = 0.35$) on the other. However, when other variables were controlled for, a positive and moderate level relationship was found between organizational citizenship behavior and trust in colleagues ($r = 0.44$), and a small and positive relationship between organizational citizenship behavior and trust in the principal ($r = 0.13$). Predictor variables are ordered by the size of their effect on organizational citizenship behaviors, as measured by standardized regression coefficients, as follows: trust in colleagues, trust in the principal, trust in stakeholders, and organizational justice.

Results of the *t*-test on the significance of regression coefficients show that trust in colleagues and trust in the principal are significant predictors of organizational citizenship behaviors. Organizational justice, which was a significant predictor of organizational citizenship behavior when considered

Table 1. Hierarchical Multiple Regression Analysis Results of Predictive Factors of Organizational Citizenship Behaviors.

Model	Variables	B	Standard Error	β	T	p	Zero-Order r	Partial r
1	Constant	32.842	1.448	–	22.681	0.00	–	–
	Organizational justice	3.766	0.367	0.430	10.269	0.00	0.43	0.43
	$R=0.43$, $R^2=0.19$, $F_{(1-464)}=105.4$, $p=0.00$							
2	Constant	22.382	1.680	–	13.322	0.00	–	–
	Trust in the principal	2.148	0.499	0.191	4.308	0.00	0.47	0.20
	Trust in colleagues	4.906	0.458	0.536	10.712	0.00	0.61	0.45
	Trust in stakeholders	-0.541	0.429	-0.057	-1.263	0.21	0.35	-0.06
	$R=0.63$, $R^2=0.40$, $F_{(3-462)}=101.8$, $p=0.00$							
3	Constant	22.362	1.680	–	13.31	0.00	–	–
	Organizational justice	0.473	0.481	0.054	0.98	0.33	0.43	0.05
	Trust in the principal	1.760	0.636	0.157	2.77	0.01	0.47	0.13
	Trust in colleagues	4.830	0.465	0.527	10.40	0.00	0.61	0.44
	Trust in stakeholders	-0.556	0.429	-0.059	-1.30	0.20	0.35	-0.06
	$R=0.63$, $R^2=0.40$, $F_{(4-461)}=76.6$, $p=0.00$							

in isolation, ceases to be a significant predictor when organizational trust variables are included in the model as well. Organizational trust and organizational justice together explain 39% of the total variance in organizational citizenship behaviors. The regression equation on the basis of these findings is as follows:

Organizational Citizenship = 22.36 + 0.47 Organizational Justice

+ 1.76 Trust in the principal + 4.83 Trust in colleagues

− 0.56 Trust in stakeholders

The analysis was repeated to see how organizational justice and organizational trust predict organizational citizenship behaviors when organizational trust is taken as a whole, this using the total score from the organizational trust scale instead of the scores for individual dimensions. Results of this analysis are reported in Table 2.

Table 2 shows that both Model 1 ($R = 0.43$, $R^2 = 0.19$, $p < 0.01$) and Model 2 ($R = 0.58$, $R^2 = 0.37$, $p < 0.01$) are significant predictors of organizational citizenship. By themselves, Model 1 explains 19% of the variation in organizational citizenship, and Model 2 explains 37% of the variation. Model 3, which predicts organizational citizenship on the basis of both organizational trust and organizational justice, is also significant ($R = 0.58$, $R^2 = 0.34$, $p < 0.01$). Models 1 and 2 together explain 34% of the variation in organizational citizenship behavior. The inclusion of organizational trust in the regression analysis brought about a 15% increase in explained variance. Positive, moderate level, and significant relationships were found to exist between organizational citizenship behavior on the one hand, and organizational justice ($r = 0.43$) and organizational trust ($r = 0.58$) on the other. However, when other variables were controlled for, a positive and moderate level relationship was found between organizational citizenship behavior and organizational trust ($r = 0.44$). Predictor variables are ordered by the size of their effect on organizational citizenship behaviors as follows: organizational trust and organizational justice.

The results of the t-test on the significance of regression coefficients show that organizational trust is a significant predictor of organizational citizenship behaviors. Organizational justice, which was a significant predictor of organizational citizenship behavior when considered in isolation, ceases to be a significant predictor when organizational trust is included in the model as well. Organizational trust and organizational justice together explain 34% of the total variance in organizational

Table 2. Hierarchical Multiple Regression Analysis Results of Predictive Factors of Organizational Citizenship Behavior.

Model	Variables	B	Standard Error	B	T	p	Zero-Order r	Partial r
1	Constant	32.842	1.448	–	22.681	0.00	–	–
	Organizational justice	3.766	0.367	0.430	10.269	0.00	0.43	0.43
			$R = 0.43$, $R^2 = 0.19$, $F_{(1-464)} = 105.4$, $p = 0.00$					
2	Constant	22.001	1.677	–	13.127	0.00	–	–
	Organizational trust	6.817	0.444	0.580	15.336	0.00	0.58	0.58
			$R = 0.58$, $R^2 = 0.37$, $F_{(1-464)} = 235.2$, $p = 0.00$					
3	Constant	21.550	1.693	–	12.73	0.00	–	–
	Organizational justice	0.770	0.437	0.088	1.76	0.07	0.43	0.08
	Organizational trust	6.139	0.587	0.522	10.46	0.00	0.58	0.44
			$R = 0.58$, $R^2 = 0.34$, $F_{(2-463)} = 119.7$, $p = 0.00$					

citizenship behaviors. The regression equation on the basis of these findings is as follows:

Organizational Citizenship = 21.55 + 0.77 Organizational Justice
+ 6.14 Organizational Trust

Relations between other variables were also examined. A high level relationship was found between organizational justice and trust in the principal ($r = 0.74$), and a moderate level relationship between organizational justice on the one hand and trust in colleagues ($r = 0.54$) and trust in stakeholders ($r = 0.40$) on the other. The relationship between organizational justice and organizational trust was found to be a moderate level one ($r = 0.66$).

CONCLUSION AND DISCUSSION

This chapter examined the relationships between organizational justice, organizational trust, and organizational citizenship behaviors in Turkish secondary schools. Prior to analyzing these relationships, participating teachers' views on organizational justice, organizational trust, and organizational citizenship behaviors were also examined.

Teachers participating in the study have positive views on organizational justice. These findings parallel those of other studies in the literature. Previous studies conducted in Turkey have found similar results (Titrek, 2009; Yılmaz, 2010a; Yılmaz & Taşdan, 2009). Organizations are interested in their employees having positive perceptions about justice, which can be defined as giving equal shares to equals, or treating people as equals (Aydın, 2002; Yılmaz, 2010a). This is because organizational justice is an important factor in interpersonal relations within an organization (Stevens & Wood, 1995), and a relative concept. For example, in a study on a group of employees who are insufficiently rewarded, Bies and Moag (1986) find that employees may perceive decisions to be just, provided that appropriate justifications are provided, even if these decisions bring negative consequences for them. That is to say, the perception of justice concerning a behavior, practice, or rule is a subjective one. Furthermore, rules and practices perceived by a majority of employees in an organization to be unjust are frequently violated no matter what the sanction is. Organizational justice perceptions of the employees are arguably among the most important determinants of their attitudes and behaviors towards an organization.

When employees have negative perceptions of organizational justice, this may result in discontent, lower work performance, and negative behaviors like aggression, theft, and lack of trust, with detrimental consequences for organizational culture (Folger & Cropanzano, 1998; Özen, 2000).

Teachers participating in the study have positive views on organizational trust in general. Secondary school teachers trust their colleagues the most, then their school principal, and finally the stakeholders. Trust in colleagues and in the principal is close to high, and trust in stakeholders is at moderate levels. In studies on state-run schools in Turkey, levels of trust in colleagues and in principals are found to be close to each other (Çokluk-Bökeoğlu & Yılmaz, 2008; Özer, Demirtaş, Üstüner, & Cömert, 2006). In this sense, the results of this study parallel those of previous studies in the literature.

The high level of trust observed among teachers is a positive phenomenon. However, it is interesting to note that teachers trust their colleagues more than they trust their principals. In private educational institutions in Turkey, especially in private training centers that prepare students for post-primary and post-secondary examinations, teachers trust their colleagues less than they trust their principals (Yılmaz, 2009). Trust in organizations is closely related to individuals' perceptions that they will not be harmed by people around them. Because most teachers employed in state run schools are tenured, there is less job-related competition among them, which may explain why teachers trust their colleagues more than they trust their principals in state run schools.

Teachers who participated in the study display high levels of organizational citizenship behavior. Previous studies conducted in Turkey also find organizational citizenship behaviors to be at high levels (Yücel, 2006; Yılmaz, 2009, 2010b; Yılmaz & Çokluk-Bökeoğlu, 2008). From the point of view of the organizations, it is important that their members engage in citizenship behaviors, because it is difficult for organizations to survive in today's complex world in the absence of organizational citizenship behaviors on the part of their members (Bateman & Organ, 1983). In addition, organizational citizenship behaviors of the employees are important for analyzing and understanding individual attitudes and behaviors within an organization.

This study also aimed to analyze the relationship between organizational citizenship behaviors on the one hand, and organizational trust and justice on the other. A positive and moderate-level relationship was found between organizational citizenship behaviors on the one hand, and organizational justice, trust in the principal, trust in colleagues, and trust in stakeholders on the other. In addition, high-level relationships were found to exist between organizational justice and trust in the principal and moderate-level relationships between organizational justice on the one hand, and trust in colleagues and trust in stakeholders, on the other. Previous studies in the literature find that perceptions of organizational justice (Cohen-Charash, & Spector, 2001; Eskew, 1993; Farh et al., 1990; Konovsky & Pugh, 1994; Organ, 1988, 1990; Organ & Ryan, 1995; Yılmaz & Taşdan, 2009) and organizational trust (Cohen-Charash & Spector, 2001; Kamer, 2001; Konovsky & Pugh, 1994; Özen, 2000) are factors in explaining organizational citizenship behaviors.

The present study found that although organizational justice is a significant predictor of organizational citizenship behaviors when considered in isolation, it is not significant as a predictor when organizational trust is controlled for. That is to say, the effect of organizational justice on organizational citizenship behaviors is mediated through organizational trust. Other studies also call attention to the mediating role of the organizational trust between organizational justice and organizational citizenship behaviors (Konovsky & Pugh, 1994; Özen, 2000). The strength of the relationship between organizational trust and justice also supports this interpretation. Trust in colleagues and trust in the principal have significant effects on citizenship behaviors. When other variables are controlled for, a positive and moderate level relationship is found between organizational citizenship behaviors and trust in colleagues, and a positive and low level relationship between organizational citizenship behaviors and trust in the principal.

Sub-dimensions of organizational trust and perceptions of organizational justice explain about two fifths of the total variance in organizational citizenship behaviors; whereas the organizational trust total score and organizational justice explain about one third of the total variance. Thus, we can argue that trust formed between employees, principals and colleagues and supported by perceptions of justice make employees to assume extra roles outside their formal job definitions. It is also understandable that trust in colleagues has a stronger effect on citizenship behaviors compared to other factors, because citizenship behaviors are voluntary extra-role behaviors to the benefit of the organization, beyond and above legal obligations, which are not required by orders, and performed without expecting any formal rewards in return. Extra-role behaviors expected of employees for the benefit of the organization have more of an interpersonal, rather than individual, character. Because they are above and beyond legal obligations, and not based on orders, they are more about relations among colleagues than relations with the principals. This, however, should not be interpreted to mean that citizenship behaviors of the employees are not affected or minimally affected by the attitudes and behaviors of the principals. It should be interpreted to mean that in organizations with high levels of trust and strong perceptions of justice, trust in colleagues is more effective in bringing about organizational citizenship behaviors, for one of the most important determinants of trust in colleagues is the behavior of the principals. If the principals are fair, then employees come to trust each other more. Future studies should examine whether and to what degree organizational trust and justice predict citizenship behaviors in organizations in which trust in principals is low.

Another factor that potentially explains the high levels of trust and citizenship behaviors among teachers is the structure of the Turkish society. The communitarian culture of Turkey (Kağıtçıbaşı, 2006) is seen by many as one of the factors leading to high levels of trust and citizenship. This is because trust tendencies and intra-group trust is stronger in communitarian societies than in individualist societies (Huff & Kelley, 2003). In communitarian cultures, individuals are very sensitive about the norms of what is called the inner group, and internalize these norms as if they are their own values (Kağıtçıbaşı, 2006), which may be one of the reasons behind high levels of citizenship behavior displayed.

The findings of this study are limited by the views of teachers working in state-run secondary schools in Kutahya provincial center. Teachers working in private schools were not included in the study. Similar studies could also be conducted in private schools, and results from the two types of schools compared. Working conditions in private schools in Turkey tend to be better than working conditions in state-run schools. Future studies can examine the relationship between organizational citizenship behaviors on the one hand, and working conditions, nature of the job, job satisfaction, level of professionalization, teacher leadership, and teacher efficacy, on the other.

This study examined the relationship between organizational citizenship behaviors, and organizational justice and trust, considered to be predictors of organizational citizenship behaviors. Further studies can examine factors like principal leadership, persuasion tactics used by principals, and power preferences, and their relationship with organizational citizenship behaviors. Because organizational citizenship behaviors are closely associated with organizational characteristics, variables such as the level of red tape, school climate, and efficient school characteristics can also be made the subject of research. Alternatively, a similar study can be conducted using qualitative research methods with a smaller group and more in-depth knowledge can be obtained by natural observation concerning the effects of organizational justice and trust on organizational citizenship behavior. This way, it would be possible to take specific aspects of education into consideration and make in-depth analyses.

ACKNOWLEDGMENTS

The authors are grateful to two anonymous reviewers and the editors of this volume for their helpful comments on earlier drafts of this chapter.

REFERENCES

Alexander, S., & Ruderman, M. (1987). The role of procedural and distributive justice in organization behavior. *Social Justice Research, 1*(2), 177–198.

Aydın, İ. (2002). *Managerial, professional and organizational ethics.* Ankara: PegemA Publishing.

Balcı, A. (2004). Practice of training the educational administrators and supervisors in Turkey: Problems and suggestions. *Contemporary Education, 29*(307), 22–40.

Bateman, T. S., & Organ, D. W. (1983). Job satisfaction and good soldier: The relationship between affect and employee citizenship. *Academy of Management Journal, 26*(4), 587–595.

Bies, R. J. (2005). Are procedural justice and interactional justice conceptually distinct? In J. Greenberg & J. A. Colquitt (Eds.), *Handbook of organizational justice* (pp. 85–112). Mahwah, NJ: Lawrence Erlbaum Associates.

Bies, R. J., & Moag, J. S. (1986). Interactional justice: Communication criteria of fairness. In R. Lewicki (Ed.), *Research on negotiation in organizations* (Vol. 1, pp. 43–55). Greenwich, CT: JAI Press.

Borman, W. C. (2004). The concept of organizational citizenship. *American Psychology Society, 13*(6), 238–241.

Brief, A. P., & Motowidlo, S. J. (1986). Prosocial organizational behavior. *Academy of Management Review, 11*(4), 710–725.

Bryk, A. S., & Schneider, B. (2003). *Trust in schools: A core resource for improvement.* New York, NY: Russell Sage Foundation.

Cohen-Charash, Y., & Spector, P. E. (2001). The role of justice in organizations: A meta-analysis. *Organizational Behavior and Human Decision Processes, 86*(2), 278–321.

Çokluk-Bökeoğlu, Ö., & Yılmaz, K. (2008). Teachers' perceptions about the organizational trust in primary school. *Educational Administration-Theory and Practice, 14*(54), 211–233.

Colquitt, J. A., Greenberg, J., & Zapata-Phelan, C. P. (2005). What is organizational justice? A historical overview. In J. Greenberg & J. A. Colquitt (Eds.), *Handbook of organizational justice* (pp. 3–56). Mahwah, NJ: Lawrence Erlbaum Associates.

Deluga, R. J. (1995). The relation between trust in the supervisor and subordinate organizational citizenship behavior. *Military Psychology, 7*(1), 1–16.

DiPaola, M. F., & Hoy, W. K. (2005). Organizational citizenship of faculty and achievement of high school students. *The High School Journal, 88*, 35–44.

DiPaola, M. F., Tarter, C. J., & Hoy, W. K. (2005). Measuring organizational citizenship in schools: The OCB scale. In W. K. Hoy & C. Miskel (Eds.), *Educational leadership and reform* (pp. 319–342). Greenwich, CT: Information Age.

DiPaola, M. F., & Tschannen-Moran, M. (2001). Organizational citizenship behavior in schools and its relation to school climate. *Journal of School Leadership, 11*(5), 424–447.

Eskew, D. E. (1993). The role of organizational justice in organizational citizenship behavior. *Employee Responsibilities and Rights Journal, 6*(3), 185–194.

Farh, J., Podsakoff, P. M., & Organ, D. W. (1990). Accounting for organizational citizenship behavior: Leader fairness and task scope versus satisfaction. *Journal of Management, 16*(4), 705–722.

Folger, R., & Cropanzano, R. (1998). *Organizational justice and human resource management.* Thousand Oaks, CA: SAGE.

Graham, J. W. (1991). An essay on organizational citizenship behavior. *Employee Responsibilities and Rights Journal, 4*, 249–270.

Greenberg, J. (1990). Organizational justice: Yesterday, today, tomorrow. *Journal of Management, 16*(2), 399–432.

Greenberg, J. (1993). Justice and organizational citizenship: A commentary on the state of the science. *Employee Responsibilities and Rights Journal, 6*(3), 249–256.

Greenberg, J. (1996). *The quest for justice on the job.* Thousand Oaks, CA: SAGE.

Hoy, W. K., Gage, Q., & Tarter, C. J. (2006). School mindfulness and faculty trust: Necessary conditions for each other? *Educational Administration Quarterly, 42*, 236–255.

Hoy, W. K., & Miskel, C. G. (2010). *Educational administration* (S. Turan, Trans. Ed.). Ankara: Nobel Publications.

Hoy, W. K., & Tarter, C. J. (2004). Organizational justice in schools: No justice without trust. *International Journal of Educational Management, 18*, 250–259.

Hoy, W. K., & Tschannen-Moran, M. (1999). Five faces of trust: An empirical confirmation in urban elementary schools. *Journal of School Leadership, 9*, 184–208.

Hoy, W. K., & Tschannen-Moran, M. (2003). The conceptualization and measurement of faculty trust in schools. In W. K. Hoy & C. Miskel (Eds.), *Studies in leading and organizing schools* (pp. 181–207). Greenwich, CT: Information Age.

Huff, L., & Kelley, L. (2003). Levels of organizational trust in individualist versus collectivist societies: A seven nation study. *Organization Science, 14*(1), 81–90.

Işık, H. (2003). From policy into practice: The effects of principal preparation programs on principal behavior. *International Journal of Educational Reform, 12*(4), 260–274.

Kamer, M. (2001). *The effect of organizational trust on organizational commitment and organizational citizenship behaviors.* Unpublished master dissertation. Marmara University, İstanbul, Turkey.

Katz, D., & Kahn, R. L. (1977). *The social psychology of organizations* (H. Can & Y. Bayar, Trans.). Ankara: TODAİE Publishing.

Kağıtçıbaşı, Ç. (2006). *New human and people.* İstanbul: Evrim.

Konovsky, M. A. (2000). Understanding procedural justice and its impact on business organizations. *Journal of Management, 26*(3), 489–511.

Konovsky, M. A., & Pugh, S. D. (1994). Citizenship behavior and social exchange. *Academy of Management Journal, 37*(3), 656–669.

Lewicki, R. J., & Bunker, B. B. (1996). Developing and maintaining trust in work relationships. In R. M. Kramer (Ed.), *Trust in organizations: Frontiers of theory and research* (pp. 114–140). Thousand Oaks, CA: SAGE.

Mishra, A. (1996). Organizational response to crisis. In R. M. Kramer & T. Tyler (Eds.), *Trust in organizations: Frontiers of theory and research* (pp. 261–287). Thousand Oaks, CA: SAGE.

MoNE (1973). Basic Law of National Education. No. 1739, Articles 26–27. Retrieved from http://okulweb.meb.gov.tr/35/02/812358/tmeb

MoNE (2009). Organization of the education system in Turkey–2008/09. Retrieved from http://sgb.meb.gov.tr/eurydice/index.htm

Moorman, R. H., & Blakely, G. L. (1995). Individualism-collectivism as an individual difference predictor of organizational citizenship behavior. *Journal of Organizational Behavior, 16*(2), 127–142.

Nyhan, R. C., & Marlowe, H. A. (1997). Development and psychometric properties of the organizational trust inventory. *Evaluation Review, 21*(5), 614–635.

Organ, D. W. (1988). *Organizational citizenship behavior: The good soldier syndrome*. Canada: Lexington Books.

Organ, D. W. (1990). The motivational basis of organizational citizenship behavior. *Research in Organizational Behavior, 12*(1), 43–72.

Organ, D. W., & Ryan, K. (1995). A meta-analytic review of attitudinal and dispositional predictors of organizational citizenship behavior. *Personnel Psychology, 48*(4), 775–802.

Özen, J. (2000). *The influential role of the employees trust in a supervisor and perceptions of organizational justice in the occurrence of the employees propensity of displaying organizational citizenship behavior*. Unpublished master dissertation. University of Akdeniz, Antalya, Turkey.

Özen, J. (2003). Organizational justice as the key to trust in organization. In F. Erdem (Ed.), *Trust in social sciences* (pp. 183–207). Ankara: Vadi Publishing.

Özer, N., Demirtaş, H., Üstüner, M., & Cömert, M. (2006). Secondary school teachers' perceptions regarding organizational trust. *Ege Education Journal, 7*(1), 103–124.

Paterson, J. M., Green, A., & Cary, J. (2002). The measurement of organizational justice in organizational change programmes: A reliability, validity and context sensitivity assessment. *Journal of Occupational and Organizational Psychology, 75*(4), 393–408.

Roch, S. G., & Shanock, L. R. (2006). Organizational justice in an exchange framework: Clarifying organizational justice distinctions. *Journal of Management, 32*(2), 299–322.

Saunders, M. N. K., & Thornhill, A. (2003). Organizational justice, trust and the management of change: An exploration. *Personnel Review, 32*(3), 360–375.

Şimşek, H. (2004). Training the educational administrators: Comparative examples and suggestions for Turkey. *Contemporary Education, 29*(307), 13–21.

Smith, C. A., Organ, D. W., & Near, J. P. (1983). Organizational citizenship behavior: Its nature and antecedents. *Journal of Applied Psychology, 68*(44), 653–663.

Stevens, E., & Wood, G. H. (1995). *Justice, ideology, and education*. New York, NY: McGraw-Hill.

Taşdan, M., & Yılmaz, K. (2008). Adaptation to Turkish of organizational citizenship and organizational justice scales. *Education and Science, 33*(150), 87–96.

Titrek, O. (2009). Employees' organizational justice perceptions in Turkish schools. *Social Behavior and Personality, 37*(5), 605–620.

Tschannen-Moran, M., & Hoy, W. K. (1998). Trust in schools: A conceptual analysis. *Journal of Educational Administration, 36,* 334–352.

Tschannen-Moran, M., & Hoy, W. K. (2000). A multidisciplinary analysis of the nature, meaning, and measurement of trust. *Review of Educational Research, 70,* 547–593.

Van Dyne, L., Graham, J. W., & Dienesch, R. M. (1994). Organizational citizenship' behavior: Construct redefinition, measurement, and validation. *Academy of Management Journal, 37*(4), 765–802.

Yücel, G. F. (2006). *Burnout and organizational citizenship behavior of teachers.* (Unpublished master dissertation). University of Afyon Kocatepe, Afyon, Turkey.

Yılmaz, K. (2004). Primary school teachers' perception about the supportive leadership behavior of school administrators and trust in school. İnönü University Journal of the Faculty of Education, 5(8), 117–131.

Yılmaz, K. (2006). Validity and reliability study of the trust scale. *Sakarya University Journal of the Faculty of Education, 11,* 69–80.

Yılmaz, K. (2009). The relationship between the organizational trust and organizational citizenship behaviors of private education center teachers. *Educational Administration – Theory and Practice, 15*(59), 471–490.

Yılmaz, K. (2010a). Secondary public school teachers' perceptions about organizational justice. *Educational Sciences: Theory and Practice, 10*(1), 579–616.

Yılmaz, K. (2010b). Public secondary school teachers' views about organizational citizenship behavior. *Ondokuz Mayıs University Journal of Education, 29*(1), 1–16.

Yılmaz, K., & Çokluk-Bökeoğlu, Ö. (2008). Organizational citizenship behaviors and organizational commitment in Turkish primary schools. *World Applied Sciences Journal, 3*(5), 775–780.

Yılmaz, K., & Taşdan, M. (2009). Organizational citizenship and organizational justice in Turkish primary schools. *Journal of Educational Administration, 47*(1), 108–126.

CHAPTER 10

TEACHERS SUPERVISING TEACHING ASSISTANTS: ASSIGNED ROLE OR DISCRETIONARY BEHAVIOUR? REFLECTIONS FROM THE UNITED KINGDOM ☆

Jill Morgan and Betty Y. Ashbaker

ABSTRACT

This chapter examines the teacher's role as supervisor of support staff (Teaching Assistants (TAs) in the UK, school paraprofessionals in the US) – a role for which there is typically little administrative or infrastructural support. Working from a UK perspective, the chapter draws on research from the UK and the US to address questions pertinent to the education systems of all countries which employ paraprofessionals: What types of behaviours do conscientious teachers engage in to provide effective supervision to paraprofessionals? How do paraprofessionals view

☆ It should be noted that the term *Teaching Assistants* denotes school-based paraprofessionals in the UK and does not include college-level support.

Discretionary Behavior and Performance in Educational Organizations: The Missing
Link in Educational Leadership and Management
Advances in Educational Administration, Volume 13, 249–274
Copyright © 2012 by Emerald Group Publishing Limited
All rights of reproduction in any form reserved
ISSN: 1479-3660/doi:10.1108/S1479-3660(2012)0000013015

the supervisory behaviours of their supervising teachers? Given the important role of paraprofessionals, the high levels of expertise required by their assigned roles, and the uneven provision for their professional development, the chapter also makes recommendations for building the teacher's supervisory role into the infrastructure of schools, rather than relying on its emergence as a discretionary behaviour.

BACKGROUND

The profile of Teaching Assistants (paraprofessionals or TAs[1]) in the United Kingdom has been greatly raised in recent years due to two government initiatives: the 2003 *National Agreement: Raising Standards and Tackling Workload* (DfES, 2003) and the introduction of the Foundation Stage/Phase in England and Wales. *The National Agreement* was designed to raise standards in schools by reducing unnecessary paperwork and bureaucracy for teachers, as historically, many of the teachers' roles have had relatively little to do with their core area of expertise: teaching and learning. What the National Agreement achieved was to:

a. allocate every teacher one half day per week of Preparation, Planning and Assessment (PPA) time – in recognition of the importance of these elements to effective teaching practice;
b. allow teachers to delegate 25 non-teaching tasks (collecting monies, photocopying, classroom displays etc.) to support staff, acknowledging that many classroom activities are not vital to pupil learning and can be performed equally well by TAs.

The National Agreement also introduced a new role for support staff: that of Cover Supervisor, which essentially authorises TAs to substitute for teachers during PPA time. This mandatory PPA time was not intended to allow teachers to prepare their TA(s) – indeed the two are mutually exclusive where the TA substitutes for the teacher. Anecdotal evidence also suggests that many TAs who work as Cover Supervisors (sometimes as their only and full-time role) are essentially functioning as teachers – planning and delivering instruction – but are allocated no PPA time to prepare for this.

The Foundation Stage/Phase[2] was introduced in England and Wales (in 2000 and 2008, respectively) to emphasise the value of learning through play and the use of outdoor as well as indoor learning environments (see Welsh Assembly Government, 2008). Based on research in other European countries (notably Sweden and Italy), the initiative sought to counteract the early formal approach to literacy and numeracy typical in the UK – a system which has apparently not enhanced the achievement of British schoolchildren in relation to their peers in countries where formal schooling begins later (OECD, 2010). The recommended ratio of 1:8 adults to children for Foundation Stage/Phase classrooms has typically not been achieved, but has led to a notable increase in the number of TAs. Government figures show the number of support staff working in schools in England almost doubled between 1995 and 2005, whereas the number of teachers increased by only 10%. More recent sources have suggested an increase of 200% in the number of TAs employed in English schools between 1999 and 2009, from 61,000 to 177,000 (www.bbc.co.uk/2/hi/uk_news/education).

TAs in the UK have come to assume a wide variety of roles (Vincett, Cremin, & Thomas, 2005), in parallel with the increasing complexity of responsibilities assigned to paraprofessionals in US classrooms (Mavropoulos, 2005). Increased attention to TA roles has naturally led to questions about their effectiveness. Blatchford et al. (2008), reporting a large-scale national study of the deployment and impact of TAs, found that the amount of individual attention or support some students received from the teacher declined when a TA was present, particularly at secondary school level, 'showing that the individualization of attention was provided by support staff at the expense of teachers' (p. 12). This is no surprise, however, it led Blatchford et al. to note a conceptual shift: 'there are grounds for the conceiving of interactions between support and pupils as an *alternative* as much as an *additional* form of support' – which was not the intended aim or rationale for the use of TAs. Roberts (2010) goes as far as to state that although the presence of a TA can reduce teacher workload and stress, and improve pupil behaviour and engagement with their work, 'pupils supported by teaching assistants may make less progress than similar peers not receiving support. In some cases, the more support pupils receive, the lower their attainment'.

Such findings are not restricted to the UK. Several US authors have noted that students receiving support from a paraprofessional are not invariably or obviously advantaged. Giangreco (2001) ascribes this in part to a 'two-pronged training trap': first, teachers can assume that paraprofessionals are well enough trained to support students, when this is typically far from true; second, no matter how little training a paraprofessional receives, teachers may feel justified in relinquishing students entirely into the hands of the 'trained' paraprofessional. Giangreco's argument is aimed at paraprofessionals who support students with special educational needs, but the point is easily generalised. When paraprofessionals do receive training, the benefits may be debatable. Such training often does not apply to their specific assignments or is simply too general to be of help (Downing, Ryndak, & Clark, 2000; Trautman, 2005). More recent research shows that inadequate training continues to be a concern. Breton (2010) surveyed paraprofessionals on a wide variety of topics including training. Nearly half (46%) of the participants rated their pre-service preparation as very poor to fair. Although this implies that more than half of paraprofessionals rated the training favourably, one must ask if it is acceptable for nearly one in every two paraprofessionals to enter the field with a perceived lack of adequate training.

SUPERVISION

A 2007 report by Estyn (the government inspectorate for schools in Wales) stated: 'The significant increase in support staff numbers means that senior teachers find it time-consuming to organise and deploy these staff'. This was – and remains – a very real concern, but the report offered the reassurance: 'there is evidence that TAs who are suitably qualified and supervised will make a difference to pupil achievement' – highlighting the importance of the twin needs of support staff, those of relevant training *and supervision*. This has been referred to as *instructional supervision* (Ashbaker & Morgan, 2006) because of the direct support to instruction that TAs now typically provide (Lasater, 2009; Welsh Government, 2008). Although the need for proper paraprofessional supervision is intuitive, Etscheidt (2005) states that paraprofessionals often work 'independently and autonomously, isolated from direction and supervision'. According to Breton (2010), many paraprofessionals receive little, if any, supervision and the quality of that supervision is inadequate. Giangreco, Yuan, McKenzie, Cameron, and Fialka (2005) state that the physical proximity between many paraprofessionals and special education teachers has decreased as more students with special needs are included in general education classrooms. As a direct result, paraprofessionals often are left with entire responsibility for directing their own work and making important instructional decisions without written plans (French, 2003) or the approval and support of a professional educator. This is an obvious weakness in a system designed to provide an individualised and focused educational programme for students with unique needs, if the individuals assigned as their major providers have not received formal training in general or special education. Logically when TAs receive training, it should be delivered in the context of their role as *support* to the teacher, pupils and prescribed curriculum, with training content restricted to material appropriate to a supportive role. The National Agreement clarified the TA's role and specified work regulations for support staff. It paid considerable attention to the tasks which teachers could delegate to TAs. However, it also required 'a proper system of direction and supervision for them' without specifying – either then or since – what that really means.

In 2007 the UK government's Department for Children Schools and Families (DCFS, 2007) published the findings from a national survey, investigating the characteristics, use and impact of support staff in schools in England and Wales. Findings of relevance include:

- 90% of TAs had some form of job description; some two-thirds had received an appraisal in the past year;
- two-thirds of TAs were supervised by a teacher; 1 in 10 stated that they received no supervision at all (more prevalent in secondary than primary schools);
- it was becoming increasingly common for schools to require specific qualifications and previous experience of TAs as a condition of employment;
- only a third of teachers who were line managers of support staff had received training for this role;
- most teachers had no allocated planning or feedback time with support staff; special schools were most likely to allocate (and fund) time for teachers to plan with TAs, secondary schools least likely;
- three-quarters of the training and development provided by teachers for support staff was informal and on the job;
- approximately half of TA participants said that they were satisfied with their job; about three-quarters stated that they felt the school appreciated their work.

In 2009, the UK government published the findings from the second wave of the national survey of support staff (Blatchford et al., 2009), which showed:

- 33% of respondents reported that support staff were involved in some way in planning with teachers, although only 6% of respondents reported that time was allocated for teachers and TAs to meet;
- teachers used feedback given to them by support staff in 24% of participating schools;

- support staff expertise was gained through training in 21% of responses; in 67% of responses support staff expertise was experiential or provided via communication with the teacher.

Blatchford et al. (2009) recommended that:

> a substantial component of all teacher training courses should involve ways of working successfully with support staff. This should recognise the reality that TAs are working in a pedagogical way with pupils, and consider in a systematic way the management of TA deployment in relation to managerial, pedagogical and curriculum concerns. (p. 133)

The National Foundation for Education Research (NFER, 2009) investigated whether schools in England encouraged collaboration between teachers and TAs, formally or informally. Two-thirds of teachers surveyed reported that their school did facilitate discussion with TAs, in order to make the best use of their skills and knowledge, although this was more common in primary (75%) than secondary schools (54%). What was unclear from this initial report was whether facilitation took the form of a time allocation, how much time was allocated or whether time allocated was used for that purpose. Pyle and Rudd (2010) provide further details of the methods the teachers used to communicate with TAs. Primary school teachers most commonly used informal conversations at the start of lessons, followed by written lesson plans or a timetabled planning session. Only a small proportion (4%) of primary school teachers reported no regular arrangements for planning with their TA. Secondary school teachers almost exclusively used informal conversations to communicate with the TA, with 20% reporting no regular arrangements for planning. This most recent research does suggest an improving picture and growing awareness of the need for teachers to communicate their intentions to TAs.

SUPERVISION: A WIDER VIEW

The situation we have described is mirrored in other countries that employ paraprofessional staff, particularly in the US (Ashbaker, Dunn, & Morgan, 2010), and much of the literature relating to supervision of TAs comes from the United States. Almost two decades ago Sergiovanni and Starratt (1993) stated that supervision, used correctly, can create powerful results in improving instruction. Likewise Glickman, Gordon, and Ross-Gordon (2001) define supervision as 'assistance for the improvement of instruction' (p. 10). More than two decades previously, Weller (1971) had recommended cycles of planning, observation and *intensive intellectual analysis of teaching performance in the interest of rational modification* (emphasis added). This referred to supervision of teachers or student teachers rather than TAs, but from about the mid-1980s, a number of scholars working with TAs developed lists of supervisory activities that closely followed these models, with the common aim of supervision improving the instruction provided to students. Sullivan and Glanz (2005) added a fourth element to Weller's cycle of clinical supervision – professional development. Thus, supervisees benefit from supervision and improve performance through planning *with the supervisor*, being observed *by the supervisor*, receiving feedback *from the supervisor*. Note the constant presence of the supervisor. Sergiovanni and Starratt (1993) listed eight phases of clinical supervision in the classroom:

1. establishment of a supervisor/supervisee relationship;
2. intensive joint planning of lessons;
3. planning a classroom observation strategy;
4. observation of the paraprofessional by the supervisor;
5. analysis of the teaching/learning process;
6. planning a conference strategy;
7. teacher-paraprofessional conference; and
8. resumption of planning.

These essentially mirror Weller's (1971) cycle of planning, observation and analysis, the results of which feed into subsequent planning. The IDEA Partnership Paraprofessional Initiative, reporting to the US Department of Education (USDE, 2001) identified supervision needs at various levels in, and aspects of the education system. They included:

1. Administrators to understand differences in staff roles and responsibilities so that staffing patterns meet individual learner needs.
2. Determining who is responsible for paraprofessional supervision (e.g. teachers, administrators, related services personnel) and when.
3. Training for personnel who have responsibility for preparing the professionals who supervise paraprofessionals.
4. Administrative support for time to plan, gather appropriate equipment and resources and develop professional environments for instruction.
5. Families to understand who is directing and monitoring the performance of paraprofessionals (pp. 4–5).

This comprehensive view highlights the extent of the infrastructure required to ensure that TAs and paraprofessionals receive the supervision they need in order to work effectively within their assigned roles.

REQUIRED OR DISCRETIONARY ROLE?

It would be appropriate to ask here whether supervising TAs is formally considered part of the teacher's role. The Standards for Practising Teachers in Wales[3] (applicable by the end of a new teacher's induction or probationary year) include as one of the professional values and attributes:

Standard 1.7: Develop effective working relationships with support staff and other professionals and understand the contribution they make to the learning, development and well-being of children and young people.

It could be argued that 'working relationships' equates with supervision (although the hierarchy and locus of responsibility of the teacher–TA relationship are not explicit). Supervision is not referred to specifically as part of the *Knowledge and Understanding* associated with this standard. However, as part of Standard 3 (Teaching: Planning, Expectations and Targets) of the same document:

Standard 3.1.5: Work effectively as a team member and collaborate with colleagues to plan work and establish targets. AND
Standard 3.1.6: Plan for support staff to be appropriately involved in supporting learning and ensure they understand the roles they are expected to fulfil.

In England the professional standards for Qualified Teacher Status (QTS) include as one of the Professional Attributes (TDA, 2007):

Have a commitment to collaboration and co-operative working.

Clarifying this rather general attribute, the list of QTS Professional Skills includes:

Work as a team member and identify opportunities for working with colleagues, sharing the development of effective practice with them, and
Ensure that colleagues working with them are appropriately involved in supporting learning and understand the roles they are expected to fulfil.

The Core Standards for teachers apply subsequent to newly acquired QTS and include the same two professional skills, but with the addition highlighted:

*Work as a team member and identify opportunities for working with colleagues, **managing their work where appropriate** and sharing the development of effective practice with them.*

This suggests a more active and deliberate approach to collaborative work, and certainly a hierarchical structure to the instructional team. Professional standards for teachers in English schools allow for five levels: QTS, Core, Post Threshold (a longevity measure for which teachers can claim pay increments by documenting competence through experience), Excellent and Advanced Skills Teacher (AST). At the Excellent level the TDA specify:

> Excellent Teachers provide an exemplary model to others through their professional expertise, have a leading role in raising standards by supporting improvements in teaching practice and support and *help their colleagues to improve their effectiveness and to address their development needs through highly effective coaching and mentoring.* (TDA, 2007, p. 4) (Emphasis added)

While this makes no specific mention of TAs or other support staff, it is clearly germane. AST standards evidence participation at the wider school level, but all levels clearly include elements of a supervisory role.

In the US, the Council for Exceptional Children (CEC, 2011) revised *Special Education Professional Ethical Principles and Practice Standards* (in the late stages of consultation and discussion as of the date of this publication) include the following specific references to the supervisory role of the special educator.

Special Education Professionals:

1. assure that special education paraeducators have appropriate training for the tasks they are assigned;
2. assign only tasks for which paraeducators have appropriately prepared;
3. provide ongoing information to paraeducators regarding their performance on assigned tasks;
4. provide timely, supportive, and collegial communications to paraeducators regarding tasks and expectations; and
5. intervene in accordance with local procedures when a paraeducator's behaviour is illegal, unethical or detrimental to individuals with exceptional learning needs.

These are standards for special educators, and indeed impetus for focusing on the employment, training and supervision of paraprofessionals in the US originated with special education, as a major employer of paraprofessional staff. Although the focus has continued with special education, federal legislation has been enacted under the umbrella of general education, notably Title I (Elementary and Secondary Education Act), as the second major employer of paraprofessionals in the US, with the 2001 re-authorisation (No Child Left Behind) requiring that paraprofessionals hired to work in Title I programmes be 'highly qualified' and work under the direction of a professional educator. Special education has also been a major employer of TAs in the UK. Indeed in most special schools,[4] the number of TAs exceeds the number of certified staff. In mainstream classrooms the support provided by TAs will typically be divided between individual support for a pupil with special educational needs and more general classroom support. Schools in England and Wales are required to appoint a Special Educational Needs Coordinator (SENCO). The SENCO role includes:

> responsibility for the day-to-day operation of provision made by the school for pupils with SEN and ... professional guidance in the area of SEN in order to secure high quality teaching and the effective use of resources to bring about improved standards of achievement for all pupils. (TTA, 1998)

The Teacher Training Agency (TTA) further states that effective coordination of SEN results in:

> learning support assistants [TAs] who ... understand their role in the school in relation to pupils with SEN; work collaboratively with the SENCO, teaching staff and staff from external agencies; through opportunities to develop their skills, become increasingly knowledgeable in ways of supporting pupils and help them to maximise their levels of achievement and independence.

Since 2010 a National Award for SEN Coordination has been established which has formalised training for SENCOs, but while leading and managing staff is one of the core functions of a SENCO, this includes all staff in the school, not only TAs or other support staff.

Two undeniable difficulties when discussing supervision for TAs are terminology and the typical working context of TAs. Many work with more than one teacher; some are assigned to a specific child because of that child's disability or special need. At secondary level this entails following the child's daily timetable through a number of different classrooms, where none of the teachers may consider themselves responsible for either child or TA. Many TAs also have more than one type of responsibility, perhaps spending a portion of the week providing general support and the rest supporting a single child, conducting small group work, or indeed under the recent legislation having total responsibility for teaching a class. Thus, the question of who is the TA's supervisor has no simple – or possibly single – answer. In addition, the term 'supervisor' is unclear in meaning. Many TAs distinguish between their line manager and supervisor, typically spending their working day with the latter, but referring to the former for organisational concerns rather than the details of their roles. Teachers may not consider themselves to be supervisors or managers of other adults. Indeed, in Minnesota, the term used is 'directing the work of [paraprofessionals]', because teachers do not supervise, as the local definition of this term includes hiring, evaluating and terminating employees.

THE ROLE OF HIGHER EDUCATION AND TEACHER TRAINING

Early research showed that training in supervision of paraprofessionals was largely absent from initial teacher training programmes in the US (Salzberg & Morgan, 1995) and the UK (Morgan & Ashbaker, 2000). This research has not been duplicated in more recent years, so hoped-for changes cannot be verified. In a large-scale survey ($n > 300$) of special education teachers in Colorado, French (2001) reported that almost 90% of respondents had acquired their knowledge of supervising paraprofessionals through 'real-life' experience rather than formal training – despite very high levels of qualifications, many years of experience as educators and a change in Colorado's endorsement requirements in 1989. Pickett, Likins, and Wallace (2003) stated:

> With rare exceptions, policies, standards, and systems for improving the performance and productivity of teacher and paraeducator teams are almost non-existent. State education agencies and/or other agencies responsible for developing and administering teacher credentialing systems have not joined forces with institutions of higher education to establish standards for licensure to ensure that teachers have the knowledge and skills they require to supervise paraeducators. Moreover paraeducator issues have yet to be addressed by various reform initiatives concerned with empowering teachers and increasing the accountability and effectiveness of education systems and practices.

In a study of States' regulations for the supervision of paraprofessionals, Hsu (2007) reported data from [State department of education] websites in relation to:

- regulations regarding supervision of paraprofessionals that align with the federal requirements;
- whether States had a definition for supervision;
- regulations regarding paraprofessional supervision;
- who had responsibility to supervise paraprofessionals;
- qualifications required of a supervisor of paraprofessionals; and

- how paraprofessionals and supervisors demonstrate appropriate supervision.

- 18 of the 50 states and the District of Columbia had information relating to paraprofessional supervision posted on their websites; of these 15 had one or more answers to the 6 key areas noted above;
- only 11 of the 50 states/DC had policies posted that were directly related to paraprofessionals;
- 9 defined 'direct supervision' in accordance with the Title I Non-Regulatory Guidance;
- 4 – Alaska, Montana, Oregon and Virginia – had specific procedures for supervising paraprofessionals;
- 15 specified who had responsibility for paraprofessional supervision; variously a teacher (sometimes specifying that they be certified, licensed or highly qualified to No Child Left Behind (NCLB) standards), a classroom teacher, or in one case the school districts;
- 4 specified the competencies supervisors must possess; and
- 4 specified how appropriate supervision should be documented. This varied from the use of a portfolio and skill inventories (MN), an approved schedule of supervision reviewed half-yearly (MT), requiring supervisors to develop and document a supervision plan (ND) and a supervision and feedback tool developed for supervisors (VA) to demonstrate appropriate supervision.

While there is some movement formalising supervision of paraprofessionals, the infrastructure at state level would still appear to be lacking, information regarding implementation is spotty and compliance with the federal regulations surely is dubious.

CONCEPTUAL FRAMEWORK

Lave and Wenger (1991) discuss the notion of situated learning and propose the concept of *Legitimate Peripheral Participation* to denote the position of a newcomer whose presence is justified and who participates in practices that are fundamental to a situation or profession, but whose participation is peripheral – not in the sense of being excluded from some inner circle (real or imagined), but because he or she is a newcomer and therefore unable as yet to participate as fully as an expert. They examine a variety of forms of apprenticeship as the means whereby a newcomer comes to participate as a full and recognised member of a learning community. We have considered elsewhere (Ashbaker & Morgan, 2009) the relevance of this framework to the working relationships of teachers and TAs, where the classroom teacher is the master or expert, to whom responsibility for developing the apprentice's (read TA's) skills and expertise naturally falls – whether there is organisational support and reward recognition for that role or not. Lave and Wenger (1991) stress the importance of the social context of learning, which presupposes communities of learners, rather than isolated individuals making lonely pilgrimages into the unknown. Where one member of the community learns, all members benefit. In this situation, peripherality can be empowering because a newcomer (or someone less expert) can participate and contribute, and with increasing intensity as skills and knowledge build. But Lave and Wenger warn that peripherality is disempowering, if the expert limits the newcomer's participation unnecessarily and literally keeps them out on the edge. Lave and Wenger also distinguish between participation as a demonstration of competence or acquired learning, and participation as learning. This is particularly apt for TAs, who participate in the instructional process from day one of hiring, learning on the job, in much the same way as student teachers, but typically without the accompanying teaching input of educational theory on which to base the very practical context of their work.

CURRENT RESEARCH

In this second half of the chapter we report a number of recent small-scale research studies relating to the teacher's supervisory responsibilities and draw from them practical ways in which the teacher's supervisory role can be recognised by and incorporated into the infrastructure of schools and therefore training and professional development for teachers.

Mavropoulos (2005) reports on the supervisory practices of special education teachers, and paraprofessionals' perceptions of that supervision. Citing Pickett's (1999) model, Mavropoulos focuses on the seventh principle governing paraprofessional employment, preparation and supervision:

Teachers/Providers responsible for supervising the work of paraeducators have the skills necessary to plan for, direct, provide on-the-job training for, monitor and evaluate the skills of paraeducators.

While these elements of the supervising teacher's role are generally agreed, several authors (e.g. Chisholm, 2002; Daniels & McBride, 2001) have suggested that *role clarification* is an additional essential element, prompting Mavropoulos to include it in his research. His data (collected from 34 teachers and 51 paraprofessionals and using a 6-point scale from *never* to *annually* and so on down to *daily*) indicated:

- Almost 40% of teachers plan *daily* or *weekly* with their paraprofessionals.
- Some 50% of teachers delegate tasks on a *daily* basis (although this may suggest lack of forward planning).
- Approximately 1 in 4 teachers report that they provide mentoring or training to their paraprofessional *daily* or *weekly*, and 1 in 2 provide such support more than once a year.
- Almost half of the teachers conduct evaluation of the paraprofessional's work at least *annually*, and 1 in 3 provide such support more frequently.

The picture however is not altogether cheerful, and suggests voids in the supervisory skills, willingness or awareness of this group of teachers. Mavropoulos (2005) administered a parallel survey to paraprofessionals working with these supervising teachers, using the same scale from *never* to *daily*. From the data it emerged that:

- 17% of paraprofessionals reported that their teachers *never* clarified roles or expectations; 24% reported that this occurred *weekly* or *daily*.
- 18% of paraprofessionals reported that their supervisor *never* planned with them; 37% reported *weekly* or *daily* planning.
- 20% reported that tasks were *never* delegated by their supervisors; 51% reported *weekly* or *daily* delegation of tasks.
- 28% reported *never* receiving mentoring or training from their supervisor; 29% received mentoring/training *weekly* or *daily*.
- 28% reported that their work was *never* evaluated or their performance monitored by their supervisor; 16% reported *weekly* or *daily* evaluation or performance monitoring.

Again, the results are not entirely negative. However, Mavropoulos reports: 'an overarching theme was that paraprofessionals perceived that special educators had limited engagement in supervisory tasks'. Statistical analysis indicated that perceptions of teachers and paraprofessionals showed no significant difference with regard to frequency of engagement in the supervisory activities of interest.

Birch and Morgan (2011) report research into the supervision experiences of TAs enrolled on a Foundation degree program in learning support in an institution of Higher Education in Wales. The Foundation degree is a two-year degree, which requires students to be simultaneously studying and working or volunteering in the field of study. Thus, all participants were TAs working in local schools while studying part-time. Questionnaires were administered to a convenience sample of students. The following points of interest emerged:

- 1 in 4 respondents stated they had no supervisor; and
- 1 in 2 respondents did not work in physical proximity with their supervisor, meaning they were unsupervised in practise even if they had a recognised supervisor; those who did work in the same physical space, did so on average for 77% of the time, leaving a quarter of their time unsupervised.

Respondents were also asked to list activities their supervisor undertook to provide supervision for them. The ensuing list was long, but condensed to issues of:

- assistance with details of assigned tasks (work to be covered by the TA, sharing lesson plans etc.);
- organisation (timetables, covering for absences etc.);
- collaboration/teamwork (planning together, discussing pupil needs);
- support (in general collegial terms, and in specific areas such as behaviour); and
- checking the TA's performance.

When asked which of these activities they considered the most helpful, TAs again most frequently cited *assistance with the details of their work*, however *collaboration/teamwork* featured more frequently than *support* or *organisation* (see Table 1).

A relatively small proportion of respondents (16%) stated that they would like additional supervision, and suggested more clearly defined roles,

Table 1. Categories of Supervision Activities Cited by TAs as (a) Undertaken by Their Supervisors and (b) Being Most Helpful.

Supervision Activities Undertaken by Teachers		Those Considered Most Helpful by TAs	
Assistance with details of TA tasks	38%	Assistance with details of TA tasks	40%
Organisation	19%	Teamwork	33%
Teamwork	19%	Support	19%
Support	17%	Organisation	8%
Checking TA's performance	7%		

greater involvement in planning and increased communication. When asked how their work was monitored or assessed, responses varied widely with some respondents referring to frequency and others to means: 1 in 4 respondents stated that their work was not assessed or monitored in any way; 19% stated that it occurred through annual appraisals, another 17% through observation and 16% through informal discussion and feedback; 14% cited paperwork. Assessments were most often conducted by the Headteacher or Deputy Headteacher.

A small number of respondents were responsible for other TAs. (This is not uncommon in UK schools, and equates with Title I in the US, where Title I teachers so-called are often not certified, but are in essence paraprofessionals with responsibility for other paraprofessionals working in the programme.) When asked what they do to supervise other TAs, responses varied widely but grouped under the themes:

- providing training/information (38% of responses, e.g. training sessions, give feedback);
- support (23% of responses, e.g. promote confidence, encourage);
- organisation (19% of responses, e.g. show where things are, explain routines);
- evaluation (9.5% of responses, e.g. appraise, observe); and
- advocating (9.5% of responses, e.g. act as a liaison to headteacher/ deputy).

This aligns more closely with what the TAs considered useful among the activities their supervisor provides, than with the list of activities undertaken on a regular basis by their supervisors.

Morgan and Ashbaker (2010) report responses from a cohort of 38 teachers and administrators representing 20 states in the US when asked: *What are the most important elements of teachers working effectively with paraprofessionals?* Responses indicated the following:

- good communication, collaboration/teamwork and providing training (for paraprofessionals) were the most frequently cited elements;
- trusting, respectful relationships were the next most frequently cited, followed by clarity of expectations/roles; and
- other elements cited included: planning together (although this could be considered a part of collaboration); professionalism on the part of both teacher and paraprofessional; the paraprofessional's level of knowledge and understanding; organisational features (such as groupings for paraprofessional's work).

Administrative support did not feature highly (2% of responses) even though the majority of the respondents held administrative positions.

POTENTIAL OBSTACLES TO EFFECTIVE SUPERVISION

Vincett et al. (2005) used observation and survey methodology to investigate collaborative practices between teachers and TAs in UK classrooms. They identify 'tensions' that can prevent or reduce the likelihood of effective collaborations between teachers and TAs:

- TAs' lack of knowledge of effective classroom practices;
- TAs' concerns over their own status;
- teachers' lack of knowledge of how best to work with TAs; and
- lack of time for teachers and TAs to meet for joint planning.

Wallace, Shin, Bartholomay, and Stahl (2003), working in the US, also identified a number of issues in relation to paraprofessional supervision:

- lack of planning time between teachers and paraprofessionals; compounded by paraprofessionals working in multiple classrooms and therefore having multiple supervisors;
- a mismatch between role assignments and training provided; more than 80% of paraprofessionals reported spending at least half of their day on instructional tasks, but only 40% reported having received training in reading, writing or maths;
- a mismatch between paraprofessionals' job description and assignments; only half reported that their job description was an accurate reflection of their duties; and
- lack of guidance for assigned work: 67% received instructions or suggestions for their work from their daily supervisor; 17% received no consistent direction.

The positive aspects of Wallace et al.'s (2003) Minnesota research included:

- those paraprofessionals who felt planning time was 'adequate' were most often likely to report that they had daily or weekly planning time with their supervisor; and
- almost 90% of the paraprofessionals reported that they felt like a valued member of the instructional team.

Special educators participating in Mavropoulos' (2005) research most frequently cited time (or lack thereof), communication and trust as potential barriers to supervision. Other obstacles included planning, training, feeling uncomfortable and inexperience. Participating paraprofessionals most often cited communication, trust and listening, followed by planning, training, time and inexperience, again showing that perceptions aligned closely.

Other research which has identified potential barriers to effective supervision cites time management, paperwork, confusion over the details of the supervisory role, and lack of confidence on the part of teachers (French, 2003). French also highlights the need for teachers to increase self-management skills in order to better manage others' time and responsibilities. Marks, Schrader, and Levine (1999) highlight the issue of time, but in the sense of the high caseloads carried by many special educators, resulting in their having little time to give to supervision, and in paraprofessionals assuming inappropriate levels of work, both in quantity and expertise.

Participants in Mavropoulos' (2005) research made suggestions for enabling supervision, with the common themes of guidance, more time to meet, communicating expectations and mentoring. Brant and Burgess (2009) report research in the UK where pre-service teachers worked as TAs as a requirement of their pre-service teacher training. This was designed to develop their understanding of how TAs influence pupil learning, and bring them to a better understanding of the needs of pupils with SEN or various additional needs. The pre-service student-teachers widely reported the intended increased understanding of pupil needs. However, many also evidenced increased awareness of the importance of collaboration between teacher and TA, as well as the complexity of the TA's role.

PERSISTENT THEMES

From the research into supervision of paraprofessionals a number of important points clearly and persistently emerge:

- the importance of each individual understanding his or her role in the work setting – and the roles of the other members of the instructional team;
- the need for clear and honest communication – including the time required to discuss planning and evaluate progress; and
- the importance of sharing information and power among team members so that no individual feels disenfranchised.

There is also noticeable emphasis on teamwork or collaborative effort, rather than a one-way model of supervision. Belbin (1995), an acknowledged expert on teamwork in the UK with a background in industry and business, states that 'teamwork is one of the most efficient ways we know of accomplishing complex tasks'. Teaching is undeniably a complex task, but we may well ask what makes collaboration an efficient way of accomplishing that task. Using the analogy of team sports Belbin suggests, 'a good team comprises players who restrict their activities so as to avoid diminishing the role of others but who play their own role with distinction'. Notably, Belbin makes no distinction between different members of the team. Even the team captain should be restricting his or her own activities so as not to diminish the other players in their assigned roles; the captain particularly must concentrate on playing his or her own role 'with distinction'. This may suggest a hands-off approach for the team leader or captain – a stand back and let them get on with it attitude that may be uncomfortable for some educators, and that may seem to contradict some of the cited research – but would depend on how the details of the captain's role were perceived.

On an organisational level, Vincett et al. (2005) offer three models for organising classroom teams that serve to overcome the tensions cited above and which also suggest a collaborative model of supervision:

Room Management where one adult is designated as learning manager and works intensively with a small group or an individual, and the other, the activity manager, provides more general supervision to the rest of the class. This model helps counteract the tension of the TA's lack of knowledge about classroom practice, but only if the teacher takes the time to discuss strengths and weaknesses of teaching sessions, and provides on-the-job training for the TA.

Zoning where the classroom is divided into learning areas or zones, with each adult taking responsibility for particular zones. Here the TA's concern about status can be counteracted if the teacher seeks and acknowledges the TA's views and shows that her opinion is valued.

Reflective Teamwork involves teacher and TA sitting together daily for approximately 15 minutes to review a previous teaching session. First the TA and then the teacher (preferably in that order) identifies two positive things from the teaching session, and two things that could be improved. These reflections feed into planning for upcoming teaching sessions. Reflective teamwork is designed to overcome the tensions of perceived lack of time for teachers and TAs to meet and plan, as teachers can usually find a 15-minute time slot during the day when pupils are working independently. It also builds the teacher's knowledge of how best to work with a TA – through trial and error, but nevertheless through regular opportunities for the teacher to offer leadership to the TA.

Senge (1990) proposes four disciplines as the basis of successful learning organisations: personal mastery, mental models, building shared vision and team learning. These disciplines closely align with much of the supervision research cited. Senge's fifth discipline is systems thinking – trying to see the bigger picture, rather than only focusing on tackling small, individual difficulties which are often caused by larger systematic flaws. This is obviously no simple matter, but we make passing reference to this aspect of Senge's thinking because of the commonalities with the other perspectives which we have discussed here and the repeated focus on working together rather than a top-down hierarchical view of supervision.

CONCLUSIONS AND IMPLICATIONS

Whitehorn (2010) notes the following remarks from Ofsted (the government inspectorate for schools in England) suggesting that effective deployment of support staff is essentially a skill: 'The quality of support for teaching and learning depend[s] very much on teachers' ability to manage and evaluate the effectiveness of members of the workforce' and concedes: 'it is a considerable challenge for teachers to direct the work of additional adults in the classroom' (p. 10). This concession may lead us to sympathise with teachers but not to let them off the supervisory hook. Glickman et al. (2001) suggest that supervision be regarded as a function and process, rather than a role or position. Mavropoulos (2005) notes that the title of supervisor is not necessary for a teacher to assume – and we might add be held accountable for – the supervisory role. Pickett and Gerlach (2003) remind us that supervision occurs at two levels, even within a school: from building level administrators, which includes the management functions of hiring and evaluation of paraprofessionals; and the ongoing delegation and supervision of the paraprofessional's daily work by teachers. At this classroom level of supervision as delegation, we posit that three elements must be present: accountability, continuing professional development (CPD) and collaboration (see Fig. 1). Of these accountability and collaboration are two-way processes, with the teacher both holding the TA accountable for standards of performance and being accountable to the TA as a deliberate supervisor, to ensure effective delivery of instruction; collaboration by definition is not a

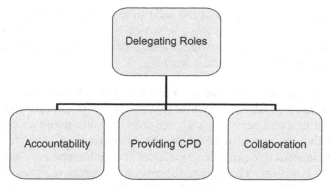

Fig. 1. Elements of the Supervisory Role as Delegation of Authority to the TA/Paraprofessional.

one-way street. Only CPD might be considered unidirectional, delivered by the supervising teacher and received by the TA. However in a situated learning paradigm, even CPD becomes two-way, with teacher and TA benefitting from each other's growing expertise, and – specific to this discussion – the teacher, by participating in the process of supervising the TA, also engaging in learning.

As a social constructivist paradigm, the principles of situated learning offer a useful approach to teachers who supervise TAs/paraprofessionals:

1. Learning as interactions between the known and unknown. This suggests the importance of the learner being aware of what he or she already knows; the need for the teacher to conduct a skills audit to ascertain what the learner knows prior to introducing new skills/knowledge; and the need for the teacher to make links for the learner between the known and the new.
2. Learning as a social process. This highlights that solitary endeavour is a poor substitute for deliberately collaborative practice; and the mere presence of another adult is insufficient – meaningful learning requires deliberate interaction focused on the common purposes of the classroom.
3. Learning as difficult to generalise. This suggests the need to be sensitive to context – ensuring that it is appropriate to the TA's cultural/linguistic background, and closely resembles the context in which the TA will use the new learning, and the importance of the teacher helping the TA to generalise principles to multiple contexts.

4. Metacognition. This suggests the need to make the TA aware of learning which is taking place, the ways in which he or she learns best and the extent and limits of her knowledge and understanding, thereby remaining aware of the need to continue learning.

Fig. 2 suggests an alternative arrangement of the elements of supervision, depicting a hierarchical relationship: that assignment of appropriate roles to the TA, as a first and necessary step, requires evaluation and accountability; that CPD then be provided based on the evaluation; and that teacher and TA engage in reflective practice to consider their effectiveness – individually and in collaboration. This again suggests an interactive, two-way supervisory process. We have referred elsewhere (Morgan & Ashbaker, 2011) to this type of process as *formative supervision* – essentially the 'intensive intellectual analysis of teaching performance in the interest of rational modification' as recommended by Weller (1971).

Teachers have the responsibility to ensure that legal and ethical guidelines are followed in their classrooms; UK and US government documentation states that TAs/paraprofessionals should be systematically supervised. While it may be the responsibility of a school's senior management team to ensure that proper systems are in place, the reality is that the teacher works with the TA on a day-to-day basis, and therefore by default becomes

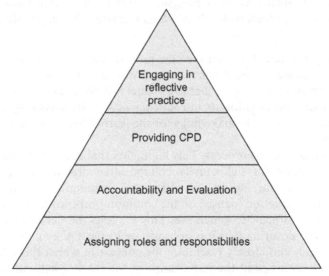

Fig. 2. A Hierarchy for the Elements of the Supervisory Role.

the TA supervisor, whether arrangements are made to support her in that role or not, and regardless of whether the title or role of *supervisor* has been bestowed. Teachers can initiate and be agents of change, but accomplishing school improvement requires school and local authority level employees to perform beyond expectations through discretionary behaviour and performance. Supervision of paraprofessional staff is hardly new – it has been a topic of serious discussion for at least three decades (Heller & Pickett, 1983) and advice has not been lacking. It is surely time to consider it as an elemental part of our education systems by developing an infrastructure that requires accountability on all levels. As Daniels and McBride (2001) assert:

> In the final analysis, schools cannot adequately function without paraprofessionals, and paraprofessionals cannot adequately function in schools that lack an infrastructure that supports and respects them as viable and contributing members of instructional teams.

NOTES

1. The preferred term for support staff in US legislation is 'paraprofessional' although as in the UK, these staff work under a wide variety of titles (paraeducator, teacher aide, instructional technician etc.); we use the terms TA (when referring to the UK) and paraprofessionals (when referring to the US).

2. In England the Foundation Stage covers the first year of compulsory schooling; in Wales the Foundation Phase covers the first three years.

3. In the UK, central (federal) government functions are partially devolved to Wales and Scotland. In Wales as of the date of this publication, the Welsh Government (formerly Welsh Assembly Government) has legislative powers in the areas of education and health. There are quite distinct differences, therefore, between some of the legal and practical structures of education in England and Wales. Scotland has more extensive legislative powers, but also has a longer history of distinct differences between the Scottish education system and England and/or Wales, dating back before devolution (legislative powers were assigned to Scotland in 1999, to Wales in 2006).

4. In the UK special schools exist largely for pupils with PMLD (Profound and Multiple Learning Difficulties) or for disabilities such as Autistic Spectrum Disorders (ASD) as inclusionary practices are encouraged, and underpinned by the provision of such contingencies as individual support by TAs in mainstream classrooms.

REFERENCES

Ashbaker, B. Y., Dunn, S. C., & Morgan, J. (2010). Paraprofessionals in special education. In P. Peterson, E. Baker & B. McGaw (Eds.), *The international encyclopedia of education* (3rd ed., pp. 780–787). Oxford, UK: Elsevier.

Ashbaker, B. Y., & Morgan, J. (2006). *Paraprofessionals in the classroom.* Boston, MA: Pearson.
Ashbaker, B. Y., & Morgan, J. (2009, March). Paraprofessionals participate in the school learning community: Legitimate peripheral participation. Paper presented at the Annual Conference of the Association of Supervision and Curriculum Development (ASCD), Orlando, FL.
Belbin, M. R. (1995). *Team roles at work.* Oxford: Butterworth-Heinemann.
Birch, A., & Morgan, J. (2011). *Teachers supervising teaching assistants: Preliminary report.* Unpublished. Swansea Metropolitan University, Swansea, UK.
Blatchford, P., Bassett, P., Brown, P., Koutsoubou, M., Martin, C., Russell, A., Webster, R., & Rubie-Davies, C. (2009). *Deployment and impact of support staff in schools.* London: DCSF. Retrieved from http://www.education.gov.uk/research/data/uploadfiles/DCSF-RR148.pdf
Blatchford, P., Bassett, P., Brown, P., Martin, C., Russell, A., Webster, R., Babayicit, S., & Haywood, N. (2008). The deployment and impact of support staff in schools and the impact of the national agreement: Results from Strand 2 Wave 1 – 2005/6 (DCSF Research Report RR027).
Brant, J., & Burgess, L. (2009). Many hands make light work: How might acting as teaching assistants, help pre-service teachers develop their understanding of pupils' learning needs in London secondary schools? *Journal of Applied Research in Education, 13,* 30–43.
Breton, W. (2010). Special education paraprofessionals: Perceptions of preservice preparation, supervision, and ongoing developmental training. *International Journal of Special Education, 25*(1), 34–45.
Chisholm, J. (2002). *Supervising paraprofessionals in middle school classrooms: A descriptive case study.* Unpublished doctoral dissertation. Virginia Polytechnic Institute and State University, Blacksburg, VA.
Council for Exceptional Children. (2011). Special education professional ethical principles and practice standards for discussion 2011: Council for exceptional children.
Daniels, V. I., & McBride, A. (2001). Paraeducators as critical team members: Redefining roles and responsibilities. *NASSP Bulletin, 85*(623), 66–74.
DCFS. (2007). *Deployment and impact of support staff in schools.* London: Author.
DfES. (2003). *Raising standards and tackling workload: A national agreement.* London: Author.
Downing, J. E., Ryndak, D. L., & Clark, D. (2000). Paraeducators in inclusive classrooms: Their own perceptions. *Remedial and Special Education, 21*(3), 171–181.
Estyn. (2007). *Standards and quality in education and training in Wales.* Cardiff, UK: Estyn.
Etscheidt, S. (2005). Paraprofessional services for students with disabilities: A legal analysis of issues. *Research and Practice for Persons with Severe Disabilities (RPSD), 30*(2), 60–80. doi:10.2511/rpsd.30.2.60
French, N. K. (2001). Supervising paraprofessionals: A survey of teacher practices. *The Journal of Special Education, 35*(1), 42–43.
French, N. K. (2003). *Managing paraeducators in your school: How to hire, train, and supervise non-certified staff.* Thousand Oaks, CA: Corwin.
Giangreco, M. F. (2001). Working with paraprofessionals. *Educational Leadership, 1*(2), 50–53.
Giangreco, M. F., Yuan, S., McKenzie, B., Cameron, P., & Fialka, J. (2005). "Be careful what you wish for …": Five reasons to be concerned about the assignment of individual paraprofessionals. *Teaching Exceptional Children, 37*(5).

Glickman, C. D., Gordon, S. P., & Ross-Gordon, J. M. (2001). *Supervision and instructional leadership: A developmental approach* (5th ed.). Boston, MA: Allyn and Bacon.

Heller, B., & Pickett, A. L. (1983). *Effective utilization of paraprofessionals by professionals training manual.* Reston, VA: Council for Exceptional Children.

Hsu, S. (2007). *Legislation, litigation, regulation, and implementation of paraprofessional supervision in school settings.* Master's thesis, Brigham Young University, Provo, UT. Retrieved from http://contentdm.lib.byu.edu/ETD/image/etd1782.pdf

Lasater, M. (2009). *RTI and the paraeducator's roles effective teaming.* Port Chester, NY: Dude Publishing.

Lave, J., & Wenger, E. (1991). *Situated learning: Legitimate peripheral participation.* Cambridge: Cambridge University Press.

Marks, S., Schrader, C., & Levine, M. (1999). Paraeducator experiences in inclusive settings: Helping, hovering, or holding their own? *Exceptional Children, 65,* 315–328.

Mavropoulos, Y. (2005). *Paraprofessional supervision: A survey of special education teachers and paraprofessionals.* Unpublished doctoral dissertation, The College of William and Mary, Williamsburg, PA.

Morgan, J., & Ashbaker, B. Y. (2000). Teacher training in relation to working with and supervising learning support assistants: A survey of institutes of higher education in the UK. *British Education Index: Education-line.* Retrieved from http://www.leeds.ac.uk/educol

Morgan, J., & Ashbaker, B. Y. (2010, March). *Leading a learning community: Teachers working effectively with paraprofessionals.* Workshop presentation at the Annual Conference of the Association of Supervision and Curriculum Development (ASCD), San Antonio, TX.

Morgan, J., & Ashbaker, B. Y. (2011). *Supporting and supervising your teaching assistant.* London: Continuum.

National Foundation for Education Research. (2009). *NFER Teacher Voice Omnibus February 2009 Survey: Classroom-based support staff and cover for unplanned absence.* Slough, UK: National Foundation for Education Research.

OECD. (2010). *PISA 2009 results: Executive summary.* Paris: OECD.

Pickett, A. L. (1999). *Strengthening and supporting teacher/provider-paraeducator teams: Guidelines for paraeducator roles, supervision, and preparation.* New York, NY: National Resource Center for Paraprofessionals.

Pickett, A. L., & Gerlach, K. (2003). *Supervising paraeducators in school settings* (2nd ed.). Austin, TX: Pro-Ed.

Pickett, A. L., Likins, M., & Wallace, T. (2003). *The employment and preparation of paraeducators: The-state-of-the-art – 2003.* New York, NY: National Resource Center for Paraprofessionals.

Pyle, K., & Rudd, P. (2010). *NFER Teacher Voice Omnibus February 2010 Survey: Performance management and various professional issues.* Manchester, UK: TDA.

Roberts, C. (2010). *A positive partnership.* Retrieved from www.tda.gov.uk/professional teacherprofessionalteacher_feb2010_tda0785.pdf. Accessed on 12 May 2011.

Salzberg, C. L., & Morgan, J. (1995). Preparing teachers to work with paraeducators. *Teacher Education and Special Education, 18*(1), 49–56.

Senge, P. M. (1990). *The fifth discipline: The art and practice of the learning organization.* London: Random House.

Sergiovanni, T., & Starratt, R. (1993). *Supervision: A redefinition* (5th ed.). New York, NY: McGraw-Hill.

Sullivan, S., & Glanz, J. (2005). *Supervision that improves teaching*. Thousand Oaks, CA: Corwin.

TDA. (2007). *Professional standards for teachers: Why sit still in your career?* London: TDA.

Trautman, M. (2005). Preparing and managing paraprofessionals. *Intervention in School and Clinic, 39*(3), 131–138.

TTA. (1998). *National standards for special educational needs co-ordinators*. London: TTA.

U.S. Department of Education. (2001). The IDEA partnership paraprofessional initiative. Report to the USDE (OSEP), Washington, DC.

Vincett, K., Cremin, H., & Thomas, G. (2005). *Teachers and assistants working together*. Buckingham, UK: Open University Press.

Wallace, T., Shin, J., Bartholomay, T., & Stahl, B. J. (2003). Knowledge and skills for teachers supervising the work of paraprofessionals. *The Council for Exceptional Children, 67*(4), 520–533.

Weller, R. (1971). *Verbal communication in instructional supervision*. New York, NY: Teachers College Press.

Welsh Assembly Government. (2008). *School support staff in Wales: Research report on the employment and deployment of support staff in schools in Wales*. Cardiff, UK: WAG.

Whitehorn, T. (2010). *School support staff topic paper*. Nottingham, UK: Department for Education.

PART III
CONCLUSIONS AND IMPLICATIONS FOR FUTURE RESEARCH

CHAPTER 11

THE POSSIBLE CONSEQUENCES OF ORGANIZATIONAL CITIZENSHIP BEHAVIORS IN DRUG AND ALCOHOL PREVENTION EDUCATION: SOME INSIGHTS FROM ISRAELI TEACHERS AND PRINCIPALS

Izhar Oplatka

ABSTRACT

The purposes of this study was to obtain a greater understanding of the consequences of teacher organizational citizenship behavior (OCB) for the teachers who perform OCBs in prevention education as well as for their classrooms and schools as perceived by the teachers and the principals themselves. Based on semi-structured interviews with 30 high-school teachers and 10 principals in the Israeli educational system, the present study found both positive and negative consequences of teacher OCB in prevention education. Among the positive consequences are

Discretionary Behavior and Performance in Educational Organizations: The Missing Link in Educational Leadership and Management
Advances in Educational Administration, Volume 13, 277–297
ISSN: 1479-3660/doi:10.1108/S1479-3660(2012)0000013016

self-fulfillment, social acknowledgment of the teacher's unique contribution, high levels of trust toward the teacher, and a sense of professional effectiveness. Among the negative consequences are negative relationships with colleagues, depletion of personal energy, and limited time with the teacher's family. Theoretical and practical insights are provided.

INTRODUCTION

While there has been considerable interest in conceptualizing the components of employee organizational citizenship behavior (OCB) and identifying the factors promoting or inhibiting the frequencies of this kind of behavior in work organizations, there remains a paucity of research on the outcomes of employee OCB, let alone of those of teacher OCB. Thus, the literature on employee OCB (including teachers) is replete with definitions, conceptualizations, factors, and variables related to OCB but lacks sufficient reference to the plausible impact of this behavior upon employees, clients, and organizations.

The current chapter focuses on the outcomes for teachers who perform OCBs in drug and alcohol prevention education based on an interpretative, qualitative study conducted among high school teachers and principals in the Israeli educational system. One of the purposes of this exploratory study was to obtain a greater understanding of the consequences of teacher OCB for the teachers who perform OCBs in prevention education as well as for their classrooms and schools as perceived by the teachers and the principals themselves.

The present study has both theoretical and practical contributions. On the theoretical level, this study used a special work task, drug and alcohol prevention education in schools, to provide insight on the perceived impact of OCB on the teachers themselves and the organizations. Researchers of OCB have long indicated that this type of behavior is critical to organizational efficiency and effectiveness because it reduces the need to allocate extra resources for maintenance functions within organizations (Bolino, 1999; Organ, 1997).

On the practical level, it is becoming important to trace the benefits of OCB for teachers and schools, especially in drug and alcohol prevention education, a kind of work task that consumes much mental and physical energy, due to schools' dependency on teachers who are committed to school goals and willing to exert considerable effort beyond minimal formal role expectations, as Somech and Bogler (2002) postulated. After all, what happens to employees after performing OCBs may affect their propensity to perform them again (Reed & Kidder, 2005). In this sense, the current study might provide policy makers and school principals with the perceived benefits of teacher OCB in prevention education, thereby enabling them to devise a system of "incentives" to persuade teachers to perform OCBs in this important education system.

In the following section, the limited research on the consequences of employee OCB in noneducation sectors and the relatively few studies on teacher OCB are discussed. The next section then goes on to depict the research methods and the main findings of this study. The chapter concludes by discussing future research directions and practical insights from this study.

CONSEQUENCES OF ORGANIZATIONAL CITIZENSHIP BEHAVIOR

It is commonly held that OCB has positive contributions to individuals (e.g., colleagues, clients) and an organization as a whole (Kidwell, Mossholder, & Bennett, 1997). Yet, much of what we know about the outcomes of OCB is speculative in nature rather than based on empirical evidence. Thus, we may point to a relationship between OCB and organizational performance and success on the one hand and individual consequences of this kind of behavior (e.g., personnel evaluations, promotion, increased self-image, etc.), on the other hand.

Several writers have postulated that OCB is likely to result in higher levels of organizational performance and task effectiveness (e.g., Bolino, 1999; Chen, 2005; Motowidlo, 2000; Organ, 1988). Activities such as volunteering, persisting, helping, following rules, and endorsing organizational objectives are considered to increase workers' productivity and contribute to organizational success. A variety of reasons underlying the connection between OCB and organizational effectiveness/productivity, although mainly speculative in nature, are suggested in the literature. For example, Bolino (1999) postulated that OCB is thought to enhance organizational performance by reducing the need to allocate scarce resources to maintenance functions within organizations, and Borman and Motowidlo (1993) believed that OCB supports the organizational, social, and psychological environment within which the technical core must function.

However, one may question the ostensibly positive relationship between OCB and organizational success/effectiveness, in that OCB may not necessarily bring about positive outcomes for the organization. Helping coworkers, for instance, may be positive when it saves the organization's time and money on training. But, when an employee devotes much time to helping others, volunteering for committees, or pursuing extra-role projects, his/her own work may be neglected or impeded. The same behavior can be positive or negative depending on the context.

Let's move now to the second type of OCB consequences: the individual-oriented outcomes. Past research and theoretical writings on OCB have pointed to a number of potential outcomes of OCB for employees who engage in this kind of behavior, including better scores in managerial evaluations of subordinate performance, indirect rewards, and employees' increased positive image in the workplace (Lovell et al., 1999; MacKenzie, Podsakoff, & Fetter, 1993; Van Scotter, 2000). It has been found that OCB has some influence on managers' evaluation of performance and other related decisions regarding their subordinates (Podsakoff, MacKenzie, Paine, & Bachrach, 2000; Van Scotter, 2000). For example, in MacKenzie et al.'s (1993) sample of 261 insurance agents, OCB accounted for 44% of the variance in performance evaluations when common method variance was not controlled.

Likewise, Haworth and Levy (2001) claimed that the decision to perform OCBs appears to be contingent on whether the performance of OCB is seen to yield a positive, valid outcome that may be instrumental in achieving some bigger goal. They indicated that only when employees believe that their managers will fairly reward such behaviors they will enact and sustain OCBs. By the same token, one potential positive outcome for employees who help others is that they are more likely to receive help in return when needed (Deckop, Cirka, & Andersson, 2003).

But, when gender differences have been considered, it has been found that performing OCB does not always improve performance appreciation. Lovell et al. (1999) showed that women received higher OCB scores than men, but did not differ from men on performance ratings. They concluded that stereotypically women are assumed to be more helpful; therefore, they receive less appreciation for performing OCB than men.

THE RESEARCH ON TEACHER OCB

The few studies focusing on teacher OCB worldwide revolved around the construction of this behavior and its antecedents in teaching. For instance, it was found that Turkish elementary schoolteacher had a moderately positive perception on OCB (Yılmaz & Tasdan, 2009), while findings from USA and Portugal indicated similar perceptions of secondary teachers in these countries toward OCB in terms of helping others and serving students' needs (Dipaola & Mendes da Costa Neves, 2009).

A broad conceptualization of the components of teacher OCB, based on interviews with Israeli teachers, supervisors, and principals, is suggested by Oplatka (2006). Among these components are supportive behaviors toward students and colleagues, initiation of changes and innovations in teaching, strong orientation toward the organization, and deep loyalty to the teaching profession. Likewise, teachers' emotional management is considered to be a discretionary, voluntary-based role element, rather than a prescribed one (Oplatka, 2007).

Several studies have shown a wide variety of variables and antecedents related to teacher OCB. Thus, results from 251 Israeli teachers have pointed to various determinants for different forms of OCB. Job satisfaction was positively related to OCB; self-efficacy was positively related only to OCBs toward the team and the organization (Somech & Drach-Zahavy, 2000). In another study, it was found that teachers who had a high sense of status in their work tended to invest in more OCBs than other teachers (Bogler & Somech, 2004). A later study among Israeli educators identified three major determinants of teacher OCB; the school principal (e.g., participative leadership), the teacher's character (e.g., open-minded), and the school's climate (Oplatka, 2006).

A survey of 447 German teachers showed that OCB is expressed differently at different levels of the organization. Christ, Van Dick, Wagner, and Stellmacher (2003) concluded that identification is an important variable that contributes to differences in OCB. Along the same line, Dipola and Tschannen-Moran (2001), who conducted research among 1,874 teachers in public schools in Ohio and Virginia, concluded that teachers work toward the achievement of overall organizational goals while helping other teachers and students. Likewise, the pervasive climate of a school is strongly related to OCB.

RESEARCH METHODS

This study employed a qualitative research methodology to collect and analyze the empirical data. Following Erickson (1986), who claimed that the conceptions in qualitative research are revealed during data analysis, no defined hypothesis was tested in the study. However, based on the literature on OCB described above, it was assumed that teachers might perform these kinds of behaviors in their work.

Context

The local Ministry of Education, through its Department for Support and Prevention, is responsible for the management and development of prevention programs in the Israeli State Education System. The prevention includes a wide variety of areas such as violence, sexual abuse, drugs, and alcohol. The activities and initiatives regarding the last two areas are conducted in close cooperation with the prevention department of the Israeli Anti-Drug Authority that is responsible for formulating national education and prevention policies and developing prevention programs.

This cooperation has led to the inclusion of a substance prevention program into the Life-Skills program, which is an inclusive part of the educational curriculum, from kindergartens to 12th grades. At each grade, the prevention program focuses on a different topic based on the age of the students, ranging from substances which are harmful to the body, cigarette smoking, and driving while intoxicated. The approach underlying these programs is comprehensive, that is, promoting a healthy lifestyle beginning as early as kindergarten children and continues until adulthood. This approach focuses on developing and using one's inherent resources and strengths. The programs and activities focus on identifying high risk factors and reinforcing protective factors and positive influences and strengths among children and youth in general and among specific high risk populations in particular (Israel Anti-Drug Authority, website: http://www.antidrugs.org.il/template/default_e.asp?maincat=46).

Junior and high schools are required by law to deliver the formal prevention programs to its students and the school counselors represent the Department of Support and Prevention in the Ministry of Education in face of the principal and the teaching staff. But, the professional educators are only responsible for prevention; treatment is at the hands of professionals out of school.

Participants

Seeking answers to the research questions, a total of 40 semi-structured interviews were conducted, 30 with secondary school teachers and 10 with secondary school principals from the State Education System, the largest one in Israel. Seven of the 30 teachers were male. The average age of the teachers was 43.51 (29–61); the average number of years in teaching was 19.44 (5–35). The sample included those who were married with children ($n = 28$) and single ($n = 2$). The teachers, who work in the Southern, Central, and Tel Aviv districts of the Israeli educational system, came from urban ($n = 23$) and rural areas ($n = 7$). Three worked in upper-class communities, 11 worked in upper middle-class communities, 9 worked in middle-class communities, while 7 worked in lower middle-class ones. They represented a highly homogenous group in terms of religiosity and class: all belonged to the middle class and were tenured.

Five of the 10 principals were male. The average age of the principals was 52 (34–64), and the average years of experience in principalship was 12.2 (5–29). They worked in the Southern, Central, and Tel Aviv districts of the Israeli educational system, and were all married with children.

Participant Selection

Due to the need to focus on a homogenous group of subjects in a qualitative inquiry that aimed at understanding a certain phenomenon profoundly (Marshall & Rossman, 1995; Paton, 2002), the teachers in this study were selected using criterion sampling, that is, all subjects who meet some criteria. Thus, the research assistant approached supervisors and other informants (e.g., school counselors), who were asked to recommend teachers with five years of teaching experience and over who were considered to do more than is formally needed in drug and alcohol prevention education, not in order to impress others, but for the sake of the whole. Informants were provided with adjectives such as caring, helpful, committed, and dedicated to prevent drug or alcohol use among their students to indicate the kind of person that the researcher was seeking, and were also asked not to recommend those who applied for principalship roles in any district.

Based on the literature on OCB, it was believed that teachers meeting the above-indicated criteria were more likely to adopt OCBs in prevention education, and therefore could provide us with much knowledge about this kind of behavior in schools. Thus, after receiving recommendations from two sources, the two to three teachers most highly recommended were contacted by telephone and a face-to-face meeting was scheduled with teachers who agreed to participate.

It is worth noting, nonetheless, that because only teachers initially recommended were interviewed, some degree of deviation may have occurred; teachers who engage in OCBs and suit the rest of the criteria specified, but were not appreciated or recognized by their principals/ counselors were excluded. Coupled with research findings that indicated that many OCBs occur out of sight of the superior (Allen, Barnard, Rush, & Russell, 2000), this potential weakness was taken into account in the interpretation of the data gathered in this study.

Procedure

One to two semi-structured, face-to-face interviews were conducted with the participants during 2009–2010, either at the respondent's home or school, in order to allow the interviewee to be in the most preferable and safest setting. This instrument was selected with the intention to enable the researcher to collect data that closely represented the personal perspectives of individual participants while concurrently benefiting from the advantage of using an "interview guide" that helps make the interviews of different individuals more systematic (Marshall & Rossman, 1995; Paton, 2002). It is important to note that the interviewer avoided using the term "OCB" or any other normatively desirable term (e.g., to assist) in order to refrain from indicating "social desirability" (Paton, 2002).

At the beginning of each interview the interviewer obtained permission to record the interview and promised complete confidentiality. In the first part of the interview, participants were asked about teachers' perceived formal duties in prevention education, in order to establish the difference between required and non-required role tasks in prevention education. The questions were shaped to inquire about specific tasks and job requirements that could be demanded and monitored by a superior.

Questions about perceptions regarding non-required tasks and role behaviors in prevention education were asked in the second part. Participants were similarly asked about behaviors they perform in drug and alcohol prevention education that they do not perceive to be part of their formal role obligations, and their motivation for performing them. In addition, they were asked about facilitating factors they perceived to be related to non-prescribed behaviors, and about the possible outcomes of their OCBs.

The manual analysis of the interview data followed the four stages described by Marshall and Rossman (1995): "organizing the data," "generating categories, themes and patterns," "testing any emergent hypotheses," and "searching for alternative explanations." This analysis aims at identifying central themes in the data, searching for recurrent experiences, feelings, and attitudes, so as to be able to code, reduce, and connect different categories to central themes. The coding is guided by the principles of "comparative analysis" (Strauss & Corbin, 1998), which includes the comparison of any coded element in terms of emergent categories and subcategories.

In order to increase trustworthiness and reliability in the research, the analysis was strengthened by structured analysis and peer review, two common indicators qualitative researchers use to build confidence in their analytic procedures (Marshall & Rossman, 1995). However, consistent with most qualitative research that assume that those studied interpret reality from multiple perspectives for varying purposes (LeCompte & Preissle, 1993), this research was interested in revealing participants' subjective ideas about reality, rather than finding some objective reality. Yet, some comparisons with the existing literature on OCB were made to intensify validity of the data.

FINDINGS

The inductive analysis of the interview data revealed several forms of teacher OCB in prevention education, including proactive responses to any suspicious signs of drug or alcohol use in students, enrichment of the formal prevention program, mentoring and listening to every student, deep involvement in school events focusing on drugs and alcohol, and incorporation of drug/alcohol-related contents in any subject matter.

When the consequences of these elements of OCB in prevention education, the focus of this chapter, were explored, they were perceived by the interviewees to have both positive and negative influences. Among the positive consequences are self-fulfillment, social acknowledgement of the teacher's unique contribution, high levels of trust toward the teacher, and a sense of professional effectiveness. Among the negative consequences are negative relationships with colleagues, depletion of personal energy, and limited time with the teacher's family.

Self-Fulfillment

The interviewees emphasized the high self-fulfillment a teacher may feel who goes beyond formal role expectations. Put simply, helping at-risk student or rescuing a child who has begun to drink alcohol excessively engenders "a sense of well-being and personal fulfillment among the teachers," as one principal (34) indicated. The teachers broadened the meaning of self-fulfillment and connected it to their OCB:

Interviewer: Why do you go beyond formal role requirement at work?
Teacher: This is the big question. Many of my friends who don't work in schools ask me all the time why I need to work so hard and do so much for the kids who are actually not my own kids. I don't know what to say. This is something that motivates me, this is something internal, it makes me happy, fulfilled (29).

Another teacher (45) explained the meaning of her self-fulfillment following her OCBs:

The reward I get is not financial, it is a huge self-fulfillment. The reward is that if a child calls me in distress, and sees me as a meaningful figure in his life, I think that for the love they give me, their gratitude, the connections I have with them many years after they graduated, this is simply amazing, stunning, this is, in fact, the appreciation they express towards me.

Indeed, the interviews are embedded with references to the high self-fulfillment the teachers feel when they engaged in OCBs. Teachers indicated that "it gives much fulfillment if you help an at-risk student," "I enjoy I can rescue a student before he becomes addicted," or "I feel I saved this child." The next quote illustrates the existential meaning the teachers feel when they engaged in OCBs:

Interviewer: I understand that you go beyond formally required in prevention education. What are the results of that?
Interviewee: I enjoy, first of all, I want to have a meaning for what I do here ... the students always ask me, I am a teacher of accounting, so they say, you can earn a lot of money as an accountant, why are you a teacher? So, I try to explain to them that I enjoy my work, that I'm happy when I can change something in their life (53).

Helping at-risk students and leading them in a positive direction in society, or simply exposing the students to the many hazards underlying the use of drug and alcohol increases the self-fulfillment of the teachers, and probably urges them to keep going beyond what is formally required of teachers by law.

Public Recognition for the Teacher's Unique Contribution

A person's need for social recognition and appreciation of his/her performance is met by some OCBs. The teachers in this study, who represent a group of self-starters, pointed to the considerable appreciation they get from their school principals and several teachers in their school, even from their peers who do not perform OCBs in school. This is evident in the following quote:

When you are a self-starter you never stop and say to yourself, I am a self-starter ... I feel I am appreciated very much, very much. People like what I do in school very much ... (46).

The teacher's perception is further supported by one of the principals (50):

Interviewer: What benefits do the teachers who go beyond formal role requirement gain? Interviewee: Much appreciation, much, much esteem. I think this is one of the sole rewards I have to give them, and I think it's of great value to them ...

Particularly, the teachers emphasized the great importance they attach to their students' recognition and appreciation of what they actually do for them. In their view, their OCBs in prevention education (and beyond) increase their students' trust in them and the students' academic success. This is manifested in the subsequent citation:

I know that at the end, the student appreciate what I do for them [because] they know I do care about them, they know I care very much about them, and their parents know it too. I'll give you an example about the boy who stayed sleeping at home and didn't come to school. We told him he isn't moving to the 12th grade if he doesn't improve his marks ... and he had to choose between his future and his drinking [of alcohol]. So, his mother came to parent meeting and was very happy to meet me because what I had done for him, [because of] my insistence on not letting him fall into alcohol ... (A teacher, 61)

The teacher's ability to be attentive to the students, a form of teacher OCB in prevention education, is considered to result in higher levels of trust between the teacher and the students. The trust is expressed by many forms of gratitude or appreciation among the students toward the teacher, as one teacher (32) indicated:

... and you should see the appreciation of the students. Do you see this clock? I got it now for my birthday from my 12th graders. They came to my home on my birthday with flowers. You see, these are the small things, not because of the gifts, but [because of] their esteem. These little things are my self-fulfillment, my happiness, this is the real approval, not a letter from the principal, not thanks from her, but from the kids ...

The trust between students and teacher leads some students, among other things, to report to the teacher about at-risk students who might become addicted to alcohol, a report that enables the teacher to further assist students in the incipient stages of their drinking/addiction. One teacher (45) remarked:

Look, I think, and this is the issue of my role definition as a homeroom teacher. I see my role as a homeroom teacher as the mother of the students in school. I speak with them at eye level, and I respect them very much, and I respect their requests, and they see how much I love my work and they respect it, and express gratitude and appreciate that ...

For these teachers, then, receiving respect and esteem from the students is a result of their OCBs in different aspects of their work, including prevention education, and also their displays of positive emotions, an element of teacher OCB found in past research.

A Sense of High Work Effectiveness

The last positive outcome of teacher OCB perceived by the interviewees in this study refers to the teacher's sense of high work effectiveness. Thus, teachers who go far beyond formal role expectations in prevention education felt that their OCBs in this sort of education influenced positively on their students, both personally and academically. For example, a teacher who initiated a meeting between his students and a formerly drug-addictive man felt that "because of me the students will not touch this garbage, as [the meeting] changed their opinions towards drugs," and another teacher believed that due to her efforts to enrich prevention education in her class, her students "feel it's really dangerous." Teacher OCB in prevention education, then, leads students to attain in-depth insights on the hazards of drug/alcohol use and even to terminate use of these materials, as one teacher (46) described:

> One of the female students, who had been hospitalized due to excessive drinking of alcohol, when I said good bye to her, I told to myself she would never come to visit the school, because my meetings with her during my attempts to stop her drinking were very difficult, very harmful, and her parents didn't cooperate. So, I said to myself she wouldn't come to visit, most of my graduates come to visit me in school. One day she came, and I told her I hadn't expected she would come to visit. She asked me why, and I explained to her what I am telling you now. She told me I was wrong. It was difficult, it was harmful, but it was also very meaningful, and I realized then that because of our meetings she forced her parents to provide her with proper treatment for withdrawal.

Additionally, the interviewees believed that their students were more successful academically and socially due to their OCBs in prevention education and in other work aspects in school. When asked to mull over the consequences of teacher OCB in prevention education, one teacher (29) said:

> Also students who didn't believe in themselves came to believe in themselves. This is something that changes their self-confidence. Students who used to do nonsense, that we thought we would see them in the streets or addicted to drugs, entered the classrooms again. My students feel they owe me, as if they learned for me. That means, I managed to

harness them. They think twice before they do any nonsense ... I had a student who tried drugs. From the moment I discovered that he used drug during the summer vacation, I told that to my principal and we invited the parents, and we began to talk with him, and talk, and he stopped. He stopped, and this is everything for me.

The academic success of a student, especially of a student who tried drugs, seems to enhance teacher work satisfaction considerably. These students are perceived as those who feel moral commitment toward the teacher who goes beyond formal role requirement and refrain from at-risk behaviors. Likewise, the teachers believed that teacher OCB in prevention education enabled them to better respond to drug and alcohol use among adolescents. In this sense, they assumed that schools in which most of the teachers go by the book in prevention education is "a school in which the average of drug users is larger as if a teacher doesn't open her eye and doesn't peek around, and isn't really involved in the prevention program, but covers the material in order to tick a 'V,' like a grocery list, then she misses the main purpose [of this program] (a teacher, 42)."

One can see the relationship constructed subjectively by the teachers in this study between their OCBs in prevention education and the school's ability to minimize drug and alcohol addiction among the students. Their optimistic belief in this relationship is reflected in an interview with a 59-year-old teacher. When asked how the school can combat drug and alcohol use among adolescents, she replied:

If [the school] decides to invest in prevention education, but to focus on it seriously, including providing resources, and not only to do a workshop and to tick a 'V' ... if you stick to the program of the Ministry of Education in drugs, the students will see it as one of many things in the school, not more than that. That's the way they will perceive it. I mean, if we talk about it again and again, and use multiple teaching methods. In one of the classes, one female student suddenly told us a personal story. She simply said: "listen folks, I was a witness yesterday to something in my family, and only yesterday I understood my teacher. I want to talk about that." At that moment, I think, it became a kind of dialogue between her and the class, and then I felt that something finally clicked among the students, I mean, I can't say that all the problems in the world have gone, and nothing will happen, but I felt that at that point, I fulfilled my mission ...

Underlying teacher OCBs in prevention education are optimism and belief in that the performance of OCBs in drug/alcohol education may make the students internalize the hazards of using these materials.

Thus far, we have discussed the perceived positive consequences of teacher OCBs in prevention education as it was revealed in the inductive analysis used in this study. The next three consequences are substantially negative and revolve around the staff, the teacher, and the teacher's family.

Negative Relationships with the Staff

Some interviewees made an association between their OCBs in prevention education and their negative relationship with their peers in the staffroom. From their point of view, due to their propensity to go beyond formal role requirements at school, they are perceived by some teachers as a queer fish. Sometimes, the teacher's unique ways to handle students are perceived as a threat to other teachers and, sometimes, the teacher's success leads some teachers to be jealous. This perceived effect is echoed in the subsequent citation:

> The teachers reject my way ... look, I'm a person who never fights, never fights with anyone. By the way, in my character I never argue about anything ... but some role incumbents who don't know how to be educators, always scream, tell me that I am a queer fish and many other insults ... (A teacher, 40)

While the teacher in the above quote is blamed for choosing unacceptable teaching methods in prevention education, sometimes teacher OCB is perceived as a threat to teachers who go by the book, and the inevitable result is conflicts among the teachers:

> When you go beyond what is expected from teachers, many teachers feel this teacher threatens them, where I am when others go beyond. This is problematic because, on one hand, you try to be a model, not that I try to say that everything is okay in my class, but to be a kind of a model of imitation or something to aspire for. On the other hand, there are teachers who feel threatened, and I pay for that and they pay. I mean, I could come and say, okay, I will be like the rest, this is what used to be so far in the school and we can go on with that. But, no, it's not me, I can't do that. (A teacher, 35)

The recurrent motive in the teachers' narratives is of anger from their colleagues due to their tendency to perform OCBs in school. The interviewees used terms such as hostility, jealousy, threat, failing, and the like to demonstrate the anger directed toward them by some colleagues in school when they receive positive feedback from principals to a degree of recoiling from any connection with them. This perceived consequence is illustrated in the interview with a 32-year-old teacher:

> Interviewer: How do the teacher relate to you, as you are a self-starter?
> Teacher: Many are deterred from that, many try to put a spoke in my wheel. I am a threat to many teachers who feel that they don't provide what is needed in the school sufficiently even after thirty years. But, I am a kind of a threat, people have words with me. I coped with a very difficult year in the school, as a member of the teacher union. In the election, people slandered me. Sometimes, the responses to my positive energy are sentences such as: what do you want with your energy? What happened to you? Instead of taking my energy positively, they reject it ...

However, when the interviewer asked the teacher if the other teachers' negative response to her is overwhelming emotionally, she surprisingly replied:

No, not at all, why? I will never be like them. It has never broken me, but it makes me think how people can be so mean, why? Instead of praying that they will gain such energy, they have such nasty comments.

This teacher's response resembles those of other interviewees who witnessed hostile responses from the staff to their OCBs but were never dissuaded by them because they got used to it and learned how to minimize their plausible negative damages. This is echoed in the following quotes:

Interviewer: How are your OCBs seen by the staff?
Teacher (46): It is hard, it is very hard, but they learned how to work with me. It is very hard. I give my work assignments [to my colleagues], my papers, my ideas, I love to give very much.

If people talk I don't hear ... so if the teachers talk, I won't hear that. No. Even if all the teachers are mean, I won't tell you it won't bother me, it will. Sometimes I say to myself I don't need to give a damn, it is annoying, I don't like the staff's talks. The kids are important to me. I put the staff aside. I also tell the teachers they are not where my head is. First of all, the kids are. (A teacher, 55)

Those who energize the teachers and empower them in front of the staff are the students and chiefly their success, on one hand, and their strong belief in their educational perspective, on the other. Nevertheless, one should bear in mind that hostile responses by the staff are not inevitable; few interviewees indicated they had never experienced such responses in the staffroom as their OCBs are not perceived negatively by their colleagues in school.

Depletion of Personal Energy

The overemphasis given by the teachers in this study to issues of drug and alcohol education is perceived to result in their depletion of personal energy. The interviewees described themselves as people who take the students' problems and difficulties to heart and waste a lot of personal energy when they are engaged in OCBs at work. The personal and mental prices paid by teachers who go beyond formal role requirement are expressed, explicitly and implicitly, by a 29-year-old teacher:

There are many days when I return home troubled. For example, yesterday I got a phone call from a mother whose daughter had run away from school a day before, and there are many problems with her. And the other teachers sit here and drink, but I am worried, and my caring is not limited to my working hours in school. There are people who maybe tell to themselves, what do I need it for? Why should I work like that? To run in the middle of the night in case one of my students needs me SOS ... I think that mentally I can't absorb all their problems. Sometimes, it seems that I am drawn so much into their problems that I have no time for all the other things in my life ... when you are so involved, their problems 'chase' after you all the time, your brain works all the time, and you think about the kids, you are worried about them, and there are moments I can't hold it anymore emotionally.

The teacher declares loudly that she can neither cope anymore with the problems of her at-risk students nor to continue caring for them excessively. Another example of the negative effect of OCBs on teachers who engaged in this kind of behaviors comes from the story of a teacher (42) who helped a family whose daughter (and a student of this teacher) had become addictive to drugs:

... This is part of you, you always think about it, all the time. I felt so sorry about this girl, because she was really a good person, a charming girl, and it hurt me. I mean, I was glad we caught her in time, I mean, in the beginning I saw it and I was happy we found her, and she wanted so much to get out of drugs, and I think that today she is fine. But, all this takes a lot of energy from you, you can't be disconnected from that ... it hurt me for her, for her parents, to see how broken her parents were, you see. This takes a lot of physical energies from you.

Another teacher (45) reported on the implications of a similar story on her, about a student who had become addictive to alcohol:

I went through a very difficult period with the student I found drinking alcohol excessively. First of all, because he pushed all the other students against me, and also because I was worried about him: what will be with him? Will he go to a treatment or not? Because his mother made a big mistake, and told him I told her about his drinking ... so, sometimes I wasn't sleeping in the night, I thought about it, I took his case with me out of school ... there is the price of anxiety, fear, energy, mental prices resulting from consistent care, what to do ... sometimes this has impact on your own mood, you wake up in the night thinking how to solve his problem ...

Furthermore, some teachers indicated that their personal prices result not only from their OCBs in prevention education which is considered to be very complex and uncertain, but also from parents of the students' incompetence to prevent drug/alcohol use among their own children. In this sense, the teacher who performs OCBs in prevention education takes on responsibility pertaining naturally to the parents themselves, and is required to cope concurrently with the student and the parents who deny the new condition of their child.

Likewise, a recurrent motive in many interviews refers to the centrality of drug/alcohol education in a teacher's mind leading him/her to devote much time and energy to this issue. This, in turn, increases the teacher's overload and curtails his/her amount of energy, as manifested clearly in the following quote:

> Many times we are drawn to situations that are far beyond our abilities. Just as I told you before, we have no formal training in prevention. We handle these issues voluntarily but sometimes there are cases that consume our energy considerably. These are many things in the school, and like the work with children and in education, in general, sometimes you become drained. I have a supportive family and good friends who support me when I am drained, so I'm re-energized, not at once, I'm not superman, but thanks for my relatives, I can come back to myself (46).

The teacher's energy-depletion is accompanied, sometimes, with a sense of frustration and helplessness resulting from the difficulty to cope successfully with drug or alcohol use. This makes it necessary to support the teachers who go beyond formal role requirements to prevent their burnout and disenchantment at a certain point in their career cycle.

The Familial Price

The last negative consequence of teacher OCB in prevention education refers to the teacher's family. Note, however, that this kind of consequence is perceived as a minor one by our interviewees. Thus, there are some interviewees who emphasized that they pay familial prices for being "self-starters" at work, while others tend to underestimate these prices, claiming they pay merely temporary and minor prices. The voice of the first group is illustrated in the following quotes:

> To do more than what is required by the book has prices, like less time for the family, even if I want or don't want. Less time for myself, I mean, I neglect many things related to the family ... (A teacher, 45)

> The only think I feel sometimes is I have no sufficient time for my own kids ... there are teachers who get home at one pm, they have nothing to do ... but I never know when my work ends, never ... so my own kids sometimes pay the price. (A teacher, 47)

Teacher OCB, then, requires much time and is done, occasionally, at the expense of the teacher's leisure time with family because the teacher cannot balance work and family demands effectively:

> I have a very supportive husband, but [teacher OCB] does have consequences. There are those days you come home frustrated and you can't leave the troubles at school. Too often I come home angry and sad, and I believe it influences my husband, my own kids ... (A teacher, 29)

In contrast, some teachers highlighted the moderate impact of teacher OCB on their familial sphere. Thus, one teacher (53) indicated succinctly that "there are times when the family pays the price, but these are times that we all have got used to already." Another teacher (42) claimed emphatically that "I don't think there are any prices at all." Having claimed that she underestimated the influence of her excessive work in prevention education on her family:

> Look, sometimes I give up on things at home because I am always busy, always at the computer, so I am less engaged in other things at home, for sure, but this is not such a huge price of course.

CONCLUDING COMMENTS

From the analysis of the interview data, a number of insights can be provided. First, among the positive consequences of teachers OCB in prevention education are attainment of self-fulfillment when teachers manage to inculcate the hazards of drug/alcohol use in the students' mind, parents' and students' awareness of the teacher's unique contribution to the students and the school, and a sense of effectiveness in the teacher's role as a result of teachers' ability to fulfill their purposes in respect to the students' healthy growth and development. These consequences align with research findings suggesting positive correlative relationships between OCB and increased positive image in the workplace (e.g., Van Scotter, 2000), greater organizational performance (e.g., Bolino, 1999), and higher job satisfaction (Somech & Drach-Zahavy, 2000).

Second, the negative consequences of teacher OCB in prevention education are found in the negative relationship that can exist between the teacher who goes beyond formal role expectations and other teachers, who express hostility, jealousy, and anger toward the teacher with OCB. Other consequences include the depletion of the teacher's physical and mental energy due to excessive treatment of at-risk students, emotional load, fatigue, frustration, disappointment, and inability to absorb the students' problems incessantly.

One can see the outcomes of teacher OCB in prevention education found in this study as a combination of consequences toward the self (self-fulfillment, public recognition, depletion of energy, familial price), toward students (a sense of high work effectiveness), and toward organization (negative relationships with staff). From this perspective it is likely that teacher OCB is of much influence on the teacher's self as four outcomes indicated by our interviewees have been referred to the teacher him/herself. Only one outcome is related to the students' own benefit and one negative outcome is related to the school as an organization. Further research could develop this perspective and examine the consequence of teacher OCB toward students and the school distinctively.

What was absent in our data is consequences of teacher OCB in prevention education that are related to positive emotions (e.g., enthusiasm, work satisfaction) that have been identified in past research (Oplatka, 2009). This might be accounted for by the kind of content teachers face when they deal with drug and alcohol education, or the negative feature of drug education that leave limited room for such emotional responses. Likewise, the interviewees' transcripts lack sufficient reference to the students' responses toward teacher OCB in prevention education to allow clear conclusion in this respect.

Evidence concerning the consequences of teacher OCB is extremely thin, however. Subsequent research on teacher OCB ought to pay more attention to independent variables of this kind of behaviors, the perceived effects of teacher OCB in different educational arenas, and the association between teachers' motives to perform OCBs and their perceived effects of these behaviors. Future research should attempt to use mixed methods to examine both the relationships between teacher OCB and a wide variety of variables and explore teachers' subjective interpretations of the benefits of OCB for students, schools, and themselves. Subsequent research should also begin to inquire into how teacher OCB is perceived by parents, principals, and teachers to better understand its effect on schools and schooling, and learn about its "image" in the school community.

Additionally, understanding the positive and negative consequences of teacher OCB is beneficial also on a practical level. Principals, supervisors, and policy makers can use this understanding to develop strategies aimed at encouraging teachers to engage in OCBs at work. Conversely, the exposure of the negative consequences may help principals to cope successfully with plausible hostile responses of teachers or work overload of teachers who perform OCBs extensively.

ACKNOWLEDGMENT

The research was supported by a grant from the Israel Anti-Drug authority. The author is indebted to its chief scientist's assistance and support in conducting the data collection.

REFERENCES

Allen, T. D., Barnard, S., Rush, M. C., & Russell, J. E. A. (2000). Ratings of organizational citizenship behavior: Does the source make a difference? *Human Resource Management Review*, *10*(1), 97–114.

Bogler, R., & Somech, A. (2004). Influence of teacher empowerment on teachers' organizational commitment, professional commitment and organizational citizenship behavior in schools. *Teaching and Teacher Education*, *20*(3), 277–289.

Bolino, M. C. (1999). Citizenship and impression management: Good soldiers or good actors. *Academy of Management Review*, *24*(1), 82–98.

Borman, W. C., & Motowidlo, S. J. (1993). Expanding the criterion domain to include elements of contextual performance. In N Schmitt & W. C. Borman (Eds.), *Personnel selection in organizations* (pp. 71–98). San Francisco, CA: Jossey-Bass.

Chen, X. P. (2005). Organizational citizenship behavior: A predictor of employee voluntary turnover. In D. L. Turnipseed (Ed.), *Handbook of organizational citizenship behavior* (pp. 435–454). New York, NY: Nova Science Publishers.

Christ, O., Van Dick, R., Wagner, U., & Stellmacher, J. (2003). When teachers go the extra mile: Foci or organizational identification as determinants of different forms of organizational citizenship behavior among schoolteachers. *British Journal of Educational Psychology*, *73*(3), 329–341.

Deckop, J. R., Cirka, C. C., & Andersson, L. M. (2003). Doing unto others: The reciprocity of helping behavior in organizations. *Journal of Business Ethics*, *47*(2), 101–113.

Dipaola, M., & Mendes da Costa Neves, P. M. (2009). Organisational citizenship behaviour in American and Portuguese public schools. *Journal of Educational Administration*, *47*(4), 490–507.

Dipola, M., & Tschannen-Moran, M. (2001). Organizational citizenship behavior in schools and its relationship to school climate. *Journal of School Leadership*, *11*, 424–445.

Erickson, F. (1986). Qualitative methods of inquiry. In M. C. Wittrock (Ed.), *Third handbook of research on teaching* (pp. 23–42). New York, NY: Macmillan.

Haworth, C. L., & Levy, P. E. (2001). The importance of instrumentality beliefs in the prediction of organizational citizenship behaviors. *Journal of Vocational Behavior*, *59*(1), 64–75.

Israel Anti-Drug Authority. *Prevention and education*. Retrieved from http://www.antidrugs. org.il/template/default_e.asp?maincat=46. Accessed on February 27, 2011.

Kidwell, R. E., Mossholder, K. W., & Bennett, N. (1997). Cohesiveness and organizational citizenship behavior: A multilevel analysis using work groups and individuals. *Journal of Management*, *23*(6), 775–793.

LeCompte, M. D., & Preissle, J. (1993). *Ethnography and qualitative design in educational research*. San Diego, CA: Academic Press.

Lovell, S. E., Kahn, A. S., Anton, J., Davidson, A., Dowling, E., Post, D., & Mason, C. (1999). Does gender affect the link between organizational citizenship behavior and performance evaluation? *Sex Roles*, *41*(5), 469–478.

MacKenzie, S. B., Podsakoff, P. M., & Fetter, R. (1993). The impact of organizational citizenship behavior on evaluations of sales performance. *Journal of Marketing*, *57*, 123–150.

Marshall, C., & Rossman, G. (1995). *Designing qualitative research*. Thousand Oaks, CA: Sage Publications.

Motowidlo, S. J. (2000). Some basic issues related to contextual performance and organizational citizenship behavior in human resource management. *Human Resource Management Review, 10*(1), 115–126.

Oplatka, I. (2006). Going beyond role expectations: Towards an understanding of the determinants and components of teacher organizational citizenship behavior. *Educational Administration Quarterly, 42*(3), 385–423.

Oplatka, I. (2007). Managing emotions in teaching: Towards an understanding of emotion displays and caring as non-prescribed role elements. *Teacher College Record, 109*(6), 1374–1400.

Oplatka, I. (2009). Organizational citizenship behavior in teaching: The consequences for teachers, pupils and the school. *International Journal of Educational Management, 23*(5), 375–389.

Organ, D. W. (1988). *Organizational citizenship behavior: The good soldier syndrome.* Lexington, MA: Lexington Books.

Organ, D. W. (1997). Organizational citizenship behavior: It's construct clean-up time. *Human Performance, 10*, 85–97.

Paton, M. Q. (2002). *Qualitative research and evaluation method.* Newbury Park, CA: Sage Publications.

Podsakoff, P. M., MacKenzie, S. B., Paine, J. B., & Bachrach, D. G. (2000). Organizational citizenship behaviors: A critical review of the theoretical and empirical literature and suggestions for future research. *Journal of Management, 26*(3), 513–563.

Reed, K. K., & Kidder, D. L. (2005). Work is its own reward: Employee perceptions about rewarding organizational citizenship behaviors. In D. L. Turnipseed (Ed.), *Handbook of organizational citizenship behavior* (pp. 243–266). New York, NY: Nova Science Publishers.

Somech, A., & Bogler, R. (2002). Antecedents and consequences of teacher organizational and professional commitment. *Educational Administration Quarterly, 38*(4), 555–577

Somech, A., & Drach-Zahavy, A. (2000). Understanding extra-role behavior in schools: The relationships between job satisfaction, sense of efficacy and teachers' extra-role behavior. *Teaching and Teacher Education, 16*, 649–659.

Strauss, A. L., & Corbin, J. (1998). *Basics of qualitative research: Techniques and procedures for developing grounded theory* (2nd ed.). Thousand Oaks, CA: Sage Publications.

Van Scotter, J. R. (2000). Relationship of task performance and contextual performance with turnover, job satisfaction, and affective commitment. *Human Resource Management Review, 10*(1), 77–93.

Yılmaz, K., & Tasdan, M. (2009). Organizational citizenship and organizational justice in Turkish primary schools. *Journal of Educational Administration, 47*(1), 108–126.

CHAPTER 12

WHAT DO WE KNOW ABOUT ASSISTANT PRINCIPALS? A CROSS-NATIONAL EXAMINATION OF THE FACTORS AFFECTING TASK PERFORMANCE, DISCRETIONARY PERFORMANCE, AND THE FUTURE CAREER ASPIRATIONS OF ASSISTANT PRINCIPALS

Ibrahim Duyar and Inayet Aydin

ABSTRACT

This study focuses on assistant principals, the "forgotten future work-force" of educational leadership. We explored the current landscape of assistant principalship within the context of work performance, including both task and discretionary performance, and the future career

Discretionary Behavior and Performance in Educational Organizations: The Missing
Link in Educational Leadership and Management
Advances in Educational Administration, Volume 13, 299–330
Copyright © 2012 by Emerald Group Publishing Limited
All rights of reproduction in any form reserved
ISSN: 1479-3660/doi:10.1108/S1479-3660(2012)0000013017

aspirations of assistant principals from a cross-national perspective. Specifically, the study aimed to fulfill the following objectives: (a) to identify the factors affecting the task and discretionary performance of assistant principals, (b) to identify the factors affecting three future career aspirations of assistant principals, and (c) to determine whether the influences of these factors differ by national origin. Personal initiative and perceived organizational support (POS) were the independent variables. This study also examined the demographic attributes of the *participants and their schools. Two randomly selected samples, which composed of 227 Turkish and 144 American assistant principals were the participants. The data-gathering instrument incorporated the revised versions of* the Personal Initiative Scale *(Fay & Frese, 2001), the* Perceived Organizational Support Scale *(Eisenberger, Huntington, Hutchison, & Sowa, 1986), and* the School Organizational Citizenship Behavior Scale *(DiPaola & Tschannen-Moran, 2001). The findings of the study showed that personal initiative and POS significantly predicted the task performance, discretionary performance, and certain future career aspirations of assistant principals. National origin appeared to be a significantly differentiating factor of the assistant principals' task performances, discretionary performances, and future career aspirations. We drew conclusions and provided suggestions for future research.*

Keywords: Assistant principals; task performance; discretionary performance/behavior; personal initiative; perceived organizational support; future career aspirations

INTRODUCTION

Assistant principalship is assumed to be the "training ground" (Kelly, 1987; Kwan, 2009) for principalship and the "entry point" (Marshall, 1992) for all administrative and executive positions in educational leadership. Despite these commonly accepted assumptions, a comprehensive review of the literature revealed a dearth of studies on assistant principalship compared with those focusing on principalship. In fact, many published work on assistant principalship have appeared in practitioner-oriented journals. Rather than focusing on identifying the standards, criteria, and conceptual frameworks of the expected roles and functions of assistant principals, these studies have attempted to determine what assistant principals do by examining their daily work practices in schools. These descriptive studies have mainly focused on the normative description of the roles played by assistant principals (Kwan, 2009). These studies have also demonstrated that the roles and tasks of assistant principals are often determined at the discretion of their principals (Marshall & Hooley, 2006). In many cases, assistant principals were assigned to tasks that the principals themselves did not want to perform (Ribbins, 1997).

More recent studies have demonstrated that the roles and tasks of assistant principals are arbitrarily assigned without much consideration for any established criteria or any proper planning process (Hess & Kelly, 2007; Kwan, 2009; Marshall & Hooley, 2006). In addition to the arbitrary and ill-defined practices in the field, the relevant literature has also shown that the roles of assistant principals lack clear direction (Mertz, 2000). Depending on their assigned roles and tasks, assistant principals were called "men in the middle" (Ribbins, 1997), "caretakers" (Koru, 1993), and "daily operations managers" (Porter, 1996). The lack of clearly defined job descriptions, unclear role expectations, and arbitrary task assignments resulted in a growing sense of dissatisfaction, anxiety, and unclear career aspirations among assistant principals (Lee, Kwan & Walker, 2009; Marshall & Hooley, 2006; Moore, 2009).

Given that assistant principals predominantly comprise the potential workforce of principalship and the entry positions for all other administrative positions in educational leadership, there is a great need for in-depth and empirical studies on assistant principalship. The current study responded to this need. Rather than providing a descriptive analysis of the roles played by assistant principals, this study examined the task performances of assistant principals from the perspective of the *Educational Leadership Policy Standards: 2008*, which were adopted by the National Policy Board for Educational Administration (Council of Chief State School Officers (CCSSO), 2008). Furthermore, this study also examined the discretionary performances of assistant principals. To our best knowledge, this aspect has not been investigated in the literature. We also investigated the future career aspirations of assistant principals to provide a comprehensive picture of the assistant principalship landscape. Most importantly, this study contributed to the existing research by studying assistant principalship from a comparative cross-national perspective for the first time.

THEORETICAL FOUNDATIONS

We identified and discussed the variables and relevant constructs that specify the focus of the study in this section. The section first establishes the dependent variables, which include work performance (i.e., task performance and discretionary behavior) and three future career aspirations of assistant principals (i.e., staying in assistant principalship, being promoted to principalship, and changing careers). In addition to the task performances of assistant principals, the current study introduces the concept of discretionary performance as a part of assistant principals' work performances. The second half of the section discusses the independent variables and their relationships, which lead to the hypotheses and research questions of the study.

Task Roles and Performances of Assistant Principals

Scholars have criticized the type and range of the *work outcomes* usually considered in work design research for being too limited in scope. Nevertheless, the traditional concepts of extrinsic *task roles* and *task performance* have remained central to the relevant research field and practice (Prabhu, 2007). Task roles and task performance are used interchangeably in performance evaluations. Task performance is defined as the expected core performances, which are usually explained in employees' formal job descriptions. Both individual task performance evaluations and studies on organizational effectiveness have emphasized the significance of individual task performance (Hoffman, Blair, Meriac, & Woehr, 2007; Motowidlo, 2003; Van Dyne, Cummings, & Parks, 1995). If task roles and/or performances are considered crucial to the effectiveness of an organization, then the following question must be answered: *what are the task roles and performances expected of assistant principals?* A historical examination of the task roles played by assistant principals will offer a good answer to this question.

The literature examining how assistant principals develop and maintain effective teaching and learning standards has evolved with the changes in education, school leadership research, and external communities (Condon & Clifford, 2010). Assistant principals were initially associated with the managerial aspects of school life. Early studies found that assistant principals' main tasks consisted of managing student discipline, student attendance, and other duties related to student affairs (e.g., managing school bus schedules) (Black, 1980; Ribbins, 1997). Hassenpflug (1991) reported that assistant principals have five major responsibilities: supervising cafeterias, enforcing student discipline, distributing textbooks, assigning lockers, and attending student activities. Similarly, Porter (1996) argued that assistant principals were responsible for administering student discipline, establishing teacher duty rosters, supervising substitute teachers, and providing instructional materials. Likewise, after conducting a meta-analysis of 26 studies, Scoggins and Bishop (1993) identified the enforcement of student discipline and student attendance as assistant principals' top two duties among their 20 most common obligations. Early studies revealed little about whether assistant principals have any influence on the overall leadership of schools.

More recent studies have started to focus on the delegation of principal responsibility to assistant principals, as their roles and tasks have become more diverse and have expanded in the wake of current accountability requirements, educational reforms, and changes in leadership perspectives (Kwan, 2009; Louis, Leithwood, Wahlstrom, & Anderson, 2010; Oliver, 2003; Weller & Weller, 2002). Recognizing that assistant principals need to receive training in areas outside of the managerial aspects of their jobs, Marshall (1992) stated, "Beyond these [managerial skills], assistant principals need to be prepared to fill roles and functions of administrators and to face the fundamental dilemmas in administration" (p. 89; cited in Oliver, 2005).

Mertz (2000) suggested that assistant principals become more involved in educational and instructional duties in addition to their managerial duties. Similarly, Hausman, Nebeker, McCreary, and Donaldson (2002) noted the increased involvement of assistant principals in curriculum and staff management. These researchers found that assistant principals have seven task roles: personnel management, student affairs, instructional leadership, professional development, resource management, public relations, and communication with stakeholders. In another study, Cranston, Tromans, and Reugebrink (2004) found that assistant principals have seven main task roles: strategic leadership, operational issues, staffing, parent and community relations, curriculum leadership, management and administration, and student affairs.

In a more recent study, Kwan (2009) studied the task roles and performances of assistant principals in Hong Kong by adopting Hausman et al.'s (2002) framework. Kwan adapted this framework to the Hong Kong context. The new and validated seven-factor model included the following factors: external communication and connection; quality assurance and accountability; teaching, learning, and curriculum; staff management; resource management; growth and development of leaders and teachers; and strategic direction and policy environment. Her study revealed that assistant principals spent most of their time in staff development followed by strategic direction and policy environment, which were once the sole domain of principals.

Scholars have also found that professional development programs for assistant principals reflect the recent changes to the task roles of assistant principals (i.e., from managerial tasks to educational and instructional leadership). In a longitudinal trend study of the professional development programs for assistant principals in California, Oliver (2005) observed that management-related professional development activities, such as legal updates, personnel procedures, and assessment procedures, dominated these programs in 2000 and 2002. In line with the national trend of focusing on educational and instructional outcomes, professional development programs for assistant principals have begun to place greater emphasis on student learning and curriculum. However, managerial skill development still dominates the professional development activities for assistant principals in most school districts.

Although scholars now better understand the task roles of assistant principals, this area of educational leadership still suffers from a lack of professional standards and criteria. As Murphy (2003) noted, "Standards for school leaders ... provide the means to shift the metric of school administration from management to educational leadership and from administration to learning while linking management and behavioral science knowledge to the larger goal of student learning" (pp. 18–19; cited in Oliver, 2005). In the absence of such norms, the best proxy for the context, measurement, and assessment of assistant principals' task performances is the professional standards developed for school principals. Borrowing from these standards makes sense because of two commonly accepted assumptions: (a) assistant principalship is the "training ground" for principalship and (b) assistant principalship is the "entry point" for all administrative positions in educational leadership.

Accordingly, the current study used the standards for principalship, which are better known as The Interstate School Leaders Licensure Consortium (ISLLC) Standards, to examine the task performances of assistant principals. The ISLLC standards have been revised several times with the following titles: Standards for School Leaders: 1996; the Standards for Advanced Programs in Educational Leadership: 2002; and Educational Leadership Policy Standards: 2008. The ISLLC standards provide guidance to state policymakers working to improve the preparation, licensure, evaluation, and professional development of educational leaders. Accordingly, states have developed their educational leadership standards in accordance with the ISLLC standards.

Discretionary Behaviors and Performances of Assistant Principals

Organizations in the 21st century operate in highly complex and dynamic environments that compel organizations to fulfill a diverse set of demands.

One ubiquitous challenge for contemporary organizations is that they have to change and adapt to increasingly dynamic environments (Fay & Sonnentag, 2010). For organizations to be competitive in such chaotic environments, their employees must do more than simply realize their task roles. As Bass stated in his seminal work (1985), a modern organization requires employees who can go well *"beyond the expectations"* of their formal job descriptions if it is to stay competitive. These employees proactively and willingly approach their work by adapting to additional roles and functions that are not prescribed by their narrowly described task roles and performances (Crant, 2000; Sonnentag, 2003).

Since Katz and Kahn (1996) and Bass (1985), several scholars have emphasized the importance of these new employee practices to the effective functioning of contemporary organizations (e.g., Chen, Eisenberger, Johnson, Ivan, & Aselage, 2009; Organ, Podsakoff, & MacKenzie, 2006). In a business environment characterized by flattened organizational structures, competition from international economies, and increased employee autonomy and responsibility, scholars have deemed the performances of discretionary work behaviors essential to effective organizational operations (Podsakoff, MacKenzie, Paine, & Bachrach, 2000). Researchers have introduced this strategic aspect of organizational behavior to the literature under different conceptions, such as *discretionary behavior* (Katz & Kahn, 1996), *extra-role behavior* (Van Dyne et al., 1995), *active performance* (Frese, 2008; Frese & Fay, 2001), *proactive performance* (Griffin, Neal, & Parker, 2007; Fay & Sonnentag, 2010), *pro-social behavior* (Brief & Motowidlo, 1986), *organizational citizenship behavior* or *good soldier syndrome* (Organ, 1988, 1997), and *contextual performance* (Borman & Motowidlo, 1993).

Although minor differences exist, all these different conceptions generally describe discretionary performance as the "individual behavior, that is discretionary, not directly or explicitly recognized by the formal reward system, and that in the aggregate promotes the effective functioning of the organization" (Organ, 1988, p. 27). In a more recent work, Organ (1997) revised the definition of discretionary behavior as "contributions to the maintenance and enhancement of the social and psychological context that supports task performance" (p. 91). He also identified discretionary behavior as an employee's "performance that supports the social and psychological environment in which task performance takes place" (p. 95). This view is aligned with Borman and Motowidlo's (1993) concept of *contextual performance*, Frese and Fay's (2001) concept of *active performance*, and Fay and Sonnentag's (2010) concept of *proactive performance*.

The relevant literature now has a consistent perspective on the classification and effects of discretionary behaviors (Hoffman et al., 2007). This perspective views *work performance* as a multidimensional notion consisting of *task performance* and *discretionary performance*. Most scholars accept the differentiation between core task performance and the various aspects of discretionary performance (Fay & Sonnentag, 2010). This view has validated the notion of *contextual performance*, which was first proposed by Borman and Motowidlo (1993) and later endorsed by Organ within the context of *organizational citizenship behaviors*. By following Organ's definition, this study treated the discretionary behaviors of assistant principals as a type of *work performance*.

Studies in the business literature and the industry have found that a strong relationship exists between employee task and discretionary performance (e.g., Campbell, 2000; Frese, 2008; Koys, 2001; Podsakoff, Whiting, Podsakoff, & Blume, 2009). By providing a meta-analytic summary of the relationship between discretionary performance and task performance, Conway (1999) found that the two constructs are empirically related yet distinct. This finding later received support from another meta-analytic study conducted by Hoffman et al. (2007). These authors found that discretionary performance and task performance are significantly correlated with one another (i.e., $r = .74$).

As Belschak and Hartog (2010) stated, discretionary employee behavior is crucial to an organization's ability to stay competitive in today's global economy. If an organization is facing difficult times and is only able to provide incentives to perform mandatory behaviors, then its employees' discretionary behaviors are of utmost importance to its viability (Tyler & Blader, 2003). This statement is particularly true in those educational organizations in which the schools operate in complex environments and in which the teachers and school administrators are expected to fulfill increasingly complex role expectations without relying on their organizations and supervisors (Somech & Drach-Zahavy, 2000; Somech & Ron, 2007). In such a fluid state, assistant principals are expected to engage in discretionary behaviors that may not be explicitly required by the formal reward system. However, their discretionary performances as aspiring leaders are essential to helping organizations effectively function and successfully respond to both current and future needs.

Although the organizational and industrial psychology literature has examined discretionary performances, few studies in the education field have examined this subject. Most of the existing studies in the education literature have focused on the discretionary performances of teachers. To the best of our knowledge, studies on the discretionary behaviors of principals and/or assistant principals do not exist.

Future Career Aspirations of Assistant Principals

Assistant principals are usually selected because of their visibility and success as school leaders. These active and innovative educators consider assistant principalship to be a necessary step in advancing their careers. Retaining these promising individuals in the system as assistant principals and/or promoting them to higher levels of leadership are the logical objectives of both the assistant principals and the school systems. Interestingly, researchers have rarely studied the recruitment, retention, and promotion of assistant principals. The existing literature found that assistant principals are feeling increasingly dissatisfied, anxious, and unclear about their future career aspirations because of the lack of clearly defined job descriptions, unclear role expectations, and arbitrary task assignments (Lee et al., 2009; Marshall & Hooley, 2006). A study revealed that secondary assistant principals were only marginally satisfied with their jobs and were not as interested in advancing their careers (Moore, 2009). Only 40% of the assistant principals expressed an intention to become promoted to principals.

Given this unstable environment, there is a great need for empirical studies that identify the factors that influence the future career aspirations of assistant principals. The current study targeted this need by examining whether the assistant principals' personal initiatives (i.e., employee), perceived organizational support (POS) (i.e., organization), and task and discretionary performances predict their future career aspirations.

We have already described the dependent variables of interest. The following sections introduce the independent variables and discuss the dynamics between them and the dependent variables.

Personal Initiatives of Assistant Principals

We are witnessing immense changes in the labor force, as contemporary jobs require greater flexibility, initiative, and consideration of global competition than before (Frese & Fay, 2001). In today's complex and competitive world, change seems to be the only constant, competition is the norm, and job security is a daydreamer's fantasy. With such a backdrop, taking charge, being proactive, and seizing the initiative are necessities rather than luxuries.

On this note, Erdogan and Bauer (2005, p. 859) state, "Organizations increasingly expect employees to fix things that they see as wrong, act on the information they have, and react to unusual circumstances by demonstrating proactive behaviors." Similarly, Crant (2000) writes the following: "Proactive people identify opportunities and act on them, show initiative, take action, and persevere until meaningful change occurs. In contrast, people who are not proactive exhibit the opposite patterns: they fail to identify, let alone seize, opportunities to change things. Less proactive individuals are passive and reactive, preferring to adapt to circumstances rather than change them" (p. 439). Thus, a proactive stance and personal initiative play important roles. As work becomes more dynamic and changeable, proactive personalities and personal initiative become even more critical determinants of organizational success and effectiveness.

Proactive behavior (Crant, 2000) conceptually overlaps with *personal initiative* (Fay & Frese, 2001), which appears more frequently in the recent literature. Despite different labels and theoretical underpinnings, these concepts, which are related to individual-level proactive behavior, typically focus on self-initiated and future-oriented behaviors that aim to change and improve the situation or oneself (Crant, 2000). Crant and Frese are two pioneers of these conceptually overlapping constructs. In the United States, Crant introduced proactive behavior. He (2000) defined proactive behavior as "taking initiative in improving current circumstances; it involves challenging the status quo rather than passively adapting present conditions" (p. 436). Proactive behavior encompasses various behaviors, such as taking charge and personal initiative, and is closely associated with flexible role expectations. Researchers have studied the effects of proactive behavior in varied fields, such as job performance (e.g., Crant, 2000) and leadership (e.g., Crant & Bateman, 2000). In a recent study, Prabhu (2007) found a robust relationship between proactive behavior and job performance after controlling for other plausible variables, such as affective commitment to change, job satisfaction, and intent to remain with the organization. In her study, proactive behavior accounted for 37.3% of the variance in job performance after controlling affective commitment to change and job satisfaction.

Similar to Crant, the European scholars Frese and Fay (2001) introduced the concept of personal initiative to the literature. They defined *personal initiative* as "work behavior characterized by its self-starting nature, its proactive approach and by being persistent in overcoming difficulties that arise in the pursuit of a goal" (p. 134). According to Frese and Fay (2001), three attributes distinguish personal initiative from other employee behaviors. First, people with personal initiatives are *self-starters* (i.e., they do something without being told or without fulfilling an explicit role requirement). Second, those with personal initiatives have *proactive* natures (i.e., they have a long-term focus and anticipate future problems or opportunities). Last, a person with personal initiative is *persistent* (i.e., he or she overcomes barriers to induce change or overcomes difficulties that arise while pursuing a goal).

Although scholars from various fields have studied personal initiative or proactive behavior, surprisingly little research on educational leadership exists. The lack of research does not suggest that personal initiative is unimportant to educational organizations. Because schools and their environments are changing fast and becoming more diverse, assistant principals must be prepared to address the situations that arise in the principal's absence or as their job responsibilities and tasks continue to change (Oliver, 2005). Personal initiative is the crucial attribute among all of the qualities that assistant principals require to become effective. One of the main reasons for this importance stems from the role ambiguity of assistant principals. Marshall and Hooley (2006) stated, "Assistant principals seldom have a consistent, well-defined job description, delineation of duties, or way of measuring outcomes from accomplishment of tasks" (p. 7). Role ambiguity indicates that the role and duties of assistant principals include many "gray areas" that include ill-defined, inconsistent, and occasionally incoherent expectations. If assistant principals wish to be effective in environments in which the roles are ambiguous, then they must understand situations and proactively and assertively take charge of certain tasks, regardless of their formal role expectations. Thus, the position of assistant principal is a tremendously challenging role that requires quickness, creativity, and most importantly, personal initiative.

By adopting Frese and Fay's view, the current study treated the personal initiative of an assistant principal as an important predictive variable of the work performances and future career aspirations of assistant principals. To date, no research is available on whether individual differences in personal initiative play an important role in assistant principals' task performances, discretionary performances, or future career aspirations.

Perceived Organizational Support

Whereas organizational psychologists have focused on individual attributes, institutional theorists emphasized the importance of organizational and contextual conditions to employees' work performances. By considering both organizations and individuals, Blau (1964) viewed work as a form of *social exchange* involving an undefined series of transactions that consequently obligates both parties involved in the social interactions. Individuals trade their work effort and loyalty for material and social rewards. Following Blau's lead, Eisenberger, Huntington, Hutchison, and Sowa (1986) considered employees' commitment to their organization to be partially based on their perceptions of the organization's commitment to them. The researchers conceptualized employees' perceptions of their organization's commitment as *"perceived organizational support"* (POS) and defined it as the employees' "global beliefs about the extent to which the organization cares about their well-being and values their contributions" (p. 501).

Employees consistently agree with statements concerning whether their organizations appreciated their contributions and would treat them favorably or unfavorably depending on the circumstances (Eisenberger et al., 1986). POS "may be used by employees as an indicator of the organization's benevolent or malevolent intent in the expression of exchange of employee effort for reward and recognition" (Lynch, Eisenberger, & Armeli, 1999, pp. 469–470). Scholars have found that POS has a positive impact on several job-related perceptions and outcomes. Employees with high levels of POS exhibited less absenteeism and were found to be more conscientious about performing their work responsibilities (Eisenberger et al., 1986).

A meta-analysis study by Rhoades and Eisenberger (2002) revealed that POS is modestly related to job performance. These authors argued that high POS leads employees to feel obligated to repay their organization for its attention to their socio-emotional needs. In turn, this heightened sense of obligation generates increased efforts and greater work performances (Eisenberger, Fasolo, & Davis-LaMastro, 1990). Studies have also shown that POS is related to the employees' intention to leave the organization and change their careers (Allen, Shore, & Griffeth, 2003).

In line with the increasing interest in discretionary performance, scholars have shown growing interest in the effects of POS on the discretionary performances of employees. According to organizational support theory, POS leads employees to feel obligated to help their organization reach its objectives by, for example, participating in extra-role behaviors, such as helping other employees (Eisenberger, Armeli, Rexwinkell, Lynch, & Rhoades, 2001). Accordingly, Eisenberger et al. (2001) found that postal employees' felt obligations to an organization mediated a positive relationship between POS and extra-role behaviors, such as helping co-workers and supervisors. By helping other employees perform their jobs more effectively, these efforts aid not only the organization but also other employees and, thus, lead to greater productivity (Bell & Mengüç, 2002; Lynch et al., 1999;

Rhoades & Eisenberger, 2002). Wayne, Shore, and Liden (1997) found a positive relationship between POS and extra-role behavior for both managers and lower level employees. These findings in other fields suggest that the nature and level of POS in schools may impact the work performances and future career aspirations of assistant principals. Unfortunately, no such study has examined this subject to date.

National Origins of Assistant Principals

The cross-cultural and cross-national studies conducted by Hofstede (2001) and House and his associates (House, Hanges, Javidan, Dorfman, & Gupta, 2004) showed that national culture plays an important role in shaping employee behaviors. The current study acknowledges that cultural factors within the context of national origin have an important impact on the personal initiatives, POS, task performances, discretionary performances, and future career aspirations of assistant principals.

Based on the relationships discussed above, the current study aimed to answer the following research questions:

1. Do Turkish and American assistant principals differ in their levels of personal initiative, POS, task-role performances, discretionary performances, and career aspirations?
2. Does a significant relationship exist between the assistant principals' personal initiatives and POS and their task performances and extra-role performances?
3. Does a significant relationship exist between the assistant principals' personal initiatives, POS, task performances, and discretionary performance and their three future career aspirations?

CONCEPTUAL AND MEASUREMENT MODEL

By adopting *social-cognitive theory* (Bandura, 2001) and systems theory, this study considered the work performances and future career aspirations of assistant principals as complex outcome variables. By utilizing an inclusive and incorporative social-cognitive perspective, we were able to incorporate the arbitrarily disconnected individual (personal initiative) and organizational antecedents (POS) in the analysis of work performances and future career aspirations of assistant principals into our framework. Fig. 1 demonstrates

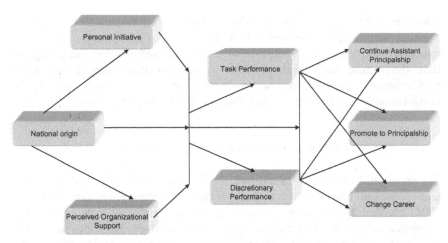

Fig. 1. Relationship Among Personal Initiative, Perceived Organizational Support, Task Performance Discretionary Performance, and Future Career Aspirations of Assistant Principals. *Note*: The arrows indicate association between variables, not the direction of causal relationship.

the conceptual framework and the hypothesized relationships among the study variables.

METHODS

This cross-national study employed a casual-comparative design. A causal-comparative design was appropriate for this study because we did not manipulate the independent variables but assumed that they were causal after the fact instead (Creswell, 2003; Lodico, Spaulding, & Voegtle, 2006). For instance, we did not manipulate the participants. The causal-comparative design helped us identify the possible causes of the observed variations (Frankel & Wallen, 2000) in the task performances, discretionary performances, and future career aspirations of the assistant principals in Turkey and United States.

Participants

The intended target populations for the study were the assistant principals of all public schools with 1–12 grades in the province of Ankara, Turkey and a southern state in the United States. We used geographical location and grade-level configuration as the two sampling criteria for our randomized cluster sampling procedure. We identified the sample size by using the *theoretical sample size table* developed by Anderson (1990). The sizes of the samples were 381 and 220 for Turkey and the United States, respectively, with a 95% confidence interval. To be included in our sample, the participants had to complete all of the sections on the questionnaire with the exception of the first section, which included the demographic attributes of the participants and their respective schools. In total, 227 and 144 surveys for Turkey and the United States, respectively, were usable. We received a total of 371 usable surveys and an overall response rate of 62% from the combined group. The response rate was slightly lower for Turkey (60%) than for the United States (65%).

Instrumentation

The current study employed a survey methodology to gather data. We used a questionnaire that incorporated three previously developed and tested questionnaires as the data-gathering instrument. Two panels of experts (i.e., one in Turkey and one in the United States) helped us develop the study questionnaire. We only included the items agreed upon by the two panels of experts in the final questionnaire. We crosschecked the accuracy of both the Turkish and English versions of the questionnaire before conducting the research.

We organized both the Turkish and English versions of the questionnaire into three sections. The first section gathered demographic data on the participants and their schools. We treated the demographic data on the participants and their schools as the control variables (covariates). The personal demographics included gender, age, educational background, and the number of years spent working as assistant principals. The school demographics consisted of school size and school configuration. Because of the lack of comparable data in Turkey, we excluded the percentage of students who received free or reduced lunches from the study.

The second section of the survey included the items used to measure the independent variables. These variables were national origin, personal initiative, and POS. We employed a dummy variable for the national origins of the assistant participants. We integrated a revised version of the *Personal Initiative Scale* (Fay & Frese, 2001) into the second section to measure the personal initiatives of the assistant principals. The sample items included "I actively attack problems" and "I take initiative immediately even if others don't." The participants rated their level of personal initiative on a four-point Likert scale (1 – *never*; 4 – *almost always*). This section also included eight items used to measure the assistant principals' POS. We employed a revised version of the *Perceived Organizational Support Scale* (Rhoades & Eisenberger, 2002) to measure POS. The sample items were "My work organization values my contribution to its well-being" and "My work organization strongly considers my goals and values." The respondents indicated the extent to which they agreed with each statement on a four-point Likert scale (1 – *never*; 4 – *almost always*).

The last section of the survey included the items used to measure the dependent variables: the task performances, discretionary performances, and future career aspirations of the assistant principals. We used the *Educational Leadership Policy Standards: ISLLC 2008* to measure the task performances of the assistant principals. By relying on a panel of experts, we identified a total of 15 items that represented the 6 ISLLC standards. The participants indicated their level of performance on a four-point Likert scale (1 – *never*; 4 – *almost always*). The section also included 10 items used to measure the discretionary performances of the assistant principals. We used *The School Organizational Citizenship Behavior Scale* developed by DiPaola and Tschannen-Moran (2001) to measure the discretionary performances of the assistant principals. The sample items included "Takes actions that protects the school from risk" and "Spreads the goodwill and positivity." The participants indicated their level of performance on a four-point Likert scale (1 – *never*; 4 – *almost always*). Finally, the section included three items used to measure the future career aspirations of the assistant principals: intent to stay as an assistant principal, to become promoted to principalship, and to change careers.

Data Analysis

Prior to conducting the statistical analyses, we examined the data for assumptions, including normality, the homogeneity of the variance–covariance matrices, and linearity. Although some of the assumptions were violated, our tests indicated that the violations were not severe. Additional tests (e.g., *Wilks' Lambda* for linearity, *Box's test* for the equality of covariance matrices, and *Levene's test* for the homogeneity of variances) also showed that the assumption violations were not severe. The violations were mainly due to the robustness of the multivariate analysis techniques (i.e., MANCOVA and hierarchical regression analysis), the skewness of the data, and the disproportionate size difference between the Turkish and American groups. The larger sample ($n_T = 227$) was 1.65 times bigger than the smaller ($n_A = 140$) sample.

The average age of the American assistant principals was 36 years old (SD = .921), and 48% of them were female (SD = .502). The average assistant principal in this group had 8.1 years of experience (SD = .889). More than three-fourths (78.5%) of the American assistant principals had only a bachelor's degree. In total, 18.8% of this group held a master's degree. The average age of the Turkish principals was 36 years old (SD = .765); only 22.9% of them were female (SD = .421). The average assistant principal in this group had 8.2 years of experience (SD = 1.046). Although 22% of the Turkish assistant principals held a master's degree, approximately two-thirds (72%) of them had only a bachelor's degree. The average school size (enrollment) in the American group was 820 students. In this group, 26% of the schools had less than 500 students, and 57% had from 501 to 1,000 students. Additionally, 32% of the schools in this group consisted of elementary schools, 21% were middle schools, and 46% were high schools. The average number of students enrolled in the Turkish schools was 865 students. In this group, 61% of the schools consisted of K-8 schools, and the remaining 39% were high schools.

We conducted reliability tests for the dependent and independent variables of the combined group and of each group separately. The Alphas for the Turkish group were .85, .85, .91, and .88 for personal initiative, POS, task performance, and discretionary performance, respectively. The Alphas for the American group were .85, .85, 90, and .87, respectively. The Alphas for the combined group were .85, .78, .90, and .87, respectively. The high Alphas for all of the groups and variables indicated that the items formed reasonably reliable scales with high internal consistencies. The task performance of the Turkish group ($\alpha = .91$) was particularly significant because the items in this scale included the ISLLC standards developed for the American group.

FINDINGS

We organized the findings of the study around three research questions.
Research Question 1: Do Turkish and American assistant principals differ in their levels of personal initiative, POS, task-role performances, discretionary performances, and three career aspirations?

A multivariate analysis of covariance (MANCOVA) answered this question. The analysis tested whether differences existed between the

Turkish and American assistant principals on a linear combination of personal initiative, POS, task performance, discretionary performance, and three future career aspirations. The demographic attributes of the participants (i.e., *age, gender, experience as assistant principal,* and *educational* background) and their schools (i.e., *school configuration* and *school size*) were included in the analyses as covariates. The MANCOVA analysis demonstrated how each dependent variable differed separately and with other groups of dependent variables interactively, across the groups.

The MANCOVA analysis yielded a significant difference, Wilk's $\Lambda = .199$, F (357, 345) = 9.83, $p = .001$. The multivariate eta was ($\acute{\eta} = .34$), which indicates a medium-sized effect (Leech, Barrett, & Morgan, 2009). The significant F indicated that significant differences existed between the Turkish and American assistant principal groups within a linear combination of seven independent variables. Further review of the MANCOVA results showed that some covariates, including age (Wilk's $\Lambda = .928$, F (357, 345) = 3.813, $p = .001$, $\acute{\eta}^2 = .07$), education (Wilk's $\Lambda = .938$, F (357,345) = 3.258, $p = .002$, $\acute{\eta}^2 = .06$), and school configuration (Wilk's $\Lambda = .957$, F (357,345) = 2.205, $p = .033$, $\acute{\eta}^2 = .04$), also exhibited significant differences between the Turkish and American assistant principals.

Table 1 demonstrates the main effects for the multivariate MANCOVA. The national origin significantly differentiated the groups' POS, task performances, discretionary performances, and aspirations to stay in the job. Similarly, in eight instances covariates also helped to differentiate the dependent variables across the groups. The multivariate eta for these covariates ranged from small to medium for the significant contributions. National origin contributed the most to the POS across the groups with an effect size of $\acute{\eta}^2 = 29$. Table 2 presents the parameter estimates. The coefficients for the linear combinations indicated that the POS ($\beta = -.674$, $p = .000$), discretionary performance ($\beta = .310, p = .002$), and intent to stay as an assistant principal ($\beta = -.547, p = .001$) significantly helped to distinguish the Turkish assistant principals from the American assistant principals. Although the number of significant covariates decreased from eight to four in the parameter estimates, the number of significantly contributing instances attributed to national origin remained unchanged at 4.

Research Question 2: Does a significant relationship exist between the assistant principals' personal initiatives and POS and their task perfor- mances and discretionary performances?

We conducted two separate hierarchical multiple regression analyses to predict the assistant principals' task performances and discretionary performances. The hierarchical multiple regression analyses allowed us to

Table 1. Linear Combination of Coefficients Distinguishing the Extent
of Personal Initiative, Perceived Organizational Support, Task
Performance, Discretionary Performance, and Three Future Career
Aspirations for Main Effects.

Dependent Variable	Source	F	p	η
Task Performance	Age	4.588	.033	.11
Promotion to Principalship	Age	13.948	.001	.18
Staying in Asst. Principalship	AP experience	4.562	.033	.11
Staying in Asst. Principalship	Education	5.153	.024	.12
Promotion to Principalship	Education	9.126	.003	.16
Task Performance	School configuration	8.815	.003	.15
Discretionary Performance	School configuration	11.314	.001	.18
Promotion to Principalship	School size	4.186	.042	.11
Perceived Organizational Support	National origin	32.698	.000	.29
Task Performance	National origin	11.110	.001	.18
Discretionary Performance	National origin	10.180	.002	.14
Staying in Asst. Principalship	National origin	6.851	.009	.18

Note: Nonsignificant sources were not shown in the table.

Table 2. Linear Combination of Coefficients Distinguishing the Extent
of Personal Initiative, Perceived Organizational Support, Task
Performance, Discretionary Performance, and Three Future Career
Aspirations for Interaction Effects.

Dependent Variable	Parameter	β	p	η
Perceived Organizational Support	National origin	−.674	.000	.29
Task Performance	Age	.066	.005	.11
Task Performance	AP experience	−.019	.003	.15
Task Performance	National origin	.321	.001	.18
Discretionary Performance	School configuration	−.147	.001	.18
Discretionary Performance	National origin	.310	.002	.17
Staying in Asst. Principalship	Education	−.199	.024	.12
Staying in Asst. Principalship	National origin	−.547	.009	.14

Note: Nonsignificant sources were not shown in the table.

test the predictions produced by the blocks of independent variables
regarding task performance and discretionary performance. The hierarchical method allowed us to control the order of the blocks of predictive
variables that we entered in the analysis. The assumption checks for

multicollinearity revealed that a high correlation existed between school configuration and discretionary performance. We eliminated school configuration because it was not one of the target variables. We kept the discretionary performance in the analysis because its tolerance (.681) was higher than the acceptable level of .44 $(1 - R^2 = 1 - .56)$.

The first analysis yielded five competing models that predicted the task performances of the assistant principals. ANOVAs for all of the models were significant, which indicates that the combination of variables in each model significantly $(p = .001)$ predicted the task performances of the assistant principals. A further review of the model summaries showed that only the first two models were significant. As Table 3 demonstrates, the first model included only the discretionary performance as the predictor of the assistant principals' task performances $F(1,358) = 416$, $p = .001$. Model 2, which included the discretionary performance and personal initiative, was better than Model 1 at predicting the task performances of the assistant principals, as the adjusted R^2 value increased from .54 to $R^2 = .56$, $F(2,357) = 232$, $p = .001$. Models 3, 4, and 5 were not significant and did not increase the R^2 value.

The hierarchical multiple regression analysis for discretionary performance yielded similar results in that it also produced five models, all of which exhibited significant ANOVAs. Significant ANOVAs indicated that the combination of variables in each model significantly $(p = .001)$ predicted the discretionary performances of the assistant principals. A further review of the model summaries showed that only the first two models were

Table 3. Hierarchical Regression Model Summary for Task Performance.

Model	R	R^2	Adjusted R^2	Std. Error of the Estimate	df1	df2	Sig. F Change
1	.733[a]	.537	.536	.27356	1	358	.000
2	.752[b]	.565	.562	.26573	1	357	.000
3	.752[c]	.565	.561	.26610	1	356	.925
4	.753[d]	.567	.562	.26591	1	355	.220
5	.757[e]	.573	.562	.26594	5	350	.429

[a]Predictors: (Constant), DP.
[b]Predictors: (Constant), DP, PI.
[c]Predictors: (Constant), DP, PI, POS.
[d]Predictors: (Constant), DP, PI, POS, Culture.
[e]Predictors: (Constant), DP, PI, POS, Culture, APExp., Education, Gender, Size, Age.

significant (see Table 4). The first model consisted of only task performance $F(1,358) = 416$, $p = .001$. Model 2, which included task performance and personal initiative, was better than Model 1 at predicting the task performances of the assistant principals, as the adjusted R^2 increased from $R^2 = .536$ to $R^2 = .56$, $F(2,357) = 241$, $p = .001$. Models 3, 4, and 5 were not significant and did not increase the R^2 value.

Research Question 3: Does a significant relationship exist between the assistant principals' personal initiatives, POS, task performances, and discretionary performances and their three future career aspirations?

To answer the above question, we conducted three separate hierarchical multiple regression analyses for each of the assistant principals' future career aspirations. The first future career aspiration represented the assistant principals' intentions to stay in their positions as assistant principals. The analysis yielded six models with significant ANOVAs at $p = .001$. The significance of the ANOVAs indicated that the combination of variables in each model significantly ($p = .001$) predicted the assistant principals' intentions to stay in their current positions. As demonstrated in Table 5, a further review of the model summaries showed that all of the models except for Model 3 were significant. Model 5 included all of the variables with a small but significant R^2 at predicting the intention to remain as an assistant principal. The variables in Model 6 accounted for 20% ($R^2 = 20$, $F(11,348) = 8.01$, $p = .009$) of the variation in the assistant principals' intentions to stay in their jobs.

Table 4. Hierarchical Regression Model Summary for Discretionary Performance.

Model	R	R^2	Adjusted R^2	Std. Error of the Estimate	df1	df2	Sig. F Change
1	.733[a]	.537	.536	.27768	1	358	.000
2	.758[b]	.575	.572	.26666	1	357	.000
3	.760[c]	.577	.574	.26626	1	356	.150
4	.760[d]	.577	.573	.26655	1	355	.636
5	.760[e]	.578	.567	.26818	5	350	.982

[a]Predictors: (Constant), TP.
[b]Predictors: (Constant), TP, PI.
[c]Predictors: (Constant), TP, PI, POS.
[d]Predictors: (Constant), TP, PI, POS, Culture.
[e]Predictors: (Constant), TP, PI, POS, Culture, APExp, Education, Gender, Size, Age.

Table 5. Hierarchical Regression Model Summary for Intent to Stay in Assistant Principalship.

Model	R	R^2	Adjusted R^2	Std. Error of the Estimate	df1	df2	Sig. F Change
1	.231[a]	.053	.051	.874	1	358	.000
2	.276[b]	.076	.071	.864	1	357	.003
3	.279[c]	.078	.070	.865	1	356	.413
4	.381[d]	.145	.135	.834	1	355	.000
5	.402[e]	.162	.150	.827	1	354	.008
6	.449[f]	.202	.177	.813	6	348	.009

[a]Predictors: (Constant), TP.
[b]Predictors: (Constant), TP, DP.
[c]Predictors: (Constant), TP, DP, PI.
[d]Predictors: (Constant), TP, DP, PI, POS.
[e]Predictors: (Constant), TP, DP, PI, POS, Culture.
[f]Predictors: (Constant), TP, DP, PI, POS, Culture, APExp., Education, Gender, Size, Age, Configuration.

Table 6. Hierarchical Regression Model Summary for Assistant Principals' Expectations to Promote Principalship.

Model	R	R^2	Adjusted R^2	Std. Error of the Estimate	df1	df2	Sig. F Change
1	.127[a]	.016	.013	1.061	1	357	.016
2	.129[b]	.017	.011	1.063	1	356	.664
3	.148[c]	.022	.014	1.061	1	355	.167
4	.282[d]	.079	.069	1.031	1	354	.000
5	.284[e]	.081	.068	1.032	1	353	.447
6	.305[f]	.093	.064	1.034	6	347	.598

[a]Predictors: (Constant), TPAVERAGE.
[b]Predictors: (Constant), TPAVERAGE, DPAVERAGE.
[c]Predictors: (Constant), TPAVERAGE, DPAVERAGE, PIAVERAGE.
[d]Predictors: (Constant), TPAVERAGE, DPAVERAGE, PIAVERAGE, POSAVERAGE.
[e]Predictors: (Constant), TPAVERAGE, DPAVERAGE, PIAVERAGE, POSAVERAGE, Culture.
[f]Predictors: (Constant), TPAVERAGE, DPAVERAGE, PIAVERAGE, POSAVERAGE, Culture. Demographics (AP experience, Education, Gender, Size, Age, Configuration)

The second future career aspiration was the assistant principals' expectations of being promoted to the principalship in the next five years. The analysis yielded six models with significant ANOVAs ($p = .001$). The significance of the ANOVAs indicated that the combination of variables in

Table 7. Hierarchical Regression Model Summary for Assistant Principals' Intent to Change Career.

Model	R	R^2	Adjusted R^2	Std. Error of the Estimate	df1	df2	Sig. F Change
1	.161[a]	.026	.023	1.174	1	358	.002
2	.206[b]	.043	.037	1.165	1	357	.013
3	.236[c]	.056	.048	1.159	1	356	.027
4	.286[d]	.082	.071	1.145	1	355	.002
5	.303[e]	.092	.079	1.140	1	354	.044
6	.459[f]	.211	.186	1.072	6	348	.000

[a]Predictors: (Constant), TP.
[b]Predictors: (Constant), TP, DP.
[c]Predictors: (Constant), TP, DP, PI.
[d]Predictors: (Constant), TP, DP, PI, POS.
[e]Predictors: (Constant), TP, DP, PI, POS, Culture.
[f]Predictors: (Constant), TP, DP, PI, POS, Culture, APExp., Education, Gender, Size, Age, Configuration.

each model significantly predicted the assistant principals' expectations of being promoted to the principalship. As demonstrated in Table 6, a further review of the model summaries showed that all six models were significant. Model 6 included all of the variables with a small but significant R^2 at predicting the participants' intentions to remain as assistant principals. The variables in Model 6 accounted for 19% ($R^2 = 20$, $F(6,348) = 9.7$, $p = .000$) of the variation in assistant principals' expectations of being promoted to the principalship.

The third future career aspiration was the intent to move out of the assistant principalship to another career. Our analyses yielded six models with significant ANOVAs. However, further analyses showed that only Models 1 and 3 were significant (Table 7). Model 3 included task performance, discretionary performance, and personal initiative. This model explained only seven percent of the variation in the assistant principals' intentions to leave the assistant principalship.

CONCLUSIONS, IMPLICATIONS, AND LIMITATIONS

The main purpose of this study was to contribute to the scant literature on assistant principalship, which currently lacks guiding professional standards, criteria, and benchmarks. In practice, principals arbitrarily assigned the roles and tasks of assistant principals without much consideration for any established criteria or proper planning process (Hess & Kelly, 2007). The assistant principals find little or no time to be involved in educational and instructional decisions because of their exhausting and rudimentary administrative duties. Furthermore, they are forced to perform arbitrary task assignments in the absence of clearly defined job descriptions and role expectations. The lack of research criticizing the current state of assistant principalship indicates that no changes will occur in the near future. This ambiguous work environment has caused assistant principals to feel increasingly dissatisfied, anxious, and unclear about their future career aspirations (Chang, Johnson, & Yang, 2007; Moore, 2009).

As the assistant principals' roles and tasks diversified and expanded in the wake of current accountability requirements, educational reforms, and changes in leadership perspectives, researchers have begun to investigate the delegation of principals' responsibilities to assistant principals (Kwan, 2009; Louis et al., 2010; Oliver, 2003; Weller & Weller, 2002). This cross-national study aimed to address the need to professionalize the assistant principalship by empirically assessing assistant principals' task performances from the perspective of the principals' professional standards. The study also investigated the discretionary performances of assistant principals and their future career aspirations in two different countries.

As the first of its type, the study showed that national origin was a significantly differentiating factor of assistant principals' POS ($p = .000$, $\dot{\eta} = .29$), task performances ($p = .001$, $\dot{\eta} = .18$), discretionary performances ($p = .002$, $\dot{\eta} = .14$), and intentions to stay in the assistant principalship ($p = .009$, $\dot{\eta} = .218$). The Turkish assistant principals ($X = 2.7$, SD = .44) received significantly less support from their organizations than their American counterparts ($X = 3.4$, SD = .59). Although both groups have similar levels of personal initiative, the low level of organizational support and certain participant and school demographics resulted in significantly lower task performances, discretionary performances, and expectations to stay in the assistant principalship for the Turkish group. Similarly, the members of this group are more inclined to change their careers than their American counterparts. These findings were in line with the relevant literature in the sense that higher POS leads to high levels of task performance (Bell & Mengüc, 2002; Lynch et al., 1999; Rhoades & Eisenberger, 2002), discretionary performance (Rhoades & Eisenberger, 2002), and intention to stay in the job (Allen et al., 2003). The findings showed that contextual factors have significant effects on assistant principals' work performances and future career aspirations. Practitioners and policymakers may enhance the assistant principals' individual performances and organizational effectiveness by improving organizational support and other contextual factors.

The study findings also showed that some participants and school demographics constituted significantly differentiating factors of the assistant principals' work performances and their future career aspirations in both groups. The effects of these variables persisted even when we included all of the factors in the equation (interaction effects). Age and experience in assistant principalship were significantly differentiating factors of the assistant principals' task performances. Interestingly, the beta coefficient for the assistant principals' experience levels and task performances was negative ($\beta = -.019$), which indicates that a negative relationship exists between these two variables. This finding conflicted with Louis et al.'s (2010) findings. Similarly, the education levels of the participants were also negatively associated with their likelihood of staying in the assistant principalship.

The findings of the study for the second research question also yielded interesting results regarding the predictive factors of the assistant principals' task performances and discretionary performances. The results of the hierarchical regression analysis showed that the assistant principals' discretionary performances and personal initiatives were two significant predictive factors of the assistant principals' task performances. In accordance with the literature (Campbell, 2000; Conway, 1999; Hoffman et al., 2007; Podsakoff et al., 2009; Prabhu, 2007), this study showed that strong empirical relationships exist between task performance and discretionary performance as well as between personal initiative and task performance (Crant, 2000; Frese, 2008; Frese & Fay, 2001). Our hierarchical regression analysis of discretionary performance confirmed these significant relationships. Task performance and personal initiative were two predictive factors of the assistant principals' discretionary performances ($R^2 = .58$, $p = .000$). Interestingly, neither national culture nor any of the demographic variables appeared to be significant predictive factors of the assistant principals' task and discretionary performances.

The findings of our hierarchical regression analysis for the three future career aspirations of the assistant principals showed that future career aspirations are more complex variables than the task or discretionary performances. Our analyses yielded five significant models. The best model showed that all of the variables except for personal initiative significantly predicted the assistant principals' intentions to stay in the assistant principalship. Similar analyses for the expectation of being promoted to the principalship yielded two statistically significant models. The best model included task performance, discretionary performance, personal initiative, and POS as the predictors of the assistant principals' expectations of being promoted to the principalship. These findings showed that a combination of numerous factors affect the assistant principals' expectations of becoming principals. Finally, the intention to change careers produced six statistically significant models. The best model included all of the independent variables and covariates. This finding was partially supported by Allen et al. (2003) and Wayne et al. (1997) on the existence of a significant relationship between POS and employees' intentions to leave the organization.

As a cross-national study in educational leadership, this study provided a major contribution to the literature by assessing the task performances of Turkish assistant principals from a conceptual perspective (i.e., ISLLC, 2008) developed for their American counterparts. The descriptive and inferential statistics indicated that the Turkish group performs core tasks similar to those of their American colleagues. The Cronbach's Alpha for the Turkish group's task performance was high ($\alpha = .91$), which indicates that a reliable scale with high internal consistency was formed for task performances as measured by ISLLC standards. The Alphas for all of the dependent and independent variables for the Turkish group were also all high (i.e., .85, .85, .91, and .88 for personal initiative, POS, task performance, and discretionary performance, respectively). Considering their Western origins, this study showed that researchers can apply these scales to a culturally diverse country, such as Turkey.

Given the absence of specific professional standards for assistant principals, this study conceptually borrowed from and applied the professional standards (i.e., ISLLC, 2008) that were developed for principals to assess the assistant principals' task performances. The Alpha for the task performances of both groups was high ($\alpha = .90$). This finding indicated that assistant principals perform tasks that are similar to those performed by principals. This finding also indicated that assistant principals execute educational and instructional tasks as well as their commonly known administrative functions. Finally, this finding empirically supported the untested assumption regarding the assistant principalship (i.e., "the assistant principalship is a training ground for the principalship"). This assumption makes sense given that assistant principals are exposed to tasks and responsibilities similar to those of the principalship, which they are preparing to assume.

The low explained variances of all of the variables in the best models for the intent to stay ($R^2 = .15$), the expectation of being promoted to the principalship ($R^2 = .8$), and the intention to change careers ($R^2 = .21$) show the complexity of future career aspirations. These results indicate that manipulating the future career aspirations of assistant principals may not be easy, especially if the organizational support is low and if the personal initiatives of the assistant principals are high.

RECOMMENDATIONS FOR POLICY AND FUTURE RESEARCH

The field of assistant principalship seems to have been abandoned by educational researchers, professional organizations, and policymakers. The existing literature on assistant principalship is limited to descriptive studies on the practices of assistant principals. Because of the lack of any conceptual and professional foundations identifying the roles and responsibilities of assistant principals, these studies have not been able to yield any comparable assessments. If the commonly accepted assumption of "the assistant principalship being the entry point to educational leadership positions" is true, then the scholarly community, professional organizations, and policymakers need to develop professional standards for this important group of professionals. Similarly, if these three communities accept the commonly accepted assumption that "the assistant principalship is the training ground for the principalship," then the communities should openly adopt the professional standards for principalship to assess assistant principals' performances. Such recognition may have significant policy implications. Primarily, the educational establishment would have to acknowledge the educational and instructional tasks performed by assistant principals. Doing so would prevent principals from giving random and arbitrary task assignments to their assistant principals.

Educational researchers must investigate many areas on assistant principalship by asking "why" and "how" questions in addition to descriptive "what" questions. The research questions may, for instance, include the following: Why do assistant principals decide to stay in their jobs or leave their field? How do they react to, survive in, or cope with an environment in which organizational support does not exist? Why do assistant principals go beyond expectations and engage in discretionary performances? How do they exhibit their personal initiatives in different environments (i.e., conducive, supportive, poor, or poisonous)? How do they interact with their fellow teachers, principals, or peers?

This study attempted to identify the influential (predictive) factors on the task performances, discretionary performances, and future career aspirations of assistant principals. Further studies are needed to identify the relational mechanisms and causal relationships among these variables. Further research can also test the construct validity of the study variables in different cultures or countries. The reliability tests for all of the study constructs yielded considerably high Alphas for each scale. Although this finding may suggest that Western constructs are applicable to culturally diverse countries, this initial interpretation must be further tested through confirmatory factor analyses for the construct validity of each study variable. Construct validity studies should utilize etic and emic approaches to capture both the culture-specific and universal components of the constructs in culturally diverse environments (Duyar, Aydin, & Pehlivan, 2009).

This study has the limitation pertinent to its self-reported and one source data. Further research should diversify the data sources to prevent possible bias and increase generalizability. The study offered a quantitative empirical methodology. Future research should also adopt qualitative methodologies to capture in-depth understanding about the processes relevant to the study constructs. Finally, the current study adopted a partial multilevel methodology through the use of hierarchical regression analysis. Future research should adopt true multilevel methodologies for the investigation, particularly cross-national investigations.

REFERENCES

Allen, D. G., Shore, L. M., & Griffeth, R. W. (2003). The role of perceived organizational support and supportive human resource practices in the turnover process. *Journal of Management, 29*(1), 99–118.

Anderson, G. (1990). *Fundamentals of educational research.* London: The Falmer Press.

Bandura, A. (2001). Social cognitive theory: An agentic perspective. *Annual Review of Psychology, 52*, 1–26.

Bass, B. M. (1985). *Leadership and performance beyond expectations.* New York, NY: Free Press.

Bell, S. J., & Mengüc, B. (2002). The employee–organization relationship, organizational citizenship behaviors, and superior service quality. *Journal of Retailing, 78*(2), 131–146.

Belschak, F. D., & Hartog, D. N. (2010). Pro-self, prosocial, and pro-organizational foci of proactive behavior: Differential antecedents and consequences. *Journal of Occupational and Organizational Psychology, 83*(2), 475–498.

Black, A. B. (1980). Clarifying the role of the assistant principal. *NASSP Bulletin, 64*(436), 33–39.

Performance Beyond Expectations 327

Blau, P. M. (1964). *Exchange and power in social life*. New York, NY: Wiley.

Borman, W. C., & Motowidlo, S. J. (1993). Expanding the criterion domain to include elements of contextual performance. In N. Schmitt & W. C. Borman (Eds.), *Personnel selection* (pp. 71–98). San Francisco, CA: Jossey-Bass.

Brief, A. P., & Motowidlo, S. J. (1986). Prosocial organizational behaviors. *Academy of Management Review, 11*, 710–725.

Campbell, D. J. (2000). The proactive employee: Managing workplace initiative. *Academy of Management Executive, 14*(3), 52–66.

Chang, C. H., Johnson, R. E., & Yang, L. Q. (2007). Emotional strain and organizational citizenship behaviors: A meta-analytic review. *Work & Stress, 21*, 312–332.

Chen, Z., Eisenberger, R., Johnson, K. M., Ivan, L. S., & Aselage, J. (2009). *Journal of Social Psychology, 149*(1), 119–124.

Condon, C., & Clifford, M. (2010). Measuring principal performance: How rigorous are commonly used principal performance assessment instruments? A Quality School Leadership Issue Brief, Learning Point. Retrieved from http://www.learningpt.org.expertise/educatorquality/school LeadersipIdentification.php/www.learningpt.org.expertise/educatorquality/schoolLeadersi pIdentification.php/. Accessed on May 28, 2011.

Conway, J. M. (1999). Distinguishing contextual performance from task performance for managerial jobs. *Journal of Applied Psychology, 84*, 3–13.

Council of Chief State School Officers (CCSSO). (2008). Educational leadership policy standards: ISLLC 2008. Washington, DC: Author. Retrieved from www.ccsso.org/Publications/ Download.cfm?Filename=ISLLC_2008final.pdf. Accessed on May 28, 2011.

Cranston, N., Tromans, C., & Reugebrink, M. (2004). Forgotten leaders: What do we know about the deputy principalship in secondary schools? *Leadership in Education, 7*(3), 225–242.

Crant, J. M. (2000). Proactive behavior in organizations. *Journal of Management, 26*, 435–452.

Crant, M. J., & Bateman, T. S. (2000). Charismatic leadership viewed from above: The impact of proactive personality. *Journal of Organizational Behavior, 21*(1), 63.

Creswell, J. W. (2003). *Research design: Qualitative and quantitative mixed method approach* (2nd ed.). Thousand Oaks, CA: Sage.

DiPaola, M., & Tschannen-Moran, M. (2001). Organizational citizenship behavior in schools and its relationship to school climate. *Journal of School Leadership, 11*(5), 424–447.

Duyar, I, Aydin, I., & Pehlivan, Z. (2009). *Analyzing principal influence tactics from a cross-cultural perspective: Do preferred influence tactics and targeted goals differ by national culture?* Educational leadership: Global context and international comparisons (pp. 191–220). Emerald: Bingley, UK.

Eisenberger, R., Armeli, S., Rexwinkell, B., Lynch, P. D., & Rhoades, L. (2001). Reciprocation of perceived organizational support. *Journal of Applied Psychology, 86*(1), 42–51.

Eisenberger, R., Fasolo, E. M., & Davis-LaMastro, V. (1990). Effects of perceived organizational support on employee diligence, innovation, and commitment. *Journal of Applied Psychology, 53*, 51–59.

Eisenberger, R., Huntington, R., Hutchison, S., & Sowa, D. (1986). Perceived organizational support. *Journal of Applied Psychology, 71*(3), 500–507.

Erdogan, B., & Bauer, T. N. (2005). Enhancing career benefits of employee proactive personality: The role of fit with jobs and organizations. *Personnel Psychology, 58*, 859–891.

Fay, D., & Frese, M. (2001). The concept of personal initiative: An overview of validity studies. *Human Performance, 14*(1), 97–124.

Fay, D., & Sonnentag, S. (2010). A look back to move ahead: New directions for research on proactive performance and other discretionary work behaviours. Special Issue: Multi-Dimensional Work Performance: Festschrift for Michael Frese. *Applied Psychology: An International Review, 59*(1), 1–20.

Frankel, J. R., & Wallen, N. E. (2000). *How to design and evaluate research in education.* New York, NY: McGraw-Hill.

Frankel, J. R., & Wallen, N. E. (2000). *Exploring research* (4th ed.). New York, NY: Prentice Hall.

Frese, M. (2008). The word is out: We need an active performance concept for modern workplaces. *Industrial and Organizational Psychology: Perspectives on Science and Practice, 1,* 67–69.

Frese, M., & Fay, D. (2001). Personal initiative: An active performance concept for work in the 21st century. In B. M. Staw & R. I. Sutton (Eds.), *Research in organizational behavior* (Vol. 23, pp. 133–187). San Diego, CA: Elsevier.

Griffin, M. A., Neal, A., & Parker, S. K. (2007). A new model of work role performance: Positive behavior in uncertain and interdependent contexts. *Academy of Management Journal, 50*(2), 327–347.

Hassenpflug, A. (1991). *NASSP Assistant Principal Special Newsletter, 7*(1), 1–7.

Hausman, C., Nebeker, A., McCreary, J., & Donaldson, G., Jr. (2002). The work life of the assistant principal. *Journal of Educational Administration, 40*(2/3), 136–158.

Hess, F. M., & Kelly, A. P. (2007). Learning to lead: What gets taught in principal-preparation programs? *Teachers College Record, 109*(1), 221–243.

Hoffman, B. J., Blair, C. A., Meriac, C. P., & Woehr, D. J. (2007). Expanding the criterion domain? A quantitative review of the OCB literature. *Journal of Applied Psychology, 92*(2), 555–566.

Hofstede, G. (2001). *Culture's consequences: Comparing values, behaviors, institutions, and organizations across nations.* Thousand Oaks, CA: Sage.

House, R. J., Hanges, P. J., Javidan, M., Dorfman, P. W., & Gupta, V. (2004). *Culture, leadership, and organizations: The GLOBE study of 62 societies.* Thousand Oaks, CA: Sage.

Katz, D., & Kahn, R. (1996). *The social psychology of organization.* New York, NY: Wiley.

Kelly, G. (1987). The assistant principalship as a training ground for the principalship. *NASSP Bulletin, 71*(501), 13–20.

Koru, J. M. (1993). The assistant principal: Crisis manger, custodian, or visionary? *NASSP Bulletin, 77*(556), 67–71.

Koys, D. J. (2001). The effects of employee satisfaction, organizational citizenship behavior, and turnover on organizational effectiveness: A unit-level, longitudinal study. *Personnel Psychology, 54,* 101–114.

Kwan, P. (2009). The vice-principal experience as a preparation for the principalship. *Journal of Educational Administration, 47*(2), 191–205.

Lee, J. C., Kwan, P., & Walker, A. (2009). Vice-principalship: Their responsibility roles and career aspirations. *International Journal of Leadership in Education, 12*(1), 187–207.

Leech, N. L., Barrett, K. C., & Morgan, G. A. (2009). *SPSS for intermediate statistics: Use and interpretation* (3rd ed.). Mahwah, NJ: Lawrence Erlbaum Associates.

Lodico, M. G., Spaulding, D. T., & Voegtle, K. H. (2006). *Method in educational research: From theory to practice.* San Francisco, CA: Jossey-Bass.

Louis, K. S., Leithwood, K., Wahlstrom, K. L., & Anderson, S. E. (2010). Investigating the links to improved student learning: Final Report of Research Findings, University of Minnesota, University of Toronto, and Wallace Foundation. Retrieved from http://www.wallacefoundation.orgwww.wallacefoundation.org. Accessed on July 23.

Lynch, P. D., Eisenberger, R., & Armeli, S. (1999). Perceived organizational support: Inferior-versus-superior performance by wary employees. *Journal of Applied Psychology, 84*, 467–483.

Marshall, C. (1992). *The assistant principal: Leadership choices and challenges.* Newbury Park, CA: Corwin Press.

Marshall, C., & Hooley, R. M. (2006). *The assistant principal: Leadership choices and challenges.* Thousand Oaks, CA: Corwin.

Mertz, N. T. (2000). Contextualizing the position of assistant principal. Paper presented at the University Council for Educational Administration Annual Meeting, Albuquerque, NM.

Moore, T. (2009). Let's end the ambiguous role of assistant principals. *Principal, 89*(1), 6666.

Motowidlo, S. J. (2003). Job performance. In W. C. Borman, D. R. Ilgen, R. J. Klimonski & Weiner (Eds.), *Handbook of psychology, 12: Industrial and organizational psychology* (pp. 39–53). Hoboken, NJ: Wiley.

Murphy, J. (2003). Reculturing educational leadership: The ISLLC standards ten years out. Retrieved from http://www.npbea.org/Resources/ISLLC_10_years_9-03.pdf. Accessed on April 19, 2011.

Oliver, R. (2003). Assistant principal job satisfaction and the desire to become principals. *NCPEA Education Leadership Review, 4*, 38–46.

Oliver, R. (2005). Assistant principal professional growth and development: A matter that cannot be left to chance. *Journal of Educational Leadership and Administration, 17*, 89–100.

Organ, D. W. (1988). *The organizational citizenship behavior: The good soldier syndrome.* Issues in Organization and Management Series. Lexington, MA: Lexington Books.

Organ, D. W. (1997). Organizational citizenship behavior: It's construct clean-up time. *Human Performance, 10*(2), 85–97.

Organ, D. W., Podsakoff, P. M., & MacKenzie, S. B. (2006). *Organizational citizenship: Its nature, antecedents, and consequences.* Thousand Oaks, CA: Sage.

Podsakoff, N. P., Whiting, S. W., Podsakoff, P. M., & Blume, B. D. (2009). Individual and organizational-level consequences of organizational citizenship behaviors: A meta-analysis. *Journal of Applied Psychology, 94*, 122–141.

Podsakoff, P. M., MacKenzie, S. B., Paine, J. B., & Bachrach, D. G. (2000). Organizational citizenship behaviors: A critical review of the theoretical and empirical literature and suggestions for future research. *Journal of Management, 26*(3), 513–563.

Porter, J. (1996). What is the role of the middle level assistant principal, and how should it change? *National Association of Secondary School Principals Bulletin, 80*(578), 25–30.

Prabhu, V. P. (2007). *Understanding the effect of proactive personality on job related outcomes in an organizational change setting.* Unpublished doctoral dissertation, Auburn University, Auburn, AL.

Rhoades, L., & Eisenberger, R. (2002). Perceived organizational support: A review of the literature. *Journal of Applied Psychology, 87*, 698–714.

Ribbins, P. (1997). Heads on deputy principalship: Impossible roles for invisible role holders? *Educational Management and Administration, 15*, 53–64.

Scoggins, A. J., & Bishop, H. L. (1993). A review of literature regarding the roles and responsibilities of assistant principals. Paper presented at the meeting of the Mid-South Educational Research Association, New Orleans, LA.

Somech, A., & Drach-Zahavy, A. (2000). Understanding extra-role behavior in schools: The relationships between job satisfaction, sense of efficacy, and teachers' extra-role behavior. *Teaching and Teacher Education, 16*, 649–659.

Somech, A., & Ron, I. (2007). Promoting organizational citizenship behavior in schools: The impact of individual and organizational characteristics. *Educational Administration Quarterly, 43*(1), 38–66.

Sonnentag, S. (2003). Recovery, work engagement, and proactive behavior: A new look at the interface between nonwork and work. *Journal of Applied Psychology, 88*(3), 518–528.

Tyler, T. R., & Blader, S. L. (2003). The group engagement model: Procedural justice, social identity, and cooperative behavior. *Personality and Social Psychology Review, 7*(4), 349–361.

Van Dyne, L., Cummings, L. L., & Parks, J. M. (1995). Extra-role behaviors: In pursuit of construct and definitional clarity (a bridge over muddied waters). In L. L. Cummings & B. M. Staw (Eds.), *Research in organizational behavior* (Vol. 17, pp. 215–285). Greenwich, CT: JAI.

Wayne, S. J., Shore, L. M., & Liden, R. C. (1997). Perceived organizational support and leadermember exchange: A social exchange perspective. *Academy of Management Journal, 40*(1), 82.

Weller, D., & Weller, S. (2002). *The assistant principal: Essentials for effective school leadership.* Thousand Oaks, CA: Corwin Press.

AUTHOR BIOGRAPHIES

Yahya Altınkurt holds Ph.D. from Anadolu University, Turkey. He is assistant professor at Dumlupınar University Faculty of Education in Kütahya. Dr. Altınkurt's research focuses on strategic planning, organizational justice, organizational citizenship, and leadership in schools. His most recent books include *Assessment of Researches of School Administration* (2008, Anadolu University Publishing coauthored with E. Ağaoğlu, M. Ceylan, E. Kesim, and T. Madden). Dr. Altınkurt's research has appeared in various journals including *Educational Sciences: Theory & Practice, Education and Science, Educational Administration: Theory and Practice, International Journal of Human Sciences, Academic Sight*.

Betty Y. Ashbaker is associate professor in the Department of Counseling Psychology and Special Education at Brigham Young University (Provo, Utah), with a broad background of experience as a special educator and school district administrator. Recipient of the 2010 Faculty Women's Scholarship Award at BYU, Dr. Ashbaker is author or coauthor of a number of books and a large number of refereed articles. Her research has appeared in a wide variety of international professional journals. In addition to her responsibilities for teaching and supervising student teachers and graduate students, she serves on many university committees, and regularly provides professional development to paraprofessional and professional educators, and school administrators. Dr. Ashbaker is a collaborative researcher with a strong focus: improving education outcomes by empowering paraprofessionals and their supervising teachers. She also specializes in research and training programs for Latino students. She is an integral part of the *Latinos in Action* group, which seeks to empower Latino youth through culture, service, and education.

Inayet Aydın holds Ph.D. from Ankara University. She is full professor at the Faculty of Educational Sciences in Ankara University. Dr. Aydın's research focuses on human resources management, staff development, stress management, professional ethics, academic ethics, public ethics, ethics training, teaching ethics, and alternative schools. Dr. Aydın's research has appeared in various journals including *Journal of Educational Administration*,

Asia Pacific Education Review, Journal of Educational Studies, Higher Education Quarterly, Educational Management Administration & Leadership, and *Education and Science.* Her invited book chapter with Ibrahim Duyar, "Analyzing Principal Influence Tactics from a Cross-cultural Perspective: Do Preferred Influence Tactics and Targeted Goals Differ by National Culture?" has appeared in the *Educational Leadership: Global Contexts and International Comparisons* by the Emerald Publishing. With this study, Dr. Aydin is recognized with the Outstanding Author Contribution Award by Emerald Publications.

Elena Belogolovsky is Ph.D. candidate in the Department of Behavioral Sciences, Faculty of Industrial Engineering and Management at the Technion – Israel Institute for Technology. She received BA degree in sociology, anthropology and educational administration from University of Haifa, Israel and MA degree in educational administration from University of Haifa, Israel. Her research interests include employees' organizational citizenship behavior, employees' perceived job breadth, employees' career stages, pay secret communication policy, pay reduction strategies, occupational stress and wellness, retirement and alcohol-related behaviors. Her most recent paper "Pay Secrecy and Individual Task Performance" coauthored with Peter Bamberger was published in *Personnel Psychology* in 2010.

Michael F. DiPaola is chancellor professor of the School of Education at The College of William & Mary. His teaching and research, in the Educational Policy, Planning & Leadership Program, has focused on the interactions of professionals in school organizations. He has studied OCB in schools for over a decade. He is the coauthor of two books, including *Principals Improving Instruction: Supervision, Evaluation, and Professional Development* with Wayne Hoy. In addition his research has been published in venues such as the *Journal of Educational Administration,* the *Journal of School Leadership,* and *The High School Journal.* Prior to accepting his position at the university in 1998, Michael's career in public schools spanned three decades. He has served as a classroom teacher, school assistant principal, high-school principal, and district superintendent.

Ibrahim Duyar is associate professor of educational leadership at the University of Arkansas at Little Rock. Dr. Duyar holds Ph.D. from the University of Wisconsin at Madison. Dr. Duyar has served as a school principal, a university professor, and a consultant in local, national, and international organizations. He worked with British Council and World

Bank in the international educational projects. He also has worked with Education Testing Service, U.S. Department of Education, and Florida Department of Education nationally. His research focuses on discretionary behavior, collective efficacy, voice and silence, and perceived organizational support in educational organizational. His research agenda resulted in numerous publications. Dr. Duyar's most recent study, "Are We Legitimate Yet? A Closer Look at the Casual Relationship Mechanisms among Principal Leadership, Teacher Self-Efficacy, and Collective Efficacy," has appeared in *Journal of Management Development* (2011). His invited book chapter with Inayet Aydin, "Analyzing Principal Influence Tactics from a Cross-cultural Perspective: Do Preferred Influence Tactics and Targeted Goals Differ by National Culture?" has appeared in the *Educational Leadership: Global Contexts and International Comparisons* by the Emerald Publications. With this study, Dr. Duyar was recognized with the Outstanding Author Contribution Award. Dr. Duyar sits on the editorial board of *Educational Administration Quarterly*. He recently served as an elected officer of the Charter Schools Research and Evaluation SIG of AERA.

Yeung Lee graduated with Ph.D. from University of Hong Kong (HKU). She is the assistant director for the Centre for Information Technology in Education at HKU. Dr. Lee's research interests include international comparative studies of pedagogical innovations and information technology, assessment for the 21st century skills, using ICT for innovative practices and e-leadership. Currently, she is involved in the IEA International Computer and Information Literacy Study in Hong Kong and one of the investigators of the Learning 2.0 project to design, implement, and evaluate an interactive learning and assessment platform for supporting enquiry learning in Liberal Studies as well as to set up a teacher professional network for curriculum and assessment innovation, and the e-learning pilot project to develop curriculum and assessment tools for Information Literacy in General Science, Mathematics, Chinese Language, and English. Her most recent publication is the impact of ICT in education policies on teacher practices and student outcomes in Hong Kong.

Noriah Abdul Malek holds Ph.D. from the University of Malaya. She is principal assistant director at the Department of Community College Education, Ministry of Higher Education, Malaysia. She is responsible for the lifelong learning program at the Ministry. Her research focuses on organizational citizenship behavior, organizational control systems, and job performance.

Jill Morgan holds Ph.D. from Utah State University. A professional educator for more than 30 years, she was formerly an elementary school teacher, and is now a senior lecturer at Swansea Metropolitan University (Wales, UK). Her responsibilities include professional development for Teaching Assistants (school paraprofessionals) and teachers, as well as teaching graduate research classes and supervision of graduate student dissertations. Her research interests lie in the dynamics of teacher-paraprofessional teams. Her most recent books (coauthored with Betty Y. Ashbaker) include *Assisting with Early Literacy Instruction: A Manual for Paraprofessionals* (2011, Allyn & Bacon), and *Supporting and Supervising your Teaching Assistant* (2009, Continuum); a second edition of *Paraprofessionals in the Classroom* (2006, Allyn & Bacon) is in press. Dr. Morgan's research has appeared in a wide variety of international journals and she regularly presents papers and workshops at international conferences. She is currently a member of the NASEN Publications Advisory Group and has reviewed submissions for *Teaching and Teacher Education, Theories and Practices in Supervision and Curriculum, Teacher Educator, Remedial and Special Education*, and *Topics in Early Childhood Special Education*.

Judy Nagy is chartered accountant and holds Ph.D. from the University of Wollongong in Australia. She is the associate professor in the Centre for Regional Engagement at the University of South Australia with responsibility for program development and teaching and learning scholarship and practice. Dr. Nagy has many years experience teaching undergraduate, postgraduate programs in Accounting, Corporate Governance and Ethics and Financial Reporting and Analysis with numerous consultancies in Financial Reporting and Analysis being developed from her MBA residential programs. She holds numerous institutional and national teaching awards including an Australian Learning and Teaching Council Citation Award and an Australian Learning and Teaching Council Excellence Award. Her research focuses on scholarship in teaching and learning with a particular focus on academic leadership and she is the project leader for two nationally funded grants from the Australian Learning and Teaching Council. Dr. Nagy's research appears in *Educational Management Administration & Leadership; Oxford Review of Education; British Journal of Educational Studies; Higher Education Research and Development and Critical Perspectives on Accounting* with chapters in various books including with (Robb, A.) The "Capture of University Education – Evidence from the Antipodes" in *The Business of Higher Education* edited by David J. Siegel and John Knapp.

Anthony H. Normore holds Ph.D. from OISE/University of Toronto. He is associate professor and program coordinator for the Educational Administration as well as program development coordinator of the doctorate degree in educational leadership at California State University Dominguez Hills in Los Angeles. Dr. Normore's research focuses on leadership development, preparation, and socialization of urban school leaders in the context of ethics and social justice. His most recent books include *Global Perspectives on Educational Leadership Reform: The Development and Preparation of Leaders of Learning and Learners of Leadership* (2010, Emerald Group Publishing); *Educational Leadership Preparation: Innovation and Interdisciplinary Approaches to the Ed.D. and Graduate Education* (2010, Palgrave MacMillan, and coauthored with Gaetane Jean-Marie, 2010); *Leadership for Social Justice: Promoting Equity and Excellence Through Inquiry and Reflective Practice* (2008, Information Age Publishing); *Leadership and Intercultural Dynamics* (2009, Information Age Publishing and coauthored with John Collard). Dr. Normore's research has appeared in various journals including *Journal of School Leadership, Journal of Educational Administration, Values and Ethics in Educational Administration, Leadership and Organizational Development Journal, Canadian Journal of Education Administration and Policy, International Journal of Urban Educational Leadership, Educational Policy, International Electronic Journal for Leadership in Learning, International Journal of the Humanities, and Journal of Research on Leadership Education.*

Izhar Oplatka holds Ph.D. from The Hebrew University of Jerusalem. He is associate professor and head of the Executive Program of Educational Administration and Leadership at The School of Education, Tel Aviv University, Israel. Dr. Oplatka's research focuses on the lives and career of schoolteachers and principals, educational marketing, gender and educational administration, and the foundations of educational administration as a field of study. His most recent books include *The Legacy of Educational Administration: A Historical Analysis of an Academic Field* (2010, Peter Lang Publishing); *The Essentials of Educational Administration* (2010, Pardes Publisher, in Hebrew); *Women Principals in a Multi-Cultural Society* (2006, Sense Publisher, with Rachel Hertz Lazarowitz). Dr. Oplatka's publications have appeared in varied international journals including *Educational Administration Quarterly, Journal of Educational Administration, Educational Management Administration & Leadership, Comparative Education Review, Teacher College Record, Canadian Journal of Education Administration and Policy, International Journal of Leadership in Education,*

Journal of Education Policy, School Leadership & Management, Urban Education, International Journal of Educational Management, and so forth.

Nancy L. Ras has been an educator for over 25 years. She began teaching English as a foreign language at the high-school level and after earning her D.Phil at the University of Sussex, she received appointments in the Graduate Leadership and Human and Community Services programs at St Mary's College of California. Her research interests include the influence of context on leadership, teacher culture, and leadership as a relational endeavor within hierarchical organizations. Nancy presents at both educational and leadership conferences worldwide, including the Asia Pacific Educational Research Conference (APERA, Singapore), the International Studying Leadership Conference (New Zealand), and the Van Leer Educational Research Conference (Jerusalem), as well as the Randall L. Tobias Multi-Sector Leadership Conference at Indiana University and the American Educational Research Association (AERA) conferences. She reviews for both the AERA and the Society for Industrial and Organizational Psychology (SIOP). Her research has been published in the *Quarterly Journal of Ideology* (2004). Dr. Ras also heads *SocioCypher Consulting, LLC* whose focus is on organizational and leadership development using social network analysis and she provides gratis leadership and organizational development to nonprofit organizations. Dr. Ras is at present pursuing a second doctoral degree in organizational psychology at Walden University.

Tamara Savelyeva is postdoctoral fellow at the number one university in Asia, the University of Hong Kong (HKU). She is focusing her leadership research on the application of ecological modeling to educational systems in order to understand how school leaders can sustain learning through information technology innovations. Prior the HKU, Dr. Savelyeva worked with Central European University, Hungary to develop leaders of sustainability and connect leadership classrooms of the Ural State University, Cornell University, University of Melbourne, University of Guadalajara, Swedish University of Ag Sciences, and Beijing Normal University. She coordinated a simultaneous implementation of this sustainable curriculum after receiving her graduate degrees from Virginia Tech and Cornell University. Dr. Savelyeva has published her research in *International Journal for Sustainability in Higher Education, Learning Environments Research, European Journal of Natural Sciences,* and *UNESCO-UNEP Russia.* Her recent book, entitled *Global Learning Environment: Innovative Concept and Interactive Model for Changing Academia and Academics* is focused on sustainable leadership research at various levels of higher education.

Anit Somech is professor and the head of Educational Management program at the University of Haifa, Israel, Department of Educational Leadership & Policy. Anit Somech received her Ph.D. degree in the Department of Industrial Engineering and Management, at the Technion, the Israel Institute for Technology, with an emphasis on Behavioral Sciences and Management. Her research interests include participative leadership, organizational citizenship behavior, stress at work, and teamwork from a multilevel perspective. Anit Somech's research has published in such outlets as the *Academy of Management Journal, Journal of Management, Journal of Organizational Behavior, Work & Stress*, and *Educational Administration Quarterly*. In addition, she serves on the editorial board of the *Educational Administration Quarterly*. Her most recent papers include *Participative Decision-Making in Schools: A Mediating-Moderating Analytical Framework for Understanding School and Teachers Outcomes* (*Educational Administration Quarterly*, 2010); *Who benefits from participative management?* (*Journal of Educational Administration*, 2010, coauthored with Pascale Benoliel); *From an Intra-Team to an Inter-Team Perspective of Effectiveness: The Role of Inter-Team Interdependence and Teams' Boundary Activities* (*Small Group Research: An International Journal of Theory, Investigation, and Application*, 2010, coauthored with Anat Drach-Zahavy); *Translating Team Creativity to Innovation Implementation: The Role of Team Composition and Climate for Innovation* (*Journal of Management*, 2010, coauthored with Anat Drach-Zahavy).

Fatt Hee Tie holds doctor of legal science from Bond University, Australia. He is associate professor at the Institute of Educational Leadership, University of Malaya in Kuala Lumpur, Malaysia. His research focusses on leadership, education law, education policy and reform, organizational control behavior, and organizational control system. His most recent book is on *Education Law in Malaysia: Principles and Practice* (2011, Sweet and Maxwell). His research has appeared in various journals including *International Journal of Educational Reform, Education and Urban Society, International Education Studies, Education and Law*, and *International Journal of Education Law and Policy*. His email is tiefh@um.edu.my.

David L. Turnipseed holds Ph. D. from the University of Alabama. He is professor of management and chair of the Management Department in the Mitchell College of Business at the University of South Alabama. His research interests are emotional intelligence, organizational citizenship behavior, and cross-cultural organization behavior. He is co-PI on a grant to study social intelligence, discretionary behavior, and success in nursing. Dr. Turnipseed's research has been published in academic journals including

Leadership and Organizational Studies, British Journal of Management, Journal of Social Behavior and Personality, Creativity and Innovation Management, Leadership and Organization Development Journal, Journal of Business Research, Psychological Reports, and *European Journal of Work and Organization Psychology.*

Elizabeth VandeWaa holds Ph.D. from Michigan State University. She is a professor in the College of Nursing at the University of South Alabama, where she is course coordinator for pharmacology. She is active in the development and delivery of continuing education courses for health care professionals, such as physicians, dentists, and nurses. Dr. VandeWaa's research has been published in various journals such as *The Journal of Parasitology, Molecular and Biochemical Parasitology, Experimental Parasitology, Toxicity and Applied Pharmacology, Parasitology Today,* and *Journal of Chemical Ecology.* Dr. VandeWaa's current research interests are pro-organizational discretionary behavior, social and emotional intelligence, and nursing success. She recently received a grant, as co-PI, to study social intelligence as a determinate of discretionary behavior and nursing success.

Kursad Yılmaz holds Ph.D. from Ankara University, Turkey. He is associate professor at Dumlupınar University Faculty of Education in Kütahya. Dr. Yılmaz's research focuses on values, management by values, organizational trust, organizational justice, and leadership in schools. His most recent books include *Values in Educational Administration* (2008, Pegem Academy Publishing); and edited books *New Approaches in Management* (2010, Pegem Academy Publishing coedited with H. B. Memduhoğlu); *Introduction to Educational Sciences* (2009, 2010, 2011 Pegem Academy Publishing coedited with H. B. Memduhoğlu); *Turkish Educational System and School Management* (2008, 2010, 2011 Pegem Academy Publishing coedited with H. B. Memduhoğlu). Dr. Yılmaz's research has appeared in various journals including *Journal of Educational Administration, Educational Planning, Higher Education Quarterly, Educational Studies, Journal of Baltic Science Education, Asia Pacific Education Review, The Asia-Pacific Education Researcher, Educational Sciences: Theory & Practice, Education and Science, Bilig – Journal of Social Sciences of the Turkish World, Educational Administration: Theory and Practice, Ankara University Journal of Faculty of Educational Sciences.*

INDEX